THE LAW RELATING TO FINANCIAL CRIME IN THE UNITED KINGDOM

Karen Harrison is Senior Lecturer in Law at the University of Hull. Her teaching and research interests focus on criminal law, penology and the sentencing and management of dangerous offenders. She has published extensively across these topics.

Nicholas Ryder is Professor in Financial Crime at Bristol Law School, University of the West of England, Bristol. He teaches and researches in the areas of commercial law, financial crime and credit unions. He has published widely on these and related areas

Comments on the 1st edition:

'It is well-written, well-researched and academically stimulating; it is one of those rare texts which you could read in one go . . . a key text for anyone interested in the legal aspects of financial crime in the UK.'

Student Law Journal

'This is a much needed and most timely book. Financial crime is a subject of increasing importance which can no longer be ignored. The authors have produced an excellent text addressing topics such as fraud, insider dealing and market abuse in a manner which combines thoroughness with accessibility. I unhesitatingly recommend the book to students as well as practitioners who are beginning to develop an interest in the subject.'

Jonathan Fisher QC, London School of Economics, UK

'Karen Harrison and Nicholas Ryder have made a major contribution to advancing our knowledge of this increasingly important area of law by providing excellent ideas and recommendations for the future. The authors are to be congratulated for their efforts and the book deserves to be widely read.'

Roman Tomasic, University of South Australia
and Durham Law School, UK

'This book comprehensively and from a practical perspective addresses financial crime in this wider and more relevant context. It provides the reader with not only the substantive law, but sets it within the relevant regulatory and enforcement environment. This work is a vital tool for anyone concerned about protecting the integrity of their institution and bringing fraudsters to book!'

Barry Rider, Centre for International Documentation
on Organised and Economic Crime, UK

THE LAW RELATING TO FINANCIAL CRIME IN THE UNITED KINGDOM

2nd edition

Karen Harrison and Nicholas Ryder

Routledge
Taylor & Francis Group

LONDON AND NEW YORK

First published 2017
by Routledge
2 Park Square, Milton Park, Abingdon, Oxon OX14 4RN

and by Routledge
711 Third Avenue, New York, NY 10017

Routledge is an imprint of the Taylor & Francis Group, an informa business

British Library Cataloguing in Publication Data
A catalogue record for this book is available from the British Library

Library of Congress Cataloging-in-Publication Data
A catalog record for this book has been requested

ISBN: 978-1-4724-6422-4 (hbk)
ISBN: 978-1-4724-6425-5 (pbk)
ISBN: 978-1-3155-5623-9 (ebk)

Typeset in Bembo
by Apex CoVantage, LLC

CONTENTS

List of abbreviations   *viii*

1   Introduction   1
    Introduction   1
    What is financial crime?   1
    The extent of financial crime   5
    The importance of financial crime regulation   8
    Contents overview   9

2   Money laundering   11
    Introduction   11
    The money laundering process   11
    What is the offence of money laundering?   13
    The extent of money laundering   19
    Policy background – where did the offence originate from?   21
    Financial institutions and regulatory bodies   24
    Financial intelligence   33
    Sentencing and recovery   36
    Future recommendations   46
    Further reading   47

3   Terrorist financing   49
    Introduction   49
    What is the offence of terrorist financing?   50
    The extent of terrorist financing   53

Policy background – where did the offence originate from?   58
Financial institutions and regulatory bodies   65
Financial intelligence   68
Sentencing and recovery   72
Future recommendations   81
Further reading   82

4   Fraud   84
Introduction   84
What is the offence of fraud?   84
Fraud and cybercrime   89
The extent of fraud   91
Policy background – where did the offence originate from?   94
Financial institutions and regulatory bodies   97
Financial intelligence   109
Sentencing and recovery   111
Future recommendations   121
Further reading   121

5   Insider dealing   123
Introduction   123
What is the offence of insider dealing?   124
The extent of insider dealing   129
Policy background   130
Financial institutions and regulatory bodies   133
Sentencing and recovery   138
Market manipulation   142
Future recommendations   146
Further reading   147

6   Market abuse   148
Introduction   148
What are the civil and criminal offences of market abuse?   148
The civil market abuse regime   153
Market abuse regulation   158
The extent of market abuse   159
Financial institutions and regulatory bodies   160
Reporting of suspicious transactions   160
Sentencing and recovery   163
Future recommendations   169
Further reading   169

7	Bribery and corruption	171
	Introduction	171
	What is the offence of bribery?	172
	The extent of bribery	180
	Policy background	182
	Financial institutions and regulatory bodies	184
	Financial intelligence	187
	Sentencing and recovery	189
	Future recommendations	198
	Further reading	199
8	The avoidance and evasion of tax	200
	Introduction	200
	What are the offences?	201
	The extent of tax evasion	203
	Policy background	205
	Financial institutions and regulatory bodies	209
	Sentencing and recovery	210
	Future recommendations	220
	Further reading	222
9	Conclusions and recommendations	223
	Money laundering	223
	Terrorist financing	225
	Fraud	227
	Insider dealing	228
	Market abuse	228
	Bribery and corruption	228
	Tax evasion/avoidance	229
	Final thoughts	230
	Bibliography	*231*
	Index	*259*

ABBREVIATIONS

AML   anti-money laundering
BEPS   base erosion and profit shifting
CIOT   Chartered Institute of Taxation
CJA   Criminal Justice Act
CMA   Competition and Markets Authority
CPS   Crown Prosecution Service
CTF   counter-terrorist financing
DPA   Deferred Prosecution Agreement
DPP   Director of Public Prosecutions
DTI   Department of Trade and Industry
ECA   Economic Crime Agency
ECHR   European Convention on Human Rights
EEC   European Economic Community
EU   European Union
FATF   Financial Action Task Force
FBI   Federal Bureau of Investigation
FCA   Financial Conduct Authority
FIU   financial intelligence unit
FSA   Financial Services Authority
FSMA   Financial Services and Markets Act
FTT   First-Tier Tribunal
GDP   gross domestic product
HMRC   HM Revenue and Customs
ICT   information and communication technology
IMF   International Monetary Fund
IRA   Irish Republican Army

ISA	individual saving account
ISIL	Islamic State of Iraq and the Levant
ISIS	Islamic State of Iraq
JMLSG	Joint Money laundering Steering Group
LIBOR	London Interbank Offered Rate
MAD	Market Abuse Directive
MAR	Market Abuse Regulation
MIB	Marketing of Investment Boards
MLRO	Money Laundering Reporting Officer
NCA	National Crime Agency
NFA	National Fraud Authority
NFIB	National Fraud Intelligence Bureau
OECD	Organisation for Economic Co-operation and Development
OFT	Office of Fair Trading
PCSU	Public and Commercial Services Union
P&O	Peninsular & Oriental Steam Navigation Company
POCA	Proceeds of Crime Act
PRA	Prudential Regulation Authority
SAR	Suspicious Activity Report
SCPO	Serious Crime Prevention Order
SEC	Security & Exchange Commission
SFO	Serious Fraud Office
SIB	Securities and Investment Board
SOCA	Serious Organised Crime Agency
SRO	self-regulating organisation
STR	suspicious transaction reporting
SYSC	Senior Management Arrangements, Systems and Controls
UK	United Kingdom
UN	United Nations
UNODC	United Nations Office on Drugs and Crime
US	United States
USA	United States of America
VAT	Value Added Tax

1

INTRODUCTION

Introduction

The second edition of this book has presented us with an ideal and unique opportunity to revisit the area of financial crime in the United Kingdom (UK) in light of several important legislative and policy developments. It has also allowed us to extend the ambit and scope of the book to include areas of financial crime that were not addressed in the first edition, namely tax evasion, market manipulation and, very briefly, cybercrime. Additionally, this new edition incorporates many important changes in the UK including the creation of the National Crime Agency (NCA); the abolition of the Financial Services Authority (FSA); the creation of the Financial Conduct Authority (FCA); the introduction of the fourth Money Laundering Directive; the increased use of financial sanctions towards those involved in market manipulation; and, the introduction of Deferred Prosecution Agreements by the Crime and Courts Act 2013. These measures fall against an uncertain political backdrop fuelled by broken promises to confront and tackle financial crime since the start of the 2007–08 financial crisis.

What is financial crime?

The term financial crime is often used in common parlance and thus is one which we assume we know its meaning, despite the fact that there is 'no internationally accepted definition'[1] of it. As outlined throughout this book, definitions are abundant for the actual offences involved, such as fraud, money laundering, terrorist financing and market abuse, but are less precise for the collective expressions of both

---

1 International Monetary Fund, *Financial system abuse, financial crime and money laundering – background paper* (International Monetary Fund: Washington, DC, 12 February 2001, 5).

financial crime and financial abuse. For a book that purports to be about financial crime however, it is important that some attempt is made at defining these latter terms. Our attempt therefore begins with the 1939 seminal definition of white collar crime provided by Professor Edwin Sutherland.[2] He defined white collar crime as 'a crime committed by a person of respectability and high social status in the course of his occupation'.[3] In his inspirational paper, Sutherland stated that:

> The present-day white-collar criminals, who are more suave and deceptive than the 'robber barons', are represented . . . [by] many other merchant princes and captains of finance and industry, and by a host of lesser followers. Their criminality has been demonstrated again and again in the investigations of land offices, railways, insurance, munitions, banking, public utilities, stock exchanges, the oil industry, real estate, reorganization committees, receiverships, bankruptcies, and politics.[4]

One of the most important parts of this definition is that white collar crime is committed by people of a high social standing.[5] This is a view supported by Kemper who noted that white collar crime refers to 'illegal behaviour that takes advantage of positions of professional authority and power – or simply the opportunity structures available within business – for personal or corporate gain'.[6] Despite its seminal status, Sutherland's definition has nevertheless been subject to a great deal of academic debate and the interpretation of the term remains 'deeply contested'.[7] For example, Bookman argued that Sutherland's definition was too narrow[8] and Podgor went so far as to argue that 'throughout the last 100 years no one could ever figure it [white

---

2 See E. Sutherland, 'The white collar criminal' (1940) *American Sociological Review*, 5(1), 1–12, at 1.

3 E. Sutherland, *White Collar Crime* (Dryden: New York, 1949, 9), as cited in S. Wilson, 'Collaring the crime and the criminal? Jury psychology and some criminological perspectives on fraud and the criminal law' (2006) *Journal of Criminal Law*, 70(1), 75–92, at 79. This is a view supported by Gottschalk who stated that 'the most economically disadvantaged members of society are not the only ones committing crime. Members of the privileged socio-economic class are also engaged in criminal behaviour. The types of crime may differ from those of the less privileged classes, such as lawyers helping criminal clients launder their money, executives bribe public officials to achieve public contracts, or accountants manipulating balance sheet to avoid taxes.' P. Gottschalk, 'Executive positions involved in white-collar crime' (2011) *Journal of Money Laundering Control*, 14(4), 300–312, at 302. For a more detailed commentary on the definitions of white collar crime see S. Simpson, 'White collar crime: A review of recent developments and promising directions for future research' (2013) *Annual Review of Sociology*, 39, 309–331, at 310–313.

4 E. Sutherland, 'The white collar criminal' (1940) *American Sociological Review*, 5(1), 2.

5 M. Benson and S. Simpson, *White-Collar Crime: An Opportunity Perspective, Criminology and Justice Series* (Routledge: London, 2009).

6 M. Kempa, 'Combating white-collar crime in Canada: Serving victim needs and market integrity' (2010) *Journal of Financial Crime*, 17(2), 252.

7 Green above, n 231 at 3. For a more detailed discussion of the problems associated with the definition of white collar crime see G. Gilligan, 'The problem of, and with, financial crime' (2012) *Northern Ireland Legal Quarterly*, 63(4), 495–508.

8 Z. Bookman, 'Convergences and omissions in reporting corporate and white collar crime' (2008) *DePaul Business & Commercial Law Journal*, 6, 347–392, at 355.

collar crime] out'.[9] White collar crime is therefore probably more encompassing than financial crime; although there is no doubt that financial crime can be classified as a form of white collar crime: a crime that is usually committed by someone who has respectability, social status and occupation.[10] White collar crime has also been referred to as 'financial crime', 'economic crime' and 'illicit finance'. Examples of white collar crime include money laundering, insider dealing, fraud and market manipulation.

In England and Wales, financial crime can be said to include 'any offence involving fraud or dishonesty; misconduct in, or misuse of information relating to, a financial market; or handling the proceeds of crime'.[11] This can therefore include such activities as money laundering and terrorist funding. The FSA offered a similar definition, stating that it is 'any offence involving money laundering, fraud or dishonesty, or market abuse'.[12] The European Commission does not appear to provide an actual definition of the term; but on looking at the legislation and Directives that have been issued to cover financial crime, it would appear that these only cover the areas of money laundering and terrorist financing.[13] The Federal Bureau of Investigation, in the United States of America (USA), has a much more far-ranging definition, including the criminal activities of corporate fraud, commodities and securities fraud, mortgage fraud, healthcare fraud, financial institution fraud, insurance fraud, mass marketing fraud and money laundering.[14] The International Monetary Fund (IMF) goes further by stating that it 'can refer to *any* non-violent crime that generally results in a financial loss' (emphasis added).[15] This can therefore include tax evasion, money laundering and financial fraud, but essentially allows for anything that causes financial harm. It further states that where the loss involves a financial institution, then the term 'financial sector crime'[16] can also be used.

Definitions of the term 'financial crime' have also been presented by academics. For example, Gottschalk states that it is 'a crime against property, involving the unlawful conversion of property belonging to another to one's own personal use and benefit', stating that it is often 'profit driven . . . to gain access to and control

---

9 E. Podgor, 'White collar crime: A letter from the future' (2007) *Ohio State Journal of Criminal Law*, 5, 247–255, at 247.

10 B. Hunter, 'White-collar offenders and desistance from crime: Stigma, blocked paths and resettlement', paper given at the University of Hull, 2010.

11 Financial Services and Markets Act 2000, s. 6(3).

12 Financial Services Authority, 'Fighting financial crime', available from http://www.fsa.gov.uk/about/what/financial_crime, accessed 21 March 2012.

13 European Commission, 'Financial crime', available from http://ec.europa.eu/internal_market/company/financial-crime/index_en.htm, accessed 21 March 2012.

14 The Federal Bureau of Investigations, 'Financial Crimes Report to the Public', available from http://www.fbi.gov/stats-services/publications/financial-crimes-report-2010–2011/financial-crimes-report-2010-2011#Financial, accessed 21 March 2012.

15 International Monetary Fund, *Financial system abuse, financial crime and money laundering – background paper* (International Monetary Fund: Washington, DC, 12 February 2001, 3).

16 *Ibid.*, 5.

over property that belonged to someone else'.[17] Pickett and Pickett define financial crime as 'the use of deception for illegal gain, normally involving breach of trust, and some concealment of the true nature of the activities'.[18] This can include fraud, insider trading, embezzlement, tax evasion, kickbacks, identity theft, cyberattacks, social engineering and money laundering. Financial Abuse is another term that is sometimes used synonymously with financial crime and is defined in the UK as:

> Financial or material abuse, including theft, fraud, exploitation, pressure in connection with wills, property or inheritance or financial transactions, or the misuse or misappropriation of property, possessions or benefits.[19]

This can therefore include the offences of: theft, forgery, fraud by abuse of position, fraud by false representation, fraud by failing to disclose information and blackmail.[20] The IMF also defines what is meant by financial abuse, but does this in rather broad terms. This is because of the fact that it argues its meaning can vary between different occasions and different jurisdictions; precisely in the same way that the term financial crime can vary. For example the government of the UK has previously included money laundering, drug trafficking, illegal capital flight, tax evasion and fraud under the term financial abuse; whilst the USA Department of State refer to it as including money laundering, tax evasion and terrorism.[21] Different jurisdictions around the world thus define the component offences (such as fraud and money laundering) differently; some make certain actions criminal whilst other countries do not. An example of the latter situation is tax evasion where some countries have very low or lax tax laws whilst others have the practical opposite. To recognise this disparity, the IMF states that financial abuse includes 'financial activities, many of which have the potential to harm financial systems, and legal activities that exploit undesirable features of tax and regulatory systems'.[22] Another term that has been used as well as or instead of financial crime is illicit finance, which has been used by the UK's Department of Treasury and Her Majesty's Treasury.[23]

A person, who has committed such offences, must therefore be able to be described as a financial criminal. Other perhaps more common terms of vernacular include that of the white collar criminal and the offender who has committed corporate crime, although as acknowledged by Croall there are also problems with

---

17 P. Gottschalk, 'Categories of financial crime' (2010) *Journal of Financial Crime*, 17(4), 441–458.

18 *Ibid.*, 441–442.

19 City of London Police, *Assessment: Financial Crime against Vulnerable Adults* (Social Care Institute for Excellence: London, November 2011, 2).

20 *Ibid.*, 3.

21 International Monetary Fund, *Financial system abuse, financial crime and money laundering – background paper* (International Monetary Fund: Washington, DC, 12 February 2001, 4).

22 *Ibid.*

23 N. Ryder, *Financial Crime in the 21st Century* (Edward Elgar: Cheltenham, 2011).

how these terms are defined.[24] For example, whilst we might often regard the white collar criminal as someone who has high social status and is respectable, powerful and at management level, this is not always true; many corporate crimes involve employees acting in the course of trade and business and their offences relate to matters of hygiene and other health and safety issues.[25] Whilst it may therefore be true, as suggested by Croall, that the vast majority of white collar crime is not undertaken by the high status offender, this is not the type of offence or offender that this book focuses upon. Therefore, for the purpose of this book, a financial criminal will be defined as someone who has committed a financial crime and who has a certain level of standing (i.e. that of management) within a business or corporation.

The extent of financial crime

Despite concerted efforts by national and international agencies such as the United Nations (UN), the Financial Action Task Force (FATF) and the IMF, it is impossible to accurately quantify the true extent of financial crime that is taking place on a daily basis around the globe. This is partly because of the fact that significant amounts of all criminal behaviour will often go undiscovered and thus unreported, but it is also because of the many methodological difficulties that are often encountered when trying to pull statistics together of this kind.[26] The only estimations that can thus be provided are those for the individual financial crimes.[27]

In the UK, for example, for the period of 2012–13, the National Fraud Authority (NFA) estimated that the cost of fraud to the UK's economy was in the region of £52 billion.[28] This is a drastic increase from the £38.4 billion quoted in 2010–11,[29] although a decrease from the record high amount of £73 billion in 2011–12.[30] The 2012–2013 figure can be broken down into losses of £20.6 billion for the public sector (predominantly through tax, benefits and tax credits and governmental frauds); £21.3 billion for the private sector (including financial services, professional services, construction and engineering, natural resources, retail, wholesale and distribution and manufacturing); £9.1 billion for UK individuals (mass marketing, rental and online tickets); and £147.3 million for the charitable sector (including identity fraud, payment/banking fraud and cyber-enabled fraud).[31] In the European Union (EU), according to a study prepared for the European Commission, fraud is estimated to range from between 0.2 and 2 per cent of gross domestic product (GDP), with the notorious examples of Barings, Drexel, Sumitomo, and Daiwa,

---

24 H. Croall, 'Who is the white-collar criminal?' (1989) *British Journal of Criminology*, 29(2), 157.

25 *Ibid.*

26 N. Ryder, *Financial Crime in the 21st Century* (Edward Elgar: Cheltenham, 2011).

27 While some examples of these are included below, a fuller assessment of the extent of each individual crime is provided throughout this book.

28 National Fraud Authority, *Annual Fraud Indicator* (National Fraud Authority: London, 2013).

29 National Fraud Authority, *Annual Fraud Indicator* (National Fraud Authority: London, 2011).

30 National Fraud Authority, *Annual Fraud Indicator* (National Fraud Authority: London, 2012).

31 National Fraud Authority, *Annual Fraud Indicator* (National Fraud Authority: London, 2013).

each involving losses in excess of US$1 billion. Fraud by banks, for example that seen by BCCI and Meridien, has contributed to considerable losses to depositors in a few countries, and seriously damaged the banking systems of some of the smaller African nations.[32]

In terms of money laundering, the FATF, on the basis of information about final sales of some illegal drugs (approximately US$120 billion a year in Europe and the USA in the late 1980s) and estimating worldwide and generalising to include all drugs, have extrapolated that on the basis of assuming that 50–70 per cent of that amount would be laundered, the approximate amount of the laundered profits could be in the region of 2 per cent of the global GDP. In one FATF member country alone, 1,233 cases of money laundering were prosecuted in one year, with a total value of US$1.6 billion. Furthermore, an Australian study, from 1995, estimated money laundering there to amount to nearly US$3 billion or about 0.75 per cent of GDP. As with all estimations of financial crime though, given that these two latter examples were based on recorded crime, the true extent of money laundering has therefore been significantly underestimated.[33] It has therefore been suggested by the United Nations Office on Drugs and Crime (UNODC) in 2009, that the amount of money laundered annually equates to 3.6% of global GDP, or approximately US$1.6 trillion.[34] This estimate by the UNODC was less than the initial estimate of Walker of US$2.85 trillion in 1995.[35] Both figures have been heavily influenced by one of the most cited and quoted estimates of money laundering that was offered by the IMF in 1998. Here, the IMF estimated that the level of money laundering was between 2–5% of the global GDP, or US$1.5 trillion.[36] However, it is extremely important to note that the calculation of the extent of money laundering on a global or even a nation state scale is fraught with methodological weaknesses. For instance, any attempt to determine the levels of money laundered is limited because there is no visible data available that can be utilised by researchers. This has been referred to as the 'shadow economy' or a nation state's 'unrecorded economic

---

32 International Monetary Fund, *Financial system abuse, financial crime and money laundering – background paper* (International Monetary Fund: Washington, DC, 12 February 2001, 11).

33 *Ibid.*

34 'Illicit money how much is out there?' (United Nations Office on Drugs and Crime, 2011), available from http://www.unodc.org/unodc/en/frontpage/2011/October/illicit-money_-how-much-is-out-there.html, accessed 13 November 2014.

35 J. Walker, 'Estimates of the extent of money laundering in and through Australia', paper prepared for Australian Transaction Reports and Analysis Centre, September 1995. Queanbeyan: John Walker Consulting Services.

36 International Monetary Fund, 'Money laundering: The importance of international countermeasures – address by Michel Camdessus, Managing Director of the International Monetary Fund', 10 February 1998, available from http://www.imf.org/external/np/speeches/1998/021098.htm, accessed 19 March 2015. It is important to note that this estimate provided by the IMF has been subjected to criticism from several commentators. See for example P. Reuter, 'Are estimates of the volume of money laundering either feasible or useful?' in B. Unger and D. van der Linds (eds.), *Research Handbook on Money Laundering* (Edward Elgar: Cheltenham, 2013, 224–231).

activity'.[37] The extent of money laundering in the UK is thus impossible to calculate and accordingly estimates vary. For example, the FSA reported that the level of laundered money in 2010 was between £23 billion and £57 billion,[38] an estimate similar to that offered by Harvey, who suggested the figure was between £19 billion and £48 billion.[39]

In contrast to the large sums of money associated with fraud and money laundering, the financing of terrorism is largely associated with smaller amounts of money. This has been referred to by some academic commentators as 'cheap terrorism'.[40] Frequently quoted examples of this include the first attack on the World Trade Center in 1993 which was estimated at a cost of only US$400,[41] the London Bishopsgate bomb in 1993 which caused over £1 billion worth of damage to property, but was estimated to only cost £3,000,[42] the Madrid train bombings which cost €8,315[43] and the London terrorist attacks in 2005 which amounted to approximately £8,000.[44] Any discussion on the estimated costs of funding acts of terrorism must briefly consider the impact of the terrorist attacks in New York and Washington on 11 September 2001. It has been suggested that the terrorist attacks of 9/11 were estimated to have cost between US$400,000 and US$500,000 over a two-year planning period.[45] This is a view supported by several commentators. For example, Lowe stated that 'terrorists need relatively small amounts of money to mount highly damaging attacks and even a terrorist spectacular like 9/11 is estimated not to have cost more than $500,000 which is minute in terms of the devastation caused'.[46]

---

37 For a more detailed commentary on the shadow economy see S. Smith, *Britain's Shadow Economy* (Clarendon Press: London, 1986).

38 Financial Services Authority, 'What Is financial crime?', available from http://www.fsa.gov.uk/pages/About/What/financial_crime/money_laundering/faqs/index.shtml, accessed 2 June 2010.

39 J. Harvey, 'An evaluation of money laundering policies' (2005) *Journal of Money Laundering Control*, 8(4), 339–345, at 340.

40 See for example N. Ryder, and U. Turksen, 'Banks in defense of the Homeland: Nexus of ethics and suspicious activity reporting' (2013) *Contemporary Issues in Law* (Special Issue on Law, Ethics and Counter-Terrorism), 12(4), 311–347 and N. Ryder, 'A false sense of security? An analysis of legislative approaches to the prevention of terrorist finance in the United States of America and the United Kingdom' (2007) *Journal of Business Law*, November, 821–850. For an interesting discussion see C. Whitlock, 'Al-Qaeda Masters Terrorism On the Cheap', 24 August 2008, available from http://www.washingtonpost.com/wp-dyn/content/article/2008/08/23/AR2008082301962.html, accessed 20 March 2015.

41 J. Gaddis, 'And now this: Lessons from the old era for the new one' in S. Talbott and N. Chander (eds.), *The Age of Terror: America and the World after September 11* (Basic Books: New York, 2001, 6).

42 HM Treasury Combating the Financing of Terrorism, *A Report on UK Action* (HM Treasury: London, 2002, 11).

43 C. Walker, 'Terrorism financing and the policing of charities: Who pays the price?' in C. King and C. Walker (eds.), *Dirty Assets – Emerging Issues in the Regulation of Criminal and Terrorist Assets* (Ashgate: Farnham, 2014, 232).

44 HM Government, *Report of the Official Account of the Bombings in London on 7th July 2005* (HM Government: London, 2006, 23).

45 National Commission on Terrorist Attacks upon the United States, *The 9/11 Commission Report* (Norton and Company: New York, 2004, 172).

46 P. Lowe, 'Counterfeiting: Linking organised crime and terrorist funding' (2006) *Journal of Financial Crime*, 13(2), 255.

Further costs associated with other elements of financial crime often include the damage caused by the financial abuse of poor regulatory frameworks, which may subsequently contribute to financial crises or undermine confidence in a country's financial system. Such losses relate to the total costs of the crises and in essence are impossible to quantify. There are also similar difficulties in attempting to estimate the effects of tax evasion, harmful tax competition and corruption.[47]

The importance of financial crime regulation

Even though financial crime is often thought to be victimless, this is far from true. As explained by the FATF, 'criminal proceeds have the power to corrupt and ultimately destabilise communities or [even] whole national economies'.[48] The integrity of a nation's financial institutions can be eroded by those organised criminals who seek to maximise their illegal profits so that they are able to enjoy the so-called champagne lifestyle,[49] and as further explained by Vaithilingam and Nair, it can weaken the financial systems which are the main players in many global financial transactions.[50] Moreover, as Ryder argues, the effects of financial crime can ultimately threaten national security on the basis that terrorists need money and resources so that they can carry out their illegal activities.[51] The IMF additionally argues that financial system abuse,

> could compromise bank soundness with potentially large fiscal liabilities, lessen the ability to attract foreign investment, and increase the volatility of international capital flows and exchange rates . . . financial system abuse, financial crime, and money laundering may also distort the allocation of resources and the distribution of wealth.[52]

Financial crime will also, almost certainly, have an adverse impact on the economies of countries. Scanlan, for example, notes how the bomb attacks in London on the 7 and 21 July 2005 and the subsequent disruption to the transport system in London, cost the UK government in excess of £3 billion.[53] In addition to this, further economic damage for a country may arise through the loss of reputation, which may prevent businesses conducting financial transactions in that country.

---

47 International Monetary Fund, *Financial system abuse, financial crime and money laundering – background paper* (International Monetary Fund: Washington, DC, 12 February 2001, 11).

48 Financial Action Task Force, *Report on Money Laundering and Terrorist Financing Typologies 2003–2004* (Financial Action Task Force: Paris, 2004).

49 N. Ryder, *Financial Crime in the 21st Century* (Edward Elgar: Cheltenham, 2011).

50 *Ibid.*

51 *Ibid.*

52 International Monetary Fund, *Financial system abuse, financial crime and money laundering – background paper* (International Monetary Fund: Washington, DC, 12 February 2001, 9).

53 G. Scanlan, 'The enterprise of crime and terror – the implications for good business: Looking to the future – old and new threats' (2006) *Journal of Financial Crime*, 13(2), 164.

The impact of financial crime can also be seen on an individual level. Although losses to individuals may be small, especially when compared to public sector and private sector losses, they can still have a significant impact on that given individual. This may include a reduced flow of wealth between generations in families and a subsequent loss of tax revenue for the government through inheritance tax. This may also have real consequences for the public purse. For example, victims of financial crime who need care in their old age may no longer have the means to pay for it themselves and so become dependent on state funding. Also, where crime is perpetrated by a professional, such as a solicitor or financial professional, there may be harm to the reputation of individuals and organisations, leading not only to a decrease in confidence and trust,[54] but as emphasised by the IMF, can consequently result in a weakening of the entire financial system.[55]

The impact of financial crime should therefore not be underestimated and can be every bit as significant as physical abuse. Deem, for example, suggests that victims of financial crime can suffer as much as those who have been victims of a violent crime.[56] Spalek notes that outrage and anger, as well as fear, stress, anxiety, and depression, were experienced by victims of the Maxwell pension fraud,[57] and how many victims of this fraud thought that their husbands' deaths had been accelerated as a result of the said events.[58]

Bearing in mind the vast figures involved in financial crime, especially when it is likely that these estimations only include the tip of the iceberg, and with such far-ranging impacts, it is essential that the UK has regulatory systems and legislation in place that effectively work to prevent and reduce the commission of such activities. The rationale of this book is therefore to look at the regulatory processes, systems and pieces of legislation that exist in the UK and offer both an assessment of these in terms of their effectiveness and a discussion on their potential reform. We hope to achieve this by not only providing a commentary on the law relating to financial crime in the UK, but also by presenting this in an innovative holistic style.

Contents overview

The contents of this book are thus divided into eight further chapters. Chapters 2 to 7 deal with the individual financial crimes of money laundering, terrorist financing, fraud, insider dealing, market abuse and bribery and corruption. Chapter 8 sees

---

54 City of London Police, *Assessment: Financial Crime against Vulnerable Adults* (Social Care Institute for Excellence: London, November 2011).

55 International Monetary Fund, *Financial system abuse, financial crime and money laundering – background paper* (International Monetary Fund: Washington, DC, 12 February 2001, 9).

56 D. Deem, 'Notes from the field: Observations in working with the forgotten victims of personal financial crimes' (2000) *Journal of Elder Abuse & Neglect*, 12(2), 33.

57 B. Spalek, *Knowledgeable Consumers? Corporate Fraud and Its Devastating Impacts, Briefing 4* (Centre for Crime and Justice Studies, 2007).

58 B. Spalek, 'Exploring the impact of financial crime: A study looking into the effects of the Maxwell scandal upon the Maxwell pensioners' (1999) *International Review of Victimology*, 6, 213.

the introduction and discussion of a new area for the book, namely tax evasion, and cybercrime is discussed in relation to fraud in Chapter 4. Each of these chapters has a similar structure. After a general introduction to the individual offence, the chapter outlines what the offence is, including relevant actus reus, mens rea and defence elements. Next follows a consideration of the extent of the financial crime in question. As noted above, this is often difficult to quantify, although through using a collection of international and national documents an attempt at this has been made. Following on from this, each chapter then turns to the question of policy background. Initially this looks at where the offence originated from but then moves onto a detailed assessment of the financial institutions and regulatory bodies that exist to control and prevent the commission of such abuse. Whether such institutions and bodies are actually achieving their listed aims is additionally analysed. Finally, each chapter looks at the sentencing options and policy applicable to each financial crime. This includes sentencing examples and provides detail on how the UK can achieve the recovery of criminal proceeds. Again the effectiveness of such options is discussed. The final chapter in the book, Chapter 9, draws together the themes of the book and makes a number of future recommendations. Our fundamental aim here is to provoke further thought and discussion, but also to offer a way forward for the regulation and prevention of financial crime in the twenty-first century.

2

MONEY LAUNDERING

Introduction

Money laundering can be defined as the process utilised by criminals to disguise or convert the proceeds of crime (dirty money) into clean money. In this sense, the term 'criminal' can include drug dealers, burglars, fraudsters, people traffickers, smugglers, terrorists, extortionists, tax evaders and illegal arms dealers, but can also include lawyers, accountants, financial experts and many other intermediaries. The laundering of money is usually achieved by placing it into the financial system where it can be transferred between different financial products and bank accounts.[1] Because of the extent and threat of the problem, the United Kingdom (UK) has adopted an aggressive policy towards the offence and is an integral member of the global battle against money laundering. The primary focus of this chapter will therefore be to cover the UK's anti-money laundering initiatives, including also an attempt at quantifying the extent of the problem. The chapter will then consider the background to the policy of criminalising and regulating money laundering, plus an evaluation of the financial institutions and regulatory bodies involved. Finally, we look at how dirty money is recovered, including a brief analysis of sentencing options and practices.

The money laundering process

Because the goal of many criminal acts is to generate a profit for the individual or group involved, the ability to change dirty money into clean untraceable money is paramount for many criminals. Money laundering is thus the process by

---

1 Financial Services Authority, 'Frequently asked questions' (Financial Services Authority, 2011), available from http://www.fsa.gov.uk/pages/About/What/financial_crime/money_laundering/faqs/index.shtml, accessed 6 June 2011.

which organised criminals and drug cartels disguise their proceeds of crime. It is of critical importance as it enables them to enjoy their profits without jeopardising their source. Money laundering is therefore a criminal activity, which involves the practice of concealing assets to avoid any discovery of the unlawful activity that fashioned them. To achieve this, the practice involves three recognisable stages: placement, layering and integration. In the first stage, the money launderer places the illegal profits of crime into, for example, the financial system.[2] This is sometimes achieved by separating larger sums of money into smaller amounts that are then deposited into several bank accounts to avoid money laundering reporting requirements. This process is commonly referred to as 'smurfing', where criminals will deposit money in a financial institution in amounts that are lower than the level at which the financial institution must complete a Suspicious Activity Report (SAR).[3] At the second step, layering, the launderer enters into several transactions to distance the illegal money from its original source. The final stage is referred to as integration, and it is at this phase of the money laundering cycle that the monies re-enter the economy. The generally accepted three stages of money laundering have however been questioned by a number of commentators. For example, Hopton suggested that the traditional money laundering process would not be applicable where money was laundered using electronic money flows and banking systems.[4] Additionally, Konningsweld questioned the conventional money laundering model and concluded that integration could be substituted with justification and investment, thus creating a four-tiered model.[5] Although there are too many money laundering mechanisms to mention them all, the most common examples in the UK include cash couriers, money transmission systems, cash-intensive businesses, shell corporations, high-value assets and property transactions.[6] Other mechanisms include investment in front companies, high levels of conspicuous consumption and moving large amounts of cash to foreign jurisdictions.[7] The National Crime Agency (NCA) has taken the view that,

> a significant amount of the criminal proceeds generated in the UK is laundered overseas, both to hide profits and pay for criminal goods. The United

---

2 For an excellent commentary on how organised criminals seek to hide their proceeds of crime at the placement stage of the layering process see J. Simser, 'Money laundering and asset cloaking techniques' (2008) *Journal of Money Laundering Control*, 11(1), 15–24.

3 For a more detailed and fascinating discussion about smurfing and money laundering see S. Welling, 'Smurfs, money laundering, and the federal criminal law: The crime of structuring transactions' (1989) *Florida Law Review*, 41, 287–339.

4 Doug Hopton, *Money Laundering: A Concise Guide for All Business* (Gower: Farnham, 2009, 3).

5 J. Koningsveld, 'Money laundering – 'You don't see it, until you understand it': Rethinking the stages of money laundering process to make enforcement more effective' in B. Unger and D van der Linde (eds.), *Research Handbook on Money Laundering* (Edward Elgar: Cheltenham, 2014, 435).

6 Financial Action Task Force, *Third Mutual Evaluation Report Anti-Money Laundering and Combating the Financing of Terrorism – United Kingdom* (Financial Action Task Force: Paris, 2007, 15).

7 National Criminal Intelligence Service, *UK Threat Assessment* (National Criminal Intelligence Service, 2007, 53).

Arab Emirates, the Far East and South East Asia (particularly Hong Kong and Singapore) and Spain are all attractive to money launderers.[8]

It is also interesting to note that one of the most common mechanisms to launder the proceeds of crime in the UK is to abuse the banking system. This point was clearly illustrated by the laundering of the proceeds of crime by General Sinai through several banks in the UK. Furthermore, the UK is regarded as 'attractive to money launderers because of the size, sophistication, and reputation of its financial markets'.[9]

What is the offence of money laundering?

The offence of money laundering is currently contained within part 7 of the Proceeds of Crime Act (POCA) 2002. This received Royal Assent on 24 July 2002 and applies to money laundering activities on or after 23 February 2003.[10] The Act contains three principal offences: i) concealing, disguising converting, transferring or removing criminal property from the jurisdiction,[11] ii) entering into or becoming concerned in an arrangement knowing or suspecting it to facilitate the acquisition, retention, use or control of criminal property on behalf of another person,[12] and iii) acquiring, using or possessing criminal property.[13] It is also an offence to be part of a conspiracy, to attempt to commit, or to counsel, aid, abet or procure any of the above. All three offences can be committed by any person, irrespective of the fact that they work within the regulated sector (including banks, insurers, accountants, credit institutions, financial institutions, lawyers, etc.) or undertake a relevant business (including casino operators, estate agents and insolvency practitioners). Other offences, mainly focused on disclosure, include failing to disclose suspicions or knowledge of money laundering,[14] failing to pass on these aforementioned disclosures to an authorised person,[15] disclosing that a person or persons are subject to an investigation because of allegations of money laundering (tipping off)[16] and, finally, making disclosures that are likely to prejudice

---

8 National Crime Agency, 'Money laundering', n/d, available from http://www.nationalcrimeagency. gov.uk/crime-threats/money-laundering, accessed 16 June 2015.

9 United States Department of State, *Department of State Bureau of International Narcotics and Law Enforcement Affairs Narcotics Control Strategy Report Volume II Money Laundering and Financial Crime* (United States Department of State: Washington, DC, 2010, 223).

10 R. Forston, 'Money laundering offences under POCA 2002' in W. Blair and R. Brent (eds.), *Banks and Financial Crime – The International Law of Tainted Money* (Oxford University Press: Oxford, 2010, 157).

11 Proceeds of Crime Act 2002, s. 327.

12 Proceeds of Crime Act 2002, s. 328.

13 Proceeds of Crime Act 2002, s. 329.

14 Proceeds of Crime Act 2002, s. 330.

15 Proceeds of Crime Act 2002, s. 331 and s. 332.

16 Proceeds of Crime Act 2002, s. 333A.

an investigation.[17] On the basis that the first three offences are the primary ones, they will be considered in more detail.

Concealing, disguising, converting, transferring or removing criminal property from the jurisdiction – section 327 POCA 2002

Section 327 of POCA 2002 generates the first of the three primary money laundering offences, with a person committing an offence if they conceal, disguise, convert, transfer or remove criminal property from England and Wales, Scotland or Northern Ireland. This also includes concealing or disguising the nature, source, location, movement, ownership or disposition of the property.[18] For the purposes of the Act, property includes money; real, personal, heritable or movable property; things in action and other incorporeal or intangible property.[19] Property is considered to be criminal property if '(a) it constitutes a person's benefit from criminal conduct or it represents such a benefit (in whole or part and whether directly or indirectly), and (b) the alleged offender knows or suspects that it constitutes or represents such a benefit.'[20] This interpretation of criminal property is somewhat contentious, mainly because its scope allows the inclusion of property from anywhere in the world.[21] Furthermore, Forston states that element (b) provides 'a somewhat artificial meaning because the knowledge of the person dealing with the property only becomes relevant at this point'.[22] Hudson, therefore, argues that the section has two specific requirements. First, that the criminal property constitutes a benefit and, second, that the defendant had suspicion or knowledge of this fact.[23]

The phrase benefit is broadly defined and is applied universally by the Act.[24] Under section 340(5) 'a person benefits from conduct if he obtains property as a result of or in connection with the conduct'.[25] The phrase includes 'not only the property that the offender directly obtained as a result of or in connection with

---

17 Proceeds of Crime Act 2002, s. 342.
18 Proceeds of Crime Act 2002, s. 327(3).
19 Proceeds of Crime Act 2002, s. 340(9).
20 Proceeds of Crime Act 2002, s. 340(3). For a critical discussion of the interpretation of this phrase see D. Bentley and R. Fisher, 'Criminal property under PCOA 2002 – time to clean up the law?' (2009) *Archbold News*, 2, 7–9.
21 Proceeds of Crime Act 2002, s. 340(9).
22 R. Forston, 'Money laundering offences under POCA 2002' in W. Blair and R. Brent (eds.), *Banks and Financial Crime – The International Law of Tainted Money* (Oxford University Press: Oxford, 2010, 163–164).
23 A. Hudson, *The Law of Finance* (Sweet and Maxwell: London, 2009, 345).
24 R. Forston, 'Money laundering offences under POCA 2002' in W. Blair and R. Brent (eds.), *Banks and Financial Crime – The International Law of Tainted Money* (Oxford University Press: Oxford, 2010, 163–164).
25 For a more detailed interpretation of this phrase see for example *R v Rowbotton* [2006] EWCA Crim 747, *R v Gabriel* [2006] EWCA Crim 229 and *R v IK* [2007] EWCA Crim 491.

the offence, but also any pecuniary advantage that he or she obtained from it'.[26] A benefit therefore includes three key concepts. The first is that any gain is directly related to criminal behaviour. The scope of section 340 is extremely wide and it is possible for *any* person to have made a gain, not just the person who committed the offence. Indeed, the Act goes as far as stating that in assessing whether or not an offence has been committed, it is immaterial 'who carried out the conduct' or 'who benefited from it' or whether the conduct occurred before or even after the passing of the Act.[27] Second, the gain must flow from the criminal activity involved. This doesn't necessarily mean just financial gain and could include improvements to someone's standard of living or profits derived from the illegal activity.[28] It can also include anything that represents a benefit,[29] with a person committing an offence if they know or suspect that what has been given to them constitutes or represents such a benefit.[30] This suggests that it could include gain that has been made in lieu of property as defined above. This would again make the provision extremely far-reaching.

Finally, it must be proven that the property or benefit derives from criminal conduct. This is defined as all conduct that constitutes a criminal offence under UK law, or would constitute an offence in the UK if the activity occurred there.[31] It is also worth noting that it is immaterial whether the criminal conduct took place prior to the POCA 2002 coming into force, as long as the laundering act took place after its commencement.[32]

Entering into or becoming concerned in an arrangement knowing or suspecting it to facilitate the acquisition, retention, use and control of criminal property on behalf of another person – section 328 POCA 2002

Section 328 POCA 2002 provides that 'A person commits an offence if he enters into or becomes concerned in an arrangement which he know or suspects facilitates (by whatever means) the acquisition, retention, use or control of criminal property by or on behalf of another person.'[33] To establish a conviction, the prosecution must prove not only that a person became concerned in an arrangement which they knew or suspected would make it simpler for another person to acquire, retain,

---

26 R. Forston, 'Money laundering offences under POCA 2002' in W. Blair and R. Brent (eds.), *Banks and Financial Crime – The International Law of Tainted Money* (Oxford University Press: Oxford, 2010, 163).

27 Proceeds of Crime Act 2002, s. 340(3)(a).

28 A. Hudson, *The Law of Finance* (Sweet and Maxwell: London, 2009, 345).

29 *Ibid.*, 344.

30 Proceeds of Crime Act 2002, s. 340(3)(b).

31 Proceeds of Crime Act 2002, s. 340(2).

32 Crown Prosecution Service, 'Proceeds of Crime Act 2002 Part 7 – money laundering offences', available from http://www.cps.gov.uk/legal/p_to_r/proceeds_of_crime_money_laundering/, accessed 6 July 2011.

33 Proceeds of Crime Act 2002, s. 328(1).

use or control criminal property, but furthermore, that the person concerned also knew or suspected that the property constituted or represented benefit from criminal conduct.[34] The offence can be committed in a number of ways and covers the situation where a third party is handling money that is derived from the proceeds of crime. Forston therefore takes the view that 'this offence is of considerable concern to those who handle or advise third parties in connection with money and other types of property'.[35] For a person to be guilty of the offence the definition of criminal property is again of central importance, as too are the concepts of knowledge and suspicion. Whilst knowledge is a fairly straightforward idea, the meaning of suspicion has caused uncertainty and anxiety, particularly in relation to what will amount to suspicion for the purposes of the offence. Harvey, for example, notes that 'suspicious itself is a wide-reaching term of which there is no objective definition: suspicious is personal and subjective and falls far short of proof based on firm evidence'.[36] Perhaps because of this subjectiveness and in an attempt to clarify meaning, the courts have defined suspicion as,

> being beyond mere speculation and based on some foundation, for example: a degree of satisfaction and not necessarily amounting to belief but at least extending beyond speculation as to whether an event has occurred or not; and, although the creation of suspicion requires a lesser factual basis than the creation of belief, it must nonetheless be built upon some foundation.[37]

In *R v DA Silva*, Longmore LJ took the view that,

> the essential element of the word 'suspect' and its affiliates, in this context, is that the defendant must think that there is a possibility, which is more than fanciful, that the relevant facts exist. A vague feeling of unease would not suffice. But the statute does not require the suspicion to be 'clear' or 'firmly grounded and targeted on specific facts', or based upon 'reasonable grounds.[38]

---

34 This section amends and updates s. 50 of the Drug Trafficking Act 1994 and s. 93A of the Criminal Justice Act 1988, s. 38 of the Criminal Law (Consolidation) (Scotland) Act 1995 and Article 46 of the Proceeds of Crime (Northern Ireland) Order 1996.

35 R. Forston, 'Money laundering offences under POCA 2002' in W. Blair and R. Brent (eds.), *Banks and Financial Crime – The International Law of Tainted Money* (Oxford University Press: Oxford, 2010, 181).

36 J. Harvey, 'Compliance and reporting issues arising for financial institutions from money laundering regulations: A preliminary cost benefit study' (2004) *Journal of Money Laundering Control*, 7(4), 333–346, at 335.

37 The Financial Services Commission, *Guidance Notes – Systems of Control to Prevent the Financial System from Being Used for Money Laundering or Terrorist Financing Activities* (Financial Services Commission, 2011, 8.1).

38 *R v DA Silva* [2006] EWCA Crim 1654. This case related to the interpretation of the phrase under the Criminal Justice Act 1988. For a more detailed discussion about the decision in this case see G. Brown, and T. Evans, 'The impact: The breadth and depth of the anti-money laundering provisions requiring reporting of suspicious activities' (2008) *Journal of International Banking Law and Regulation*, 23(5), 274–277.

Furthermore, Lord Hope in *R v Sail (Abdulrahman)* stated,

> the assumption is that the person has a suspicion, otherwise he would not be thinking of doing what the statute contemplates. The objective test is introduced in the interest of fairness, to ensure that the suspicion has a reasonable basis for it. The subjective test – actual suspicion – is not enough. The objective test – that there 'were reasonable grounds for it – must be satisfied too.[39]

Moreover, according to the Court of Appeal in *K v National Westminster Bank, HMRC, SOCA,*[40] the interpretation of suspicion is the same in civil law as it is in criminal law. Applying case law, we therefore have what is often referred to as the 'more than fanciful possibility test'.[41] Therefore, Hudson takes the view that 'the defendant must have actual suspicion and also [that] there must have been a reasonable basis for having that suspicion, as well as the property being used for criminal purposes'.[42]

Section 328 has also caused problems with respect to what an arrangement is, particularly with regard to those working within the legal profession. For example in *P v P*[43] Dame Butler-Sloss, in the Family Division of the High Court, held that a legal professional, if acting for a client in divorce proceedings, is required to investigate the financial affairs of both parties in some detail, and any irregularity such as an over-claimed benefit payment or undeclared value added tax transaction requires the solicitor to stop proceedings whilst they makes their disclosure to the relevant body and await guidance. This caused Collins and Kennedy to note that 'many professionals will soon be committing criminal offences if they fail to report suspicions about money laundering activity'.[44] Further clarity was however provided the following year in *Bowman v Fels,*[45] a Court of Appeal judgment, which disapproved of *P v P*. In this case, the judgment concerned two important points. The first, at the very centre of the appeal, related to 'whether s. 328 applies to the ordinary conduct of legal proceedings or any aspect of such conduct – including, in particular, any step taken to pursue proceedings and the obtaining of a judgement'.[46] In its decision, the Court of Appeal made it clear that the proper interpretation of section 328 did not cover or affect legal proceedings. The Court arguably came to this decision through its interpretation of 'being concerned in an arrangement', with Brooke LJ stating that there was a 'strong argument for a restricted understanding of the concept',[47] and saying that 'as a matter of ordinary language, our impression

---

39 *R v Sail (Abdulrahman)* [2006] UKHL 18, para. 52.
40 [2006] EWCA Civ 1039.
41 The Financial Services Commission, *Guidance Notes – Systems of Control to Prevent the Financial System from Being Used for Money Laundering or Terrorist Financing Activities* (Financial Services Commission, 2011, 8.1).
42 A. Hudson, *The Law of Finance* (Sweet and Maxwell: Hebden Bridge, 2009, 350).
43 [2004] Fam 1.
44 J. Collins and A. Kennedy, 'The cheat, his wife and her lawyer' (2003) *Taxation*, November, 136.
45 [2005] EWCA Civ 226.
46 [2005] EWCA Civ 226, para. 52.
47 [2005] EWCA Civ 226, para. 63.

on reading s. 328 was and remains that, whatever Parliament may have had in mind by the phrase "entering into or becomes concerned in an arrangement which . . . facilitates" it is most unlikely that it was thinking of legal proceedings'.[48] Ordinary legal activities, such as securing injunctive relief, steps needing to be taken in litigation, dividing assets in accordance with judgment, alternative dispute resolutions and securing freezing orders, therefore fall outside what is considered under section 328 to be an arrangement.

Acquiring, using or possessing criminal property – section 329 POCA 2002

The third principal money laundering offence is found in section 329(1) of POCA 2002.[49] This section provides that a person commits an offence if they acquire, use or have in their possession criminal property. For the purposes of the offence, possession means physical custody. For a person to be convicted of an offence, it has to be proven that the property handled is criminal property and that it comprises a benefit. Furthermore, the prosecution has to prove that the defendant knows or suspects that the property is obtained from criminal conduct.

Defences

A person does not commit an offence under section 327 POCA 2002 if 'he makes an authorised disclosure under section 338 and (if the disclosure is made before he does the act mentioned in subsection (1)) he has the appropriate consent'.[50] This is known as the consent defence[51] and relates to consent given to the defendant that they can proceed on the basis of the authorised disclosure. An authorised disclosure is 'a disclosure to a constable, a customs officer or a nominated officer by the alleged offender that property is criminal property',[52] with the defence also applying to situations whether the defendant intended to make a disclosure but had a reasonable excuse for not doing so: the reasonable excuse defence. Furthermore, a person does not commit an offence if

a)   he knows or believes on reasonable grounds, that the relevant criminal conduct occurred in a particular country or territory outside the United Kingdom, and
b)   the relevant criminal conduct –

    (i)   was not, at the time it occurred, unlawful under the criminal law then applying in that country or territory, and
    (ii) is not of a description prescribed by an order made by the Secretary of State.[53]

---

48 [2005] EWCA Civ 226, para. 64.
49 This unifies and replaces Drug Trafficking Act 1994, s. 51 and Criminal Justice Act 1988, s. 93B.
50 Proceeds of Crime Act 2002, s. 327(2).
51 See *Hosni Tayeb v HSBC Bank plc* [2004] EWHC 1529.
52 Proceeds of Crime Act 2002, s. 338(1).
53 Proceeds of Crime Act 2002, s. 327(2A).

Finally, and applying only to deposit taking institutions, a body does not commit an offence if 'a) it does the act in operating an account maintained with it, and b) the value of the criminal property concerned is less than the threshold amount determined under s. 339A for the act'.[54] This is currently set at £250 and has been at this level since 1 July 2005. Similar defences also exist for section 328 and section 329 offences.

In addition to those defences outlined above, and only in relation to a section 329 offence, section 329(2)(c) provides the adequate consideration defence. This covers those people who have accepted dirty money for ordinary consumable goods and/ or services. In such cases, the person receiving the money is not obliged to question the source of it.[55] It can also be relied upon by professional advisors who have received money for or on account of costs (unless it is a gross overpayment of the services given), but will not apply if the defendant knows or suspects that the payment will help another to carry out criminal conduct. If this is the case, the person is treated as not having paid proper consideration.[56] Employees working within the regulated sector may also have a defence if they can prove that they have received inadequate training from their employers on matters of money laundering and/or their requirements to disclose.

The extent of money laundering

Because of the secretive nature of money laundering, it is extremely difficult to measure the true extent of the problem, with many previous attempts proving largely unsuccessful.[57] This is further hampered by the fact there are so many different ways that organised criminals launder money, as discussed above. Despite these difficulties there have been claims that money laundering is one of the world's largest industries, with an International Monetary Fund (IMF) assessment in 1998 suggesting that it was equal to 2–5 per cent of global gross domestic product (GDP).[58] Furthermore, Spalek claims that the amount is approximately US$500 billion per year;[59] Maylam argues that it could be as much as US$1.5 trillion[60] whilst Walker

---

54 Proceeds of Crime Act 2002, s. 327(2C).

55 Annotation notes to Proceeds of Crime Act 2002, s. 327.

56 Crown Prosecution Service, 'Proceeds of Crime Act 2002 Part 7 – money laundering offences', available from http://www.cps.gov.uk/legal/p_to_r/proceeds_of_crime_money_laundering/, accessed 6 July 2011.

57 For an excellent discussion of this very point see B. Unger, *The Scale and Impacts of Money Laundering* (Edward Elgar: Cheltenham, 2007).

58 Financial Services Authority, 'Frequently asked questions' (Financial Services Authority: London, 2011), available from http://www.fsa.gov.uk/pages/About/What/financial_crime/money_laundering/faqs/index.shtml, accessed 6 June 2011.

59 R. Spalek, 'Regulation, White–collar crime and the Bank of Credit and Commerce International' (2001) *Howard Journal of Criminal Justice*, 40, 166–179, at 167.

60 S. Maylam, 'Prosecution for money laundering in the UK' (2002) *Journal of Financial Crime*, 10, 157–158, at 158.

estimates that in fact it could be nearer US$2.85 trillion.[61] The United Nations Office on Drugs and Crime (UNODC) agreed with the IMF 2–5 per cent of global GDP, estimating that this equates to an annual amount of between US$800 billion and US$2 trillion.[62] Additionally, the UNODC reported that in 2009 the estimated amount of money laundered by criminals 'was $1.6 trillion, or 2.7% global GDP'.[63] The report added that this was still consistent with the earlier and often cited figure of the IMF's original 'consensus range'.[64]

Figures for the UK are fairly disparate. It was once thought that the amount of money laundered on an annual basis in the UK ranged from £19 billion to £48 billion,[65] although HM Treasury took the view that 'each year £10 billion of illicit funds passed through the regulated sector'.[66] Other estimates include Yeandle et al., who concluded that the amount of money laundered is approximately £25 billion,[67] with Transparency International arguing that the annual amount is nearer £48 billion.[68] These figures, which were based on a 1999 HM Customs and Excise assessment, would now produce estimates of between £23 billion and £57 billion.[69] Although, if we take the IMF estimation of between 2 and 5 per cent GDP and base it on the GDP figures for the UK in 2010 (£1,473 billion[70]) we are looking at between £29.46 billion and £73.65 billion. In 2014, when the GDP in the UK was £1,732 billion,[71] this amounted to between £34.64 billion and £86.6 billion. The amount of money involved is therefore of epic proportions and requires an effective monitoring and prevention strategy.

---

61 J. Walker, 'Modelling global money laundering flows – some findings', available from http://www.johnwalkercrimetrendsanalysis.com.au/ML%20method.htm, accessed 6 June 2011.

62 United Nations Office on Drugs and Crime, 'Money-laundering and globalization', available from http://www.unodc.org/unodc/en/money-laundering/globalization.html, accessed 6 July 2011.

63 United Nations Office on Drugs and Crime, *Estimating Illicit Financial Flows Resulting from Drug Trafficking and Other Transnational Organised Crimes* (United Nations Office on Drugs and Crime, 2011, 5).

64 *Ibid.*

65 J. Harvey, 'An evaluation of money laundering policies' (2005) *Journal of Money Laundering Control*, 8(4), 339–345, at 340.

66 Financial Conduct Authority, *Anti-Money Laundering Annual Report 2012/13* (Financial Conduct Authority: London, 2013, 3). Also see HM Treasury, *The Financial Challenge to Crime and Terrorism* (HM Treasury: London, 2007).

67 M. Yeandle, M. Mainelli, A. Berendt, and B. Healy, *Anti-Money Laundering Requirements: Costs, Benefits and Perceptions* (Corporation of London, 2005, 15).

68 Transparency International, 'Corruption statistics', n/d, available from http://www.transparency.org.uk/corruption/statistics-and-quotes/uk-corruption, accessed 16 June 2016.

69 Financial Services Authority, 'Frequently asked questions' (Financial Services Authority, 2011), available from http://www.fsa.gov.uk/pages/About/What/financial_crime/money_laundering/faqs/index.shtml, accessed 6 June 2011.

70 UK Public Spending, 'UK gross domestic product', available from http://www.ukpublicspending.co.uk/downchart_ukgs.php?title=UK%20Gross%20Domestic%20Product&year=1950_2010&chart=, accessed 6 June 2011.

71 UK Public Spending, 'UK gross domestic product', available from http://www.ukpublicspending.co.uk/, accessed 23 July 2015.

Policy background – where did the offence originate from?

The origins of the UK's money laundering policy are to be found not in the European Union (EU), but in the declaration of the 'war on drugs' by President Richard Nixon in the 1970s. President Ronald Regan and subsequent United States (US) administrations have continued to follow the model used. This is not surprising as money laundering is inherently linked with the sale, production and manufacture of illegal narcotic substances, which resulted in its prevention being pushed to the top of the international community's criminal justice agenda in the 1980s. This community, largely led by the United Nations (UN) and the EU, introduced a wide range of legislative measures that aimed to tackle money laundering and the problems it presents. These measures included, for example, the UN Convention against Illicit Traffic in Narcotic Drugs and Psychotropic Substances, which is more commonly referred to as the Vienna Convention.[72] The Vienna Convention provides that signatories must criminalise the laundering of drug proceeds, implement instruments to allow for the determination of jurisdiction over the offence of money laundering, permit the confiscation of the proceeds of the sale of illegal drugs and/or materials used in their manufacturing, introduce mechanisms to facilitate extradition matters and provide measures to improve mutual legal assistance. The UK signed the Vienna Convention in December 1988 and ratified it in June 1991.[73] The impact of the Vienna Convention is illustrated by the Criminal Justice (International Co-operation) Act 1990,[74] part two of which is entitled the Vienna Convention. It is also important to note that the Convention only applies to drug trafficking offences. The scope of the UN's legislative measures was therefore extended by the UN Convention against Transnational Organised Crime, or the Palermo Convention,[75] to include the 'proceeds of serious crime'.[76] The UK signed the Palermo Convention in December 2000, and ratified it in February 2006.[77] Evidence of its influence is illustrated by the fact that it is referred to in the Serious Organised Crime and Police Act 2005.[78] The scope of the UN's legislative remit to tackle money laundering was extended by the introduction of its

---

72 United Nations Convention against Illicit Traffic in Narcotic Drugs and Psychotropic Substances (1988).

73 Financial Action Task Force, *Third Mutual Evaluation Report Anti-Money Laundering and Combating the Financing of Terrorism – United Kingdom* (Financial Action Task Force: Paris, 2007, 250).

74 Booth *et al.* noted that this Act was 'enacted partly to enable the United Kingdom to implement the Vienna Convention'. See R. Booth, S. Farrell, G. Bastable, and N. Yeo, *Money Laundering Law and Regulation a Practical Guide* (Oxford University Press: Oxford, 2011, 15).

75 United Nations Convention against Transnational Organized Crime, G.A. Res. 55/25, U.N. GAOR, 55th Sess., Supp. No. 49, Vol. I, at 43, U.N. Doc. A/55/49.

76 R. McDonnell, 'UN anti-money laundering initiatives' in W. Muller, C. Kalin, and J. Goldsworth (eds.), *Anti-Money Laundering International Law and Practice* (John Wiley and Sons: Chichester, 2004, 51).

77 Financial Action Task Force, *Third Mutual Evaluation Report Anti-Money Laundering and Combating the Financing of Terrorism – United Kingdom* (Financial Action Task Force: Paris, 2007, 250).

78 Serious Organised Crime and Police Act 2005, s. 95.

within the strategy'.[94] Furthermore, in its 2007 Mutual Evaluation Report the FATF concluded that the UK was fully compliant on 19 out of the 40 Recommendations, largely compliant on nine, partially compliant on nine and non-compliant on only three.[95] The report concluded that the UK has a far-reaching AML legislative framework that fully complies with both the Vienna and Palermo conventions.[96] The UK's current AML and counter-terrorist financing measures will again be assessed by the FATF in 2016.[97]

In addition to the Recommendations, another important industry guideline is the Basel Committee on Banking Regulation and Supervisory Principles. The Committee has published a Statement of Principles, which is consistent with the Recommendations, and also a number of best practice papers that highlight ways to prevent the financial system becoming an instrument for financial crime clients.[98] The UK is a member of the Basel Committee on Banking Supervision and a founding member of the Egmont Group of FIUs. The objective of the Egmont group is to 'increase and improve the communication between FIUs worldwide to help fight what is recognised as a universal problem'.[99] The UK's AML policy has therefore been influenced by the legislative and preventative measures of the international community and by international best practices and industry guidelines. The UK's money laundering policy is managed and implemented by several government departments, financial regulatory and law enforcement agencies, many of which are considered below.

Financial institutions and regulatory bodies

HM Treasury and the Home Office

HM Treasury is the leading money laundering authority in the UK and is responsible for the implementation of the Money Laundering Directives and the execution of the UN's financial sanctions regime. It is the UK's representative at the FATF and sanctions the industry guidelines on compliance with money laundering controls.[100] The importance of the role of HM Treasury is illustrated by the publication

---

94 HM Treasury, 'Appointment of the UK president of the Financial Action Task Force', available from http://www.gov-news.org/gov/uk/news/appointment_uk_president_financial_action/36083.html, accessed 3 July 2011.

95 Financial Action Task Force, *Third Mutual Evaluation Report Anti-Money Laundering and Combating the Financing of Terrorism – United Kingdom* (Financial Action Task Force: Paris, 2007, 10–15).

96 *Ibid.*

97 For the purpose of this review the FATF will be using its new methodology that was adopted in February 2013. See Financial Action Task Force, Methodology for Assessing Technical Compliance with the FATF Recommendations and the Effectiveness of AML/CFT Systems (Financial Action Task Force: Paris, 2013).

98 M. Simpson, 'International initiatives' in M. Simpson, N. Smith, and A. Srivastava (eds.), *International Guide to Money Laundering Law and Practice* (Bloomsbury Professional: Haywards Heath, 2010, 202).

99 *Ibid.*

100 Financial Action Task Force, *Third Mutual Evaluation Report Anti-Money Laundering and Combating the Financing of Terrorism – United Kingdom* (Financial Action Task Force: Paris, 2007, 24).

of its money laundering strategy,[101] where the objective is to create an effective AML framework that seeks to achieve an appropriate balance between tackling money laundering whilst preventing the imposition of burdensome compliance regulations. In relation to this, HM Treasury has taken the view that,

> [t]he existing [AML] regime consists of measures ranging from provisions in the criminal law to punish money launderers and to deprive them of their proceeds, to the obligation on the financial services industry and certain other sectors and professions to identify their customers and to report suspicious activities when necessary.[102]

The objective of HM Treasury is thus to safeguard 'the integrity of the financial system from exploitation by criminals and terrorists. It does this by deploying financial tools to deter, detect and disrupt crime and security threats. The approach taken is effective and proportionate to the risks posed as well as engaging with business, law makers and law enforcers.'[103] This is clearly illustrated by the publication of its second strategy document in 2007 which outlined how the government intended to tackle the problems associated with money laundering and the financing of terrorism.[104]

HM Treasury co-chairs the Money Laundering Advisory Committee with the Home Office, which is a 'forum for all relevant stakeholders [including] financial institutions, trade and consumer organisations, government and law enforcement representatives'.[105] The Money Laundering Advisory Committee 'advises the government on its approach to preventing money laundering in the UK . . . members include representatives from law enforcement, government, industry and regulators. The Committee reviews industry guidance before it is approved by the Treasury.'[106] Furthermore, HM Treasury also provides a critical role in selecting and appointing controllers of the AML sector. This role has resulted in the publication of an annual AML report which outlines good practices in the AML arena.[107] Furthermore, HM

---

101 HM Treasury, *The Financial Challenge of Terrorism and Crime* (HM Treasury: London, 2007, 77).
102 *Ibid.*, 11.
103 HM Treasury, *The Financial Challenge of Terrorism and Crime* (HM Treasury: London, 2007).
104 *Ibid.*
105 Oxford Analytica Ltd., 'Country report: Anti-money laundering rules in the United Kingdom' in M. Pieith and G. Aiolfi (eds.), *A Comparative Guide to Anti-Money Laundering a Critical Analysis of Systems in Singapore, Switzerland, the UK and the USA* (Edward Elgar: Cheltenham, 2004, 271).
106 HM Treasury, 'Policy paper: Preventing money laundering', 5 June 2013, available from https://www.gov.uk/government/publications/preventing-money-laundering/preventing-money-laundering#financial-action-task-force-fatf, accessed 1 July 2015.
107 See HM Treasury, *Anti-Money Laundering and Counter Terrorist Finance Supervision Report 2010–11* (HM Treasury: London, 2011). Since the publication of the first report, HM Treasury have published three further reports. See HM Treasury, *Anti-Money Laundering and Counter Terrorist Finance Supervision Report 2011–12* (HM Treasury: London, 2012), HM Treasury, *Anti-Money Laundering and Counter Terrorist Finance Supervision Report 2012–13* (HM Treasury: London, 2012) and HM Treasury, *Anti-Money Laundering and Counter Terrorist Finance Supervision Report 2013–14* (HM Treasury: London, 2013).

Treasury plays a very important role in ensuring that businesses comply with the AML regulations. For example, HM Treasury approves guidance that is written by the business sector, and the UK courts are obliged to take these guidance notes into consideration. This includes the guidelines for credit and financial institutions,[108] auditors,[109] insolvency practitioners,[110] external auditors,[111] tax advisors,[112] independent legal professionals,[113] trust or company service providers,[114] high-value dealers,[115] casinos[116] and all property professionals.[117] HM Treasury also issues Advisory Notices on countries that are deemed to have weak AML and CTF systems.[118] The Counter-Terrorism Act 2008 provides that firms are obliged to embark on further due diligence obligations with financial transactions involving bodies or persons from those named countries.[119] In this role, HM Treasury is further supported by the Home Office, which is responsible for managing police forces in England and Wales, and NCA, which acts as the UK's FIU. In relation to money laundering, the Home Office manages the asset recovery scheme and the mutual legal assistance regime.

The Financial Services Authority

Between 1997 and 2012 the Financial Services Authority (FSA) was an integral part of the UK's AML system and it could be said that it was a key policymaker. The

---

108 Joint Money Laundering Steering Group, *Prevention of Money Laundering/Combating Terrorist Financing: Guidance for the UK Financial Sector: Parts 1–3* (Joint Money Laundering Steering Group: London, 2014).
109 *Ibid.*
110 The Consultative Committee of Accountancy Boards, *Anti-Money Laundering Guidance for the Accountancy Sector* (Consultative Committee of Accountancy Boards: London, 2007).
111 *Ibid.*
112 Financial Reporting Council, *Money Laundering Guidance for Auditors on UK Legislation: Practice Note 12 (Revised)* (Financial Reporting Council: London, 2010).
113 See for example, International Bar Association, the American Bar Association and the Council of Bars and Law Societies of Europe, *A Lawyer's Guide to Detecting and Preventing Money Laundering* (International Bar Association, the American Bar Association and the Council of Bars and Law Societies of Europe: London, 2014).
114 HM Revenue and Customs, *Anti-Money Laundering Guidance for Trust or Company Service Providers* (HM Revenue and Customs: London, 2010).
115 HM Revenue and Customs, 'Notice MLR9b: Money laundering regulations registration guide for high value dealers', 13 September 2013, available from https://www.gov.uk/government/publications/notice-mlr9b-money-laundering-regulations-registration-guide-for-high-value-dealers/notice-mlr9b-money-laundering-regulations-registration-guide-for-high-value-dealers, accessed 1 July 2015.
116 The Gambling Commission, *Money Laundering: The Prevention of Money Laundering and Combating the Financing of Terrorism Guidance for Remote and Non-Remote Casinos Second Edition* (The Gambling Commission: London, 2013).
117 Royal Institute for Chartered Surveyors, *Money Laundering Guidance* (Royal Institute for Chartered Surveyors: London, 2011).
118 HM Treasury, *Advisory Notice on Money Laundering and Terrorist Financing Controls in Overseas Jurisdictions* (HM Treasury: London, 2015).
119 For a more detailed discussion see M. Goldby, 'The impact of Schedule 7 of the Counter-Terrorism Act 2008 on banks and their customers' (2010) *Journal of Money Laundering Control*, 13(4), 351–371 and G. Rees and T. Moloney, 'The latest efforts to interrupt terrorist supply lines: Schedule 7 to the Counter-Terrorism Act 2008' (2010) *Criminal Law Review*, 2, 127–135.

Authority was established following a number of high-profile financial scandals between the 1970s and 1990s, which were arguably caused by poor banking regulation by the Bank of England. The FSA were therefore given extensive rule making and enforcement powers under the Financial Services and Markets Act (FSMA) 2000. Under this Act the FSA had a duty to reduce financial crime by ensuring that financial institutions had systems and practices in place that protected them against being used by financial criminals as vehicles to launder money. Financial crime is broadly defined within the FSMA 2000 as incorporating any offence including fraud or dishonesty,[120] misconduct in, or misuse of information relating to, a financial market,[121] or handling the proceeds of crime.[122] The principal objective of the FSA was, therefore, to focus on the AML systems and controls that the regulated sector had in place.[123] Under the FSMA 2000 the FSA made rules in relation to the prevention and detection of money laundering.[124] The rule making powers of the FSA were originally contained in the Money Laundering Sourcebook,[125] but these were detailed, burdensome and very similar to those in the Money Laundering Regulations 1993. The Money Laundering Sourcebook was therefore replaced by a principles-based approach in the Senior Management Arrangements, Systems and Controls (SYSC) part of the FSA's *Handbook*.[126]

The most important tools that the FSA had in the fight against money laundering were its extensive investigative and enforcement powers.[127] The FSA had the ability to require information from firms,[128] to appoint investigators,[129] to obtain the assistance of overseas financial regulators[130] and provide appointed investigators with additional powers.[131] Furthermore, the FSA became a prosecuting authority in respect of certain money laundering offences.[132] These powers applied whether

---

120 Financial Services and Markets Act 2000, s. 6 (3)(a).
121 Financial Services and Markets Act 2000, s. 6 (3)(b).
122 Financial Services and Markets Act 2000, s. 6 (3)(c).
123 A. Proctor, 'Supporting a risk-based anti-money laundering approach through enforcement action' (2004) *Journal of Financial Regulation and Compliance*, 13(1), 10–14, at 11. Members of the regulated sector are defined in the Financial Services and Markets Act 2000 (Regulated Activities) Order 2001, S.I. 2001/544.
124 Financial Services and Markets Act 2000, s. 146.
125 Financial Services Authority, *Money Laundering Handbook* (Financial Services Authority, 2006). The FSA adopted the Money Laundering Regulation 1993 via the Financial Services and Markets Act 2000 Regulations (Relating to Money Laundering Regulations) 2001, S.I. 2001/1819.
126 The FSA Handbook contains the FSA's legal rules and guidance on a wide range of measures and can be accessed from http://www.fsa.gov.uk/Pages/handbook/index.shtml.
127 J. Bagge, 'The future for enforcement under the new Financial Services Authority' (1998) *The Company Lawyer*, 19(7), 194–197, at 195.
128 Financial Services and Markets Act 2000, ss. 165–166.
129 Financial Services and Markets Act 2000, ss. 167–168.
130 Financial Services and Markets Act 2000, s. 169.
131 Financial Services and Markets Act 2000, s. 172.
132 The prosecutorial powers of the FSA were confirmed by the Supreme Court in *R v Rollins* [2010] UK SC 39.

or not the entity to be prosecuted was actually regulated by the FSA.[133] The FSA also had the power to impose a financial penalty where it established that there had been a contravention by an authorised person of any requirement imposed under the FSMA 2000.[134] For example, the FSA fined firms' Money Laundering Reporting Officers (MLRO) and imposed a series of fines on firms that had breached their AML rules even where there was no evidence of money being laundered.[135]

At the time of writing the first edition of this book, the FSA remained the UK's financial regulatory agency. However, following the introduction of the Financial Services Act in 2012, the FSA was abolished and replaced by the Financial Conduct Authority (FCA) and the Prudential Regulation Authority (PRA). Therefore, the next section of the chapter provides a commentary on the role of the FCA towards countering the threat posed by money laundering.

The Financial Conduct Authority

The origins of the FCA can be traced back to the 2007–08 financial crisis and the clear failings of the FSA, as graphically illustrated by the near collapse of Northern Rock. One of the most important sections of the 2010 Coalition government's agreement was the desire to reform the then system of banking regulation. The Coalition agreement provided 'we will reform the regulatory system to avoid a repeat of the financial crisis. We will bring forward proposals to give the Bank of England control of macro-prudential regulation and oversight of micro-prudential regulation.'[136] This was more commonly referred to as the 'tripartite' system of banking regulation that was administered by HM Treasury, the FSA and the Bank of England. In June 2010, the Chancellor of the Exchequer George Osborne MP outlined in greater detail the Coalition government's financial services policy. Of particular relevance to this chapter was the decision to abolish the FSA and transfer its supervisory powers to the Bank of England,[137] create a Financial Policy Committee within the Bank of England, establish the PRA that would be responsible for the day-to-day supervision of financial institutions, establish the Consumer Protection Markets Authority that would regulate the conduct of all financial services firms, establish the Economic Crime Agency (ECA), create the Independent Commission on Banking and introduce a specific bank levy.[138] The Financial Services

---

133 Financial Services and Markets Act 2000, s. 402 (1)(a).

134 Financial Services and Markets Act 2000, s. 206 (1).

135 See FSA Press Release, 'FSA fines Alpari and its former money laundering reporting officer, Sudipto Chattopadhyay for anti-money laundering failings', 5 May 2010, available from http://www.fsa.gov.uk/pages/Library/Communication/PR/2010/077.shtml, accessed 6 July 2011.

136 HM Government, *The Coalition: Our Programme for Government* (HM Government: London, 2010, 9).

137 See HM Treasury, *A New Approach to Financial Regulation: Consultation on Reforming the Consumer Credit Regime* (HM Treasury: London, 2010).

138 HM Treasury, 'Financial Services Policy Agenda', available from http://www.hm-treasury.gov.uk/fin_policy_agenda_index.htm, accessed 19 July 2011.

Act 2012 resulted in the transformation of the tripartite system of banking regulation into what has become referred to as the 'twin peaks' approach.

In relation to money laundering, the FCA has adopted a very similar approach as that practised by the FSA. According to its website, the FCA describes itself as 'the competent authority for supervising compliance of most credit and financial institutions with the Money Laundering Regulations'.[139] In the latest version of the SYSC part of the *Handbook*, the regulated sector is required to have in place systems and controls that are appropriate for the firm to conduct its business.[140] This includes: a requirement to carry out regular assessments of the adequacy of AML systems so as to protect themselves from being used to further financial crime;[141] allocation of a director or senior manager with overall responsibility for establishing and maintaining an AML system; and, the appointment of a MLRO.[142] The SYSC regime thus seeks to provide the regulated sector with an even higher degree of flexibility, which allows regulated firms to identify the risks and determine how they can best allocate their resources in areas that are most vulnerable. This approach seeks to encourage and enable the regulated sector to target their resources most appropriately on activities at risk from money laundering, thus reducing AML compliance costs. Furthermore, regulated firms are required to 'establish, implement and maintain adequate policies and procedures sufficient to ensure compliance of the firm including its managers, employees and appointed representatives (or where applicable, tied agents) with its obligations under the regulatory system and for countering the risk that the firm might be used to further financial crime'.[143]

Additionally, the SYSC part of the *Handbook* requires that a regulated firm 'must ensure the policies and procedures established under SYSC 6.1.1R include systems and controls that (1) enable it to identify, assess, monitor and manage *money laundering* risk; and (2) are comprehensive and proportionate to the nature, scale and complexity of its activities.'[144] Furthermore, a 'firm must carry out a regular assessment of the adequacy of these systems and controls to ensure that they continue to comply with SYSC 6.3.1 R'.[145] The *Handbook* also provides that 'A firm must allocate to a director or senior manager (who may also be the money laundering reporting officer) overall responsibility within the firm for the establishment and maintenance of effective anti-money laundering systems and controls.'[146] Finally, an authorised firm is also required to appoint an MLRO who is responsible for maintaining the firm's compliance the rules.[147]

---

139   Financial Conduct Authority, 'Anti-money laundering', 14 November 2011, available from https://www.fca.org.uk/firms/being-regulated/meeting-your-obligations/firm-guides/systems/aml, accessed 24 June 2015.

140   Financial Services Authority, *FSA Handbook* (Financial Services Authority, 2006, SYSC 3.1.1).

141   *Ibid.*, SYSC 3.2.6 C.

142   *Ibid.*, SYSC 3.2.6 H and I.

143   *Ibid.*, SYSC 6.1.1.

144   *Ibid.*, SYSC 6.3.1.

145   *Ibid.*, SYSC 6.3.3.

146   *Ibid.*, SYSC 6.3.8.

147   *Ibid.*, SYSC 6.3.9.

The Serious Organised Crime Agency

The Serious Organised Crime Agency (SOCA) was the UK's FIU and as such administers the assets recovering provisions under the POCA 2002.[148] It took over this role from the National Criminal Intelligence Service in 2005. SOCA was created by the Serious Organised Crime and Police Act 2005 and at that time was a major part of the then government's organised crime strategy. SOCA has three objectives: i) to tackle serious organised crime, ii) to gather information relating to crime, and iii) other general considerations. In relation to organised crime, the Act states that SOCA has the function of preventing and detecting serious organised crime, in addition to contributing to the reduction of such crime and the mitigation of its consequences.[149] Furthermore, section 3 provides that in relation to information on serious crime the function of SOCA is the 'gathering, storing, analysing and disseminating [of] information relevant to (a) the prevention, detection, investigation or prosecution of offences, or (b) the reduction of crime in other ways or the mitigation of its consequences'.[150]

The National Crime Agency

In May 2010, the Coalition government (Conservatives and Liberal Democrats) published its Coalition agreement, which contained a commitment to tackle economic crime. The agreement proposed that the roles of the Serious Fraud Office (SFO), the FSA and the Office of Fair Trading would be merged into the ECA. The Chancellor of the Exchequer stated 'we take white collar crime as seriously as other crime and we are determined to simplify the confusing and overlapping responsibilities in this area in order to improve detection and enforcement'.[151] It was made clear that the government's ambition was to get serious about white collar crime, including fraud, insider dealing, bribery, corruption and, for the purposes of this chapter, money laundering. The government has therefore arguably recognised that the existing multiplicity of disparate agencies has led to conflicting priorities and ineffective outcomes. The proposal to create a one-stop shop has been advocated for many years but has been given fresh impetus by the Policy Exchange research note on Fighting Fraud and Financial Crime.[152] This paper argued that the interests of fraud detection, investigation and prosecution would be better served by a unified approach mandated to tackle economic crime. The Coalition government proposed that the ECA would be led by the Home Office, which historically has

---

148 However, it is important to note that it is likely this role will transfer to the National Crime Agency during the next parliamentary year.
149 Serious Organised Crime and Police Act 2005, s. 2(1)(a) and (b).
150 Serious Organised Crime and Police Act 2005, s. 3(1)(a) and (b).
151 HM Treasury, 'George Osborne, Chancellor of the Exchequer: Speech at the Lord Mayor's dinner for bankers & merchants of the City of London, at Mansion House', 16 June 2010, available from http://www.hm-treasury.gov.uk/press_12_10.htm, accessed 26 June 2010.
152 J. Fisher and T. Sumpster, *Fighting Fraud and Financial Crime* (Policy Exchange, 2010, London 12).

adopted a piecemeal approach towards tackling financial crime.[153] To further this endeavour, the Home Office began a consultation process with key stakeholders and expected the 'initial elements of the ECA' to be in place by 2011.[154]

However, before this could take place, in June 2010, the Home Secretary announced the creation of the NCA which has been set up to tackle organised crime, fraud, cybercrime, maintain border protection and protect children and young people. The NCA is divided into four distinct divisions: i) Organised Crime Command, ii) Border Policing Command, iii) Economic Crime Command, and iv) the Child Exploitation and Online Protection Centre.[155] The Home Office initially envisaged the role of the Economic Crime Command to 'ensure a coherent approach to the use of resources focused on economic crime across the full range of agencies deploying them'.[156] Furthermore, it is hoped that it will 'maintain an overview' of a wide range of economic crime agencies including the City of London Police and SFO.[157] The NCA was officially launched following the enactment of the Crime and Courts Act 2013. The 2013 Act gave the NCA several objectives including the crime reduction function and[158] the criminal intelligence function.[159] In relation to money laundering, the Crime and Courts Act states that the NCA will have the functions conferred by the POCA 2002, which includes its role as FIU and the management of the confiscation of the proceeds of crime. According to the NCA's website, it acts as the 'UK Financial Intelligence Unit [and] receives, analyses and distributes financial intelligence gathered from Suspicious Activity Reports'.[160]

HM Revenue and Customs

HM Revenue and Customs (HMRC) plays an important role in the prevention of money laundering on the basis that it is a designated supervisory authority under the Money Laundering Regulations 2007. It is responsible for high-value dealers, money services businesses, auditors, bill payment service providers and telecommunications firms.

Crown Prosecution Service

The Crown Prosecution Service (CPS) was established by the Prosecution of Offences Act 1985 and is one of the prosecuting authorities in the UK in relation

153 Home Office, 'Economic crime press release', 17 January 2011, available from http://www.homeoffice.gov.uk/media-centre/news/economic-crime, accessed 22 January 2011.
154 Ibid.
155 The Home Office, *The National Crime Agency – A Plan for the Creation of a National Crime-Fighting Capability* (Home Office: London, 2011).
156 Ibid., 20.
157 Ibid.
158 Crime and Courts Act 2013, s. 1(4).
159 Crime and Courts Act 2013, s. 1(5).
160 National Crime Agency, 'UK Financial Intelligence Unit', n/d, available from http://www.nationalcrimeagency.gov.uk/about-us/what-we-do/specialist-capabilities/ukfiu, accessed 25 June 2015.

to the offences of money laundering. In conjunction with the FCA, it initiates criminal proceedings on receiving financial intelligence from the NCA.

British Bankers Association and Building Societies Association

The British Bankers Association, created in 1919, is the leading trade association for banks operating in the UK. It has approximately 300 members and its principle purpose being to combat money laundering. In this role it has produced AML guidelines for banks, which are published by the Joint Money Laundering Steering Group (JMLSG). The Building Societies Association performs a very similar role to the British Bankers Association in that it seeks to tackle money laundering by providing AML guidance notes, information and the latest money laundering trends. This is similarly disseminated via the JMLSG.[161]

Joint Money Laundering Steering Group

The JMLSG consists of 17 of the leading UK trade associations in the financial services industry.[162] Its objective is to disseminate good practice among the financial services sector; to counter the threat posed by money laundering; and, to provide workable and practical assistance in interpreting the 2007 Money Laundering Regulations. This is achieved by issuing detailed guidance notes, which are regularly amended to coincide with the publication and implementation of new Money Laundering Regulations.[163] Leong notes that its aim is 'to provide an indication of good generic industry practice and a base from which management can develop tailored policies and procedures that are appropriate to their businesses'.[164] Hopton furthermore argues that 'they are also a good source of industry practice and provide management with advice and assistance'.[165] Importantly, the FSA previously recommended that firms should 'read the JMLSG guidance notes in conjunction with the FSA's rules'.[166]

Finance and Leasing Association

The Finance and Leasing Association is the trade association for the asset, consumer and motor finance industries in the UK. Members come from the banking sector,

---

161 Building Societies Association, 'Financial crime prevention', available from http://www.bsa.org. uk/policy/policyissues/fcpandphysec/financialcrime.htm, accessed 1 July 2011.

162 Joint Money Laundering Steering Group, 'Who are the members of the JMLSG?', available from http://www.jmlsg.org.uk/bba/jsp/polopoly.jsp?d=777&a=9907, accessed 18 June 2010.

163 D. Hopton, *Money Laundering a Concise Guide for All Businesses* (Gower: Farnham, 2009, 43).

164 A. Leong, 'Chasing dirty money: Domestic and international measures against money laundering' (2007) *Journal of Money Laundering Control*, 10(2), 140–156, at 144–145.

165 D. Hopton, *Money Laundering a Concise Guide for All Businesses* (Gower, 2009, 43).

166 Oxford Analytica Ltd., 'Country report: Anti-money laundering rules in the United Kingdom' in M. Pieith and G. Aiolfi (eds.), *A Comparative Guide to Anti-Money Laundering a Critical Analysis of Systems in Singapore, Switzerland, the UK and the USA* (Edward Elgar: Cheltenham, 2004, 276).

subsidiaries of banks and building societies, the finance divisions of retail companies and a number of independent firms. The Finance and Leasing Association represents its members on a wide range of AML initiatives, including the City of London Police's Economic Crime Unit; SOCA's work in non-fiscal and identification related crime; the National Fraud Authority's (NFA) work, which includes coordinating the fight against financial crime and fraud between the National Fraud Reporting Centre and the National Fraud Intelligence Bureau; and, the work of JMLSG.

Association of British Insurers

The Association of British Insurers is the trade association for the UK's insurance industry. It has over 400 members who are authorised by the FCA and are bound by its AML rules.

Royal Institute of Chartered Surveyors

The Royal Institute of Chartered Surveyors is an industry representative for estate agents and other specialised firms involved in land, construction and environmental issues. It publishes AML guidance notes and liaises with the National Association of Estate Agents.[167] Its members are bound by the Money Laundering Regulations 2007 and rely on guidance notes provided by SOCA, the Office of Fair Trading (OFT), HMRC and HM Treasury.

The Law Society England and Wales

The Law Society represents solicitors in England and Wales and is committed to assisting solicitors to meet their AML obligations.[168] Solicitors are bound by the Money Laundering Regulations 2007, with guidance on this issued by the Law Society via an AML practice note published in 2009.[169]

Financial intelligence

With the existence of so many authorities and bodies involved in AML measures, one of the most important and traditional money laundering countermeasures is the use of financial intelligence. The UK introduced its first money laundering reporting requirements by virtue of the Drug Trafficking Offences Act 1986 which has since been amended by the POCA 2002 and the Money Laundering Regulations 2007. A wide range of financial institutions in the regulated sector are thus

167 Royal Institute of Chartered Surveyors, *Money Laundering Guidance* (Royal Institute of Chartered Surveyors: London, 2010).
168 The Law Society. 'Anti-money laundering', available from http://www.lawsociety.org.uk/products andservices/antimoneylaundering.page, accessed 1 July 2011.
169 The Law Society, *Anti-Money Laundering Practice Note* (The Law Society: London, 2009).

required to report any allegations of money laundering to the NCA. The 2007 Regulations, as described above, were introduced to implement the Third Money Laundering Directive,[170] with its purpose being to 'impose standards of behaviour governing "know your client" regulations in relation to customers'.[171] The 2007 Regulations apply to a wide range of financial services institutions, including credit institutions,[172] financial institutions,[173] auditors,[174] insolvency practitioners,[175] external accountants,[176] tax advisers,[177] independent legal professionals,[178] trust or company service providers,[179] estate agents,[180] high-value dealers[181] and casinos.[182] For institutions in the financial services sector, Regulation 7 additionally requires them to apply customer due diligence measures where they suspect the transaction concerns money laundering or terrorist financing, or where they distrust a customer's identification. Customer due diligence measures are defined in Regulation 5 as:

(a) Identifying the customer and verifying the customer's identity on the basis of documents, data or information obtained from a reliable and independent source;

(b) Identifying, where there is a beneficial owner who is not the customer, the beneficial owner and taking adequate measures, on a risk-sensitive basis, to verify his identity, so that the relevant person is satisfied that he knows who the beneficial owner is, including, in the case of a legal person, trust, or similar legal arrangement, measures to understand the ownership and control structure of the person, trust or arrangement; and

---

170 Council Directive (EC) 2005/60 of 26 October 2005, [2005] OJ L309/15.

171 A. Hudson, *The Law of Finance* (Sweet and Maxwell: London, 2009, 360).

172 As defined in Article 4(1)(a) of the Banking Consolidation Directive 2000/12/EC of the European Parliament and of the Council of 20 March 2000 relating to the taking up and pursuit of the business of credit institutions.

173 This is defined as an undertaking, including a money service business, when it carries out one or more of the activities listed in points 2 to 12 and 14 of Annex 1 to the Banking Consolidation Directive.

174 An auditor is defined as 'any firm or individual who is a statutory auditor within the meaning of Companies Act 2006'.

175 Any person who acts as an insolvency practitioner within the meaning of Insolvency Act 1986, s. 388 as amended by Insolvency Act 2000, s. 3.

176 This is a firm or sole practitioner who by way of business provides accountancy services to other persons. Money Laundering Regulations 2007, regulation 3(7).

177 This is defined as a firm or sole practitioner who by way of business provides advice about the tax affairs of other persons, when providing such services. Money Laundering Regulations 2007, regulation 3(8).

178 An independent legal professional is a firm or sole practitioner who provides services of a legal nature concerning the sale and acquisition of real property, the administration of client money and other related activities. Money Laundering Regulations 2007, regulation 3(9).

179 A trust or company service provider is defined as a firm or sole practitioner who provides business services relating to the formation of legal entities or acts as an agent for another party to operate as a director or other relevant position within a company. Money Laundering Regulations 2007, regulation 3(10).

180 As defined by the Estate Agents Act 1979, s. 1.

181 A high-value dealer is a business or sole trader that deals in goods where the payment/s is at least 15,000 euros in total. Money Laundering Regulations 2007, regulation 3(12).

182 A casino holds an operating licence by virtue of the Gambling Act 2005, s. 65(2).

(c) Obtaining information on the purpose and intended nature of the business relationship.

This means that the firm is required to authenticate the identity of the customer and monitor their business relationships (Regulation 8). Moreover, casinos are under an individual obligation to determine the identity of customers by virtue of Regulation 10. The 2007 Regulations also impose obligations relating to record-keeping (Regulation 19), policies and procedures (Regulation 20) and staff training (Regulation 21) and contain provisions and obligations relating to supervision and registration (Regulations 23–36), creating enforcement powers for supervisors (Regulations 34–47), provisions for the recovery of penalties and charges (Regulation 48) and impose an obligation on some public authorities to report suspicions of money laundering or terrorist financing (Regulation 49).

If a firm suspects that it is being used for the purposes of money laundering, it is required to notify its MLRO who will complete a SAR and file it with the NCA, which determines if further action is to be taken. The overall effectiveness of the SAR regime has been questioned. For example, its deficiencies include an ineffective SARs database, weak monitoring of enforcement outcomes, inadequate training and a lack of governmental support for the scheme.[183] It has also been suggested that SARs are underused by law enforcement agencies, and law enforcement bodies continue to have poor management information on how SARs are utilised.[184] Despite these criticisms, the existence of these reporting requirements has created a fear factor in the regulated sector and has thus resulted in a significant increase in the number of SARs submitted to the NCA.[185] The accountancy firm KPMG noted that the number of SARs submitted between 1995 and 2002 increased from 5,000 to 60,000.[186] In 2008, SOCA reported that it had received 210,524 SARs,[187] which increased to 240,582 in 2010,[188] 247,601 in 2011,[189] 278,665 in 2012,[190] 316,527 in 2013[191] and 354,186 in 2014.[192]

This increase is directly attributable to the threat of sanctions by such organisations as the FCA, which, in the regulated sector, has adopted a tactic that has been

---

183 KPMG, *Money Laundering: Review of the Reporting System* (KPMG, 2003, London, 14).

184 *Ibid*.

185 R. Sarker, 'Anti-money laundering requirements: Too much pain for too little gain' (2006) *Company Lawyer*, 27(8), 250–251, at 251.

186 KPMG, *Money Laundering: Review of the Reporting System* (KPMG, 2003, London, 14).

187 Serious Organised Crime Agency, *The Suspicious Activity Reports Regime Annual Report 2008* (Serious Organised Crime Agency: London, 2008, 15).

188 Serious Organised Crime Agency, *The Suspicious Activity Reports Regime Annual Report 2010* (Serious Organised Crime Agency: London, 2010, 4).

189 Serious Organised Crime Agency, *The Suspicious Activity Reports Regime Annual Report 2011* (Serious Organised Crime Agency: London, 2011, 10).

190 Serious Organised Crime Agency, *The Suspicious Activity Reports Regime Annual Report 2012* (Serious Organised Crime Agency: London, 2012, 12).

191 National Crime Agency, *The Suspicious Activity Reports Regime Annual Report 2013* (National Crime Agency: London, 2013, 6).

192 National Crime Agency, *The Suspicious Activity Reports Regime Annual Report 2014* (National Crime Agency: London, 2014, 7).

referred to as defensive or preventative reporting.[193] Reporting entities have also complained about the significant increase in compliance costs,[194] which has resulted in suggestions that the AML reporting requirements should be abandoned and that the resources should be redirected elsewhere. Estimates of the compliance costs vary. For example, the British Bankers Association claim that their members spend £250 million each year in complying with the regulations,[195] whilst KPMG estimate that annual costs are nearer £90 million.[196] Such costs also appear to be rising exponentially each year. From survey data collected by KPMG, respondents in 2004 felt that compliance costs had increased by 61 per cent.[197] Three years later average costs had again increased by 58 per cent, had increased by 45 per cent over the next three years and by 53 per cent over the subsequent four years. Furthermore, research has suggested that the AML costs in the UK are higher than in other European countries including Germany, France and Italy.[198] In its 2004 AML strategy paper, HM Treasury asserted that one of the fundamental aims of its policy was to ensure that the compliance costs imposed were proportionate. We would argue, however, that this is simply not the case.

Sentencing and recovery

Criminal powers of prosecution

Because of the importance of and devastating effect caused by money laundering it is perhaps unsurprising that the maximum penalty for the offences contained within sections 327–329 of the POCA 2002 is 14 years,[199] although in the USA this maxima is set at 20 years.[200] In all cases, a fine can be imposed instead of or as well as imprisonment. Whilst in the UK, there is no maximum fine, the maximum financial penalty in the USA for money laundering is set at $500,000 or twice the value of the property involved in the crime.[201] It is also worth noting that in addition to the courts, and under the Money Laundering Regulations 2007 section 15(1), the Commissioners

---

193 A. Leong, 'Chasing dirty money: Domestic and international measures against money laundering' (2007) *Journal of Money Laundering Control*, 10(2), 140–156, at 142.

194 Home Office, *Report on the Operation in 2004 of the Terrorism Act 2000* (Home Office: London, 2004, 19–20).

195 *Ibid.*

196 KPMG, *Money Laundering: Review of the Reporting System* (KPMG, 2003, London, 46–47).

197 KPMG, 'Global anti-money laundering survey' (KPMG, 2014) available from https://www.kpmg.com/KY/en/IssuesAndInsights/ArticlesPublications/PublishingImages/global-anti-money-laundering-survey-v3.pdf.

198 M. Yeandle, M. Mainelli, A. Berendt, and B. Healy, *Anti-Money Laundering Requirements: Costs, Benefits and Perceptions* (Corporation of London, 2005).

199 Proceeds of Crime Act 2002, s. 334(1).

200 Australian Government and Australian Institute of Criminology, *Charges and Offences of Money Laundering* Transnational Crime Brief No. 4 (Australian Institute of Criminology: Canberra, 2008).

201 C. van Cleef, H. Silets, and P. Motz, 'Does the punishment fit the crime' (2004) *Journal of Financial Crime*, 12(1), 57.

TABLE 2.1 Money laundering prosecutions and convictions in the UK from 1999 to 2007[202]

	1999	2000	2001	2002	2003	2004	2005	2006	2007
Prosecutions	126	129	182	256	300	552	1,327	2,379	2,318
Convictions	39	50	75	86	123	207	595	1,273	1,348
Convictions (%)	30.95	38.76	41.21	33.59	41	37.5	44.84	53.51	58.15

may impose a penalty of such amount as they consider appropriate, not exceeding £5,000, on a person to whom Regulation 5 (requirement to be registered) applies or where that person fails to comply with any requirements in Regulations 5, 6 (supplementary information), 9 (fees) or 10 (entry, inspection, etc).

Prosecution for money laundering has been fairly prevalent. In 2008 the total numbers of offences charged by the CPS under sections 327, 328 and 329 of the POCA 2002 was 5,660. This increased to 5,760 in 2009 and to 6,134 in 2010. 2011 and 2012 saw slight decreases to 5,973 and 5,730 respectively.[203] Detailed above in Table 2.1, is the number of money laundering convictions in the UK between 1999 and 2007. These have steadily increased each year, although in 2008 decreased slightly to 1,286.[204]

When deciding on the length of sentence to impose, the court, as in all sentencing decisions, must take into account the seriousness of the offence, balancing it with other issues such as mitigating factors and the existence of a guilty plea.[205] It will also consider precedent and the existence of guideline judgments. For example, *R v Basra*[206] provides general advice concerning the sentencing of money laundering offences and *R v El-Delbi*[207] concentrates on the proceeds of drug trafficking. In the circumstances of the latter case the Court of Appeal advised that:

> Those who launder large sums that are the proceeds of drug trafficking play an essential role in enabling the drugs conspiracy to succeed and, as such, can expect severe sentences comparable to those given to others playing a significant role in the supply of drugs.

---

202 A. O. Alkaabi, G. Mohay, A. Mccullagh, and N. A. Chantler, 'Comparative analysis of the extent of money laundering in Australia, UAE, UK and the USA' (20 January 2010) paper for Finance and Corporate Governance Conference 2010, available from http://ssrn.com/abstract=1539843, accessed 6 July 2011.

203 HC Deb, 7 November 2013, c265W.

204 HC Deb, 26 July 2010, c689W.

205 For more on this complicated process see K. Harrison, 'Sentencing financial crime in England and Wales' in N. Ryder (ed.), *Financial Crime in the 21st Century – Law and Policy* (Edward Elgar: Cheltenham, 2011).

206 [2002] 2 Cr. App. R. (S) 100.

207 [2003] EWCA Crim 1767.

However, it has to be borne in mind that Parliament has provided different upper limits to a judge's sentencing process for dealing in Class A drugs (life imprisonment) and money laundering (14 years).

There will be no direct arithmetical relationship between the sums recovered by Customs or shown to be involved; nonetheless sentences very close to the maximum have to be reserved for cases where the evidence establishes laundering on a very large scale.[208]

To further aid with the often difficult decision of sentence length, the Sentencing Council has recently (in 2014) issued a definitive guideline to help sentencers in fraud, money laundering and bribery offences.[209] Described in more detail in Chapter 4, the court must first work out how serious the offence is, through assessing culpability and harm caused or that which was risked being caused, and then use published sentencing starting points and category ranges to come up with the most appropriate sentence. Other factors, such as aggravating factors, mitigation and the existence of a guilty plea, are also taken into account. If, for example, the offence caused a loss of £30 million and culpability was deemed to be high, then the starting point is 10 years custody, with a category range of 8–13 years in custody.[210] It is worth noting that the 14-year maxima can still be achieved if there are aggravating factors and 'consecutive sentences for multiple offences may be appropriate where large sums are involved'.[211] At the lower end, for an offence that caused £5,000 worth of loss and where the offender had medium culpability, the starting point is a high-level community order, with the category range being a low-level community order to one year in custody.[212]

Perhaps different to other financial crimes (see Chapter 4), the court does appear to be using its maxima when it comes to sentencing those convicted of money laundering offences. For example, Ussama El-Kurd,[213] in 1999, was sentenced to the maximum penalty of 14 years imprisonment and fined £1 million for being involved in a £70 million money laundering operation. The operation was described as the largest in Europe, with El-Kurd being the first person in England and Wales to be convicted solely on money laundering charges, that is, not additionally connected to other drug or terrorist offences.[214] Likewise, Tarsemwal Lal Sabharwal[215] received 12 years imprisonment for the laundering of over £53 million

208 Sentencing Guidelines Council, 'Guideline Judgments Case Compendium', available from http://sentencingcouncil.judiciary.gov.uk/docs/web_case_compendium.pdf, accessed 6 June 2011.
209 Sentencing Council, *Fraud, Bribery and Money Laundering Offences Definitive Guideline* (Sentencing Guidelines Secretariat: London, 2014).
210 *Ibid.*, 37.
211 *Ibid.*, 38.
212 *Ibid.*, 37.
213 *R v Ussama-el-Kurd* [2001] Crim. L.R. 234 (CA).
214 BBC News, 'UK Maximum sentence for money launder' (*BBC Online Network*, 25 February 1999), available from http://news.bbc.co.uk/1/hi/uk/285759.stm, accessed 6 June 2011.
215 *R v Tarsemwal Lal Sabharwal* [2001] 2 Cr. App. R. (S) 81.

of drug trafficking proceeds. Whilst the Court of Appeal acknowledged that this was at the top end of sentencing, it stated that the offence was also at the top end in terms of seriousness[216] and that it thus felt that the model of just deserts had been properly applied. Similarly, David Simpson[217] received 11 years imprisonment for the laundering of money worth £2.5 million. The Court of Appeal acknowledged that he was not the most seriously involved in the scam, but his role was still said to be 'crucial and pivotal'.[218]

At the other end of the spectrum is the case of Philip Griffiths,[219] a solicitor, who received a term of six months imprisonment for failing to disclose a financial transaction where he had reasonable grounds for knowing or suspecting that it involved money laundering. Whilst the judge acknowledged that Griffiths had lost his practice, had not made any money out of the transaction (apart from his usual conveyancing fee), and the dramatic impact it had had on his health and life, it was still felt that a custodial sentence was proportionate and justified. Leveson J argued, '[o]rganising the cover-up or laundering the proceeds of crime is always particularly serious, especially if organised or set up as an operation. Custodial sentences are absolutely inevitable in almost every case, if not every case.'[220] This was also shown in *R v Duff*[221] where the Court of Appeal upheld a six-month custodial sentence against a solicitor who had failed to report the fact that he had received £70,000 from a client to invest in a joint business, and that the client was later charged with drugs offences.[222] Even though he took advice from another solicitor as to his duty to notify and consulted the Law Society's guidance notes, the Court still held that the sentence was not 'in any way excessive'.[223] What is interesting here, therefore, is the penalising of someone who fails to act, rather than punishing someone for committing a positive act. In English and Welsh criminal law, there are very few situations where a failure to act will initiate criminal proceedings, although being under a duty to act is obviously one such exception. The fact that the government has created such a duty and that a failure in this duty has been criminalised and severely punished shows how serious the government is in tackling this particular crime.[224]

In addition to terms of imprisonment and/or financial penalties, the courts will also endeavour to recover the proceeds of criminal conduct and/or monitor the offender's financial and business practices after their conviction and/or release from custody. This is achieved through ancillary orders. Such orders can be described as ancillary in that they are often given in addition to the other more general

---

216 *R v Tarsemwal Lal Sabharwal* [2001] 2 Cr. App. R. (S) 375.
217 *R v Simpson* [1998] 2 Cr. App. R. (S) 111.
218 *R v Simpson* [1998] 2 Cr. App. R. (S) 114.
219 *R v Griffiths (Philip)* [2006] EWCA Crim 2155.
220 *Ibid.*, at para. 11.
221 [2003] 1 Cr. App. R. (S) 88.
222 *R v Duff* [2003] 1 Cr. App. R. (S) 471.
223 *Ibid.*
224 For the relevant provisions see Proceeds of Crime Act 2002, ss. 327–330.

sentencing penalties, rather than instead of. Many of these orders will be assessed through this book, with this chapter concentrating on the recovery of the proceeds of crime. This is largely achieved through the implementation of a confiscation order,[225] which can be made against any convicted offender who is thought to have a criminal lifestyle. The interpretation of the phrase 'criminal lifestyle' is extremely contentious, with the provisions contained within section 10 of the POCA 2002 often described as draconian.[226] In deciding whether the offender had such a life-style, the sentencing court will use the assumptions as set out in section 10. These are as follows:

> The first assumption is that any property transferred to the defendant at any time after the relevant day was obtained by him –
>
> (a) as a result of his general criminal conduct, and
> (b) at the earliest time he appears to have held it.
>
> The second assumption is that any property held by the defendant at any time after the date of conviction was obtained by him –
>
> (a) as a result of his general criminal conduct, and
> (b) at the earliest time he appears to have held it.
>
> The third assumption is that any expenditure incurred by the defendant at any time after the relevant day was met from property obtained by him as a result of his general criminal conduct.
>
> The fourth assumption is that, for the purpose of valuing any property obtained (or assumed to have been obtained) by the defendant, he obtained it free of any other interests in it.

If such a lifestyle is found and in addition the offender financially benefitted from it, the court can decide what recoverable amount it believes is appropriate and just in the circumstances and then make an order to ensure that such a payment is made. The recoverable amount is equal to that which the offender has benefitted from, unless such an amount is unavailable. If this is the case, then the recoverable amount is either the available amount or if no money is available a nominal amount.[227] Priority of available funds is given first to court-sanctioned financial penalties,[228] with confiscation expected to be achieved within six months.[229] This can be extended to up to 12 months if the Crown Court believes that exceptional circumstances warrant such an extension. Upon the making of a confiscation order

---

225 Proceeds of Crime Act 2002, ss. 6–13.
226 For more on this see R. Alexander, 'Corruption as a financial crime' (2009) *Company Lawyer*, 30(4), 98 and J. L. Masters, 'Fraud and money laundering: The evolving criminalization of corporate non-compliance' (2008) *Journal of Money Laundering Control*, 11(2), 103.
227 Proceeds of Crime Act 2002, s. 7.
228 Proceeds of Crime Act 2002, s. 9.
229 Proceeds of Crime Act 2002, s. 11.

the court should also order a period of imprisonment which will be served if the payment is not made, with the maximum default periods being outlined in section 139(4) of the Powers of the Criminal Courts (Sentencing) Act 2000. As mentioned above, the order is ancillary to imprisonment with the effect of a confiscation order having no bearing on the custodial term.[230] The existence of such an order is especially important when HM Treasury currently estimates that serious crime involves approximately £5 billion of assets that are in a seizable form.[231]

In order to try to ensure that available assets exist at the time of sentencing, as soon as a defendant begins to be investigated for a financial crime, the court can issue a restraint order,[232] if there are 'reasonable grounds to suspect that the alleged offender has benefitted from his criminal conduct'.[233] The main purpose of a restraint order is to prevent the disposal of criminal assets, and can be made even before the defendant has been charged with a criminal offence, provided that this is the expected course of action. If such an order is made, it can instruct a defendant to not only disclose the nature and whereabouts of their assets, but also to relocate assets back within the jurisdiction of England and Wales. The order will apply to all realisable property held by the defendant and can additionally include any property that is transferred to them after the order has been made. When deciding which property to seize, the court must take into account the cost of reasonable living and legal expenses and, if appropriate, allow the defendant to continue in the course of their trade, business, profession or occupation.[234] Since June 2015 the court also has to ensure that the defendant has the means to make any relevant legal aid payments that they are liable for.[235]

Civil powers of financial penalties

The FSA and now the FCA, as part of its 'credible deterrence' policy, has traditionally favoured imposing financial sanctions on firms and individuals as opposed to instigating criminal proceedings.[236] This policy has been summarised by Peat and Mason.

> The normal sanction imposed on a firm is a financial penalty; the firm pays the fine and then carries on with its normal business. In contrast a sanction imposed on an individual may have longer-lasting consequences, for example a prohibition order may prevent an individual from working in the

---

230 *R v Rogers* [2001] EWCA Crim 1680.

231 HM Treasury, *The Financial Challenge of Terrorism and Crime* (HM Treasury: London, 2007).

232 Proceeds of Crime Act 2002, s. 41.

233 Proceeds of Crime Act 2002, s. 40.

234 Proceeds of Crime Act 2002, s. 41.

235 Proceeds of Crime Act 2001, s. 41 (2A).

236 Financial Services Authority, 'Delivering credible deterrence', speech by Margaret Cole, Director of Enforcement, FSA, Annual Financial Crime Conference, 27 April 2009, available from http://www.fsa.gov.uk/library/communication/speeches/2009/0427_mc.shtml, accessed 8 March 2013.

financial services industry for a period of years, and this has a greater deterrent effect.[237]

It has been argued that the objective of the credible deterrence policy is to 'deliver a message that breaches of law and/or regulation will result in offenders suffering "meaningful consequences" including imprisonment'.[238] Teasdale stated that the 'credible deterrence agenda has relied upon not only securing meaningful convictions, judgments and regulatory decisions, but also upon clearly advertising them; to the regulated community to dissuade similar behaviour, and to the wider world to engender consumer and market confidence'.[239] Lewis *et al.* stated that the FSA 'levied large fines and, at worst, bans, on firms and relevant approved individuals who breached its rules – sometimes regardless of whether the breach has resulted in actual harm to customers'.[240] This point is clearly illustrated by the significant increase in the use of financial sanctions by the FSA since the start of the financial crisis.[241] Srivastava *et al.* stated that 'financial sanctions have assumed greater political importance in recent years and as a result there has been increased focus on the part of the FSA in ensuring that firms understand their obligations under the various financial sanctions regimes'.[242] For example, in 2007 the regulatory agency imposed a total of £5.3 million in financial sanctions.[243] A year later, the FSA reported that the figure had increased to £22.7 million,[244] with further increases seen in 2009 to £35 million.[245] This increase continued in 2010 (£89.1m)[246] and although there was a slight dip in 2011 (£66.1m)[247] a monumental increase was recorded in 2012. For this time period the FSA imposed financial sanctions that amounted to £311.5

237 R. Peat, and I. Mason, 'Credible deterrence in action: The FSA brings a series of cases against traders' (2009) *Company Lawyer*, 30(9), 278–279, at 278.

238 A. Srivastava, I. Mason, M. Simpson, and M. Litt, 'Financial crime' (2011) *Compliance Officer Bulletin*, 86(May), 8.

239 S. Teasdale, 'FSA to FCA: Recent trends in UK financial conduct regulation' (2011) *Journal of International Banking Law and Regulation*, 26(12), 583–586, at 585.

240 A. Lewis, R. Pretorius, and E. Radmore, 'Outsourcing in the financial services sector' (2013) *Compliance Officer Bulletin*, 106(May), 1–34, at 3.

241 For a more detailed commentary on the approach adopted by the Financial Services Authority towards imposing financial sanctions see Financial Services Authority, *Financial Services Firms' Approach to UK Financial Sanctions* (Financial Services Authority: London, 2009).

242 A. Srivastava, I. Mason, M. Simpson, and M. Litt, 'Financial crime' (2011) *Compliance Officer Bulletin*, 86(May), 7.

243 Financial Services Authority, 'FSA Fines Table 2007', n/d, available from http://www.fsa.gov.uk/about/press/facts/fines/2007, accessed 8 March 2013.

244 Financial Services Authority, 'FSA Fines Table 2008', n/d, available from http://www.fsa.gov.uk/about/press/facts/fines/2008, accessed 8 March 2013.

245 Financial Services Authority, 'FSA Fines Table 2009', n/d, available from http://www.fsa.gov.uk/about/press/facts/fines/2009, accessed 8 March 2013.

246 Financial Services Authority, 'FSA Fines Table 2010', n/d, available from http://www.fsa.gov.uk/about/press/facts/fines/2010, accessed 8 March 2013.

247 Financial Services Authority, 'FSA Fines Table 2011', n/d, available from http://www.fsa.gov.uk/about/press/facts/fines/2011, accessed 8 March 2013.

million,[248] the majority of which were associated with the London Interbank Offered Rate (LIBOR) scandal. This monumental rise, however, has not abated, and in 2013, the total amount of fines imposed was £474.2 million,[249] which rose further in 2014 to £1.4 billion.[250] During 2012 and 2013 regulatory agencies 'handed out a record [of] £312m in fines, more than triple the previous high number of £89m'.[251] Teasdale described these decisions as an example of 'an increase in the FSA's [and FCA's] readiness to take decisive action'[252] and is testament to the credible deterrent policy.

There are also several sanctions that the regulators can impose on an MLRO who has breached the AML regulations, including private warnings, public statements of misconduct, unlimited financial penalties and prohibition orders.[253] The first example of the FSA imposing a financial penalty on an MLRO occurred in October 2008, when Michael Wheelhouse was fined £17,500 for 'not having adequate anti-money laundering systems and controls in place for verifying and recording clients' identities'.[254] The FSA stated:

> It is vital to the integrity of the UK's financial markets that regulated firms are not used by criminals to launder money. Senior management must implement and follow procedures that meet our requirements so that the risks their firms face are properly managed. This fine is a warning to firms and individuals about the importance of complying with our rules in this area and we will not hesitate to clamp down on failures, where necessary.[255]

Furthermore, in May 2010, the FSA imposed a financial penalty (£140,000) on Alpari (UK) Ltd for failing to have in place adequate AML systems and controls. More importantly, the FSA imposed a financial penalty of £14,000 on Alpari's former MLRO, Sudipto Chattopadhyay, who had failed to broaden the firm's AML compliance levels after its customers increased from 400 to over 11,000. The FSA stated that 'as its MLRO during this period with responsibility for compliance

248 Financial Services Authority, 'FSA Fines Table 2012', n/d, available from http://www.fsa.gov.uk/about/press/facts/fines/2012, accessed 8 March 2013.

249 Financial Conduct Authority, 'Fine table – 2013', 18 November 2013, available from http://www.fca.org.uk/firms/being-regulated/enforcement/fines/2013, accessed 3 July 2015.

250 Financial Conduct Authority, 'Fine table – 2014', 7 January 2015, available from http://www.fca.org.uk/firms/being-regulated/enforcement/fines/2014, accessed 3 July 2015.

251 Financial Conduct Authority, 'The changing face of financial crime', 1 July 2013, available from http://www.fca.org.uk/news/speeches/the-changing-face-of-financial-crime, accessed 8 July 2013.

252 S. Teasdale, 'FSA to FCA: Recent trends in UK financial conduct regulation' (2011) *Journal of International Banking Law and Regulation*, 26(12), 583–586, at 584.

253 C. Foster, 'Developments in accountability for the Money Laundering Reporting Officer in the United Kingdom' (2001) *Journal of International Financial Markets*, 3(3), 113–117, at 116.

254 Financial Services Authority, 'FSA fines firm and MLRO for money laundering controls failings', 29 October 2009, available from http://www.fsa.gov.uk/pages/library/communication/pr/2008/125.shtml, accessed 3 July 2015.

255 FSA/PN/125/2008 20 October 2008.

oversight and money laundering reporting, Chattopadhyay was accountable for these breaches and therefore also received a financial penalty for the failings'.[256] Another example of the FSA utilising its tougher stance on breaches of the Money Laundering Regulations and imposing a financial penalty is the case involving Habib Bank AG Zurich. The FSA fined the company £525,000 and its MLRO, Syed Itrat Hussainn, £17,500 for a 'failure to take reasonable care to establish and maintain adequate anti-money laundering systems and controls'.[257] The *Law Society Gazette* described this penalty as a case that 'is likely to raise concerns among those fulfilling the role at law firms'.[258] Other high-profile cases include Coutts & Company, which was fined £8.75 million;[259] EFG Private Bank, which was fined £4.2 million;[260] and, Guaranty First Bank (UK) Ltd, which was fined £525,000. The Guaranty First Bank received its fine because the bank had 'failed to take reasonable care to establish and maintain effective anti-money-laundering systems and controls in relation to customers that were identified . . . as presenting a higher risk of money-laundering or terrorist financing . . . for the purposes of the 2007 Regulations, including those customers deemed to be a politically exposed person'.[261]

The FCA has continued with this punitive stance. In January 2014 it imposed a financial penalty of £7.6 million on Standard Bank Plc for not complying with the 2007 Money Laundering Regulations because it 'failed to take reasonable care to ensure that all aspects of its AML policies were applied appropriately and consistently to its corporate customers'.[262] As a result of its investigation, the FCA concluded that Standard Bank Plc had not regularly undertaken the enhanced due diligence measures prior to commencing a business relationship with corporate customers who had an association with politically exposed persons. Furthermore, the FCA determined

256 Financial Conduct Authority, 'FSA fines Alpari and its former money laundering reporting officer, Sudipto Chattopadhyay for anti-money laundering failings', 5 May 2010, available from http://www.fsa.gov.uk/pages/library/communication/pr/2010/077.shtml, accessed 3 July 2015.

257 Financial Services Authority, 'FSA fines Habib Bank AG Zurich £525,000 and money laundering reporting officer £17,500 for anti-money laundering control failings', 15 May 2012, available from http://www.fsa.gov.uk/library/communication/pr/2012/055.shtml, accessed 3 July 2015.

258 J. Raynor, 'FSA fines anti-money laundering officer £14k', 20 May 2010, available from http://www.lawgazette.co.uk/news/fsa-fines-anti-money-laundering-officer-14k/55555.fullarticle, accessed 3 July 2015. Also see Herbert Smith, 'FSA fines MLRO and firm for failure to comply with anti-money laundering requirements' (2009) *Law & Financial Markets Review*, 3(1), 79–82 and Herbert Smith, 'FSA fines bank and its former MLRO for failure to comply with anti-money laundering requirements' (2012) *Law & Financial Markets Review*, 6(4), 311–314.

259 Financial Services Authority, 'Coutts fined £8.75 million for anti-money laundering control failings', 26 March 2012, available from http://www.fsa.gov.uk/library/communication/pr/2012/032.shtml, accessed 3 July 2015.

260 Financial Services Authority, 'FSA final notice 2013: EFG Private Bank Ltd', 31 May 2013, available from http://www.fca.org.uk/your-fca/documents/final-notices/2013/fsa-final-notice-2013-efg-private-bank-ltd, accessed 3 July 2015.

261 Financial Conduct Authority, 'Final notice on Guaranty First Bank (UK) Ltd', 8 August 2013, available from http://www.fca.org.uk/your-fca/documents/final-notices/2013/guaranty-trust-bank-uk-limited, accessed 3 July 2015.

262 Financial Conduct Authority, 'Standard Bank PLC fined £7.6m for failures in its anti-money laundering controls', 23 January 2014, available from https://www.fca.org.uk/news/standard-bank-plc-fined-for-failures-in-its-antimoney-laundering-controls, accessed 3 July 2015.

that the bank did not consistently keep up the 'appropriate level of ongoing monitoring for existing business relationships by keeping customer due diligence up to
date'.[263] Despite the level of these fines it can still be argued that the financial penalties imposed by the FSA and FCA since the start of the financial crisis are insufficient
and represent an insignificant percentage of the annual profits of the guilty firms.
Despite producing a series of media friendly headlines, the FCA has arguably under-
performed, given its vast array of other enforcement measures. However, Srivastava
et al. have defended the past enforcement activities of the FSA by stating:

> The FSA has been criticised for making ineffective use of its enforcement pow-
> ers and, particularly, for its reluctance to use criminal enforcement powers. In
> fairness to the FSA, one of the major innovations under FSMA was the FSA's
> power to impose civil fines for market abuse and thereby overcome the signifi-
> cant evidential difficulties associated with prosecuting insider dealing under the
> Criminal Justice Act 1993. It is therefore not surprising that the FSA chose
> to focus on the use of its civil powers during its early years. In response to the
> criticisms that it has received, the FSA has more recently increased its use of
> criminal prosecutions. This initiative has been particularly notable in cases of
> insider dealing where the FSA has secured a number of convictions.[264]

Despite this defence, we would argue that more could still be done.

TABLE 2.2 Recent money laundering cases

Offence: Money Laundering
Legislation: sections 327, 328 and 329 Proceeds of Crime Act 2002
Maximum Penalty: 14 years imprisonment

Name	Date	Sentence	Brief Details
Liam James Renolds	17.8.2015	four years	Pleaded guilty to importing and supplying Class A and Class B drugs and laundering the profits.
Johannes Franciscus Franken	16.6.2015	five years four months	Pleaded guilty to five counts of fraud by false representation and laundering the profits. He was an accountant employed by BMW and altered supplier invoices so that they were paid into his account. Fraud amounted to £5.9 million.
Bulbinder Singh Sandhu	13.3.2015	two years	Pleaded guilty to fraudulently obtaining VAT repayments from HMRC amounting to £670,000 and the laundering of said money.
Wendy Ann Smith	27.11.2014	two years	Found guilty of conspiracy to defraud and launder money.

(Continued)

---

263 *Ibid.*
264 A. Srivastava, I. Mason, M. Simpson, and M. Litt, 'Financial crime' (2011) *Compliance Officer Bulletin*,
     86(May), 8.

TABLE 2.2 (*Continued*)

Name	Date	Sentence	Brief Details
John Paul Clark	31.10.14	25 years	Pleaded guilty to Class A and B drug offences in addition to money laundering. He was the head of an international criminal gang who imported and supplied drugs worth over £11 million. The sentencing judge, Judge Timothy Clarkson said:'This is an instance of money laundering on a very large scale, all related to the vast profits flowing from your drug dealing operations . . . your culpability is clearly high . . . You were the head of this drug-dealing enterprise. You played a leading role and were responsible for activities within it . . . You enjoyed a very high level of luxury in your life with beautiful houses, rental properties, dressing in designer clothes and owning expensive cars . . . you travelled abroad and were in frequent contact with those involved.'[265]
Chukwuka Ugwu	17.10.14	322 days	Pleaded guilty to money laundering after defrauding more than £200,000 from individuals who he had meet on the dating website match.com. This is interesting in that he was also convicted on money laundering.
Adewunmi Nusi	17.10.2014	one year eight months	Also involved in the above.
Monty Peter Emu	17.10.2014	three years six months	Also involved in the match.com scam.
Emmanuel Oko	17.10.14	eight years	Pleaded guilty to the above scam and also fraud by false representation.
Tatiana Daniella Oprea	17.10.2014	eight months	Pleaded guilty to money laundering and conspiring to facilitate breaches of UK immigration laws.

Future recommendations

The UK's money laundering policy is generally compliant with the international measures outlined at the start of this chapter. Its policy is well managed by HM Treasury and now assisted by the FCA, which has undertaken the regulatory functions of the FSA. At the time of writing this book, in early 2016, the EU has finally agreed to the contents of the Fourth Money Laundering Directive that Member States are required to implement by 2017. This will be implemented by the

---

265 http://www.thelawpages.com/court-cases/John-Paul-Clark-14294-1.law.

UK government and it will continue to correctly assert that its money laundering regime is the 'gold standard' and that it continues to exceed the requirements from the EU. There has been little or no difference in the measures used by the FCA, which has continued to pursue its pre-placement AML policy. It is likely that the FCA will continue to impose financial sanctions for authorised firms that breach its extensive money laundering rules and there appears to be little or no appetite for the FCA to instigate criminal proceedings for the money laundering offences under POCA 2002. The most significant change since the first edition of this book has been the creation of a new FIU – the NCA – by virtue of the Crime and Courts Act 2013. However, it is important to stress that the role of the NCA will be very similar to that of SOCA, and little alteration is therefore expected here. The authors would recommend that the FCA should continue to use its credible deterrence strategy and imposed financial sanctions on firms that have breached their pre-placement obligations. However, it is strongly asserted that there is no reason why the FCA shouldn't instigate more criminal proceedings for money laundering following the decision of the Supreme Court in *R v Rollins* and such activity is therefore strongly encouraged.

Further reading

R. Alexander, *Insider Dealing and Money Laundering in the EU: Law and Regulation* (Ashgate: Farnham, 2007).

P. Alldridge, *Money Laundering Law* (Hart: Oxford, 2003).

T. Bennett, *Money Laundering Compliance* (Bloomsbury Professional: Haywards Heath, 2015).

W. Blair and R. Brent, *Banks and Financial Crime: The International Law of Tainted Money* (Oxford University Press: Oxford, 2008).

R. Booth, S. Farrell, G. Bastable, and N. Yeo, *Money Laundering Law and Regulation a Practical Guide* (Oxford University Press: Oxford, 2011).

D. Demetis, *Technology and Anti-Money Laundering a Systems Theory and Risk-Based Approach* (Edward Elgar: Cheltenham, 2010).

J. Fisher, *Money Laundering and Practice* (Oxford University Press: Oxford, 2009).

M. Gallant, *Money Laundering and the Proceeds of Crime – Economic Crime and Civil Remedies* (Edwards Elgar: Cheltenham, 2005).

W. Gilmore, *Dirty Money – The Evolution of International Measures to Counter Money Laundering and the Financial of Terrorism* (Council of Europe: Brussels, 2003).

D. Hopton, *Money Laundering a Concise Guide for All Business* (Gower: Farnham, 2009).

M. Levi, 'Money laundering and its regulation' (2002) *The ANNALS of the American Academy of Political and Social Science*, 582(1), 181–194.

M. Levi and P. Reuter, 'Money laundering' (2006) *Crime and Justice*, 34(1), 289–375.

N. Ryder, *Money Laundering – An Endless Cycle? A Comparative Analysis of the Anti-Money Laundering Policies in the United States of America, the United Kingdom, Australia and Canada* (Routledge: London, 2012).

G. Stessens, *Money Laundering – A New International Law Enforcement Model* (Cambridge University Press: Cambridge, 2000).

B. Unger, *The Scale and Impacts of Money Laundering* (Edwards Elgar: Cheltenham, 2007).

B. Unger and J. Ferwerda, *Money Laundering in the Real Estate Eector* (Edward Elgar: Cheltenham, 2011).

A. Verhage, *The Anti-Money Laundering Complex and the Compliance Industry* (Routledge: London, 2011).

J. Walker, 'How big is global money laundering?' (1999) *Journal of Money Laundering Control,* 3(1), 25–37.

3

TERRORIST FINANCING

Introduction

Prior to the terrorist attacks in the United States of America (USA) on 11 September 2001 (9/11), the international community's attitude towards financial crime focused on the prevention of money laundering, the illegal drugs trade and fraud. One of the consequences of 9/11, however, was a fundamental change in attitudes towards implementing counter-terrorist financing (CTF) laws. Terrorist financing has been defined widely and we include some of those definitions here. For example, the International Convention for the Suppression of Terrorist financing defines it as including 'assets of every kind, whether tangible or intangible, movable or immovable, however acquired, and legal documents or instruments in any form'.[1] It has also been defined as the 'raising, moving, storing and using of financial resources for the purposes of terrorism',[2] and by the World Bank as providing 'the financial support, in any form, of terrorism or of those who encourage, plan, or engage in it'.[3] Furthermore, the International Monetary Fund (IMF) has stated that terrorist financing 'involves the solicitation, collection or provision of funds with the intention that they may be used to support terrorist acts or organizations'.[4] Terrorist financing has also been referred to as 'reverse money laundering', which is a practice

---

1 International Convention for the Suppression of the Financing of Terrorism (1999) Art.1 para.1. Hereinafter 'International Convention'.

2 Charity Commission, 'Compliance toolkit: Protecting charities from harm', (2009 Module 7, page 1) available from http://www.charity-commission.gov.uk/Library/tkch1mod7.pdf, accessed 17 June 2011.

3 The World Bank, *Reference Guide to Anti-Money Laundering and Combating the Financing of Terrorism* (World Bank: Washington, DC, 2006, 19).

4 International Monetary Fund, 'Anti-money laundering/combating the financing of terrorism – topics', available from http://www.imf.org/external/np/leg/amlcft/eng/aml1.htm#financingterrorism, accessed 26 June 2014. Hereinafter 'IMF'.

whereby 'clean' or 'legitimate' money is acquired and then funnelled to support acts of terrorism.[5] As detailed in the previous chapter, money laundering involves the conversion of 'dirty' or 'illegal' money into clean money via its laundering through three recognised phases.

For the purposes of terrorist financing, terrorism is defined as the use or threat of action which involves serious violence against a person; serious damage to property; endangers a person's life; creates a serious risk to the health or safety of the public; or is designed to seriously interfere or disrupt an electronic system.[6] Such attacks, including the aforementioned 9/11, caused the international community, and largely led by the USA, to instigate the so-called financial war on terrorism.[7] The United Kingdom (UK), principally influenced by the international legislative measures introduced by the United Nations (UN), the European Union (EU) and the Recommendations of the Financial Action Task Force (FATF), has consequentially implemented several pieces of controversial legislation aimed at combating terrorist financing. Such measures include the Terrorism Act 2000, the Anti-Terrorism Crime and Security Act 2001, the Prevention of Terrorism Act 2005, the Counter-Terrorism Act 2008 and the Terrorist Asset-Freezing (Temporary Provisions) Act 2010. The primary aim of this chapter will therefore be to cover these important pieces of legislation, including also an attempt at quantifying the extent and level of terrorist financing. The chapter will then consider the background to the policy of criminalising and regulating the problem, plus evaluate the financial institutions and regulatory bodies involved. Finally we look at how terrorist assets are recovered.

What is the offence of terrorist financing?

The principal criminal offences relating to terrorist financing can be found in sections 15–18 of the Terrorism Act 2000, which received Royal Assent on 20 July 2000. These include: raising, receiving or providing funds for the purpose of terrorism;[8] using or possessing funds for the purpose of terrorism;[9] becoming involved in an arrangement which makes funds available for the purposes of terrorism;[10] and, facilitating the laundering of terrorist property and money.[11] Additional offences include failing to disclose information about the occurrence of terrorist financing[12] and, for those working in the regulated financial sector, the

---

5 For a more detailed discussion of this process see S. Cassella, 'Reverse money laundering' (2003) *Journal of Money Laundering Control*, 7(1), 92.
6 Terrorism Act 2000, s. 1.
7 For a more detailed discussion see Nicholas Ryder, *The Financial War on Terror: A Review of Counter-Terrorist Financing Strategies Since 2001* (Routledge: London, 2015).
8 Terrorism Act 2000, s. 15.
9 Terrorism Act 2000, s. 16.
10 Terrorism Act 2000, s. 17.
11 Terrorism Act 2000, s. 18.
12 Terrorism Act 2000, s. 19 and s. 21A.

offence of tipping off.[13] Interestingly, and in accordance with section 63 of the Terrorism Act 2000, if a person does anything outside of the UK that would have been an offence under sections 15–18 of the Act within the UK, they will also be guilty of an offence. Only the four principal offences will be discussed further.

Fund-raising – section 15 Terrorism Act 2000

The offence of fund-raising is committed if a person facilitates the raising of money for the purposes of terrorism. This can be done through inviting another to provide money or property, receiving such money or other property or through providing money or other property. In all three circumstances the person must either intend that the money (or property) to be used to fund terrorist activity or have reasonable cause to suspect that it may be used for this purpose. Consideration is not a requisite factor, with the Act defining the provision of money or property to include where it is 'given, lent or otherwise made available'.[14]

Use and possession – section 16 Terrorism Act 2000

The second terrorist financing offence covers the situation where a person uses money or other property for terrorist purposes, or has in their possession money or property which they intend to be used in this way or has reasonable cause to suspect this to be the case.

Funding arrangements – section 17 Terrorism Act 2000

The next offence is found in section 17 of the Terrorism Act 2000, which deals with funding arrangements. Under this section, an offence is committed if a person enters into or becomes concerned in an arrangement and as a result of this arrangement money or other property is made available for the funding of terrorism. As with the other offences, the person needs to either know that the money or property is to be used in this way, or have reasonable cause to suspect that it is to be used for this purpose.

Money laundering – section 18 Terrorism Act 2000

The final principal offence is concerned with money laundering. This is committed if a person deals with terrorist property in a way that conceals it, removes it from the jurisdiction, or transfers it to another person. For the purposes of this section, terrorist property is defined to include '(a) Money or other property which is likely to be used for the purposes of terrorism (including any resources of a proscribed organisation), (b) Proceeds of the commission of acts of terrorism, and (c) Proceeds

---

13 Terrorism Act 2000, s. 21D.
14 Terrorism Act 2000, s. 15(4).

of acts carried out for the purposes of terrorism'.[15] Unlike the other offences, there is no need to show intention, knowledge or reasonable suspicion. In fact, section 18(2) creates a defence whereby a person is not guilty of the offence if they can prove either that they did not know that the arrangement related to terrorist property, or had no reasonable cause to suspect this to be so.

Defences

In relation to these four principal offences, the defence of express consent exists.[16] This relates to the situation where an individual is working in cooperation with the police and has express permission to continue with their terrorist financing activities. Originally this defence only applied where a person made a disclosure *after* becoming involved in an arrangement or transaction, through his own initiative and as soon as was deemed to be reasonably practicable.[17] This has now been extended to widen and include the defences of prior consent, consent and reasonable excuse. These were introduced by the Terrorism Act 2000 and Proceeds of Crime Act 2002 (Amendment) Regulations 2007 (which came into force on 26 December 2007) and are found in sections 21ZA, 21ZB and 21ZC of the Terrorism Act 2000. The prior consent defence can be relied upon where a person makes a disclosure to an authorised person *before* becoming involved in a transaction or an arrangement, and the person then becomes involved in such an arrangement with the consent of this authorised officer.[18] For the purposes of the defence an authorised officer is defined as 'a National Crime Agency officer authorised for the purposes of this section by the Director General of that Agency'.[19]

Similarly, the consent defence is valid where a person is already involved in a transaction or arrangement and makes a disclosure during this stage and the person then acts with the consent of an authorised officer.[20] This is only valid if the person involved can prove that there was a reasonable excuse for their failure to make an advance disclosure, the disclosure was made as soon as reasonably practicable and was of their own volition.[21] A person cannot rely on the defences of either prior consent or consent if the authorised officer forbids the continued involvement of the person in the arrangement or transaction. Finally, the reasonable excuse defence may be used if a person intended to make a disclosure of the kind mentioned above, and even though they did not, there was a reasonable excuse for not doing so.[22] Other defences relate to those working within the regulated sector, who have failed to make disclosures of activity that they know, suspect or have reasonable grounds

---

15 Terrorism Act 2000, s. 14.
16 Terrorism Act 2000, s. 21.
17 Terrorism Act 2000, s. 21(3).
18 Terrorism Act 2000, s. 21ZA(1).
19 Terrorism Act 2000, s. 21ZA(5).
20 Terrorism Act 2000, s. 21ZB(1).
21 Terrorism Act 2000, s. 21ZB(2).
22 Terrorism Act 2000, s. 21ZC.

for knowing or suspecting relate to terrorist financing. These can be found in sections 21A, 21B, 21E, 21F and 21G of the Terrorism Act 2000. Sections 21A and 21B will be discussed in more detail below. Without doubt, the aim of all of these defences is the discovery of offending behaviour.

The extent of terrorist financing

The extent of terrorist financing can be contrasted with the other types of financial crime discussed in this book because the objective of a terrorist is not to hide the proceeds of their illegal activity but to use the finances to promote a distorted ideology via a terrorist attack. As previously outlined, this is often known as reverse money laundering and was deemed by President George Bush to be more of a threat to USA national security than actual money laundering. Gurung, Wijaya and Rao described reverse money laundering as stemming from 'legitimate sources i.e. the fund is obtained to do illegal activity in comparison to money laundering where money is generated from criminal procedures and made legitimate'.[23] Similarly, Hardouin stated that '[t]errorists practice reverse money laundering since they transform clean money into dirty money whereas in the case of organized crime things are happening just the other way round'.[24] Therefore, this chapter adopts the opposite stance to the other chapters in this book and briefly highlights the estimated costs of a number of terrorist attacks but also considers the plethora of sources that are used to finance these attacks.

Already mentioned above, one of the most well-known and damaging to life terrorist attacks to date was a series of four coordinated suicide attacks against USA landmarks in Washington, Arlington County and New York on 11 September 2001. In total, 2,996 people were killed and at least US$10 billion worth of infrastructure and property damage caused. Despite the magnitude of this loss, it is thought that the attacks cost approximately US$500,000. Similarly and with reference to the four coordinated attacks on the public transport system in London on 7 July 2005 where 52 people died and more than 700 were injured, it has been estimated that this only cost the terrorists £8,000.[25] Some commentators, however, disagree, arguing that the London bombings were more likely to have cost between £100 and £200.[26] Furthermore, whilst the Bishopsgate bomb in London in 1993 caused over £1 billion of property damage, it was estimated to have only cost the terrorists £3,000.[27] Because

---

23 J. Gurung, M. Wijaya, and A. Rao, 'AMLCTF compliance and SMEs in Australia: A case study of the prepaid card industry' (2010) *Journal of Money Laundering Control*, 13(3), 199.

24 P. Hardouin, 'Banks governance and public-private partnership in preventing and confronting organized crime, corruption and terrorism financing' (2009) *Journal of Financial Crime*, 16(3), 206.

25 M. Levi, 'Combating the financing of terrorism: A history and assessment of the control of threat finance' (2010) *British Journal of Criminology*, 50, 650.

26 See M. Evans, 'Shortage of money led to 7/7 security failures' *The Times* (London, 11 May 2006); M. Townsend, 'Leak reveals official story of London bombings' *The Observer* (London, 9 April 2006).

27 HM Treasury, *Combating the Financing of Terrorism: A Report on UK Action* (HM Treasury: London, 2002, 11).

of the relatively small amounts of money involved, such attacks have become known as 'cheap terrorism', with another example being the first attack on the World Trade Center in 1993, in which six people were murdered and over 1,000 were injured at an estimated cost of only US$400.[28] Other examples include the Oklahoma City bombing (US$5,000),[29] the Boston Marathon bombings ($50)[30] and the train bombings in Madrid (€8,315).[31] More recent examples of the concept of cheap terrorism include the murder of Lee Rigby in May 2013,[32] the Charlie Hebdo murders in Paris in January 2015[33] and the terrorist attack on the Tunisian resort of Sousse later that same year.[34] Such estimates must, however, be treated with an element of caution as there are 'few reliable data on the cost of attempting terrorist attacks'.[35] Despite this caution Waszak claims that 'the cost of making a suicide bomb can be as low as $5, while the deployment of a suicide bomber including transportation and reconnaissance, can cost as little as $200'.[36]

The prevention of terrorist financing is very difficult due to not only the low financial costs involved, but also to the extensive array of financial tools used to fund such attacks.[37] Historically, terrorists have relied on two main sources of funding: state and private sponsors.[38] State-sponsorship of terrorism is where national governments provide logistical and financial support to terrorist organisations.[39] The true extent of state-sponsored terrorism is impossible to determine, yet it has been suggested that state sponsors do provide substantial support to terrorists.[40] However, there is evidence to suggest that the extent of state-sponsored terrorism has declined and it is now more likely that terrorists will receive funding from private sponsors

---

28 J. Gaddis, 'And now this: Lessons from the old era for the new one' in S. Talbott and N. Chander (eds.), *The Age of Terror: America and the World After September 11* (Basic Books: New York, 2001, 6).

29 NBC News, 'The McVeigh Tapes: Confessions of an American terrorist', available from http://www.nbcnews.com/id/36135258/ns/msnbc_tv/#.VDJpOU10zIU, accessed 6 October 2014.

30 *Ibid.*

31 Clive Walker, *Terrorism and the Law* (Oxford University Press: Oxford, 2011, 232).

32 See generally BBC News, 'Lee Rigby murder: Adebolajo and Adebowale jailed', available from http://www.bbc.co.uk/news/uk-26357007, accessed 10 August 2015.

33 See CNN, 'A timeline of the Charlie Hebdo terror attack', available from http://edition.cnn.com/2015/01/08/europe/charlie-hebdo-attack-timeline/, accessed 10 August 2015.

34 See BBC, 'Tunisia beach massacre 'linked' to museum killings', available from http://www.bbc.co.uk/news/uk-33791293, accessed 10 August 2015.

35 J. Prober, 'Accounting for terror: debunking the paradigm of inexpensive terrorism', 1 November 2005, available from http://www.washingtoninstitute.org/policy-analysis/view/accounting-for-terror-debunking-the-paradigm-of-inexpensive-terrorism, accessed 11 August 2014.

36 J. Waszak, 'The obstacles to suppressing radical Islamic terrorist financing' (2004) *Case Western Reserve Journal of International law*, 36, 673.

37 See M. Levitt, 'Stemming the follow of terrorist financing: practical and conceptual challenges' (2003) *The Fletcher Forum of World Affairs*, 27(1), 64.

38 I. Bantekas, 'The international law of terrorist financing' (2003) *American Journal of International Law*, 97(2), 315.

39 A. Chase, 'Legal mechanisms of the international community and the United States concerning the state sponsorship of terrorism' (2004) *Virginia Journal of International Law*, 45, 41.

40 *Ibid.*

or donors.[41] This perceived decline in state-sponsored terrorism has forced terrorist organisations to diversify their funding activities and, in effect, become self-funding. Lee, for example, has stated that the al-Qaeda 'network increasingly is shifting to non-bank methods of moving and storing value and is relying on a decentralised structure of largely self-financing cells'.[42] The self-sufficiency of terrorist cells was also recognised by the official report on the terrorist attacks on London on 7 July 2005.[43] Terrorists have therefore been forced to deploy several mechanisms to raise additional funds, including the collection of membership dues and/or subscriptions; the sale of publications; speaking tours; cultural and social events; door-to-door solicitation within the community; appeals to wealthy members of the community; and, donations of a portion of personal earnings.[44] Alldridge takes the view that other sources of funding include 'kidnapping for ransom, armed robbery, extortion and drug trading',[45] whilst Lowe argues that terrorists fund some activities via counterfeiting.[46] It has also been reported that another source of funding for terrorist groups is conflict diamonds, and that this source of funding has been used by al-Qaeda and Hamas.[47] This all means that terrorists are able to 'manipulate an expanding array of tools to shield their wealth, without regard to international borders'.[48] Terrorists are also utilising new electronic technologies to transfer money over the internet to conceal their true origin.[49] In addition to the above, it has also been mooted that al-Qaeda has obtained monies from both charitable contributions and from legitimate companies.[50] Terrorists have also acquired funding through traditional criminal activities, including benefit and credit card fraud, identity theft, the sale of counterfeit goods and drug trafficking.[51]

The threat posed by the wide range of sources available to terrorists has been clearly illustrated by the activities of several terrorist groups. For example, the so-called

---

41 See for example M. Basile, 'Going to the source: Why al-Qaeda's financial network is likely to withstand the current war on terrorist financing' (2004) *Studies in Conflict & Terrorism*, 27, 183.

42 R. Lee, *Terrorist Financing: The US and International Response Report for Congress* (Congressional Research Service: Washington, DC, 2002, 19).

43 House of Commons, *Report of the Official Account of the Bombings in London on 7th July 2005* (House of Commons: London, 2005, 23).

44 I. Bantekas, 'The international law of terrorist financing' (2003) *American Journal of International Law*, 97, 315.

45 Peter Alldridge, *Money Laundering Law* (Hart: Oxford, 2003, 215).

46 P. Lowe, 'Counterfeiting: Links to organised crime and terrorist funding' (2006) *Journal of Financial Crime*, 13(2), 255.

47 Global Witness, *Broken Vows – Exposing the Loupe Holes in the Diamond Industry's Efforts to Prevent the Trade in Conflict Diamonds* (Global Witness Publishing Inc.: London, 2003, 2).

48 K. Alexander, 'The international anti-money laundering regime: The role of the Financial Action Task Force' (2001) *Journal of Money Laundering Control*, 4(3), 231.

49 R. Lee, *Terrorist Financing: The US and International Response Report for Congress* (Congressional Research Service: Washington, DC, 2002, 22).

50 N. Ryder, 'Danger money' (2007) *New Law Journal*, 157, 7300; Supp (Charities Appeals Supplement), 6, 8.

51 C. Linn, 'How terrorist exploit gaps in US anti-money laundering laws to secrete plunder' (2005) *Journal of Money Laundering Control*, 8(3), 200.

Islamic State of Iraq (ISIS) and Levant have exploited the political and security weaknesses in Iraq by using a very wide range of sources to fund their activities. It has been reported that since the ISIS takeover of Mosul in June 2014, ISIS 'insurgents [have] seized as much as $400 million from the central bank . . . and reportedly emptied the vaults in all the other banks in a city of more than one million residents'.[52] It has been estimated that the total assets of ISIS amounted to US$900 million prior to its capturing of Mosul, and that they now exceed US$2 billion. Such figures must however be treated with caution, as it is impossible to know the true wealth of ISIS. It is true, however, and as Jones notes, that 'ISIS has been catapulted into a position of unrivalled wealth'.[53] The position has become even more threatening because of its seizure and control of several affluent oil fields[54] and an acknowledgement that ISIS is 'well-funded . . . thanks to a raging criminal enterprise of extortion, bank robbery and petty theft, as well as donations from well-heeled sponsors throughout the Arab world'.[55] ISIS has also been boosted by 'citizens in Saudi Arabia and Kuwait [who] have quietly funnelled vast sums of money to and joined the ranks of ISIS and other jihadist groups'.[56] Jones, citing Zelin, adds:

> They're [ISIS] probably the richest jihadi organization ever seen . . . they get their money from trafficking weapons, kidnappings for ransom, counterfeit currencies, oil refining, smuggling artefacts that are thousands of years old and from taxes that they have for areas they are in – either on businesses, or at checkpoints or on ordinary people.[57]

Another terrorist group that has utilised a vast array of sources is Al Shabaab, a Somali-based militant Islamist group, that has obtained funding from the illegal smuggling of ivory.[58] It has been asserted that Al Shabaab receives '£365,000 per

---

52 R. Nordland, and A. Rubin, 'Iraq insurgents reaping wealth as they advance', available from http://www.nytimes.com/2014/06/21/world/middleeast/isis-iraq-insurgents-reaping-wealth-as-they-advance.html?_r=0, accessed 26 June 2014.

53 S. Jones, 'Diverse funding and strong accounting give ISIS unparalleled wealth', available from http://www.ft.com/cms/s/0/21e8c922-f95d-11e3-bb9d-00144feab7de.html?siteedition=uk#axzz35pfchnAb, accessed 27 June 2014.

54 See M. Tran, 'ISIS insurgents attack Iraq's biggest oil refinery', available from http://www.theguardian.com/world/2014/jun/18/isis-fighters-iraq-oil-refinery-baiji, accessed 27 June 2014.

55 Fox News, 'Extortion, bank robbery fuel ISIS bloody drive to establish Sharia caliphate', available from http://www.foxnews.com/world/2014/06/14/extortion-bank-robbery-fuel-isis-bloody-drive-to-establish-sharia-caliphate/, accessed 27 June 2014.

56 A. Hauslohner, 'Jihadist expansion in Iraq puts Persian Gulf states in a tight spot', available from http://m.washingtonpost.com/world/jihadist-expansion-in-iraq-puts-persian-gulf-states-in-a-tight-spot/2014/06/13/e52e90ac-f317-11e3-bf76-447a5df6411f_story.html, accessed 27 June 2014.

57 S. Jones, 'Diverse funding and strong accounting give ISIS unparalleled wealth', available from http://www.ft.com/cms/s/0/21e8c922-f95d-11e3-bb9d-00144feab7de.html?siteedition=uk#axzz35pfchnAb, accessed 27 June 2014.

58 V. Doshi, 'Elephant Campaign: How Africa's "white gold" funds the al-Shabaab militants', available from http://www.independent.co.uk/voices/campaigns/elephant-campaign/elephant-campaign-how-africas-white-gold-funds-the-alshabaab-militants-9102862.html, accessed 27 June 2014.

month from ivory alone, enough to support around 40 per cent of the salaries paid to militants. Other sources of the group's revenue include exporting charcoal and collecting zakat, an informal Islamic tithe.'[59] Harnish noted that Al Shabaab 'has the funds, weapons, technical expertise, and human resources needed to conduct operations. It raises money by taxing international aid organizations, collecting zakat from citizens, receiving remittances from abroad, and receiving financial support from Eritrea.'[60] It has also been estimated that 'Al Shabaab earned more than $25m a year from illicit exports of charcoal to Gulf Arab states and from taxing the trucking of charcoal to the Somali ports of Kismayu and Barawe.'[61] The UN noted that Al Shabaab receives a lot of its funding via charcoal exports and the illegal importation of contraband sugar.[62] Bergen and Sterman noted that Al Shabaab has also received donations from supporters within the USA.[63] For example, in October 2011 two women were convicted of 'providing material support to a designated terrorist organization'.[64] The Council of Foreign Relations noted that:

> Al-Shabaab has benefited from several different sources of income over the years, including revenue from other terrorist groups, state sponsors, the Somali diaspora, charities, piracy, kidnapping, and the extortion of local businesses. Saudi Arabia, Yemen, Syria, Iran, Qatar, and Eritrea have been cited as prominent state backers.[65]

Another example of a terrorist group that has been able to exploit a wide range of sources of funding is Boko Haram, 'an Islamist movement based primarily in the north-eastern region of Nigeria'.[66] It has been suggested that Boko Haram are funded

---

59 *Ibid.*

60 C. Harnish, *The Terror Threat from Somalia – The Internationalization of Al Shabaab – A Report of the Critical Threats Project of the American Enterprise Institute* (American Enterprise Institute: Washington, DC, 2010, 2).

61 W. Maclean, 'Shabaab finances face squeeze after Kenya attack', available from http://www.reuters. com/article/2013/09/26/us-kenya-attack-shabaab-funding-idUSBRE98P05Z20130926, accessed 27 June 2014.

62 United Nations, *Report of the Monitoring Group on Somalia and Eritrea Pursuant to Security Council Resolution 2060 (2012): Somalia* (United Nations: New York, 2012).

63 P. Bergen, and D. Sterman, 'Al-Shabaab backed by money from US', available from http://www.cnn. com/2013/09/29/opinion/bergen-shabaab-fundraising/, accessed 27 June 2014.

64 Federal Bureau of Investigation, 'Two Minnesota women convicted of providing material support to al Shabaab', available from http://www.fbi.gov/minneapolis/press-releases/2011/two-minnesota-women-convicted-of-providing-material-support-to-al-shabaab, accessed 15 October 2014. Also see Federal Bureau of Investigation, 'San Diego jury convicts four Somali immigrants of providing support to foreign terrorists', available from http://www.fbi.gov/sandiego/press-releases/2013/san-diego-jury-convicts-four-somali-immigrants-of-providing-support-to-foreign-terrorists, accessed 15 October 2014.

65 J. Masters, 'Al-Shabab', available from http://www.cfr.org/somalia/al-shabab/p18650, accessed 27 June 2014.

66 E. Foster-Bowser, and A. Sanders, 'Security threats in the Sahel and beyond: AQIM, Boko Haram and al Shabaab', available from http://reliefweb.int/sites/reliefweb.int/files/resources/Full_Report_3818. pdf, accessed 30 September 2014.

'through black market dealings, local and international benefactors, and links to al-Qaida and other well-funded groups in the Middle East'.[67] The Inter-Governmental Action Group Against Money Laundering in West Africa noted that Boko Harem has been partly financed through private donors and misapplied charitable donations.[68] Interestingly, the FATF has provided several examples of how Boko Haram acquires its financing, including the sale of goods and other lucrative activities, business profits/logistical support, contributions from members of a terrorist group, begging by vulnerable persons, extortion of civilians by means of intimidation, arms smugglers, cash couriers and financial contributions of political leaders.[69] In relation to contributions from political leaders the FATF stated that Boko Haram 'exploits the security challenges in the north to coerce some governors to co-operate in exchange for peace in their states. The case also reveals the need to enhance the personal security of government officials who may be intimidated and exploited by terrorist groups for protection fees'.[70] The US Department of State noted that Boko Haram acquires funding via 'commercial activities such as telecommunications; abuse of the Nigerian financial system; illegal fundraising; extortion; cash couriers, including the use of female cash couriers; and the active assistance of local politicians in raising funds. Kidnapping for ransom [is] also a source of terrorist financing.'[71] Furthermore, it has been suggested that Boko Haram, like other terrorist groups, have engaged in criminal activities such as bank robberies and stolen oil to fund their activities.[72] The prevention and detection of terrorist finances is therefore extremely difficult if not impossible because of the extensive financial tools used to fund terrorist operations.

Policy background – where did the offence originate from?

Due to the 'Troubles' in Northern Ireland and other terrorist activities in mainland Britain, the UK has significant experience of tackling domestic acts of terrorism. Consequently, the evolution of its terrorist-related measures and policies can be traced back to its initial efforts to tackle terrorism in the early part of the twentieth

---

67 T. McCoy, 'Paying for terrorism: Where does Boko Haram gets its money from?', available from http://www.independent.co.uk/news/world/africa/paying-for-terrorism-where-does-boko-haram-gets-its-money-from-9503948.html, accessed 27 June 2014.

68 Inter-governmental Action Group Against Money Laundering in West Africa, *Threat Assessment of Money Laundering and Terrorist Financing in West Africa* (Inter-governmental Action Group Against Money Laundering in West Africa, 2010, 94).

69 Financial Action Task Force, *FATF Report – Terrorist Financing in West Africa* (Financial Action Task Force: Paris, 2013, 16).

70 *Ibid*, 23.

71 Department of State, *Country Reports on Terrorism 2013* (Department of State: Washington, DC, 2014, 40).

72 House of Representatives Committee on Homeland Security Subcommittee on Counterterrorism and Intelligence, *Boko Haram Emerging Threat to the U.S.* (Homeland U.S. House of Representatives Committee on Homeland Security Subcommittee on Counterterrorism and Intelligence: Washington, DC, 2011, 18).

century.[73] The two central legislative pillars of the UK's counter-terrorist efforts are therefore the Northern Ireland (Emergency Provisions) Act 1973[74] and the Prevention of Terrorism (Temporary Provisions) Act 1974.[75] Since these formative Acts, more recentpieces of legislation and the UK's CTF policy has been heavily influenced by drug trafficking legislation. Donohue stated that the UK's 'anti-terrorist finance regime has exhibited an almost symbiotic relationship between anti-drug and anti-terrorist finance measures since the mid-1980s, leading to a steady expansion in the number and range of related offences, investigatory authorities, regulatory provisions, and powers of forfeiture'.[76] For example, the Drug Trafficking Offences Act 1986 contained a series of statutory provisions that permitted the confiscation of the proceeds of drug trafficking offences.[77] Furthermore, the scope of a limited number of criminal offences covered by the Drug Trafficking Offences Act 1986 was extended to all 'non-drug' indictable offences and specific summary offences by the Criminal Justice Act 1988.[78] Further amendments were also introduced by the Drug Trafficking Act 1994[79] and the Proceeds of Crime Act 1995.[80]

Despite the enactment of such progressive and wide-ranging pieces of legislation, terrorist financing continued, which in 2000 led the then Labour government to review the UK's confiscation regime.[81] The report recommended that an 'Asset Confiscation Agency' should be created and that both the money laundering and confiscation regime should be consolidated under one piece of legislation. These recommendations were eventually enacted via the Proceeds of Crime Act 2002.[82] The drug-related mechanisms also influenced the CTF provisions in the Prevention of Terrorism Act 1989,[83] and as Donohue stated, the Act 'drew inspiration from these anti-drug laws'.[84] For example, the Prevention of Terrorism (Temporary Provisions) Act 1989 introduced specific provisions under Part III to criminalise

73 Laura Donohue, *The Cost of Counterterrorism – Power, Politics and Liberty* (Cambridge University Press, 2008, 129).
74 For an excellent discussion of the Northern Ireland (Emergency Provisions) Act 1973 see B. Dickson, 'Northern Ireland emergency legislation – the wrong medicine?' (1992) *Public Law*, Winter, 592.
75 Laura Donohue, *The Cost of Counterterrorism – Power, Politics and Liberty* (Cambridge University Press, 2008, 130).
76 *Ibid.*, 123.
77 Drug Trafficking Act 1986, s. 1.
78 Criminal Justice Act 1988, ss.71–89.
79 Drug Trafficking Act 1994, ss.1–41.
80 Proceeds of Crime Act 1995, ss.1–2.
81 Cabinet Office, *Recovering the Proceeds of Crime – A Performance and Innovation Unit Report* (Cabinet Office: London, 2000, 118–120).
82 For a more detailed discussion of the confiscation regime under the Proceeds of Crime Act 2002 see N. Ryder, 'To confiscate or not to confiscate? A comparative analysis of the confiscation of the proceeds of crime legislation in the United States of America and the United Kingdom' (2013) *Journal of Business Law*, 8, 767.
83 For a more detailed discussion see B. Rider, 'Taking money launderers to the cleaners: Part 2' (1996) *Private Client Business*, 3, 205–206.
84 Laura Donohue, *The Cost of Counterterrorism – Power, Politics and Liberty* (Cambridge University Press, 2008, 133).

the financing of terrorism[85] and the control of terrorist finances[86] as well as imposing forfeiture and criminal penalties on those found guilty of this offence.[87] Using such legislation, the UK has achieved some success in Northern Ireland against the Irish Republican Army (IRA) by virtue of the offences created.[88] However, its effectiveness was still questioned and thus resulted in a review of the UK's terrorist policy by the Home Office in 1998. The Consultation Paper concluded that the terrorist financing provisions contained several weaknesses including the fact that there were only four terrorist financing convictions between 1978 and 1989.[89] Bell argued in 2003 that 'there have been no successful prosecutions for terrorist funding offences in Northern Ireland over the last 30 years and the forfeiture provisions under the Prevention of Terrorism (Temporary Provisions) Act 1989 have never been utilised'.[90] The Home Office therefore recommended that the scope of the terrorist financing provisions should be extended to fund-raising for all terrorist purposes. The Criminal Justice Act 1993, therefore, added separate provisions to counteract terrorist financing under Part IV,[91] lowered the standard of proof from criminal to civil standards,[92] and brought the legislation more in line with anti-money laundering measures. Additionally, following the Omagh bombings in 1998, the Criminal Justice (Terrorism and Conspiracy) Act 1998 allowed courts to grant a forfeiture order for any property connected with proscribed terrorist organisations.[93] Therefore, it is evident that the UK already had a robust attitude towards disrupting terrorist finances and recognised it as a separate offence to money laundering, even before there was international action on the issue. This can be seen further by the fact that the UK was one of the few Member States that signed and ratified the 1999 UN Convention on the Suppression of the Financing of Terrorism before 9/11. This was signed 10 January 2000 and ratified 7 March 2001.

The subsequent legislation to the UN Convention was the Terrorism Act 2000, which was, and still is, the cornerstone of the UK's CTF strategy. Part III of the Act significantly extends provisions relating to terrorism to include international terrorism and persons residing outside the UK.[94] This allays previous criticism of UK legislation that it focused too heavily on Northern Ireland and other parts of the UK. The provisions therefore include, as noted above, offences of fund-raising[95]

---

85 Prevention of Terrorism (Temporary Provisions) Act 1989 (repealed), s. 9.

86 Prevention of Terrorism (Temporary Provisions) Act 1989 (repealed), s. 9; s. 11.

87 Prevention of Terrorism (Temporary Provisions) Act 1989 (repealed), s. 13.

88 For a more detailed discussion of terrorist funding in Northern Ireland see W. Tupman, 'Where has all the money gone? The IRA as a profit-making concern' (1998) *Journal of Money Laundering Control*, 1(4), 303.

89 *Ibid*.

90 R. Bell, 'The confiscation, forfeiture and disruption of terrorist finances' (2003) *Journal of Money Laundering Control*, 7(2), 113.

91 As amendments to the Northern Ireland (Emergency Provisions) Act 1991.

92 Criminal Justice Act 1993, s. 37(2).

93 Criminal Justice (Terrorism and Conspiracy) Act 1998, s. 4(3).

94 Terrorism Act 2000, s. 1(4)(a),(c) and (d).

95 Terrorism Act 2000, s. 15.

and money laundering,[96] and cover the issues of confiscation, seizure of cash during an investigation[97] and penalties of forfeiture if convicted.[98] Accordingly, the UK is one of the few countries that has properly separated CTF legislation and is thus one of the most advanced in the application of financial weapons against terrorist organisations. In 2002, HM Treasury published a report that outlined the important contribution made by the UK government towards targeting the sources of terrorist financing.[99] Building on this leadership, in 2007 the government also launched the financial challenge to crime and terrorism, which 'sets out for the first time how the public and private sector would come together to deter terrorists from using the financial system, detect them when they did, and use financial tools to disrupt them'.[100] In 2010, HM Treasury stated that 'the government's aim is to deprive terrorists and violent extremists of the financial resources and systems needed for terrorist-related activity, including radicalisation'.[101] In terms of CTF legislation, the UK is therefore a world leader.

International CTF measures

The term 'terrorist finance' was adopted by the UN in its seminal Declaration to Eliminate International Terrorism in 1994.[102] This was soon followed by General Assembly Resolution A/RES/51/210, which provided that Member States were to 'take steps to prevent and counteract, through appropriate domestic measures, the financing of terrorists and terrorist organizations'.[103] The scope of this Resolution, however, was limited to terrorist bombings and nuclear terrorism. The al-Qaeda bombings in Kenya and Tanzania in 1998 therefore resulted in a rethink and the subsequent passing of Resolution A/RES/52/165 in 1997 and Resolution A/RES/53/108 in 1998. These highlighted the need to counter terrorist financing, as well as a suggestion to form a Convention against the financing of terrorism.[104] Consequently, as mentioned above, the International Convention for the Suppression of the Financing of Terrorism 1999 defines funds for terrorism to include 'assets of every kind, whether tangible or intangible, movable or immovable,

---

96 Terrorism Act 2000, s. 18.

97 Terrorism Act 2000, ss. 24–26.

98 Terrorism Act 2000, s. 23.

99 HM Treasury, *Combating the Financing of Terrorism: A Report on UK Action* (HM Treasury: London, 2002, 11).

100 HM Treasury, *The Financial Challenge to Crime and Terrorism* (HM Treasury: London, 2007).

101 *Ibid.*, 5.

102 Annex to Resolution 49/60, Measures to eliminate international terrorism, 9 December 1994, 49/60.

103 A/RES/51/210, 88th Plenary Meeting of General Assembly, 17th December; also see A/RES/45/121 of 14 December 1990.

104 A/RES/52/165 15 December 1997, para. 3 on pledge to prevent terrorist financing; A/RES/53/108, 8 December 1998, para. 11 on a draft International Convention against terrorist financing.

however acquired, and legal documents or instruments in any form'.[105] The 1999 Convention therefore criminalised the collection or distribution of funds that were to be used in an act of terrorism,[106] and also outlined measures for the freezing and forfeiture of funds used for terrorist acts.[107] Despite the importance of preventing terrorist financing, only 41 Member States signed the Treaty, and only six ratified it.[108]

Additionally, it is also important to consider the impact of UN Security Council Resolution 1267, which was adopted on 15 October 1999. This Resolution created a sanctions regime that included both individuals and entities associated with al-Qaeda, Osama bin Laden and/or the Taliban. The scope and breadth of the sanctions regime is extensive and it applies to all parts of the world. This obligation has commonly been referred to as the 'Sanctions Regime', which has been amended on numerous occasions by other UN Security Council Resolutions including resolutions 1333 (2000),[109] 1390 (2002),[110] 1455 (2003),[111] 1526 (2004),[112] 1617 (2005),[113] 1735 (2006),[114] 1822 (2008),[115] 1904 (2009),[116] 1989 (2011)[117]and 2083 (2012).[118] Furthermore, Resolution 1267 stipulates that a Committee of the Security Council is established to ensure that the obligations outlined in the previous paragraph 4 of Resolution 1267 are followed. Additionally, the Committee 'maintains

105 Article 1, para. 1 of the Convention, The United Nations (1999).
106 Article 2(1)(a) and (b), also request under Article 4 for domestic states to criminalise terrorist financing, 1999 United Nations Convention for the Suppression of Terrorist Financing, adopted by UN in Resolution 54/109, 9 December 1999.
107 See in general Article 8, 1999 Convention.
108 A. Leong, 'Chasing dirty money: Domestic and international measures against money laundering' (2007) *Journal of Money Laundering Control*, 10(2), 145.
109 United Nations, 'United Nations Security Council Resolution 1333', available from http://www.state.gov/documents/organization/5265.pdf, accessed 23 November 2014.
110 United Nations, 'United Nations Security Council Resolution 1390', available from http://daccess-dds-ny.un.org/doc/UNDOC/GEN/N02/216/02/PDF/N0221602.pdf?OpenElement, accessed 23 November 2014.
111 United Nations, 'United Nations Security Council Resolution 1455', available from http://www.un.org/ga/search/view_doc.asp?symbol=S/RES/1455(2003), accessed 23 November 2014.
112 United Nations, 'United Nations Security Council Resolution 1526', available from http://www.state.gov/j/ct/rls/other/un/66955.htm, accessed 23 November 2014.
113 United Nations, 'United Nations Security Council Resolution 1617', available from http://www.state.gov/j/ct/rls/other/un/65909.htm, accessed 23 November 2014.
114 United Nations, 'United Nations Security Council Resolution 1735', available from http://eurasiangroup.org/files/documents/oon_eng/1735_20_2006_20eng.pdf, accessed 23 November 2014.
115 United Nations, 'United Nations Security Council Resolution 1822', available from http://eurasiangroup.org/files/documents/oon_eng/1735_20_2006_20eng.pdf, accessed 23 November 2014.
116 United Nations, 'United Nations Security Council Resolution 1904', available from http://eurasiangroup.org/files/documents/oon_eng/1735_20_2006_20eng.pdf, accessed 23 November 2014.
117 United Nations, 'United Nations Security Council Resolution 1989', available from http://www.sipri.org/databases/embargoes/un_arms_embargoes/taliban/UNSCR1989.pdf, accessed 23 November 2014.
118 United Nations, 'United Nations Security Council Resolution 2083', available from http://www.sipri.org/databases/embargoes/un_arms_embargoes/taliban/UNSCR1989.pdf, accessed 23 November 2014.

a list of individuals and entities with respect to Al-Qaida and other individuals, groups, undertakings and entities associated with them . . . states may request the Committee to add names to the Al-Qaida Sanctions List. The Committee also considers submissions by States to delete names from the Al-Qaida Sanctions List.'[119]

Another important CTF measure was UN Security Council Resolution 1269, which was universally adopted in October 1999 and which condemned the rising and intensifying acts of international terrorism. In particular, Security Council Resolution 1269 asked nation states to completely implement the UN's anti-terrorist conventions. Specifically, the Resolution provided that countries should 'cooperate with each other, particularly through bilateral and multilateral agreements and arrangements, to prevent and suppress terrorist acts, protect their nationals and other persons against terrorist attacks and bring to justice the perpetrators of such acts'.[120] Furthermore, nation states should 'prevent and suppress in their territories through all lawful means the preparation and financing of any acts of terrorism'.[121] Countries are required to 'deny those who plan, finance or commit terrorist acts safe havens by ensuring their apprehension and prosecution or extradition'.[122] Additionally, they must 'take appropriate measures in conformity with the relevant provisions of national and international law, including international standards of human rights, before granting refugee status, for the purpose of ensuring that the asylum-seeker has not participated in terrorist acts'.[123] Finally, countries should exchange information in accordance with international and domestic law, and cooperate on administrative and judicial matters.[124] What is interesting to note here is the second part of paragraph four that provides that countries are required to 'prevent and suppress in their territories through all lawful means the preparation and financing of any acts of terrorism'.[125] Although UN Security Council Resolution 1269 doesn't specifically provide for examples or requirements for 'lawful means', it does illustrate the continued importance of combating the financing of terrorism.

The terrorist attacks of 9/11, as outlined above, led to a monumental shift in attitudes towards the detection and prevention of terrorist financing. The Convention therefore served as a precedent for UN Security Council Resolution 1373.[126] This imposes four obligations on members of the UN:[127] i) it specifically requires states to thwart and control the financing of terrorism;[128] ii) it criminalises the collection

---

119 The United Nations, 'General information on the on the work of the Committee' available from http://www.un.org/sc/committees/1267/information.shtml, accessed 9 September 2014.

120 United Nations Security Council Resolution 1269, paragraph 4.

121 *Ibid.*

122 *Ibid.*

123 *Ibid.*

124 *Ibid.*

125 *Ibid.*

126 P. Binning, 'In safe hands? Striking the balance between privacy and security – anti-terrorist finance measures' (2002) *European Human Rights Law Review*, 6, 737.

127 See Cabinet Office, *The UK and the Campaign against International Terrorism – Progress Report* (Cabinet Office: London, 2002, 24).

128 S.C. Res, 1373, U.N. SCOR, 56th Sess., 4385th Mtg. Article 1(a).

of terrorist funds in states territory;[129] iii) it freezes funds, financial assets and economic resources of people who commit or try to commit acts of terrorism;[130] and,
iv) it prevents any nationals from within their territories providing funds, financial
assets and economic resources to people who seek to commit acts of terrorism.[131]
Resolution 1373 is therefore the most important international legislative measure
that seeks to prevent terrorist financing, with the obligation on Member States to
freeze assets described as absolute in compelling collective application.[132] In contrast
to the 1999 Convention, all 191 Member States have submitted reports to the UN
Security Council Counter-Terrorism Committee on the actions they have taken
to suppress international terrorism, including how they have gone about blocking
terrorist finances as required by Resolution 1373.[133]

It has been suggested by the FATF that the UK's CTF policy can be divided
into three parts 'to deter, through the establishment of enforceable safeguards
and supervision; to detect, using the financial intelligence generated by money
laundering controls to identify and target criminals and terrorist financiers; and
to disrupt, maximising the use of available penalties such as prosecutions or asset
seizures.'[134] Furthermore, the Home Office stated that the UK's CTF policy was
aimed at:

> preventing terrorists from using common methods to raise funds, or using
> the financial system to move money, making it harder for terrorist networks
> to operate by reducing the resources available for propaganda, recruitment,
> facilitation, training, and support of families, as well as harder for extremists
> to mount attacks, targeting the raising and movement of money in and out of
> the UK by terrorists and disrupting the funding of bodies such as Al Qa'ida,
> using financial intelligence and financial investigation methods to support
> counter-terrorist investigations and implementing asset freezes to prohibit
> anyone from dealing with the funds or economic resources belonging to or
> owned, held or controlled by a designated person.[135]

Building on this leadership, in 2007 the government launched the financial challenge to crime and terrorism, which 'sets out for the first time how the public and
private sector would come together to deter terrorists from using the financial

---

129 S.C. Res, 1373, U.N. SCOR, 56th Sess., 4385th Mtg. Article 1(b).
130 S.C. Res, 1373, U.N. SCOR, 56th Sess., 4385th Mtg. Article 1(c).
131 S.C. Res, 1373, U.N. SCOR, 56th Sess., 4385th Mtg. Article 1(5).
132 See A. Kruse, 'Financial and economic sanctions – from a perspective of international law and
     human rights' (2005) *Journal of Financial Crime*, 12(3), 218.
133 The White House, *Progress Report on the Global War on Terrorism* (The White House, 2003, 6).
134 Financial Action Task Force, *Third Mutual Evaluation Report Anti-Money Laundering and Combating
     the Financing of Terrorism – The United Kingdom of Great Britain and Northern Ireland* (Financial Action
     Task Force: Paris, 2007).
135 Home Office, 'Counter terrorist finance strategy', available from https://www.gov.uk/government/
     publications/counter-terrorist-finance-strategy, accessed 15 July 2014.

system, detect them when they did, and use financial tools to disrupt them'.[136] In 2010 HM Treasury stated that 'the government's aim is to deprive terrorists and violent extremists of the financial resources and systems needed for terrorist-related activity, including radicalisation'.[137] These measures were supported by the publication of several policy documents aimed at tackling international terrorism.[138] This was further strengthened by the Strategy for Countering International Terrorism[139] and the publication of the National Security Strategy in 2010.[140] This was accompanied by the publication of the Strategic Defence and Security Review,[141] and the publication of CONTEST, the UK's new counter-terrorism strategy.[142] These strategy documents were followed by the introduction of several pieces of terrorist-related legislation, which included the Protection of Freedoms Act 2012,[143] the Terrorism Prevention of Investigations Measures Act 2011,[144] the Communications Data Bill,[145] the Justice and Security Act 2013[146] and the Data Retention and Investigatory Powers Act 2014.

Financial institutions and regulatory bodies

HM Treasury

HM Treasury is the leading CTF government department in the UK and is responsible for the execution of the UN's financial sanctions regime.[147] Explained in more

---

136 HM Treasury, *The Financial Challenge to Crime and Terrorism* (HM Treasury: London, 2007).
137 *Ibid.*, 5.
138 HM Government, *Countering International Terrorism: The United Kingdom's Strategy* (HM Government: London, 2006).
139 HM Government, *The United Kingdom's Strategy for Countering International Terrorism* (HM Government: London, 2009).
140 HM Government, *A Strong Britain in an Age of Uncertainty: The National Security Strategy* (HM Government: London, 2010). In this document, the government identified a total of 15 risks presented by terrorism and concentrated on four, which it identified as the most pressing. These included acts of terrorism that directly affect the UK or its interests, attacks on UK cyberspace, a major accident or natural hazard and military action between countries that involves the UK and its allies.
141 HM Government, *Securing Britain in an Age of Uncertainty: The Strategic Defence and Security Review* (HM Government: London, 2010).
142 HM Government, *CONTEST – The United Kingdom's Strategy for Countering Terrorism* (HM Government: London, 2011).
143 For an excellent discussion of this legislation see E. Cape, 'The counter-terrorism provisions of the Protection of Freedoms Act 2012: Preventing misuse or a case of smoke and mirrors?' (2013) *Criminal Law Review*, 5, 385.
144 For a more detailed discussion see C. Walker, and A. Horne, 'The Terrorism Prevention and Investigations Measures Act 2011: One thing but not much the other?' (2012) *Criminal Law Review*, 6, 421.
145 For a brief commentary see E. Parris, and S. Briskman, 'The draft Communications Data Bill: An overview' (2012) *E-Commerce Law & Policy*, 14(7), 14.
146 For a discussion of this Bill see M. Chamberlain, 'The Justice and Security Bill' (2012) Civil Justice Quarterly, 31(4), 424.
147 Financial Action Task Force, *Third Mutual Evaluation Report Anti-Money Laundering and Combating the Financing of Terrorism – United Kingdom* (Financial Action Task Force: Paris, 2007, 24).

detail below, HM Treasury in association with the Home Office implements the UK's terrorist financing policy. This is further evidence of how the Coalition government extended the remit of the Home Office to tackle all aspects of financial crime, including money laundering and fraud. This is especially so since the creation of the National Crime Agency (NCA). Nonetheless, the objective of HM Treasury, as highlighted in Chapter 2, is to safeguard 'the integrity of the financial system from exploitation by criminals and terrorists. It does this by deploying financial tools to deter, detect and disrupt crime and security threats. The approach taken is effective and proportionate to the risks posed as well as engaging with business, law makers and law enforcers.'[148] This is clearly illustrated by the publication of its CTF strategy document in 2007 which outlined how the government intended to tackle the financing of terrorism.[149] In an attempt to achieve these objectives, HM Treasury has created the Asset Freezing Unit. This is responsible for:

- domestic legislation on financial sanctions;
- the implementation and administration of domestic financial sanctions;
- domestic designations under the Terrorist Asset-Freezing etc. Act 2010;
- providing advice to Treasury ministers;
- the implementation and administration of international financial sanctions in the UK;
- working in conjunction with the Foreign and Commonwealth Office on the design of individual financial sanctions regimes and listing decisions at the UN and European Union (EU);
- working with international partners to develop the international frameworks for financial sanctions; and,
- licensing exemptions to financial sanctions.[150]

Furthermore, the Unit,

- issues Notices and notifications advising of the introduction, amendment, suspension or lifting of financial sanctions regimes with a view to making bodies and individuals likely to be affected by financial sanctions aware of their obligations;
- provides on the financial sanctions home page of the Treasury website a consolidated list of financial sanctions targets which consists of the names of individuals and entities that have been listed by the UN, EU and/or the UK under legislation relating to a specific financial sanctions regime;

---

148 HM Treasury, *The Financial Challenge to Crime and Terrorism* (HM Treasury: London, 2007, 11).
149 HM Treasury, *Combating the Financing of Terrorism: A Report on UK Action* (HM Treasury: London, 2002, 11).
150 HM Treasury, 'Asset freezing unit', available from http://www.hm-treasury.gov.uk/fin_sanctions_afu.htm, accessed 14 March 2015.

- provides on the financial sanctions home page of the Treasury website an investment ban list in relation to the EU measures against Burma/Myanmar;
- processes applications for licences to release frozen funds or to make funds available to designated/restricted persons; and,
- responds to reports and queries from financial institutions, companies and members of the public concerning financial sanctions.[151]

Home Office

The Home Office is responsible for i) managing the police in England and Wales, ii) the NCA, and iii) tackling organised crime, counter-terrorism, crime and immigration. As mentioned above, the Coalition government published its counter-terrorism strategy, or CONTEST, as it is referred to by the Home Office, in 2011.[152] This is administered and coordinated by the Home Office's Office for Security and Counter-Terrorism. In particular, this office is responsible for supporting the Home Secretary and other government departments in relation to CONTEST; is required to deliver certain parts of the counter-terrorism strategy; must supervise the UK Security Service; and, coordinates counter-terrorism crisis management.[153] The strategy has four important objectives listed under the sound bites of pursue, prevent, protect and prepare. It therefore aims to: i) Pursue: to stop terrorist attacks; ii) Prevent: to stop people becoming terrorists or supporting terrorism; iii) Protect: to strengthen our protection against a terrorist attack; and iv) Prepare: to mitigate the impact of a terrorist attack. Despite these laudable aims, the strategy fails to provide any significant detail as to how the Home Office actually intends to combat and prevent the financing of terrorism.

Foreign and Commonwealth Office

The Foreign and Commonwealth Office is responsible for the implementation of several UN money laundering legislative provisions. It performs the same function in relation to CTF policy and is responsible for the ratification of UN treaties and the implementation of UN Security Council resolutions. In relation to the UK's counter-terrorism strategy, the Foreign and Commonwealth Office organises the delivery of CONTEST overseas.

National Crime Agency

The NCA is the UK's Financial Intelligence Unit (FIU) and as such administers the reporting obligations under the Proceeds of Crime Act 2002. It also manages the

---

151   *Ibid.*
152   Home Office, *The United Kingdom's Strategy for Countering Terrorism* (Home Office: London, 2011).
153   *Ibid.*, 123.

reporting of suspected instances of terrorist financing from a wide range of financial services bodies and other relevant professions. The NCA was created by the Crime and Courts Act 2013.

Financial intelligence

As with other financial crimes, financial intelligence is extremely important if the CTF policy is to be effective. Schedule 2, Part III, of the Anti-terrorism, Crime and Security Act 2001 therefore inserts section 21A into the Terrorism Act 2000 and creates the offence of failing to disclose in the regulated sector. A person commits an offence under this section if three conditions are met: i) the accused knows or suspects, or has reasonable grounds for knowing or suspecting that a person has committed an offence under sections 15–18 of the Terrorism Act 2000;[154] ii) the information or other matter upon which the accused has based their knowledge or suspicion, or which gives reasonable grounds for such knowledge of suspicion came to him in the course of a business that operates within the regulated sector;[155] and, iii) the accused does not disclose the information or other matter to a constable or nominated officer (normally a money laundering reporting officer) as soon as practicable after they received the information.[156] A person does not commit an offence if they had a reasonable excuse for not disclosing the information or other matter or they are a professional legal adviser and the information or other matter came to them in privileged circumstances.[157] Lord Carlile argued that these reporting obligations are 'still [an] under-publicised duty, to which the only major statutory exception is genuine legal professional privilege'.[158]

Furthermore, the Anti-terrorism, Crime and Security Act 2001 amends the Terrorism Act 2000 by inserting a further defence of protected disclosures.[159] For this to be utilised, three conditions must be met. The first condition is that the information or other matter disclosed came to the person making the disclosure (the discloser) in the course of a business in the regulated sector.[160] The second condition is that the information or other matter causes the discloser to know or suspect, or gives them reasonable grounds for knowing or suspecting that a person has committed an offence as outlined above under sections 15–18 of the Terrorism Act 2000.[161] The third and final condition is that the disclosure is made to a constable

---

154 Terrorism Act 2000, s. 21A(2).
155 Terrorism Act 2000, s. 21A(3).
156 Terrorism Act 2000, s. 21A(4).
157 Terrorism Act 2000, s. 21A.
158 Home Office, Report on the Operation in 2004 of the Terrorism Act 2000 (Home Office: London, 2004, 24).
159 Terrorism Act 2000, s. 21B.
160 Terrorism Act 2000, s. 21B(2).
161 Terrorism Act 2000, s. 21B(3).

or a nominated officer as soon as is practicable after the information or other matter comes to the discloser.[162]

An individual or organisation that suspects that an offence has been committed under the Terrorism Act 2000 is required to complete a Suspicious Activity Report (SAR). The UK has a long history of imposing reporting requirements on financial institutions where there is a risk of money laundering or terrorist financing. For example, the first money laundering reporting requirements were contained in the Drug Trafficking Offences Act 1986, which was amended by the Criminal Justice Act 1993. These reporting obligations have since become mandatory and have been consolidated by the Proceeds of Crime Act 2002 and the Money Laundering Regulations 2007.[163] The Anti-terrorism, Crime and Security Act 2001 makes it a criminal offence to fail to disclose knowledge or suspicion that another person has committed an offence under sections 15–18 of the Terrorism Act 2000.[164] Binning described this offence as almost identical to the offence of failing to disclose information under the Proceeds of Crime Act 2002.[165] An individual or organisation that suspects that an offence has been committed under the Terrorism Act 2000 is thus legally required to complete a SAR, which is then sent via a Money Laundering Reporting Officer (MLRO) to the NCA for processing, who will determine whether or not to pass the information on to the police for further investigation. Lord Carlisle commented that 'there are concerns in the business sector about difficulties of compliance and the serious consequences that may flow from this'.[166] It has also been argued that the reporting requirements under the Anti-terrorism, Crime and Security Act 2001 are difficult to understand and that they are not working.

The number of terrorist-related SARs submitted between 2007 and 2008 was 956.[167] This decreased slightly to 703 between 2008 and 2009.[168] Since then there has been an annual increase in the number of SARs received. In 2008, the UK FIU received 210,524 SARs.[169] This rose to 240,582 SARs in 2010,[170] to 247,601 in

---

162 Terrorism Act 2000, s. 21B(4).

163 S.I. 2007/2517.

164 Anti-terrorism, Crime and Security Act 2001, Schedule 2 Pt III.

165 Proceeds of Crime Act 2002 ss. 330–332.

166 Home Office, *Report on the Operation in 2004 of the Terrorism Act 2000* (Home Office: London, 2004, 19–20).

167 Serious Organised Crime Agency, *The Suspicious Activity Reports Regime Annual Report 2008* (Serious Organised Crime Agency: London, 2008, 42).

168 Serious Organised Crime Agency, *The Suspicious Activity Reports Regime Annual Report 2009* (Serious Organised Crime Agency: London, 2010, 14).

169 Serious Organised Crime Agency, *The Suspicious Activity Reports Regime Annual Report 2008* (Serious Organised Crime Agency: London, 2009, 15).

170 Serious Organised Crime Agency, *The Suspicious Activity Reports Regime Annual Report 2010* (Serious Organised Crime Agency: London, 2011, 4).

2011,[171] to 278,665 in 2012,[172] to 316,527 in 2013[173] and to 354,186 in 2014.[174] The number of suspected instances of terrorist financing in 2013 numbered 856 SARs, an increase of 23% from 2012, representing 0.27% of the total number of submitted SARs to the NCA.[175]

In addition to the traditional means of gathering financial intelligence via the use of SARs, the Terrorism Act 2000 contains a number of statutory measures that related to financial information orders. Elabag stated that 'Schedule 6 to the Terrorism Act 2000 deals with orders empowering the police to require financial institutions to supply customer information relevant to terrorist investigation'.[176] A police officer can apply for an order that could 'require a financial institution [to which the order applies] to provide customer information for the purposes of the investigation'.[177] The order could apply to '(a) all financial institutions, (b) a particular description, or particular descriptions, of financial institutions, or (c) a particular financial institution or particular financial institutions'.[178] If a financial institution fails to comply with the financial information order it is guilty of a criminal offence.[179] However, the financial institution does have a defence to breaching the financial information order if it can illustrate that either the '(a) information required was not in the institution's possession, or (b) that it was not reasonably practicable for the institution to comply with the requirement'.[180] Binning noted that financial information orders are 'available for general criminal money laundering and criminal benefit investigations under the Proceeds of Crime Act 2002. They are also available for use in mutual assistance requests to enable information to be passed to overseas investigators without the knowledge of the account holder.'[181]

Furthermore, the Terrorism Act 2000 permits the use of account monitoring orders.[182] Account monitoring orders have been described as draconian[183] and their

---

171 Serious Organised Crime Agency, *The Suspicious Activity Reports Regime Annual Report 2011* (Serious Organised Crime Agency: London, 2012).

172 *Ibid.*

173 National Crime Agency, *Suspicious Activity Reports (SARs) Annual Report 2013* (National Crime Agency: London, 2014).

174 National Crime Agency, *Suspicious Activity Reports (SARs) Annual Report 2014* (National Crime Agency: London, 2015).

175 National Crime Agency, *Suspicious Activity Reports (SARs) Annual Report 2013* (National Crime Agency: London, 2014).

176 O. Elagab, 'Control of terrorist funds and the banking system' (2006) *Journal of International Banking Law and Regulation*, 21(1), 40.

177 Terrorism Act 2000, Schedule 6, para. 1(1).

178 Terrorism Act 2000, Schedule 6, para. 1(1)(a).

179 Terrorism Act 2000, Schedule 6, para. 1(3).

180 *Ibid.*

181 P. Binning, 'In safe hands? Striking the balance between privacy and security – anti-terrorist finance measures' (2002) *European Human Rights Law Review*, 6, 747.

182 Terrorism Act 2000, Schedule 6A.

183 S. Gentle, 'Proceeds of Crime Act 2002: Update' (2008) *Compliance Officer Bulletin*, 56 (May), 31.

relationship with civil liberties has been questioned on several occasions.[184] An account monitoring order can be granted by a judge if they are satisfied that '(a) the order is sought for the purposes of a terrorist investigation, (b) the tracing of terrorist property is desirable for the purposes of the investigation, and (c) the order will enhance the effectiveness of the investigation'.[185] There must also be reasonable grounds for suspecting that the named person in the application 'has benefitted from criminal conduct in a confiscation investigation [or has] committed a money laundering offence in a money laundering investigation'.[186] There must also be reasonable grounds to believe that the account information that is subsequently produced will be of 'substantial value to the investigation'.[187] Under the order, a financial institution is required to provide information on a specified account for a specified period of time, although this cannot be for more than 90 days.[188]

One of the most controversial pieces of CTF legislation that has been enacted in the UK is the Counter-Terrorism Act 2008. In relation to tackling terrorist financing, the Act 'has added to those financial provisions in significant ways. The Act implements a new regime of financial directions in Schedule 7 . . . the scheme is very wide-ranging in application and effect.'[189] Goldby stated that the Counter-Terrorism Act 'provides new anti-money laundering and counter-terrorism financing provisions applicable to the private sector'.[190] Schedule 7 of the 2008 Act therefore provides HM Treasury with the ability to give a direction to either a person or a financial institution where the FATF has requested actions to be pursued against a country because of the terrorist financing or money laundering risks it presents. The direction will contain a precise legal obligation on the financial services sector in relation to a transaction of business with a government of a country, a person undertaking a business in a country or a person resident or business incorporated in country. Finally, HM Treasury may impose a direction against a country where it believes there is substantial risk to the UK because of the development, manufacturing or facilitation of nuclear, radiological, biological or chemical weapons there, or the facilitation of such development. The second part of Schedule 7 outlines the people who can be subject to the direction and that it may be issued to people working in the financial sector. Schedule 7 of the Counter-Terrorism Act 2008 provides for the requirement of a direction and the obligations that can be imposed. For example, the obligations can be imposed on transactions, business

184 See T. Johnson, 'Civil recovery: Is the erosion of individual rights justified?' (2011) *Civil Justice Quarterly*, 30(2), 136.
185 Terrorism Act 2000, Schedule 6, para. 2A.
186 Home Office, *Financial Orders Under Part 8 of the Proceeds of Crime Act 2002* (Home Office: London, 2015, 27).
187 *Ibid.*
188 *Ibid.*
189 G. Rees and T. Moloney, 'The latest efforts to interrupt terrorist supply lines: Schedule 7 to the Counter-Terrorism Act 2008' (2010) *Criminal Law Review*, 2, 127.
190 M. Goldby, 'The impact of Schedule 7 of the Counter-Terrorism Act 2008 on banks and their customers' (2010) *Journal of Money Laundering Control*, 13(4), 352.

relationships with a person carrying on business in the country, the government of the country, or a person resident or business incorporated in the country. It is very likely that once a direction has been imposed by virtue of Schedule 7 of the Counter-Terrorism Act 2008 the recipient will be required to improve their due diligence measures. Part 5 of Schedule 7 permits the relevant enforcement agency to obtain information and Part 6 permits the use of financial sanctions on those who fail to observe the directions. Rees and Moloney state that:

> The powers of the Treasury have been significantly extended . . . [it] can now choose whether to follow the recommendations of the FATF or can simply make its own mind up as to whether a state, or elements of it, pose a terrorist, money laundering or proliferation risk to the interests of the United Kingdom.[191]

The powers of HM Treasury under Schedule 7 of the Counter-Terrorism Act 2008 were challenged in *Bank Mellat v HM Treasury (No. 2)*.[192] Here, the Supreme Court determined that the directions authorised by HM Treasury under Schedule 7 breached Article 6 of the European Convention of Human Rights and the rules of natural justice.[193] HM Treasury challenged the open judgment of the Supreme Court, and the Court of Appeal recently determined that HM Treasury should disclose and grant Bank Mellat access to the documents that were used to impose the sanctions.[194]

Sentencing and recovery

Criminal prosecution

A defendant who has been found guilty of any of the four principal terrorist financing offences, as outlined above, is liable to a maximum term of 14 years imprisonment and/or an unlimited fine,[195] the same as that for the offence of money laundering. Despite this penalty and the devastating effects of the crime, there have been very few UK prosecutions for terrorist financing. Between 11 September 2001 and 31 December 2007, only 74 terrorist financing charges were made in Great Britain, making up only 17 per cent of all charges made under the

---

191 G. Rees and T. Moloney, 'The latest efforts to interrupt terrorist supply lines: Schedule 7 to the Counter-Terrorism Act 2008' (2010) *Criminal Law Review*, 2, 135.
192 [2013] UKSC 38 and 39; [2013] 3 W.L.R. 179.
193 For a more detailed discussion of this case see C. Sargeant, 'Two steps backward, one step forward – the cautionary tale of Bank Mellat (No 1)' (2013) *Cambridge Journal of International and Comparative Law*, 3(1), 111.
194 *Bank Mellat v HM Treasury* [2015] EWCA Civ 1052.
195 Terrorism Act 2000, s. 22.

Terrorism Act 2000.[196] Furthermore, in 2007, the Crown Prosecution Service prosecuted only three defendants under section 17 of the Terrorism Act 2000 and in 2008, only four defendants under section 15.[197] Between September 2001 and 2009, only 11 people were convicted under sections 15–19 of the Terrorism Act 2000.[198] As Robinson claims, terrorist money laundering prosecutions in Great Britain have 'mostly failed'.[199]

It is unclear why the prosecution rate has been so low, although one reason may be because in order to prove the offences under Part III of the Terrorism Act 2000 the prosecution has to prove the terrorist element. For instance, for a section 17 offence it is necessary to prove that the defendant not only became involved in a funding arrangement but that they knew or suspected that the proceeds of the arrangement were for the purposes of terrorism. Whilst the defendant may have suspected that the arrangement was illegal in some way, it is harder to prove that the suspicion was one of actual terrorism rather than drug trafficking, human trafficking or some other crime.[200] Because of the small numbers involved, there are no sentencing guidelines for these offences and no published cases relating to sentencing practice. The only guidance, to the authors' knowledge, is contained in section 30 of the Counter-Terrorism Act 2008, which states that if an offence has a terrorist connection, the court must treat that as an aggravating factor and sentence accordingly.

Examples of sentencing for section 15 offences include two Algerian men, Benmerzouga and Meziane, who were sentenced in 2003 to 11 years imprisonment for raising over £200,000 for purposes of terrorism through a credit card fraud.[201] Similarly, in 2007, Hassan Mutegombwa received ten years for inviting someone to provide money for the purposes of terrorism,[202] indicating that the judges involved thought that these two offences were serious enough to warrant lengthy terms of incarceration. Despite these examples, more usual sentences would appear to be much shorter. For example, in 2008, Abu Izzadeen was sentenced to four and a half years for inciting terrorism and terrorist fund-raising, Shah Jala Hussain

---

196 P. Sproat, 'Counter-terrorist finance in the UK: A quantitative and qualitative commentary based on open-source materials' (2010) *Journal of Money Laundering Control*, 13(4), 315.

197 House of Lords, 'Money laundering and the financing of terrorism: European Union Committee', 2009, available from http://www.publications.parliament.uk/pa/ld200809/ldselect/ldeucom/132/9031811.htm, accessed 24 June 2011.

198 HC Deb, 5 February 2010, c586w.

199 P. Sproat, 'Counter-terrorist finance in the UK: A quantitative and qualitative commentary based on open-source materials' (2010) *Journal of Money Laundering Control*, 13(4), 320.

200 R. Alexander, 'Money laundering and terrorist financing: Time for a combined offence' (2009) *Company Lawyer*, 30(7), 202.

201 The Telegraph, 'Two al-Qa'eda terrorists jailed for 11 Years', available from http://www.telegraph.co.uk/news/1426290/Two-al-Qaeda-terrorists-jailed-for-11-years.html, accessed 28 June 2011.

202 Metropolitan Police, 'Operation Overamp: Hassan Mutegombwa', available from http://www.powerbase.info/images/6/6c/Metropolitan_Police_Service_Press_Release_on_Conviction_of_Hassan_Mutegombwa.pdf, accessed 28 June 2011.

received two years and three months for terrorist fund-raising whilst Simon Kee-ler received two and a half years and Abdul Muhid two years imprisonment for the same offence.[203] In March 2011, Rajib Karim was sentenced to three years impris-onment for an offence under section 15(3) of the Terrorism Act 2000, although because of other terrorist offences his total sentence was one of 30 years.[204] These cases would therefore suggest that the usual sentence for a fund-raising offence is an immediate custodial sentence of between two and three years.

The final mechanism that the sentencing court has at its disposal is a notifica-tion requirement, which is found under Part 4 of the Counter-Terrorism Act 2008. For the purposes of this chapter, notification requirements apply to the fund-raising offences detailed above and found under sections 15–18 of the Ter-rorism Act 2000.[205] To be made subject to these requirements the individual must be i) 16 or over at the time of being dealt with,[206] ii) have been convicted of an applicable offence under the Act, and iii) have either been sentenced to an indeter-minate prison term[207] or a hospital order.[208] The consequence of the requirement is that the individual concerned must notify the police of certain information within three days of being sentenced. Such information includes their date of birth, national insurance number, full name and any other names previously used, home address and any other prescribed information.[209] The requirements are very similar in nature to the notification requirements applicable for sex offenders and, as under that legislation,[210] the individual concerned has an ongoing duty to ensure that any changes to previously submitted information are updated as soon as possible.[211] Annual re-notification of current information to the police is also required.[212] The length of time during which an individual is obliged to notify the police of such information will depend on the initial sentence. Imprisonment or custody for life, detention at Her Majesty's pleasure, detention in a young offenders institution for 10 years or more and imprisonment in a young offenders' institution for public protection purposes will result in a 30-year notification period.[213] A 15-year notification period applies when the individual was imprisoned in a young offender institution for a term of at least five years but less than 10.[214] Failure to

---

203 BBC News, 'Arrogant Muslim preacher jailed', available from http://news.bbc.co.uk/1/hi/uk/7354397.stm, accessed 28 June 2011.
204 Metropolitan Police, 'Man jailed for 30 years for terrorism offences', available from http://content.met.police.uk/News/Man-jailed-for-30-years-for-terrorism-offences/1260268719101/1257246745756, accessed 28 June 2011.
205 Counter-Terrorism Act 2008, s. 41.
206 Counter-Terrorism Act 2008, s. 44.
207 This includes custody for life and also custody under dangerous offender provisions.
208 Counter-Terrorism Act 2008, s. 45.
209 Counter-Terrorism Act 2008, s. 47.
210 Sexual Offences Act 2003, s. 80.
211 Counter-Terrorism Act 2008, s. 48.
212 Counter-Terrorism Act 2008, s. 49.
213 Counter-Terrorism Act 2008, s. 53(2).
214 Counter-Terrorism Act 2008, s. 53(3).

comply with initial notification, notification of changes, periodic notification and any other requirements added to the order can subject individuals to a maximum of five years custody and/or a financial penalty.[215] Schedule 4 of the Act also makes provisions for those offenders who were convicted of terrorist financing offences outside of the UK.[216] This applies to both UK nationals and foreign nationals who either intend to come to or who are already in the UK. In addition to basic notification, those subject to Part 4 of this Act may also be subject to foreign travel restrictions. Again, similar to provisions legislated for sex offenders,[217] individuals can be restricted from a) travelling to a named country outside of the UK, b) travelling to any country outside of the UK except those named within the order, and c) travelling outside of the UK.[218] In case we were in any doubt, such legislation clearly reminds us that those offenders who knowingly help to fund terrorism are dangerous to the public.

Civil recovery

Despite the lack of sentencing guidance, there does appear to be more emphasis placed on recovery. This is not surprising when we bear in mind that the overall aim of CTF legislation is to prevent the funding of terrorism. It is perhaps predictable, then, that there has been a glut of initiatives and orders that enable the recovery of money and/or property that was intended for use in terrorism. For example, the Terrorism Act 2000, as amended by the Counter-Terrorism Act 2008, states that if a person is convicted of an offence under sections 15–19, any property connected with the offence can be the subject of a criminal forfeiture order.[219] The court also has the option of a confiscation order under the Proceeds of Crime Act (POCA) 2002 (see Chapter 2), although if the court has the choice between the two, it may be better to opt for the forfeiture order as this deprives the defendant of the title of designated assets, whilst a confiscation order is only an order to pay a sum of money and is enforced as if it were a fine. A person subject to a forfeiture order is required to give to a police officer all property that is specified in the order.[220] The Terrorism Act 2000 also allows for Orders in Council, which have the effect of giving foreign forfeiture orders recognition in England and Wales.

Furthermore, the Anti-terrorism, Crime and Security Act 2001 authorises the seizure of terrorist cash anywhere in the UK;[221] the freezing of funds at the start of a terrorist-related investigation;[222] and, as highlighted above, the monitoring

---

215 Counter-Terrorism Act 2008, s. 54.
216 Counter-Terrorism Act 2008, s. 57.
217 Sexual Offences Act 2003, s. 122C.
218 Counter-Terrorism Act 2008, s. 58.
219 Terrorism Act 2000, s. 23.
220 Terrorism Act 2000, Schedule 4.
221 Anti-terrorism Crime and Security Act 2001, Schedule 1, Part 2.
222 Anti-terrorism Crime and Security Act 2001, ss. 4–16.

of suspected accounts.[223] It is worth noting that the Anti-terrorism, Crime and Security Act 2001 received Royal Assent on 14 December 2001, only 94 days after the 9/11 attacks in New York and Washington and thus could be described as having been rushed through Parliament. Nevertheless, the first recovery mechanism is provided for under Part I of the Act, which allows for the civil seizure and forfeiture of terrorist cash. For the purposes of the Act, terrorist cash is defined to include cash which '(a) is intended to be used for the purposes of terrorism, (b) consists of resources of an organisation which is a proscribed organisation, or (c) is, or represents, property obtained through terrorism'.[224] The cash must have been found in the UK and can include coins and notes in any currency, postal orders, bankers' drafts, cheques of any kind, bearer bonds and bearer shares.[225] The Act permits the authorised officer to seize cash if they have reasonable grounds for suspecting that it is terrorist cash.[226] Initially, this is only for a period of 48 hours, but can be extended by a magistrates' court, acting in a civil capacity, to a maximum of two years.[227] If the period of seizure is for longer than 48 hours, then the cash must be placed in an interest-bearing account. Any interest earned on the sum will be added to the capital either when the money is forfeited or released.[228] Between 2001 and 31 January 2007, £469,000 worth of cash was seized under terrorism legislation and £1.4 million of terrorist funds under the POCA 2002.[229]

Additionally, Part II of the Anti-terrorism, Crime and Security Act 2001 allows HM Treasury to freeze the assets of known or suspected terrorists. These are known as freezing orders, although they are sometimes referred to as asset freezing orders, freezing injunctions or Mareva[230] orders. An order can be made, if two statutory requirements are met. First, HM Treasury must reasonably believe that action threatening the UK's economy or the life or property of UK nationals or residents has taken place or is likely to take place. Interestingly, the Act provides that HM Treasury is not required to prove actual detriment to freeze the assets of a suspected terrorist, but that a threat is sufficient. There is no condition that there should be a suspicion of criminal activity, nor a condition that any criminal activity exists. The second element is that the persons involved in the action are resident outside of the UK or are an overseas government.[231] Under the Act, a freezing order prohibits the person from making funds available to or for the benefit of a person or persons

---

223 Anti-terrorism, Crime and Security Act 2001, Schedule 2, Part 1.
224 Anti-terrorism, Crime and Security Act 2001, s. 1(1).
225 Anti-terrorism, Crime and Security Act 2001, Schedule 1, para. 1.
226 Anti-terrorism, Crime and Security Act 2001, Schedule 1, para. 2.
227 Anti-terrorism, Crime and Security Act 2001, Schedule 1, para. 3.
228 Anti-terrorism, Crime and Security Act 2001, Schedule 1, para. 4.
229 P. Sproat, 'Counter-terrorist finance in the UK: A quantitative and qualitative commentary based on open-source materials' (2010) *Journal of Money Laundering Control*, 13(4), 324.
230 See *Mareva Compania Naviera SA v International Bulkcarriers SA* [1980] 1 All E.R. 213.
231 Anti-terrorism, Crime and Security Act 2001, s. 4(1)(a) and (b).

specified in the order,[232] which can include people in and outside of the UK.[233] The order is an interim order and as such must be kept under constant review by the Treasury.[234] It can last for no longer than two years[235] and, interestingly, binds not just the person named in the order, but also third parties with knowledge of it.[236] White argues that whilst the order is powerful, it is generally regarded by the courts as draconian and therefore is only used in exceptional circumstances.[237] An example of such an order, however, is the Landsbanki Freezing Order 2008.[238] This was made in October 2008 against the Icelandic bank, Landsbanki, after it was revealed that local councils in the UK had deposited approximately £800 million in the failing bank during the credit crunch.[239] The order froze funds owned, held and controlled by the bank and lasted until 15 June 2009.[240] Furthermore, following 9/11, HM Treasury and the Bank of England froze the assets of over 100 organisations and 200 individuals, including over £100 million of Taliban and al-Qaeda assets.[241]

The UK has additionally implemented the Terrorism (United Nations Measures) Order 2006 to give legal effect to Security Council Resolution 1373.[242] The Order also gives effect to the enforcement of EC Regulation 2580/2001, which permits for the designation of people within this regulation for such measures that relate to, inter alia, the freezing of funds, financial assets and economic resources. HM Treasury took the view that the aim of the Order was enhanced to provide further restrictions on making funds, economic resources and financial services available to anyone who has been designated in the UK by the Treasury as a person suspected of committing, attempting to commit, participating in or facilitating acts of terrorism. By virtue of Article 4 of the Order, HM Treasury has the power to designate a person if four conditions are met. These are that HM Treasury has reasonable grounds to suspect that a person is or may be: (a) a person who commits, attempts to commit,

---

232 Anti-terrorism, Crime and Security Act 2001, s. 5(1).
233 Anti-terrorism, Crime and Security Act 2001, s. 5(2).
234 Anti-terrorism, Crime and Security Act 2001, s. 7.
235 Anti-terrorism, Crime and Security Act 2001, s. 8.
236 S. White, 'Freezing injunctions: A procedural overview and practical guide', 2005, available from http://www.parkcourtchambers.co.uk/seminar-handouts/16.11.05%20Commercial-Chancery %20_S%20White_.pdf, accessed 24 June 2011.
237 *Ibid.*
238 The Landsbanki Freezing Order 2008, S.I. 2008/2668.
239 For an excellent discussion of the use of the powers under the Anti-terrorism, Crime and Security Act 2001 see G. Lennon, and C. Walker, 'Hot money in a cold climate' (2009) *Public Law*, January, 37.
240 HM Treasury, 'The Landsbanki freezing order', 2011, available from http://www.hm-treasury.gov. uk/fin_stability_landsbanki.htm, accessed 24 June 2011.
241 HM Treasury, *Combating the Financing of Terrorism: A Report on UK Action* (HM Treasury: London, 2002, 9).
242 S.I. 2006/2657.

participates in or facilitates the commission of acts of terrorism; (b) a person named in the Council Decision; (c) a person owned or controlled, directly or indirectly, by a designated person; or (d) a person acting on behalf of or at the direction of a designated person. Under Article 5 of the Order, HM Treasury is required to make appropriate measures to publicise the direction or to notify specific people and to inform the person identified in the direction.

Furthermore, under Article 7 of the 2006 Order, a person is prohibited from '[d]ealing with funds, financial assets and economic resources of anyone who commits, attempts to commit, participates in or facilitates the commission of acts of terrorism; designated persons; anyone owned or controlled by them or anyone acting on their behalf of or at their direction.'[243] The Article makes it a criminal offence to contravene this prohibition. Article 8 of the Order additionally prohibits making funds, financial assets, economic resources or financial services available to anyone in respect of whom Article 7 applies. Similarly, contravention of this prohibition is also a criminal offence.

The legality of the Terrorism (United Nations Measures) Order 2006 was challenged in *A v HM Treasury*.[244] Here, the appellants required orders from the court to quash the freezing of their assets under the aforementioned Order.[245] Collins J decided that the orders granted should be set aside, against five of the applicants, on three grounds: i) parliamentary approval should have been sought; the orders should not have been made by Order in Council; ii) it was impossible to determine how the test adopted by HM Treasury (that it had reasonable grounds for suspecting the applicants were committing terrorists acts) could represent a necessary means of applying the relevant UN Resolution; and iii) the 2006 Order created criminal offences that contravened the principle of legal certainty. The interpretation of the phrase 'economic resources' was crucial in the case, and the Court decided that the definition of this phrase meant that the family members of the applicants did not know if they were breaching the Order or if they needed a licence from HM Treasury.[246] HM Treasury appealed to the Court of Appeal,[247] who considered four issues:

1   Was the 2006 Terrorism Order unlawful and should it be quashed?
2   What was impact of the lack of procedural safeguards in the 2006 Order?
3   Did the offences created under Articles 7 and 8 of the Order satisfy the principles of legal certainty and proportionality?

---

243   *Ibid.*
244   [2008] EWHC 869.
245   One of the applicants unsuccessfully argued that an order granted against himself by the Al-Qaeda and Taliban (United Nations Measures) Order 2006, S.I. 2006/2952 should be set aside.
246   For a more detailed discussion of this issue see *M v HM Treasury* [2008] UKHL 26.
247   *A v HM Treasury* [2008] EWCA Civ 1187.

4   Whether the Al-Qaeda and Taliban (UN Measures) 2006 was unlawful because
     a person placed on the UN Sanctions Committee list had no appeal mechanism
     against that decision.

The Court of Appeal held that the reasonable ground test adopted by HM Treasury
did not go beyond the ambit of Resolution 1373, but the requirement in the 2006
Order of 'or may be' did go further than the Resolution. Therefore, it determined
that the directions granted by HM Treasury were quashed. The Court of Appeal
further stated that the courts must be relied on to guarantee that satisfactory procedural protection is upheld for applicants under the Order[248] and that the provisions
of the licensing system under the Order were proportionate and legally certain.
Finally, it held that the Al-Qaeda and Taliban (United Nations Measures) 2006 was
lawful.

   In response the government has introduced the Terrorism (United Nations Measures) Order,[249] which provides that a direction will cease to have effect 12 months
after it was made, although HM Treasury still has ability to renew a direction.[250] The
Order revises the prohibition on making funds, economic resources and financial
services available for the benefit of a designation person so that they only apply if
the designated person obtains, or is able to obtain, a significant financial benefit. The
ban on making funds, economic resources and financial assets available directly to
a designated person, as outlined above, is unaltered. Furthermore, the 2009 Order
changes the prohibition on making economic resources available to a designated
person by providing a defence to that person if they did not know and had no
reasonable cause to suspect that the economic resources which they provided to a
designated person would be likely to be exchanged or used in exchange for funds,
goods or services. The Financial Services Secretary to the Treasury, Lord Myners,
took the view that 'overall, these changes will improve the operation of the asset-
freezing regime, ensure that it remains fair and proportionate and help facilitate
effective compliance by ensuring that prohibitions are more tailored and clearer in
how they apply'.[251] The matter finally came before the Supreme Court who considered the legitimacy of the Terrorism (United Nations Measures) Order and the
Al-Qaeda and Taliban (United Nations Measures) Order 2006. Despite what had
been said by the Court of Appeal, the Supreme Court determined that both of the
Orders were ultra vires, and HM Treasury swiftly responded by implementing the
Draft Terrorist Asset-Freezing Bill (2010) and implementing the Terrorist Asset-
Freezing (Temporary Provisions) Act 2010.

---

248 The Court of Appeal stated that the method adopted should be comparable with that adopted in
     Secretary of State for the Home Department v MB [2008] 1 AC 440.
249 S.I. 2009/1747.
250 S.I. 2009/1747, Article 5.
251 HC Debates 15 July 2009: Column WS96.

TABLE 3.1 Recent terrorist financing cases

Offence: Fund-raising for the purposes of terrorism/Funding arrangements
Legislation: sections 15 and 17 Terrorism Act 2000
Maximum Penalty: 14 years imprisonment

Name	Date	Sentence	Brief Details
Hana Khan	26.3.2015	21 months (suspended)	Found guilty of two counts of fund-raising by sending £1,000 to her boyfriend in Syria. Judge Gerald Gordon described her case as exceptional as she had not been radicalised.
Ali Asim	6.2.2015	one year nine months	Pleaded guilty to sending £300 to a British jihadist in Syria. Mr Justice Jeremy Baker said: '. . . although the sum involved was limited, I consider that bearing in mind the purpose for which you were aware these funds were to be provided, this offence is so serious that only a sentence of immediate custody can be justified.'[252]
Amal El-Wahabi	13.11.2014	two years four months	Found guilty of making £15,800 available for her husband who was in Syria and had converted to Islam. She was the first British woman to be convicted of a terror offence since the conflict in Syria began.
Rahin Ahmen	26.4.2013	12 years	Pleaded guilty to fund-raising but also two counts of engaging in conduct in preparation for acts of terrorism.
Mujahid Hussain	26.4.2013	four years	Pleaded guilty to fund-raising and possessing/ collecting a record of information likely to be useful to a person committing or preparing an act of terrorism.
Mohammed Shafik Ali	1.8.2012	three years	Pleaded guilty to fund-raising £3,000, which he intended to send to his brother in Syria to help with acts of terrorism.
Mohammed Shabir Ali	1.8.2012	three years	Brother of the above and also involved.
Rajib Karim	18.3.2011	30 years	Pleaded guilty to fund-raising, collecting record of information likely to be useful in committing or preparing an act of terrorism and three counts of engaging in conduct in preparation for acts of terrorism. He was found guilty of another four. He was a software engineer at British Airways Plc and passed on sensitive information to help prepare for terrorist acts.

252 http://www.thelawpages.com/court-cases/Ali-Asim-14760–1.law.

Name	Date	Sentence	Brief Details
Abu Izzadeen	18.4.2008	four years six months (two years for fund-raising)	Found guilty of fund-raising and incitement to commit an act of terrorism. Convictions related to a series of speeches made at a London mosque.
Simon Keeler	18.4.2008	As above	Connected to the above incidents
Abdul Mahid	18.4.2008	two years	Also connected to the above incident but only found guilty of fund-raising.

Future recommendations

The UK has attempted to adopt a very robust policy towards the financing of terror-ism and introduced counter-terrorist related legislation prior to the terrorist attacks in September 2001. Importantly, these measures were aimed at tackling the threat posed by domestic and *not* international terrorism. The Prevention of Terrorism (Temporary Provisions) Act introduced a series of CTF-related measures that predated the inter-national Convention by nearly a decade. These measures were intended to counteract the threat posed by the IRA and other domestic terrorist-related entities. However, a detailed review of the effectiveness of these provisions by the Home Office deter-mined that they were not fit for purpose and should be reformed. This resulted in the introduction of the Terrorism Act 2000 that repealed the terrorist financing provi-sions of the Prevention of Terrorism (Temporary Provisions) Act 1989. The Terrorism Act 2000 was amended by the Anti-terrorism, Crime and Security Act 2001 and several related statutory instruments that were introduced following 9/11. These leg-islative measures expanded the criminal offence of the financing of terrorism, required reporting entities to submit reports to the NCA that related to allegations of suspicious transactions for the purposes of supporting or funding terrorism, the introduction of the UN sanctions regime and measures that allowed for the freezing of terrorist assets.

Despite the plethora of CTF legislation, this chapter has presented evidence that questions the effectiveness of the implementation of the 'financial war on terrorism' in the UK. For example, prosecutors are reluctant to enforce the criminal offences created by the Terrorism Act 2000. The ability of HM Treasury to freeze the assets of terrorists was dealt a monumental blow following the decision of the Supreme Court in *A v HM Treasury*. Furthermore, it is also noted that the amount of money that has been frozen since 9/11 can be classified as derisory. It has been suggested that these measures represented a new and innovative way to tackle the financing of ter-rorism following 9/11. However, as demonstrated in the first part of this chapter, the UK had already introduced a series of legislative measures that allowed authorities to tackle the financing of terrorism as advocated by the financial war on terrorism.

The effectiveness of the UK's stance towards the financing of terrorism has also been limited by political infighting within government over the creation of a single Economic Crime Agency. This was proposed before the general election in 2010 and was subsequently adopted by the Coalition government as part of their Coalition agreement.[253] However, the idea was rejected by the then Home Secretary, Theresa May MP, who opted to prioritise the creation of the NCA following the enactment of the Courts and Crime Act 2013. The role of the NCA is divided into four 'Commands', one of which tackles 'Economic Crime'. This disjointed approach towards establishing a single economic crime agency that exclusively deals with all aspects of financial crime has adversely affected the ability of the UK to tackle the financing of terrorism. For example, the Home Affairs Select Committee stated that the effectiveness of the UK's CTF strategy is also adversely affected by 'the fact that in the UK, the responsibility for countering terrorism finance is spread across a number of departmental departments and agencies with no department in charge of overseeing the policy'.[254] This was supported by Anderson who noted 'the fact that asset-freezing is administered by a different department from other counter-terrorism powers means however that extra effort may be required if asset-freezing is always to be considered as an alternative to or in conjunction with other possible disposals for those believed to be engaged in terrorism'.[255] Those who fund terrorism are dangerous offenders and the policy and practice in the UK therefore needs to recognise this.

Further reading

O. Akindemowo, 'The pervasive influence of anti-terrorist financing policy: Post 9/11 non-bank electronic money issuance' (2004) *Journal of International Banking Law and Regulation*, 19(8), 289–297.

R. Alexander, 'Money laundering and terrorist financing: Time for a combined offence' (2009) *Company Lawyer*, 30(7), 200–204.

P. Alldridge, *Money Laundering Law* (Hart: Oxford, 2003).

A. Arabinda, *Targeting Terrorist Financing – International Co-Operation and New Regimes* (Routledge: Abingdon, 2009).

D. Aufhauser, 'Terrorist financing: Foxes run to ground' (2003) *Journal of Money Laundering Control*, 6(4), 301–305.

R. Bell, 'The confiscation, forfeiture and disruption of terrorist finances' (2003) *Journal of Money Laundering Control*, 7(2), 105–125.

T. Bierseker, and S. Eckert, *Countering the Financing of Terrorism* (Routledge: Abingdon, 2008).

P. Binning, 'In safe hands? Striking the balance between privacy and security – anti-terrorist finance measures' (2002) *European Human Rights Law Review*, 6, 737–749.

W. Blair, and R. Brent, *Banks and Financial Crime: The International Law of Tainted Money* (Oxford University Press: Oxford, 2008).

S. Cassella, 'Reverse money laundering' (2003) *Journal of Money Laundering Control*, 7(1), 92–94.

A. Culley, 'The international convention for the suppression of the financial of terrorism: A legal tour de force?' (2007) *Dublin University Law Journal*, 29, 397–413.

A. Culley, 'A windfall for counter-Terrorist financing of small change? Post 9/11 asset freezing and forfeiture under the microscope' (2008) *Dublin Law Journal*, 30, 353–366.

Y. Danziger, 'Changes in methods of freezing funds of terrorist organisations since 9/11: A comparative analysis' (2012) *Journal of Money Laundering Control*, 15(2), 210–236.

---

253 Policy Exchange, *Fighting Fraud and Financial Crime* (Policy Exchange: London, 2010).

254 Home Affairs Select Committee, *Counter-Terrorism Seventeenth Report of Session 2013–14* (Home Affairs Select Committee: London, 2014, 49).

255 D. Anderson, *Third Report on the Operation of the Terrorist Asset-Freezing Etc. Act 2010* (HM Government: London, 2013, 13).

L. Donohue, 'Anti-terrorist finance in the United Kingdom and United States' (2006) *Michigan Journal of International Law*, Winter, 27, 303–435.

L. Donohue, 'Constitutional and legal challenges to the anti-terrorist finance regime' (2008) *Wake Forest Law Review*, 43, 643–689.

L. Donohue, *The Cost of Counterterrorism – Powers, Politics and Liberty* (Cambridge University Press: Cambridge, UK, 2008).

J. D'Souza, *Terrorist Financing, Money Laundering, and Tax Evasion* (Taylor and Francis Group: New York and London, 2011).

O. Elagab, 'Control of terrorist funds and the banking system' (2006) *Journal of International Banking Law and Regulation*, 21(1), 38–44.

M. Gallant, 'Promise and perils: The making of global money laundering, terrorist finance norms' (2010) *Journal of Money Laundering Control*, 13(3), 175–183.

W. Gilmore, *Dirty Money – The Evolution of International Measures to Counter Money Laundering and the Financial of Terrorism* (Council of Europe: Strasbourg, 2003).

M. Goldby, 'Anti-money laundering reporting requirements imposed by English law: Measuring effectiveness and gauging the need for reform' (2013) *Journal of Business Law*, 4, 367–397.

M. Goldby, 'The impact of Schedule 7 of the Counter-Terrorism Act 2008 on banks and their customers' (2010) *Journal of Money Laundering Control*, 13(4), 351–371.

J. Gurule, 'The demise of the U.N. economic sanctions regime to deprive terrorist of funding' (2009) *Case Western Reserve Journal of International Law*, 4, 19–63.

J. Gurule, *Unfunding Terror – The Legal Response to the Financing of Global Terrorism* (Edward Elgar: Cheltenham, 2008).

J. Horgan and M. Taylor, 'Playing the "green card" – financing of the provisional IRA: Part 1' (1999) *Terrorism and Political Violence*, 11(2), 1–38.

J. Horgan and M. Taylor, 'Playing the "green card" – financing of the provisional IRA: Part 2' (2003) *Terrorism and Political Violence*, 15(2), 1–60.

J. Johnson, 'Is the global financial system AML/CTF prepared?' (2008) *Journal of Financial Crime*, 15(1), 7–21.

V. Mitsilegas and B. Gilmore, 'The EU legislative framework against money laundering and terrorist finance: A critical analysis in the light of evolving global standards' (2007) *International & Comparative Law Quarterly*, 56(1), 119–140.

M. O'Neill, *The Evolving EU Counter-Terrorism Legal Framework* (Routledge Cavendish: London, 2012).

T. Parkman and G. Peeling, *Countering Terrorist Finance – A Training Handbook for Financial Services* (Gower: Aldershot, 2007).

S. Ramage, '2008 amendments of the Proceeds of Crime Act 2002 and other legislation that combats terrorist financing' (2008) *Criminal Lawyer*, 182, 1–5.

A. Richard, *Fighting Terrorist Financing: Transatlantic Co-Operation and International Institutions* (Centre for Transatlantic Relations: Washington DC, 2005).

N. Ryder, 'A false sense of security? An analysis of legislative approaches towards the prevention of terrorist finance in the United States and the United Kingdom' (2007) *Journal of Business Law*, November, 821–850.

P. Sproat, 'Counter-terrorist finance in the UK: A quantitative and qualitative commentary based on open-source materials' (2010) *Journal of Money Laundering Control*, 13(4), 315–335.

W. Tupman, 'Ten myths about terrorist financing' (2009) *Journal of Money Laundering Control*, 12(2), 189–205.

C. Walker, 'The legal definition of "terrorism" in United Kingdom law and beyond' (2007) *Public Law*, Summer, 331–352

C. Walker, *Terrorism and the Law* (Oxford University Press: Oxford, 2011).

4

FRAUD

Introduction

International efforts to tackle financial crime have in the most part concentrated on money laundering arising from the manufacture and sale of illegal narcotics and the financing of terrorism, as outlined in the two previous chapters. This is largely due to the United States of America (USA) led 'war on drugs' and the 'financial war on terrorism'. Fraud however is another financial crime of epic proportions and as noted by Wright is 'becoming the crime of choice for organised crime and terrorist funding'.[1] This chapter therefore identifies the anti-fraud measures adopted in the United Kingdom (UK). Its primary focus will be to consider the strategic goals of the UK's fraud policy in light of the publication of the Fraud Review in 2006 and the National Fraud Strategy and attempt to quantify the extent of the problem. The chapter will then consider background to the policy of criminalising and regulating fraud, plus evaluate the financial institutions and regulatory bodies involved. Finally, we look at how the proceeds of fraudulent activity are recovered, including a brief analysis of sentencing options and practices. Fraud is increasingly being committed through the use of information and communication technology (ICT) and this chapter also considers this element of cybercrime.

What is the offence of fraud?

As outlined below, and since 15 January 2007, there is now a single primary offence of fraud, contained in section 1 of the Fraud Act 2006. The offence can be committed in three different ways: by a false representation;[2] by a failure to disclose

---

1 R. Wright, 'Developing effective tools to manage the risk of damage caused by economically motivated crime fraud' (2007) *Journal of Financial Crime*, 14(1), 17–27, at 18.

2 Fraud Act 2006, s. 2.

information when there is a legal duty to do so;[3] and, by abuse of position.[4] There are also a number of secondary offences including the possession or control of articles for use either in the course of or in connection with frauds;[5] the making, adapting, supplying or offering to supply articles for use in frauds;[6] participating in fraudulent trading as a sole trader;[7] and, obtaining services dishonestly where the defendant either intends not to pay or not to pay in full.[8] For reasons of space, only the primary offence will be discussed in detail.

Fraud by false representation – section 2 Fraud Act 2006

To make out an offence under section 2 of the Fraud Act 2006, the defendant must have not only dishonestly made a false representation but to have also intended, by making that representation, to either make a gain (for themself or any other person) or to cause or expose an individual to the risk of a loss. The offence is entirely offender focused; as long as a false representation is actually made and the requisite dishonest intention (mens rea) element exists, the offence is made out. There is no need, therefore, to prove that an actual gain or loss was achieved, making this offence a conduct crime rather than a result crime and arguably much wider than the offences under the Theft Acts of 1968 and 1978. The second major change in the legislation is that the concept of deception has been removed entirely. Ormerod therefore argues that it 'is overbroad, based too heavily on the ill-defined concept of dishonesty, too vague to meet the obligation under Art. 7 of the ECHR [European Convention on Human Rights], and otherwise deficient in principle'.[9]

For reasons of clarity, a representation is stated to be 'any representation as to fact or law, including a representation as to the state of mind of (a) the person making the representation, or (b) any other person'.[10] This can be either express or implied[11] and achieved through both words and conduct, including body language, identity and items of clothing.[12] A representation made by implied conduct, for example, would include the dishonest use of a credit card, in the sense that the individual is falsely representing the fact that they have the authority to use the card.[13] A representation can also be made through an omission. Interestingly, the representation does not have to be made to a person and includes the situation where information

---

3 Fraud Act 2006, s. 3.
4 Fraud Act 2006, s. 4.
5 Fraud Act 2006, s. 6.
6 Fraud Act 2006, s. 7.
7 Fraud Act 2006, s. 9.
8 Fraud Act 2006, s. 11.
9 D. Ormerod, 'The Fraud Act 2006 – criminalising lying?' (2007) *Criminal Law Review*, March, 193–219, at 219.
10 Fraud Act 2006, s. 2(3).
11 Fraud Act 2006, s. 2(4).
12 Crown Prosecution Service, 'The Fraud Act 2006' 2008, available from http://www.cps.gov.uk/legal/d_to_g/fraud_act/, accessed 8 June 2011.
13 See *R v Lambie* [1982] AC 449.

is submitted to a 'system or device designed to receive, convey or respond to communications (with or without human intervention)'.[14] This would include CHIP and PIN devices or ATM machines. If the representation is made to a machine, for practical purposes the offence can only be made out where the representation has been submitted; so in the case of using an email, when the email is actually sent. Representations are deemed to be false when they are either misleading or untrue and the defendant knows or thinks this to be the case.[15] To aid in the interpretation of this, the concept of knowledge has been defined by the House of Lords (now Supreme Court) in *R v Montila (Steven William)*:[16]

> A person may have reasonable grounds to suspect that property is one thing (A) when in fact it is something different (B). But that is not so when the question is what a person knows. A person cannot know that something is A when in fact it is B. The proposition that a person knows that something is A is based on the premise that it is true that it is A. The fact that the property is A provides the starting point. Then there is the question whether the person knows that the property is A.[17]

This would suggest a fairly stringent test, although the Crown Prosecution Service (CPS) believes that in practice it will be no more burdensome than proving the nature of deception in previous obtaining by deception cases. For example, it claims that 'where a debit or credit card has been used fraudulently, evidence of the rightful owner and that he or she did not carry out the transaction' will suffice.[18]

In terms of mens rea (guilty mind), the prosecution has to show that the defendant dishonestly made the false representation. As with the offence of theft under section 1 of the Theft Act 1968, dishonesty, if denied by the defendant, is defined by the Ghosh Test,[19] although the situations where the defendant is not dishonest under section 2 Theft Act 1968 do not apply. The prosecution must also prove that there was an intention to make a gain or intent to cause a loss (or risk the causing of a loss). Both gain and loss are defined in section 5 of the Fraud Act 2006. A gain includes 'keeping what one has, as well as a gain by getting what one does not have'[20] and a loss includes 'getting what one might get, as well as a loss by parting

---

14 Fraud Act 2006, s. 2(5).

15 Fraud Act 2006, s. 2(2).

16 [2004] UKHL 50.

17 *R v Montila (Steven William)* [2004] UKHL 50.

18 Crown Prosecution Service, 'The Fraud Act 2006', 2008, available from http://www.cps.gov.uk/legal/d_to_g/fraud_act/, accessed 8 June 2011.

19 [1982] 1 QB 1053: in determining whether the prosecution had proved that a defendant was acting dishonestly, a jury had first of all to decide whether according to the ordinary standards of reasonable and honest people what was done was dishonest; if it was not dishonest by those standards, that was the end of the matter and the prosecution failed. If, however, it was dishonest by those standards, then the jury had to consider whether the defendant himself had to have realised that what he was doing was by those standards dishonest.

20 Fraud Act 2006, s. 5(3).

with what one has'.[21] Both refer to money and other property[22] and additionally include losses and gains that are temporary or permanent.[23] Interestingly, however, the term gain does not have to mean profit and can include the situation where a person obtains money they were actually entitled to receive.[24]

Fraud by failing to disclose information – section 3 Fraud Act 2006

Fraud by failing to disclose information, under section 3 of the Fraud Act 2006, is essentially a crime of lying by omission. The defendant must have dishonestly failed to disclose to another person information that they were under a legal duty to disclose and by this failure intended to make a gain for themself or another, or cause a loss or the risk of a loss to another. As with the offence under section 2 above, the offence is offender focused with it being unnecessary to prove either that someone was misled or that a loss or gain was actually made. Once more this makes the offence easier to prove than the deception offences it replaces. The extent and nature of the legal duty is not defined in the Act, although the Explanatory Notes do provide examples of when a duty might exist, including the intentional failure to disclose a heart condition when applying for life insurance. It could also encompass the situation as in *R v Firth*[25] where a consultant failed to inform a hospital that he was using National Health Service (NHS) facilities for private patients. Furthermore, the Law Commission stated:

> Such a duty may derive from statute (such as the provisions governing company prospectuses), from the fact that the transaction in question is one of the utmost good faith (such as a contract of insurance), from the express or implied terms of a contract, from the custom of a particular trade or market, or from the existence of a fiduciary relationship between the parties (such as that of agent and principal).
>
> For this purpose there is a legal duty to disclose information not only if the defendant's failure to disclose gives the victim a cause of action for damages, but also if the law gives the victim a right to set aside any change in his or her legal position to which he or she may consent as a result of the non-disclosure. For example, a person in a fiduciary position has a duty to disclose material information when entering into a contract with his or her beneficiary, in the sense that a failure to make such disclosure will entitle the beneficiary to rescind the contract and to reclaim any property transferred under it.[26]

---

21 Fraud Act 2006, s. 5(4).
22 Defined as real, personal, things in action and other intangible property – Fraud Act 2006, s. 5(2).
23 Fraud Act 2006, s. 5(2)(b).
24 *Attorney General Reference (no. 1 of 2001)* [2002] 3 All E.R. 840, CA.
25 (1990) 91 Cr App R 217.
26 Law Commission 'Fraud. Report on a reference under section 3(1)(e) of the Law Commissions Act 1965', Law Commission Report No 276, Cm 5560 (2002), paras 7.28 and 7.29.

The information that is not disclosed does not have to be material or relevant; there is no de minimis provision and it is not a defence to claim ignorance of the duty or incompetence in supplying information.[27] For any of these issues to make a difference the defendant would have to prove that the failure was not carried out dishonestly. Other terms under the offence have the same meaning as those discussed above.

Fraud by abuse of position – section 4 Fraud Act 2006

The third and final way in which fraud can be committed under section 1 of the Fraud Act 2006 is by abuse of position. For the offence to have been committed the defendant must occupy a position 'in which he is expected to safeguard, or not act against, the financial interests of another person';[28] they must dishonestly abuse this position; and through this abuse intend to either make a gain for themself or another or cause a loss or risk the causing of a loss.[29] Similar to the other provisions, this can also be carried out through omission rather than by a positive act.[30] Also, as with the other two offences, this too is offender focused. With regard to the position that the defendant must occupy, the Law Commission has stated:

> The necessary relationship will be present between trustee and beneficiary, director and company, professional person and client, agent and principal, employee and employer, or between partners. It may arise otherwise, for example within a family, or in the context of voluntary work, or in any context where the parties are not at arm's length. In nearly all cases where it arises, it will be recognised by the civil law as importing fiduciary duties, and any relationship that is so recognised will suffice . . . The question whether the particular facts alleged can properly be described as giving rise to that relationship will be an issue capable of being ruled on by the judge and, if the case goes to the jury, of being the subject of directions.[31]

Whilst this position is a position of trust, it arguably falls short 'of one where there is a legal duty or an entitlement to single minded loyalty',[32] thus making it more of

---

27 Crown Prosecution Service, 'The Fraud Act 2006', 2008, available from http://www.cps.gov.uk/legal/d_to_g/fraud_act/, accessed 8 June 2011.

28 Fraud Act 2006, s. 4(1)(a).

29 Fraud Act 2006, s. 4.

30 Fraud Act 2006, s. 4(2).

31 Law Commission 'Fraud. Report on a reference under section 3(1)(e) of the Law Commissions Act 1965', Law Commission Report No 276, Cm 5560 (2002), para. 7.38.

32 Crown Prosecution Service, 'The Fraud Act 2006', 2008, available from http://www.cps.gov.uk/legal/d_to_g/fraud_act/, accessed 8 June 2011.

a moral rather than a legal obligation. The CPS has therefore put together a non-exhaustive list of examples including:

- an employee of a software company who uses their position to clone software products with the intention of selling the products on their own behalf;
- where a person is employed to care for an elderly or disabled person and has access to that person's bank account but abuses that position by removing funds for their own personal use;
- an Attorney who removes money from the grantor's accounts for his own use. The Power of Attorney allows them to do so but when excessive this will be capable of being an offence under section 4;
- an employee who fails to take up the chance of a crucial contract so that an associate or rival company can take it up instead;
- an employee who abuses their position to grant contracts or discounts to friends, relatives and associates;
- a waiter who sells their own bottles of wine passing them off as belonging to the restaurant;
- a tradesperson who helps an elderly person with odd jobs, gains influence over that person and removes money from their account; and,
- the person entrusted to purchase lottery tickets on behalf of others.[33]

Despite this guidance on the term 'position', there is no aid as to the meanings of 'abuse' or 'financial interests', which leads to the presumption that they should take their ordinary meaning. Other terms including dishonesty and intending to make a loss or gain have the same interpretation as discussed above.

Fraud and cybercrime

In October 2015, for the first time, the Office of National Statistics in England and Wales issued crime statistics that included cybercrime. The data collected between May and August 2015 show that there were 2.5 million incidences of cybercrime (with the majority of these relating to where a computer or internet-enabled device was infected by a virus) and over five million cases of online fraud.[34] A consideration of fraud in the twenty-first century must now therefore include fraud committed as a cybercrime.

Despite cybercrime being currently heralded as 'Britain's most common criminal offence',[35] there is no determined definition of what it actually is. This is largely

---

33 *Ibid.*

34 Office for National Statistics, 'Improving crime statistics in England and Wales', 2015, available from http://www.ons.gov.uk/ons/rel/crime-stats/crime-statistics/year-ending-june-2015/sty-fraud.html, accessed 1 December 2015.

35 http://www.techweekeurope.co.uk/security/firewall/ons-cybercrime-crime-offences-178956, accessed 1 December 2015.

because of the fact that it is a collection of offences, the common denominator of which is the fact that they are committed using ICT.[36] Thomas and Loader argue that it is those 'computer-mediated activities which are either illegal or considered illicit by certain parties and which can be conducted through global electronic networks'.[37] The government in its Cyber Crime Strategy in 2014 defined cyber-crime as

> falling into one of two categories: new offences committed using new tech-nologies, such as offences against computer systems and data, dealt with in the Computer Misuse Act 1990, and old offences committed using new technol-ogy, where networked computers and other devices are used to facilitate the commission of an offence.[38]

Furnell[39] helps to explain this distinction further by categorising cybercrime into computer-assisted crimes and computer-focused crimes. The former are crimes that predate the internet, but which are now being committed using ICT. Examples include money laundering, hate speech, fraud and sexual harassment.[40] Computer-focused crimes, however, are those that have only developed since the widespread use of ICT and the internet. Cybercrime can therefore amount to hacking, which is breaking into computer systems to change data or to steal and transferring illegal images. Such activities can be achieved through phishing emails, peer-to-peer net-working and malicious software that infects the user's computer.[41] Other examples include online auction scams where the seller asks the victim to transfer money into a bank account, or where they pretend to be acting on behalf of a reputable charity but instead are pocketing the money.[42]

Further definitions of cybercrime look at the relationship between the offender and victim, rather than exclusively focusing on the actual technology.[43] One such definition comes from Wall who divides cybercrime into four areas:

1   Cyber-trespass – crossing boundaries into other people's property and/or caus-ing damage, e.g. hacking, defacement, viruses.
2   Cyber-deceptions and thefts – stealing (money, property), e.g. credit card fraud, intellectual property violations (a.k.a. 'piracy').
3   Cyber-pornography – breaching laws of obscenity and decency.

---

36 M. Yar, *Cybercrime and Society* (Sage: London, 2006).
37 D. Thomas, and B. Loader (eds.), *Cybercrime: Law Enforcement, Security and Surveillance in the Informa-tion Age* (Routledge: London, 2000, 3).
38 Home Office, *Cyber Crime Strategy, Cm 7842* (HMSO: London, 2010, 9).
39 S. Furnell, *Cybercrime: Vandalizing the Information Society* (Addison-Wesley: London, 2002, 22).
40 M. Yar, *Cybercrime and Society* (Sage: London, 2006).
41 Home Office, *Cyber Crime Strategy, Cm 7842* (HMSO: London, 2010).
42 Action Fraud, 'Types of Fraud', 2015, available from http://www.actionfraud.police.uk/fraud-az-online-fraud, accessed 1 December 2015.
43 M. Yar, *Cybercrime and Society* (Sage: London, 2006).

4   Cyber-violence – doing psychological harm to, or inciting physical harm against others, thereby breaching laws relating to the protection of the person, e.g. hate speech, stalking.[44]

Yar has subsequently added a fifth, namely 'Crimes against the state, those activities that breach laws protecting the integrity of the nation and its infrastructure (e.g. terrorism, espionage and disclosure of official secrets)'.[45] On the basis that this book concerns the subject matter of financial crime it will only be the second category of offences that we will consider in more detail.

The government acknowledges that financially based cybercrime is largely committed by 'serious organised criminals, who target government, business and the public to obtain money or goods'.[46] The most financially profitable cybercriminal activity is 'conducted with multi-skilled, virtual criminal networks, whose structures are different to traditional organised crime groups';[47] members will rarely meet and may not even now each other's identity. The main purpose of such activity is financial gain, but some of this 'profit' may also be used to fund terrorist activities. In terms of financial crime committed using ICT, the government argues that there are two main offences: online fraud and identity theft.[48] Online frauds can include debit and credit card frauds, non-delivery fraud, lottery scams, online auctions and fraud involving fake watches, clothing and goods.[49] It can also cover account takeover, business opportunity fraud, health scams, holiday fraud, loan scams, mass marketing fraud, rental fraud, land banking scams, domain name scams, charity donation fraud, work from home scams, vehicle matching scams and identity fraud.[50]

Despite the fact that cybercrime is overtaking physical crime in the UK, there have been very few new pieces of legislation to cover it. The vast majority of prosecutions for financial-based cybercrimes and certainly those in relation to fraud have therefore taken place under section 2 of the Fraud Act 2006, as detailed above.

The extent of fraud

The international profile of fraud has increased significantly during the last two decades.[51] This is due, in part, to instances of global corporate fraud relating to the

---

44 D. Wall, 'Cybercrimes and the Internet' in D. Wall (ed.), *Crime and the Internet* (Routledge: London, 2001, 3–7).

45 M. Yar, *Cybercrime and Society* (Sage: London, 2006, 11).

46 Home Office, *Cyber Crime Strategy, Cm 7842* (HMSO: London, 2010, 11).

47 *Ibid.*

48 Home Office, *Cyber Crime Strategy, Cm 7842* (HMSO: London, 2010).

49 *Ibid.*

50 Action Fraud, 'Online fraud', 2016, available from http://www.actionfraud.police.uk/fraud-az-online-fraud, accessed 9 February 2016.

51 For an interesting discussion of the historical development of fraud see G. Robb, *White-Collar Crime in Modern England – Financial Fraud and Business Morality 1845–1929* (Cambridge University Press: Cambridge, UK, 1992).

collapse of the Bank of Credit and Commerce International,[52] Barings Bank,[53] Enron[54] and WorldCom.[55] Additionally, there have been a number of fraudulent schemes that have targeted individuals, including the Ponzi fraud schemes by Bernard Madoff and Alan Stanford.[56] Large-scale fraud has also occurred in the European Union (EU) following the collapse of Parmalat and Vivendi,[57] and Jérôme Kerviel's fraudulent investments that cost SocGEN £3.7 billion.[58] The USA has witnessed high-profile frauds, including Aldephia Communications, Qwest Communications International Inc, America Online, Xerox and Tyco International.[59] Furthermore, as a result of the recent global financial crisis, mortgage fraud has become another major worldwide concern. For example, prior to the onset of the financial crisis, the Federal Bureau of Intelligence (FBI) estimated that the extent of mortgage fraud in 2006 was $4.2 billion.[60] It was declared to be an 'escalating problem' in 2007,[61] and in 2008, the reported losses from mortgage fraud increased by 83 per cent to $1.4 billion.[62] In 2009, the FBI, citing 'Core Logic', estimated that the total amount

52 For an excellent discussion see A. Arora, 'The statutory system of the bank supervision and the failure of BCCI' (2006) *Journal of Business Law*, August, 487–510.

53 For a general commentary of the collapse of Barings Bank L. see L. Proctor, 'The Barings collapse: A regulatory failure, or a failure of supervision?' (1997) *Brooklyn Journal of International Law*, 22, 735–767.

54 Generally see T. Hurst, 'A post-Enron examination of corporate governance problems in the investment company industry' (2006) *The Company Lawyer*, 27(2), 41–49.

55 See J. Sidak, 'The failure of good intentions: The WorldCom fraud and the collapse of American telecommunications after deregulation' (2003) *Yale Journal on Regulation*, 20, 207–261.

56 It has been reported that the total losses in the Madoff scandal could have exceeded $50bn. See T. Anderson, H. Lane and M. Fox, 'Consequences and responses to the Madoff fraud' (2009) *Journal of International Banking and Regulation*, 24(11), 548–555, at 548. Allen Stanford was convicted of 'one count of conspiracy to commit wire and mail fraud, four counts of wire fraud, five counts of mail fraud, one count of conspiracy to obstruct an SEC [Security & Exchange Commission] investigation, one count of obstruction of an SEC investigation, and one count of conspiracy to commit money laundering'. See Federal Bureau of Investigation, 'Allen Stanford convicted in Houston for orchestrating $7 billion investment fraud scheme', 6 March 2012, available from http://www.fbi.gov/houston/press-releases/2012/allen-stanford-convicted-in-houston-fororchestrating-7-billion-investment-fraud-scheme, accessed 4 June 2012.

57 M. Abarca, 'The need for substantive regulation on investor protection and corporate governance in Europe: Does Europe need a Sarbanes-Oxley?' (2004) *Journal of International Banking Law and Regulation*, 19(11), 419–431, at 419.

58 J. Haines, 'The National fraud strategy: New rules to crack down on fraud' (2009) *Company Lawyer*, 30(7), 213.

59 M. Lunt, 'The extraterritorial effects of the Sarbanes-Oxley Act 2002' (2006) *Journal of Business Law*, May, 249–266, at 249.

60 Federal Bureau of Investigation, 'Mortgage Fraud Report 2006', May 2007, available from http://www.fbi.gov/stats-services/publications/mortgage-fraud-2006/2006-mortgage-fraud-report, accessed 23 May 2013.

61 Federal Bureau of Investigation, 'Mortgage Fraud Report 2007', April 2008, available from http://www.fbi.gov/stats-services/publications/mortgage-fraud-2007, accessed 18 October 2013.

62 Federal Bureau of Investigation, 'Mortgage Fraud Report 2008', n/d, available from http://www.fbi.gov/stats-services/publications/mortgage-fraud-2008/2008-mortgage-fraud-report, accessed 17 June 2013.

of losses related to mortgage fraud had increased to $14 billion.[63] 'Core Logic' esti-
mated that the extent of mortgage fraud in 2011 was US$12 billion.[64] In its 2012
mortgage fraud report, 'Core Logic' projected that that the level of mortgage fraud
had increased to US$13 billion.[65] This statistical data is supported by research cited
by Creseny et al. who concluded that 'mortgage fraud is more prevalent now than
in the heyday of the origination boom and that it will continue to rise'.[66] The UK
has also experienced large-scale instances of fraud, with examples including Polly
Peck,[67] Independent Insurance,[68] the Mirror Group Pension Scheme,[69] the Guinness share-trading fraud[70] and the collapse of Barlow Clowes.[71]

Despite this collection of large-scale frauds, the calculation of global and/or
national fraud, like other types of financial crime, is fraught with methodological
difficulties.[72] Indeed, the Fraud Review stated that 'there are no reliable estimates
of the cost of fraud to the economy as a whole',[73] although it has been argued that
'in monetary terms, fraud is on a par with Class A drugs'.[74] It was conservatively
suggested that in 2005 the cost of fraud amounted to £13.9 billion in the UK.[75] In
2010 the National Fraud Authority (NFA) noted that the figure was nearer £30.5
billion,[76] with this figure increasing year on year. For example, the NFA estimated
that fraud in the UK had increased to £38.4 billion in 2011[77] and had reached £73
billion in 2012.[78] Despite these incremental increases, the NFA noted that the level
of fraud had dropped to £52 billion in 2013.[79] This decrease was also noted by

---

63 Federal Bureau of Investigation, '2009 Mortgage Fraud Report Year in Review', n/d, available from
    http://www.fbi.gov/stats-services/publications/mortgage-fraud-2009, accessed 17 June 2013.
64 CoreLogic, 2011 Mortgage Fraud Trends Report (Irvine, 2011, 1).
65 Ibid.
66 See note 23 above, at 226.
67 J. Gallagher, J. Lauchlan and M. Steven, 'Polly Peck: The breaking of an entrepreneur?' (1996) Journal
    of Small Business and Enterprise Development, 3(1), 3–12.
68 R v Bright [2008] 2 Cr. App. R. (S) 102.
69 R. Sarker, 'Maxwell: Fraud trial of the century' (1996) Company Lawyer, 17(4), 116–117.
70 R. Sarker, 'Guinness – pure genius' (1994) Company Lawyer, 15(10), 310–312.
71 A. Doig, Fraud (Willan Publishing: Cullompton, 2006, 9–12).
72 Attorney General's Office, Fraud Review – Final Report (Attorney General's Office, 2006, 21). For a
    more detailed examination of the problems associated with determining extent of fraud see M. Levi
    and J. Burrows, 'Measuring the impact of fraud in the UK: A conceptual and empirical journey'
    (2008) British Journal of Criminology, 48(3), 293–318.
73 M. Levi, and J. Burrows, 'Measuring the impact of fraud in the UK: A conceptual and empirical
    journey' (2008) British Journal of Criminology, 48(3), 293–318, at 297.
74 R. Sarker, 'Fighting fraud – a missed opportunity?' (2007) Company Lawyer, 28(8), 243–244, at 243.
75 M. Levi, J. Burrows, M. Fleming and M. Hopkins, The Nature, Extent and Economic Impact of Fraud in
    the UK (ACPO, 2007, London, iii).
76 National Fraud Authority, National Fraud Authority Annual Fraud Indicator (National Fraud Authority:
    London, 2010, 7).
77 National Fraud Authority, Annual Fraud Indicator 2011 (National Fraud Authority: London, 2011, 3).
78 National Fraud Authority, Annual Fraud Indicator 2012 (National Fraud Authority: London, 2012, 3).
79 National Fraud Authority, Annual Fraud Indicator 2013 (National Fraud Authority: London, 2013, 2).

CIFAS which concluded that there was an 11 per cent drop in the levels of fraud in 2013.[80]

Although large-scale frauds, as mentioned above, often make the headlines, it should not be forgotten how extensive the offence is on an everyday level. In fact this is one of the few financial crimes covered in this book that is commonly committed by people not connected to the banking/financial or related sectors. For the year ending June 2015, a total of 599,689 fraud offences were recorded in England and Wales, which is equivalent to 10 offences per 1,000 head of population. On a comparative basis with the previous year (2013–2014) this represents an increase of 9 per cent.[81] The threat of fraud cannot therefore be underestimated, and with suggestions that terrorists are increasingly using it to fund their illegal activities,[82] it is imperative that we have effective anti-fraud policies and procedures in place.

Policy background – where did the offence originate from?

The Fraud Review

The international fraud policy can be contrasted with its money laundering and terrorist financing policies due to the lack of international legislative measures from the United Nations (UN) and EU. Both institutions have developed anti-fraud policies that concentrate on their own finances but they have tended to steer away from initiating a global legislative regime.[83] In 2006, fraud became a major policy goal of the Labour government and is now a major concern for the current Conservative government. This is the result of the publication of the Fraud Review,[84] which was asked to recommend ways to reduce the threat posed by fraud. In particular, the Fraud Review was asked to identify the extent of fraud, what role the government should play in tackling it and how the government could obtain value for money.[85] Unsurprisingly, and in light of our comments above, the Review was unable to accurately outline the extent of fraud. In relation to its second task, however, it concluded that the government has two functions: i) to protect public money from fraudsters; and, ii) to protect consumers and businesses against fraud. The Review

---

80 CIFAS, 'Fraud decrease serves as vindication and warning says Cifas', 21 January 2014, available from https://www.cifas.org.uk/twentythirteen_fraudtrends, accessed 20 August 2015.

81 Office for National Statistics, 'Crime in England and Wales, year ending June 2015' (*ONS*, 15 October 2015) available from http://www.ons.gov.uk/ons/rel/crime-stats/crime-statistics/year-ending-june-2015/stb-crime—ye-june-2015.html#tab-Fraud, accessed 12 November 2015.

82 N. Ryder, 'A false sense of security? An analysis of legislative approaches to the prevention of terrorist finance in the United States of America and the United Kingdom' (2007) *Journal of Business Law*, November, 821–850, at 825.

83 For a more detailed discussion see N. Ryder, *Financial Crime in the 21st Century: Law and Policy* (Edward Elgar: Cheltenham, 2011, 97–102).

84 The government announced that it intended to introduce a radical overhaul of the laws on fraud in its 2005 general election manifesto. Labour Party, *Labour Party Manifesto – Britain Forward Not Back* (Labour Party, London, 2005).

85 *Ibid.*, 4–5.

recommended that the government should adopt a holistic approach towards fraud and develop a national strategy. Furthermore, it recommended the creation of the NFA to develop and implement the strategy. It also suggested that a National Fraud Reporting Centre should be created so that businesses and individuals could report fraud, a suggestion that resulted in the creation of the National Fraud Intelligence Bureau (NFIB). The NFIB is thus the agency dedicated to analysing and assessing fraud, employing analysts from both law enforcement and the private sector. The Review also suggested that a national lead police authority should be established based on the City of London Police.[86]

In an attempt to carry forward these aims, the NFA was given three objectives:[87] i) to create a criminal justice system that is sympathetic to the needs of the victims of fraud by ensuring that the system operates more effectively and efficiently;[88] ii) to attempt to discourage organised criminals from committing fraud in the UK; and, iii) to increase the public's confidence in the response to fraud.[89] A significant measure introduced by the NFA to achieve this was the publication of the National Fraud Strategy.[90] This provides the NFA with five objectives, including tackling the threat of fraud, acting effectively to pursue fraudsters and holding them to account, improving the support available to victims, reducing the UK's exposure to fraud and targeting action against fraud more effectively.[91] Parallels can, therefore, be drawn between the UK's fraud, money laundering and counter-terrorist financing policies as a result of the publication of this strategy document. However, it must be pointed out that the NFA was abolished by the Coalition government in March 2014, with its functions transferred to the National Crime Agency (NCA) and the Home Office.[92]

Background to the Fraud Act 2006

Prior to the Fraud Act 2006, the UK's legislative framework concerning fraudulent activity comprised eight statutory deception offences in the Theft Acts of 1968 and 1978 and the common law offence of conspiracy to defraud.[93] The 98 offences cre-

---

86 Attorney General's Office, *Fraud Review – Final Report* (Attorney General's Office, 2006, 10).
87 National Fraud Strategic Authority, *The National Fraud Strategy – A New Approach to Combating Fraud* (National Fraud Strategic Authority, 2009, 10).
88 For a more detailed discussion of how this is to be achieved see The Attorney General's Office, *Extending the Powers of the Crown Court to Prevent Fraud and Compensate Victims: A Consultation* (Attorney General's Office, 2008).
89 National Fraud Strategic Fraud Authority, 'UK toughens up on fraudsters with new anti-fraud authority', available from http://www.attorneygeneral.gov.uk/NewsCentre/Pages/UKToughens UpOn%20FraudstersWithNewAnti-FraudAuthority.aspx, accessed 2 October 2008.
90 National Fraud Strategic Authority, *The National Fraud Strategy – A New Approach to Combating Fraud* (National Fraud Strategic Authority, 2009, 3).
91 *Ibid.*
92 See HM Government, 'National Fraud Authority', n/d, available from https://www.gov.uk/government/organisations/national-fraud-authority, accessed 20 August 2015.
93 The Theft Act 1986 was the creation of the Criminal Law Revision Committee, Theft and Related Offences, Cmnd. 2977, May 1966. Other noteworthy attempts to tackle fraud before the Theft Act were the Prevention of Fraud (Investments) Act 1958 and the Financial Services Act 1986.

ated by the Theft Acts were difficult to enforce[94] and, as stated by Ormerod, 'were notoriously technical. Although overlapping, they were over-particularised, creating a hazardous terrain for prosecutors who, in charging, could be tripped up by something as subtle as the fraudster's method of payment. The interpretive difficulties were substantial.'[95] This led to the introduction of the Theft Act 1978, although unfortunately, this did little to rectify the problems.[96] The Home Office noted that it 'is not always clear which offence should be charged, and defendants have successfully argued that the consequences of their particular deceptive behaviour did not fit the definition of the offence with which they have been charged'.[97] In 1998, the then Home Secretary Jack Straw MP asked the Law Commission to examine the law on fraud. Specifically, the Law Commission were asked

> to examine the law on fraud, and in particular to consider whether it: is readily comprehensible to juries; is adequate for effective prosecution; is fair to potential defendants; meets the need of developing technology including electronic means of transfer; and to make recommendations to improve the law in these respects with all due expedition. In making these recommendations to consider whether a general offence of fraud would improve the criminal law.[98]

In 1999 the Law Commission published a Consultation Paper that distinguished between two types of fraudulent offences – dishonesty and deception.[99] The Law Commission concluded that whilst the concerns expressed about the existing law were valid, they could be met by extending the existing offences in preference to creating a single offence of fraud.[100] The Law Commission published its final report in 2002, which led to the Fraud Bill.[101] The Fraud Act came into force on 15 January 2007[102] and, as explained above, overhauls and widens the criminal offences

---

94 See generally P. Kiernan and G. Scanlan, 'Fraud and the law commission: The future of dishonesty' (2003) *Journal of Financial Crime*, 10(3), 199–208.

95 D. Ormerod, 'The Fraud Act 2006 – criminalising lying?' (2007) *Criminal Law Review*, March, 193–219, at 200.

96 For a useful discussion of the law of theft see A. Doig, *Fraud* (Willan Publishing: Cullompton, 2006, 22–35).

97 *Ibid.*, 22–35. For a more detailed illustration of this problem see generally *R v Preddy* [1996] AC 815, 831.

98 HC Debates 7 April 1998 c.176–177WA.

99 The Law Commission, *Legislating the Criminal Code Fraud and Deception – Law Commission Consultation Paper No 155* (Law Commission, 1999).

100 The Law Commission also published an informal discussion paper in 2000. See Law Commission, 'Informal discussion paper: Fraud and deception – further proposals from the criminal law team' (Law Commission, 2000).

101 For an analysis of the Law Commission's report see P. Kiernan and G. Scanlan, 'Fraud and the law commission: The future of dishonesty' (2003) *Journal of Financial Crime*, 10(3), 199–208.

102 Fraud Act 2006 (Commencement) Order 2006, S.I. 2006/3500.

available in respect of fraudulent and deceptive behaviour.[103] Dennis argued that the Act 'represents the culmination of a law reform debate that can be traced back more than 30 years'.[104] Scanlan took the view that the Fraud Act 2006 'provides prosecutors with a broad range offences of fraud'.[105] This clearly represents a significant improvement on the statutory offences of the Theft Acts and the common law offences of conspiracy to defraud.

Financial institutions and regulatory bodies

Serious Fraud Office

As with other financial crime offences, there is also a broad range of regulatory agencies that attempt to combat fraud, with the most prominent being the Serious Fraud Office (SFO). It was established following an era of financial deregulation in the 1980s; an era that resulted in London attracting 'foreign criminals, including "mademen" from the US Mafia, the "Cosa Nostra", who were now in London taking advantage of the new climate of enterprise, offering securities scams, commodity futures trading frauds and other forms of investment rip-offs'.[106] Bosworth-Davies noted that 'almost overnight, London became the fraud capital of Europe and every con-man, snake-oil, salesman, grafter and hustler turned up'.[107] To tackle these problems the government decided to create an independent governmental department that had both investigative and prosecutorial powers.[108] This was achieved through the Criminal Justice Act 1987, which was influenced by the Fraud Trials Committee Report, commonly known as the Roskill Report.[109] The Roskill Committee, set up in 1983, considered the introduction of more effective means of fighting fraud through changes to the law and criminal proceedings. The Committee was asked to 'consider in what ways the conduct of criminal proceedings in England and Wales arising from fraud can be improved and to consider what changes in existing law and procedure would be desirable to secure the just, expeditious and economical disposal of such proceedings'.[110] In its assessment of the then situation, it criticised the staffing levels of the agencies policing fraud and argued that there

---

103 NB: not all of the offences under the Theft Act 1968 have been abolished. For example, false accounting (Theft Act 1968, s. 17), the liability of company directors (Theft Act 1968, s. 18), false statements by company directors (Theft Act 1968, s. 19) and dishonest destruction of documents (Theft Act 1968, s. 20(1)).

104 I. Dennis, 'Fraud Act 2006' (2007) *Criminal Law Review*, January, 1–2, at 1.

105 G. Scanlan, 'Offences concerning directors and officers of a company: Fraud and corruption in the United Kingdom – the present and the future' (2008) *Journal of Financial Crime*, 15(1), 22–37, at 25.

106 R. Bosworth-Davies, 'Investigating financial crime: The continuing evolution of the public fraud investigation role – a personal perspective' (2009) *Company Lawyer*, 30(7), 195–199, at 196.

107 *Ibid.*

108 See generally R. Wright, 'Fraud after Roskill: A view from the Serious Fraud Office' (2003) *Journal of Financial Crime*, 11(1), 10–16.

109 Roskill, *Fraud Trials Committee Report* (HMSO: London, 1986).

110 *Ibid.*

was a great deal of overlap between them. The Roskill Committee concluded that 'co-operation between different investigating bodies in the UK was inefficient, and the interchange of information or assistance between our law enforcement authorities was unsatisfactory'.[111] The Committee made 112 recommendations, of which all but two were implemented.[112] Its main recommendation was the creation of a new unified organisation responsible for the detection, investigation and prosecution of serious fraud cases.

The result was the SFO, which has jurisdiction in England, Wales and Northern Ireland, but not Scotland.[113] It is headed by a director, who is appointed and accountable to the Attorney General. Under the Criminal Justice Act, the SFO has the ability to search property and compel persons to answer questions and produce documents, provided the SFO have reasonable grounds to do so.[114] However, it is important to note that following the formation of the UK's first Coalition government in 2010, the SFO suffered a significant reduction in its annual budget. For example, the annual budget of the SFO in 2007–08 was £43.3 million and in 2008–09 stood at £53.2 million. In 2009–10, however, the figure was reduced to £40.1 million; was £35.5 million in 2010–11; £31.5 million in 2011–12; £34.8 million in 2012–13; £32.1 million in 2013–14 and £30.8 million in 2014–15.[115] Over six years the SFO has therefore lost £22.4 million. The decision to reduce the budget, at a time when white collar crime has increased and the duties of the SFO have been expanded to incorporate the enforcement of the Bribery Act 2010, has unsurprisingly been questioned and criticised.[116]

According to its website, the SFO work as part of the criminal justice system and they seek to reduce fraud and corruption, delivering justice and maintaining

---

111 *Ibid.*
112 For a detailed commentary of the Roskill Commission see M. Levi, 'The Roskill Fraud Commission revisited: An assessment' (2003) *Journal of Financial Crime*, 11(1), 38–44.
113 Criminal Justice Act 1987, s. 1.
114 Criminal Justice Act 1987, s. 2. It is important to note that the SFO has other investigative and prosecutorial powers under the Fraud Act 2006, the Theft Act 1968, the Companies Act 2006, the Serious Crime Act 2007, the Serious Organised Crime and Police Act 2005, the Proceeds of Crime Act 2002 and the Regulation of Investigatory Powers Act 2000.
115 Serious Fraud Office, *Serious Fraud Office Annual Report and Accounts 2011–2012* (Serious Fraud Office: London, 2012, 7). Also see for example A. Purkiss, 'U.K. fraud office hit by budget cuts, staff losses', 28 March 2011, available from http://www.bloomberg.com/news/2011-03-28/u-k-fraud-office-hit-by-budget-cuts-staff-losses-ft-reports.html, accessed 30 June 2013.
116 See for example B. Masters, 'Fraud watchdog weakened by budget cuts', 27 March 2011, available from http://www.ft.com/cms/s/0/8221aba2–58b5–11e0–9b8a-00144feab49a.html#axzz2XgX4w3hV, accessed 30 June 2013, J. Russel, 'The case to answer for the Serious Fraud Office', 26 May 2012, available from http://www.telegraph.co.uk/finance/financial-crime/9292046/The-case-to-answer-for-the-Serious-Fraud-Office.html, accessed 30 June 2013, J. Armitage, 'Cuts hamper fight against crime, warns SFO director', 5 April 2012, available from http://www.independent.co.uk/news/business/news/cuts-hamper-fight-against-crime-warns-sfo-director-7619339.html, accessed 30 June 2013.

confidence in the UK's business and financial institutions.[117] In determining whether or not to investigate an allegation of fraud, the SFO use the following list of criteria:

- cases which undermine UK commercial/financial Plcs in general, and the City of London in particular;
- cases where the actual or potential loss involved is high;
- cases where actual or potential harm is significant;
- cases where there is a very significant public interest element; and
- new species of fraud.[118]

Following a number of high-profile failed prosecutions, the effectiveness of the SFO has, however, been questioned. Mahendra, for example, describes the notorious failures of the SFO as reminiscent of 'watching the England cricket team – a victory being so rare and unexpected that it was a cause of national rejoicing'.[119] Indeed, Wright notes that 'because the SFO operates in the spotlight, the beam falls on the unsuccessful as well as the victorious. Indeed it shines with blinding brightness on the ones that get away.'[120] The prosecutorial inadequacies of the SFO were also highlighted by the Review of the Serious Fraud Office.[121] The Review compared the performance of the SFO with the US Attorney's Office for the Southern District of New York and the Manhattan District Attorney's Office and concluded that 'the discrepancies in conviction rates are striking'.[122] The Review noted that between 2003 and 2007 the SFO's average conviction rate was 61 per cent, whilst the conviction rates in the two aforementioned cases studied were 91 per cent and 97 per cent respectively.[123]

In an attempt to try to allay some of this criticism and in the wake of the collapse of the Jubilee Line fraud trial,[124] in September 2007 the CPS announced the creation of the Fraud Prosecution Unit. This is now referred to as the Fraud Prosecution Division.[125] The Division limits its involvement to those suspected cases involving the corruption of public officials, fraud on government departments, fraud on overseas governments, complicated money laundering cases and any other

---

117 Serious Fraud Office, 'What we do and who we work with', n/d, available from http://www.sfo. gov.uk/about-us/what-we-do-and-who-we-work-with.aspx, accessed 20 August 2015.

118 Serious Fraud Office, 'Serious Fraud Office [SFO] case selection', n/d, available from http://www. sfo.gov.uk/fraud/sfo-confidential – giving-us-information-in-confidence/serious-fraud-office-[sfo]-case-selection.aspx, accessed 20 August 2015.

119 B. Mahendra, 'Fighting serious fraud' (2002) *New Law Journal*, 152(7020), 289.

120 R. Wright, 'Fraud after Roskill: A view from the Serious Fraud Office' (2003) *Journal of Financial Crime*, 11(1), 10–16, at 10.

121 J. de Grazia, *Review of the Serious Fraud Office – Final Report* (Serious Fraud Office: London, 2008).

122 *Ibid.*, 3–4.

123 J. de Grazia, *Review of the Serious Fraud Office – Final Report* (Serious Fraud Office: London, 2008).

124 J. Masters, 'Fraud and money laundering: The evolving criminalisation of corporate non-compliance' (2008) *Journal of Money Laundering Control*, 11(2), 103–122, at 104.

125 Crown Prosecution Service, 'DPP announces new head of Fraud Prosecution Division' 2009, available from http://www.cps.gov.uk/news/press_releases/136_09/, accessed 22 January 2010.

matter that it feels is within its remit. Such cases must also exceed £750,000.[126] In October 2008, HM CPS Inspectorate concluded there 'has been a positive direction of travel in terms of successful outcomes (convictions), which stood at a creditable 85% of the defendants proceeded against in 2007–08; underlying casework quality, which is characterised by strong legal decision-making and active case progression; and the development of management systems and leadership profile'.[127] Bosworth-Davies has therefore taken the view that 'it [the SFO] was not the great success that Roskill envisaged, and its activities were marked out by 20 years of professional jealousy and internal squabbling among its component teams'.[128] Conversely, the performance of the SFO is hampered by the complexity of the crimes it investigates.[129] Raphael notes that the SFO is 'always kept short of resources and instead of being a unified fraud office, was just another, more sophisticated, prosecution agency'.[130] The ability of the SFO to tackle fraud and bribery has thus been limited by a series of controversial budget cuts first imposed by the Coalition government but unfortunately maintained by the current Conservative government. If we continue to expect the SFO to effectively carry out its job then it is clear that we need to ensure that it is properly funded and resourced so that it is capable of doing this.

Regulatory agencies

In addition to the SFO, a number of financial regulatory agencies also exist to tackle fraud. By virtue of the Financial Services and Markets Act 2000, the Financial Services Authority (FSA) was given a statutory objective to reduce financial crime, which included fraud.[131] Its fraud policy was divided into four parts: i) a direct approach,[132] ii) increased supervisory activity,[133] iii) promoting a more joined up approach,[134] and iv) FSA Handbook modifications.[135] The FSA, for example,

---

126 *Ibid.*

127 HM Crown Prosecution Service, Inspectorate, *Review of the Fraud Prosecution Service* (HM Crown Prosecution Service Inspectorate: London, 2008, 5).

128 R. Bosworth-Davies, 'Investigating financial crime: The continuing evolution of the public fraud investigation role – a personal perspective' (2009) *Company Lawyer*, 30(7), 195–199, at 198.

129 R. Wright, 'Fraud after Roskill: A view from the Serious Fraud Office' (2003) *Journal of Financial Crime*, 11(1), 10–16, at 10.

130 *Ibid.*

131 Financial Services Authority, 'Developing our policy on fraud and dishonesty – discussion paper 26' (Financial Services Authority: London, 2003).

132 This would have seen the FSA focusing its efforts on specific types of fraud or dishonesty that constitute the greatest areas of concern, and where the FSA can make a difference.

133 This would include, for example, considering the firms' systems and controls against fraud in more detail in terms of supervisory work, including how firms collect data on fraud and dishonesty.

134 The third approach would involve the FSA liaising closely with the financial sector and other interested parties to achieve a more effective approach towards fraud prevention in the financial services sector.

135 The final proposed method would include codification and clarification of the relevant fraud risk management provisions of the *Handbook*.

requires senior management to take responsibility for managing their own risk of fraud by having in place effective controls and instruments that are proportionate to the risks they face.[136] It also works to improve whistle-blowing arrangements, amend the financial crime material contained within the FSA Handbook and ensure that the financial services sector, trade associations and the government continue to communicate the risk of fraud to their customers and consumers.[137]

To implement this policy the FSA was given an extensive array of enforcement powers, some of which it has utilised to combat fraud. It is a prosecuting authority for both money laundering and certain fraud-related offences,[138] and has the power to impose a financial penalty where it establishes that there has been a contravention by an authorised person of any requirement.[139] For example, the FSA fined Capita Financial Administration Limited £300,000 for poor anti-fraud controls in 2006,[140] and in May 2007 fined BNP Paribas Private Bank £350,000 for weaknesses in its systems and controls which allowed a senior employee to fraudulently transfer £1.4 million out of the firm's clients' accounts without permission.[141] Furthermore, it has fined the Nationwide Building Society £980,000 for 'failing to have effective systems and controls to manage its information security risks',[142] and Norwich Union Life, £1.26 million for not 'having effective systems and controls in place to protect customers' confidential information and manage its financial crime risks'.[143]

In addition to fining, the FSA also has the power to ban authorised persons and firms from undertaking any regulated activity.[144] For example, in 2008 the FSA fined and/or banned 12 mortgage brokers for submitting false mortgage applications, prohibited another 24 brokers from working and issued fines in excess of £500,000.[145] In the first half of 2009 the level of fines imposed by the FSA had

---

136 Financial Services Authority, 'The FSA's new approach to fraud – Fighting fraud in partnership', speech by Philip Robinson, 26 October 2004, available from http://www.fsa.gov.uk/library/communication/speeches/2004/sp208.shtml, accessed 3 August 2011.

137 *Ibid.*

138 For example, in 2008 the FSA successfully prosecuted William Radclyffe for offences under the Theft Acts, the Financial Services Act 1986 and the Financial Services and Markets Act 2000. Financial Services Authority, 'Fake stockbroker sentenced to 15 months', available from http://www.fsa.gov.uk/pages/Library/Communication/PR/2008/011.shtml, accessed 28 March 2010.

139 Financial Services and Markets Act 2000, s. 206(1).

140 Financial Services Authority, 'FSA fines Capita Financial Administrators Limited £300,000 in first anti-fraud controls case', available from http://www.fsa.gov.uk/pages/Library/Communication/PR/2006/019.shtml, accessed 16 March 2006.

141 Financial Services Authority, *Financial Services Authority Annual Report 2007/2008* (Financial Services Authority, 2008, 23).

142 Financial Services Authority, 'FSA fines Nationwide £980 000 for information security lapses', available from http://www.fsa.gov.uk/pages/Library/Communication/PR/2007/021.shtml, accessed 14 February 2007.

143 Financial Services Authority, 'FSA fines Norwich Union Life £1.26m', available from http://www.fsa.gov.uk/pages/Library/Communication/PR/2007/130.shtml, accessed 4 November 2009.

144 Financial Services and Markets Act 2000, s. 56.

145 National Fraud Strategic Authority, *The National Fraud Strategy – A New Approach to Combating Fraud* (National Fraud Strategic Authority, 2009, 16).

already exceeded this figure. In addition to imposing sanctions on fraudsters the FSA has also enabled victims of fraud to recover losses suffered at the hands of companies involved in share fraud activity. For example, in February 2010 the FSA recovered £270,000 for defrauded investors who were advised to buy shares in Eduvest plc.[146] Although historically the FSA has concentrated is financial crime policy on money laundering, largely at the expense of fraud, in order to meet its statutory objective to reduce financial crime, its recent efforts to tackle fraud, especially mortgage fraud, have been fast tracked.

Additionally, the FSA has the ability to prosecute for a wide range of criminal activities.[147] For example the FSA can prosecute carrying on or purporting to carry on a regulated activity without authorisation or exemption,[148] making false claims that the person or organisation is authorised or exempt,[149] communicating an invitation or inducement to engage in investment activity in breach of the restrictions on financial promotion,[150] misleading the FSA and other contraventions in relation to the exercise of Treaty rights,[151] performing or agreeing to perform functions in breach of a prohibition order[152] and failing to register a copy of listing particulars on or before publication.[153] Furthermore, the FSA is able to pursue criminal proceedings where someone offers securities to the public before publishing a prospectus required by listing rules,[154] issuing an advertisement, or other information specified in the listing rules, without prior approval or authorisation from the competent authority,[155] failing to cooperate with, or giving false information to, FSA-appointed investigators,[156] failing to comply with provisions about control over authorised persons,[157] carrying on, or purporting to carry on, business in contravention of a consumer credit prohibition,[158] making false claims to be a person to whom the general prohibition does not apply,[159] providing false or misleading information to an auditor,[160] disclosing confidential information,[161] failure by a director of an insurer carrying on long-term insurance business to notify the FSA of a general

---

146 Financial Services Authority, 'FSA returns £270 000 to victims of share fraud', available from http://www.fsa.gov.uk/pages/Library/Communication/PR/2010/032.shtml, accessed 21 March 2010.
147 Financial Services and Markets Act 2000, ss. 401 and 402.
148 Financial Services and Markets Act 2000, s. 23.
149 Financial Services and Markets Act 2000, s. 24.
150 Financial Services and Markets Act 2000, s. 25.
151 Financial Services and Markets Act 2000, Schedule 4, para. 6.
152 Financial Services and Markets Act 2000, s. 56(4).
153 Financial Services and Markets Act 2000, s. 83(3).
154 Financial Services and Markets Act 2000, s. 85(2).
155 Financial Services and Markets Act 2000, s. 98(2).
156 Financial Services and Markets Act 2000, s. 177.
157 Financial Services and Markets Act 2000, s. 191.
158 Financial Services and Markets Act 2000, s. 203(9).
159 Financial Services and Markets Act 2000, s. 333.
160 Financial Services and Markets Act 2000, s. 346.
161 Financial Services and Markets Act 2000, s. 352.

meeting to propose a resolution for voluntary winding up,[162] misleading statements and practices offences[163] and misleading the FSA.[164] Additionally, the FSA is able to commence prosecutions for insider dealing,[165] money laundering[166] and terrorist financing.[167] However, there is some *uncertainty* if the FSA is able to enforce its *own* fraud policy and instigate criminal proceedings.[168] For example, the FSA has stated that 'we cannot prosecute most types of fraud and dishonesty . . . in contrast with money laundering; we have no direct powers to prosecute fraud or dishonesty offences. Prosecution is the responsibility of other law enforcement agencies.'[169] This explanation was reiterated by Lord Turner, the former Chairman of the FSA, who said:

> My understanding is that the FSA is *not* able to bring a criminal case in the UK. If it falls within the category of fraud, which is a general category of malfeasance quite separate from financial regulation, the Serious Fraud Office has a right to look at it, and we have been in contact with the SFO throughout this. I think that it announced a week or so ago that it would increase its focus on this issue. In the UK, this issue – as I understand it, but I would defer to my legal expert here – is *not* one where we, the FSA, have an ability to bring a criminal case.[170]

Further uncertainty was also expressed by Tracey McDermott of the FSA who added 'we are *not* a general fraud prosecutor . . . we have spent quite a lot of time and energy on prosecuting both section 397 offences and indeed insider dealing offences . . . we do *not* have a remit to prosecute false accounting, conspiracy'.[171] However, based on the following cases, it is strongly suggested that the FSA *does*

---

162 Financial Services and Markets Act 2000, s. 366(3).
163 Financial Services and Markets Act 2000, s. 397.
164 Financial Services and Markets Act 2000, s. 398.
165 Financial Services and Markets Act 2000, s. 402 (1)(a). For a more detailed discussion of this section see D. Ormerod, 'Prosecution: Insider dealing – Criminal Justice Act 1993 s. 61' (2009) *Criminal Law Review*, 6, 445–449.
166 Financial Services and Markets Act 2000, s. 402 (1)(b). For a general discussion of the ability of the FSA to initiate prosecutions for money laundering see N. Taylor, 'FSA prosecutions: Offences of money laundering – power to prosecute' (2010) *Criminal Law Review*, 10, 772–775.
167 Financial Services and Markets Act 2000, s. 402 (1)(c). For a detailed discussion of this see M. Goldby, 'The impact of Schedule 7 of the Counter-Terrorism Act 2008 on banks and their customers' (2010) *Journal of Money Laundering Control*, 13(4), 351–371.
168 The fraud policy of the FSA can be divided into four parts and includes a direct approach, increased supervisory activity, promoting a more joined up approach and *Handbook* modifications. See N. Ryder, *Financial Crime in the 21st Century: Law and Policy* (Edward Elgar: Cheltenham, 2011, 130).
169 Financial Services Authority, 'Developing our policy on fraud and dishonesty – discussion paper 26' (Financial Services Authority, London, 2003, 18).
170 HM Treasury Select Committee, *Fixing LIBOR: Some Preliminary Findings* (HM Treasury: London, 2012, 102) (emphasis added).
171 *Ibid*.

have the regulatory remit to prosecute certain fraudulent activity. For example, in March 2000 the FSA *successfully* prosecuted Paul Haslam for breaches of the Banking Act 1987.[172] Furthermore, in February 2008 the FSA successfully prosecuted William Anthony 'Robin' Radclyffe, who was convicted after pleading guilty to a series of offences under the Theft Acts, the Financial Services Act 1986 and Financial Services and Markets Act 2000. The defendant, who was not authorised by the FSA, made a series of false and misleading statements to his clients.[173] Margaret Cole, the then Director of FSA, said 'our prosecution of this case is indicative of the FSAs determination to deter wrongdoing of this sort'.[174]

Financial Conduct Authority

As outlined in the first edition of this book, the FSA had a statutory objective to reduce financial crime under the Financial Services and Markets Act 2000. Following the near collapse of Northern Rock and the damning criticism of the performance of the FSA in the prelude, during and following the 2007–08 financial crisis, the Coalition government announced that it intended to create a new system of financial regulation under the control of the Bank of England. The FSA was replaced by the Financial Conduct Authority (FCA), by virtue of the Financial Services Act 2012, and is obliged to tackle fraud through its statutory objective to reduce the risk of financial crime. It is also important to note that this also overlaps with the FCA's consumer protection objective. One of the first issues that the FCA concentrates on in relation to fraud is data security, which it defines as:

> the way that firms put in place systems and controls to prevent their consumers' personal details, such as address, date of birth, national insurance number, earnings, account details, etc, from being accessed by criminals. Information

---

172 Section 35 of the Banking Act 1987 provides that a person commits the offence of fraudulent inducement if a person '(a) makes a statement, promise or forecast which he knows to be make a deposit, misleading, false or deceptive, or dishonestly conceals any material facts; or (b) recklessly makes (dishonestly or otherwise) a statement, promise or forecast which is misleading, false or deceptive, is guilty of an offence if he makes the statement, promise or forecast or conceals the facts for the purpose of inducing, or is reckless as to whether it may induce, another person (whether or not the person to whom the statement, promise or forecast is made or from whom the facts are concealed) – (i) to make, or refrain from making, a deposit with him or any other person; or (ii) to enter, or refrain from entering, into an agreement for the purpose of making such a deposit'.

173 Financial Services Authority, 'Fake stockbroker sentenced to 15 months', 13 February 2008, available from http://www.fsa.gov.uk/library/communication/pr/2008/011.shtml, accessed 12 November 2012.

174 *Ibid.* Also see K. Griffiths, 'Fraudulent broker gets 15 months', 14 February 2008, available from http://www.telegraph.co.uk/finance/markets/2784369/Fraudulent-broker-gets-15-months.html, accessed 12 November 2012.

must be kept secure because consumers can be vulnerable and criminals can use it to commit offences such as identity theft.[175]

Firms regulated by the FCA are required to 'safeguard their consumers data and we require firms to have adequate systems and controls in place to discharge these responsibilities'.[176] Failure to comply with these obligations could render a firm subject to the imposition of a financial penalty by the FCA. For example, the Nationwide Building Society was fined £980,000 for 'failing to take reasonable care to organise and control its affairs responsibly and effectively, with adequate risk management systems. Nationwide did not take reasonable care to ensure that it had effective systems and controls to manage the risks relating to information security.'[177] Furthermore, the FSA fined Zurich Insurance £2.275 million for 'failing to take reasonable care to establish and maintain systems and controls that were appropriate to its business; and failing to take reasonable care to establish and maintain effective systems and controls to counter the risk that Zurich UK might be used to further financial crime'.[178]

The FCA has adopted a joined-up approach towards tackling mortgage fraud by implementing the Information from Lenders Scheme.[179] Under this scheme, lenders are encouraged to inform the FCA about any 'intermediaries they suspect of being involved in mortgage fraud'.[180] At first glance, this appears to be an appropriate mechanism to tackle mortgage fraud. However, the reporting system is entirely voluntary and can be contrasted with the mandatory reporting obligations imposed on similar firms for money laundering and the financing of terrorism as discussed in Chapters 2 and 3. Furthermore, the voluntary scheme that has been adopted by the FCA can be contrasted with the stance adopted in the USA where firms have a legal obligation to report alleged instances of mortgage fraud.[181] The FCA has used its extensive enforcement powers and has banned 67 intermediaries and imposed financial penalties in excess of £2 billion.[182] These figures can be distinguished from the USA where, in August 2014,

---

175 Financial Conduct Authority, 'Data security', 28 January 2015, available from https://www.fca.org.uk/about/what/enforcing/data-security, accessed 20 August 2015.

176 *Ibid.*

177 Financial Services Authority, 'Final notice: Nationwide Building Society', 14 February 2007, available from http://www.fsa.gov.uk/pubs/final/nbs.pdf, accessed 20 August 2015.

178 *Ibid.*

179 Financial Conduct Authority, 'Fighting mortgage fraud', 1 May 2015, available from https://www.fca.org.uk/about/what/enforcing/fraud/mortgage, accessed 20 August 2015.

180 *Ibid.*

181 For a more detailed discussion of mortgage fraud in the USA see N. Ryder, *The Financial Crisis and White Collar Crime: The Perfect Storm* (Edward Elgar: Cheltenham, 2014, 47–58).

182 Financial Conduct Authority, 'Fighting mortgage fraud', 1 May 2015, available from https://www.fca.org.uk/about/what/enforcing/fraud/mortgage, accessed 20 August 2015.

Bank of America was fined approximately £17 billion to settle allegations of mortgage fraud.[183]

An important part of the FCA's role towards fighting fraud is the enforcement of its rules so that authorised firms are not exploited by financial criminals. The FCA seeks to ensure that authorised firms:

- take appropriate steps to protect themselves against fraud;
- put in place systems and controls to mitigate financial crime risk effectively;
- can detect and prevent money laundering; and
- understand that the FCA will use its enforcement powers against them if they use corrupt or unethical methods.[184]

If the FCA determines that a firm has breached its fraud regulations there are a vast array of enforcement powers that it can utilise. The most frequently used power has been its ability to impose financial penalties, as will be illustrated in Chapters 5 and 6. Another important part of the FCA's stance towards tackling fraud involves working with regulated firms, trade associations, the NCA,[185] the Fraud Advisory Panel[186] and key service providers in the financial services sector. Furthermore, the FCA also undertakes a number of preventative measures to make investors aware of possible fraudulent scams.[187] Finally, the FCA provides a list of unauthorised firms and individuals to avoid.[188]

National Fraud Authority

One of the most important agencies established to tackle fraud is the NFA.[189] The objectives of the NFA are threefold: i) creating a criminal justice system that is sympathetic to the needs of fraud victims by ensuring that the system operates more effectively and efficiently,[190] ii) discouraging organised criminals from

---

183 Department of Justice, 'Bank of America to pay $16.65bn in historic Justice Department settlement for financial fraud leading up to and during the financial crisis', 21 August 2014, available from http://www.justice.gov/opa/pr/bank-america-pay-1665-billion-historic-justice-department-settlement-financial-fraud-leading, accessed 20 August 2015.

184 Financial Conduct Authority, 'Enforcing our rules and fighting financial crime', 28 January 2015, available from https://www.fca.org.uk/about/what/enforcing/, accessed 21 August 2015.

185 National Crime Agency, 'About us', n/d, available from http://www.nationalcrimeagency.gov.uk/about-us, accessed 21 August 2015.

186 *Ibid.*

187 Financial Conduct Authority, 'How to avoid investment scams', 27 November 2014, available from https://www.fca.org.uk/consumers/scams/how-to-avoid-scams, accessed 21 August 2015.

188 Financial Conduct Authority, 'Unauthorised firms and individuals to avoid', n/d, available from https://www.fca.org.uk/consumers/protect-yourself/unauthorised-firms/unauthorised-firms-to-avoid, accessed 21 August 2015.

189 National Fraud Strategic Authority, *The National Fraud Strategy – A New Approach to Combating Fraud* (National Fraud Strategic Authority, 2009, 10).

190 For a more detailed discussion of how this is to be achieved see the Attorney General's Office, *Extending the Powers of the Crown Court to Prevent Fraud and Compensate Victims: A Consultation* (Attorney General's Office: London, 2008).

committing fraud in the UK, and iii) increasing the public's confidence in the response to fraud.[191] Professor Barry Rider states that the NFA

> has an impressive list of strategic aims: tackling the key threats of fraud that pose the greatest harm to the United Kingdom; the pursuit of fraudsters effectively, holding them to account and improving victim support; the reduction of the UK's exposure to fraud by building, sharing and acting on knowledge; and securing the international collaboration necessary to protect the UK from fraud.[192]

The NFA's Interim Chief Executive Sandra Quinn has boldly claimed that 'we can respond quickly and effectively to the fraud threat'.[193] This level of optimism was not shared by Bosworth-Davies who stated that the NFA 'will last about as long as the unlamented Asset Recovery Agency'.[194] Despite this pessimism, an important measure introduced by the NFA was the publication of the National Fraud Strategy, which is an integral part of the government's fraud policy.[195] Under this strategy the NFA is required to,

1   tackle the threats presented by fraud;
2   act effectively to pursue fraudsters and hold them to account;
3   improve the support available to victims;
4   reduce the UK's exposure to fraud by building the nation's capability to prevent it; and,
5   target action against fraud more effectively by building, sharing and acting on knowledge and securing the international collaboration necessary to protect the UK from fraud.[196]

Despite the fanfare announcement by the government that it had created the NFA, the one fundamental question that must be asked is whether it will actually make any difference towards the overall effectiveness of the UK's fraud policy. If we are to believe that the extent of fraud in the UK is somewhere between £14 and £30 billion, how is it possible for one agency to make any valuable dent in this statistic if it only has a budget of £29 million over a three-year period. More resources are therefore urgently required. The NFA was abolished by the Coalition government

---

191 National Fraud Strategic Fraud Authority, 'UK toughens up on fraudsters with new anti-fraud authority', available from http://www.attorneygeneral.gov.uk/NewsCentre/Pages/UKToughens UpOn%20FraudstersWithNewAnti-FraudAuthority.aspx, accessed 2 October 2008.

192 B. Rider, 'A bold step?' (2009) *Company Lawyer*, 30(1), 1–2, at 1.

193 National Fraud Strategic Authority, *The National Fraud Strategy – A New Approach to Combating Fraud* (National Fraud Strategic Authority, 2009, 16).

194 R. Bosworth-Davies, 'Investigating financial crime: The continuing evolution of the public fraud investigation role – a personal perspective' (2009) *Company Lawyer*, 30(7), 195–199, at 199.

195 National Fraud Strategic Authority, *The National Fraud Strategy – A New Approach to Combating Fraud* (National Fraud Strategic Authority, 2009, 3).

196 *Ibid.*, 16.

in March 2013, with its functions being transferred to the NCA or Home Office. Thus, the UK's counter-fraud policy is now without an agency to develop and monitor its strategy. It will be interesting to see if during the lifetime of the Conservative government the remit of the NCA will expand to include fraud if the Home Secretary decides to revive efforts to abolish the SFO.[197]

Effectiveness

In the UK, for example, there is a considerable degree of overlap between the SFO and the FCA, with both having extensive investigative and prosecutorial powers that seek to achieve the same objective. The failures of the SFO are well documented, whilst the FCA's effectiveness must be questioned because of the uncertainty over its ability to prosecute allegations of fraud. In the previous edition of the book we recommended that a single financial crime agency should be established to coordinate the UK's fraud policy with extensive investigative and prosecutorial powers. Such an idea was mooted by Fisher, who recommended the creation of a 'single "Financial Crimes Enforcement Agency" to tackle serious fraud, corruption and financial market crimes'.[198] This recommendation was supported by the Conservative party whilst in opposition before the 2010 general election, who suggested the establishment of an Economic Crime Agency (ECA) that would do the work of the SFO, the Fraud Prosecution Service and the Office of Fair Trading. In 2010 the then Shadow Chancellor George Osborne MP stated 'we are very, very bad at prosecuting white-collar crime. We have six different government departments, eight different agencies and the result is that these crimes go unpunished.'[199] Following the 2010 general election the Coalition government outlined its desire to create a single agency to tackle financial crime, stating, as mentioned in Chapter 2: 'We take white collar crime as seriously as other crime, so we will create a single agency to take on the work of tackling serious economic crime that is currently done by, among others, the Serious Fraud Office, Financial Services Authority and Office of Fair Trading.'[200] Whilst such rhetoric sounds promising, the financial crisis could have scuppered the government's plans to create such an agency.[201] The Fraud Advisory Panel writing in March 2010 took the view that because of the current climate

---

197 C. Binham and H. Warrell, 'Theresa May revives attempt to abolish SFO', 5 October 2014, available from http://www.ft.com/cms/s/0/e15dc7c0–4ae9–11e4-b1be-00144feab7de.html#axzz3jLhJ8iis, accessed 21 August 2015.

198 J. Fisher, *Fighting Fraud and Financial Crime A New Architecture for the Investigation and Prosecution of Serious Fraud, Corruption and Financial Market Crimes* (Policy Exchange, 2010, London, 3).

199 Times Online, 'Conservatives confirm plans for single Economic Crime Agency', available from http://timesonline.typepad.com/law/2010/04/conservatives-confirm-plans-for-single-economic-crime-agency.html, accessed 26 April 2010.

200 HM Government, *The Coalition: Our Programme for Government* (HM Government: London, 2010, 9).

201 D. Leigh and R. Evans, 'Cost of new economic crime agency could prove prohibitive', available from http://www.guardian.co.uk/business/2010/jun/02/economic-crime-agency-scheme-cost, accessed 12 July 2010.

the time was just not right for an ECA.[202] However, as highlighted in Chapter 2, the NCA has been established to oversee and manage the UK's fight against financial crime, via its Economic Crime Command. Since its creation in 2013 the NCA has concentrated on managing the UK's confiscation regime and acting as the financial intelligence unit, which has included some fraud-related matters. However, the NCA has been criticised for being 'incompetent' in how it contributed towards the collapse of a £40 million fraud trial in December 2014.[203] Therefore the anti-fraud agencies discussed in this chapter face an extremely uncertain future.

Financial intelligence

The UK has a strong history of utilising financial intelligence as part of its broader financial crime strategy, a point clearly illustrated by the anti-money laundering reporting provisions of the Proceeds of Crime Act (POCA) 2002 and the duty to report any suspected instances of terrorist financing under the Terrorism Act 2000. The Fraud Review noted that

> Fraud is massively underreported. Fraud is not a police priority, so even when reports are taken, little is done with them. Many victims don't report at all. So the official crime statistics display just the tip of the iceberg and developing a strategic law enforcement response is impossible because the information to target investigations does not exist.[204]

If a suspected fraud is committed against a bank it is reported to its Money Laundering Reporting Officer (MLRO). Successful frauds are reported to the NCA. Conversely, it is the decision for individual banks to determine whether or not to report the fraud to the police. In 2007 the Home Office announced that victims of credit card, cheque and online banking fraud are able to report the matter to their banks and other financial institutions.[205] However, although still important, the obligation to report allegations of fraud is not as straightforward. The primary statutory obligation for reported instances of fraud is contained under the POCA 2002.[206] It is a criminal offence under the Act to fail to disclose via a Suspicious Activity Report (SAR) where there is knowledge, suspicion or reasonable grounds to know or suspect that a person is laundering the proceeds of criminal conduct. Successful

202 See generally Fraud Advisory Panel, *Roskill Revisited: Is There a Case for a Unified Fraud Prosecution Office?* (Fraud Advisory Panel: London, 2010).

203 M. Evans, 'Judge blasts National Crime Agency after blunders cause case to collapse', 2 December 2014, available from http://www.telegraph.co.uk/news/uknews/crime/11268097/Judge-blasts-National-Crime-Agency-after-blunders-cause-case-to-collapse.html, accessed 21 August 2015.

204 General's Office, *Fraud Review – Final Report* (Attorney General's Office: London, 2006, 7).

205 Home Office, 'Fraud', available from http://www.crimereduction.homeoffice.gov.uk/fraud/fraud17.htm, accessed 7 December 2009.

206 Proceeds of Crime Act 2002, s. 330.

fraud is defined as money laundering for the purpose of this Act.[207] Furthermore, the Act specifies that members of the regulated sector are required to report their suspicions as soon as reasonably practical to the NCA via their MLRO. There is no legal obligation to report unsuccessful or attempted frauds to the authorities because any attempted frauds will not give rise to any legal criminal proceedings, and therefore fall outside the scope of the mandatory reporting obligations under the POCA 2002. Ultimately, the decision whether or not an investigation will be conducted lies with the police. The Home Office has advised that the police should only investigate where there are good grounds to believe that a criminal offence has been committed.[208]

Furthermore, members of the regulated sector are obliged to report fraud to the FCA in the following circumstances:

1   they become aware that an employee may have committed a fraud against one of its customers; or
2   they become aware that a person, whether or not employed by it, may have committed a fraud against it; or
3   they consider that any person, whether or not employed by it, is acting with intent to commit a fraud against it; or
4   they identify irregularities in its accounting or other records, whether or not there is evidence of fraud; or
5   they suspect that one of its employees may be guilty of serious misconduct concerning his honesty or integrity and which is connected with the firm's regulated activities or ancillary activities.[209]

In determining whether or not the matter is significant, the firm must consider:

1   the size of any monetary loss or potential monetary loss to itself or its customers (either in terms of a single incident or group of similar or related incidents);
2   the risk of reputational loss to the firm; and
3   whether the incident or a pattern of incidents reflects weaknesses in the firm's internal controls.[210]

Such notifications are required 'as the FSA [now FCA] needs to be aware of the types of fraudulent and irregular activity which are being attempted or undertaken, and to act, if necessary, to prevent effects on consumers or other firms'.[211] To help

---

207   It is important to note that the Proceeds of Crime Act 2002 applies to serious crime, which includes fraud.
208   Home Office, *Home Office Circular 47/2004 Priorities for the Investigation of Fraud Cases* (Home Office: London, 2004).
209   SUP 15.3.17R.
210   SUP 15.3.18G.
211   SUP 15.3.19G.

with this endeavour, each notification 'should provide all relevant and significant details of the incident or suspected incident of which the firm is aware'.[212] Furthermore, if the firm has suffered significant financial losses as a result of the incident, or may suffer reputational loss, the FCA will question 'whether the incident suggests weaknesses in the firm's internal controls'.[213] If the fraud is committed by an FCA Approved Person,[214] the FCA has the power to withdraw its authorisation, and the possibility of prosecution becomes real.

It can therefore be seen that the UK's policy towards fraud has gained momentum both under the previous governments and a willingness shared by the new Conservative administration. However, there is still scope for improvement in the initiatives introduced to tackle fraud. For example, the effectiveness of the criminalisation of fraud has been limited by the inadequacies of the Theft Acts and the common law offences, a position that has been improved by the introduction of the Fraud Act. However, following the collapse of several high profile instances of fraud, concerns still remain about the enforcement of these offences by the SFO and the CPS. Whilst it is simply too early to determine if the Fraud Act has made any difference to the prosecution of fraudsters, the Coalition government must be commended for recognising the need to create a single ECA, as long as this actually happens. This will be a factor for the current Conservative government to decide upon. In addition to the creation of such an agency the government also needs to tackle the reporting of instances of suspicious fraudulent activities, which is fragmented with a number of different reporting mechanisms available, causing yet more confusion and delay.

Sentencing and recovery

Under section 1(3) of the Fraud Act 2006, the maximum term of imprisonment for a fraud offence is 10 years. This can be contrasted with the USA, where for securities fraud, mail fraud and wire fraud the maxima is 20 years imprisonment.[215] As with other financial offences in the UK, an offender can also receive an unlimited fine. During 2008 and 2009 there were 14,238 prosecutions in the UK under sections 1–4 of the Fraud Act 2006, resulting in 11,133 convictions and a conviction rate of 78.2 per cent.[216] In 2009, of the 14,688 offenders who were sentenced for fraud, 2,654 were sentenced to immediate imprisonment with an average custodial term of 12.2 months. These figures have remained fairly static over the last few years; for example, in 2011, 14,887 were sentenced, with 2,947 receiving a custodial

---

212 *Ibid.*

213 SUP 15.3.20G.

214 An approved person is an individual who has been approved by the FSA to perform controlled functions, which relates to the carrying on of a regulated activity by a firm. See Financial Services and Markets Act 2000, s. 59.

215 Australian Government and Australian Institute of Criminology, *Charges and Offences of Money Laundering* Transnational Crime Brief No. 4 (Australian Institute of Criminology: Canberra, 2008).

216 HL Deb, 18 May 2011, c338W.

term, with the average length of that term being 14.9 years. Likewise in 2013, of the 12,095 offenders sentenced for fraud, 2,535 offenders were sent to prison with their average custodial term being 14.9 months.[217] Furthermore, in 2010–11 the SFO took 17 complex fraud cases to trial, achieving at least one conviction in every case. This included 31 defendants (both individual and corporate) and amounted to a conviction rate of 84 per cent.[218] When contrasted with the 50 per cent conviction rate for money laundering (see Chapter 2), this is significantly better.

Unlike the financial crimes previously considered, a fair amount of judicial guidance exists in relation to deciding what length of sentence should be imposed for the offence of fraud. Originally, this was provided in the form of Court of Appeal guideline judgments.[219] For example, in *R v Feld*[220] factors held to be relevant to sentencing fraud included:

- The amount involved and the manner in which the fraud is carried out.
- The period over which the fraud is carried out and the degree of persistence with which it is carried out.
- The position of the accused within the company and his measure of control over it.
- Any abuse of trust which is revealed.
- The consequences of the fraud.
- The effect on public confidence in the City and the integrity of commercial life.
- The loss to small investors, which will aggravate the fraud.
- The personal benefit derived by a defendant.
- The plea.
- The age and character of the defendant.[221]

Moreover, in *R v Barrick*,[222] Lane LCJ set out a number of factors that should be taken into account when sentencing professional people for offences of fraud:

- The quality and degree of trust reposed in the offender including his rank.
- The period over which the fraud or the thefts have been perpetrated.
- The use to which the money or property dishonestly taken was put.
- The effect upon the victim.
- The impact of the offences on the public and public confidence.

217 HC Deb, 23 June 2014, c3W.
218 HC Deb, 24 May 2011, c775.
219 See *R v Barrick* (1985) 7 Cr. App. Rep. (S) 142; *R v Stewart* [1987] 2 All E.R. 383; *R v Clark* [1988] 2 Cr. App. Rep. (S) 95; *R v Stevens and others* [1993] 14 Cr. App. R. (S) 372; *R v Palk and Smith* [1997] 2 Cr. App R. (S) 167; *R v Feld* [1999] 1 Cr. App. R. (S) 1; *R v Roach* [2002] 1 Cr. App. R. (S) 12.
220 [1999] 1 Cr. App. R. (S) 1.
221 [1999] 1 Cr. App. R. (S) 4.
222 (1985) 7 Cr. App. Rep. (S) 142.

- The effect on fellow-employees or partners.
- The effect on the offender himself.
- His own history.
- Those matters of mitigation special to himself such as illness; being placed under great strain by excessive responsibility or the like; where, as sometimes happens, there has been a long delay, say over two years, between his being confronted with his dishonesty by his professional body or the police and the start of his trial; finally, any help given by him to the police.[223]

Interestingly, Lane LCJ also warned how 'professional men should expect to be punished as severely as others: in some cases, more severely'[224] and gave some recommendations as to appropriate sentencing starting points,[225] which were subsequently updated in *R v Clark*:[226]

- Where the amount is not small, but is less than £17,500, terms of imprisonment from the very short up to 21 months will be appropriate.
- Cases involving sums between £17,500 and £100,000, will merit two to three years.
- Cases involving sums between £100,000 and £250,000, will merit three to four years.
- Cases involving between £250,000 and £1 million will merit between five and nine years.
- Cases involving £1 million or more will merit ten years or more.
- Where the sums involved are exceptionally large, and not stolen on a single occasion, or the dishonesty is directed at more than one victim or group of victims, consecutive sentences may be called for.[227]

Other guideline judgments relevant to fraud include *R v Palk and Smith*[228] (fraudulent trading), *R v Stevens and others*[229] (mortgage fraud) and *R v Roach*[230] (obtaining a money transfer by deception).

---

223 (1985) 7 Cr. App. Rep. (S) 147.
224 (1985) 7 Cr. App. Rep. (S) 143; this was also supported in the later case of *R v Stewart* [1987] 2 All E.R. 383.
225 'Where the amounts involved could not be described as small but were less than £10,000 or thereabouts, terms of imprisonment ranging from the very short up to about eighteen months were appropriate. Cases involving sums of between about £10,000 and £50,000 would merit a term of about two or three years' imprisonment. Where greater sums were involved, for example those over £100,000, then a term of three and a half to four years would be justified'. (1985) 7 Cr. App. Rep. (S) 143–144.
226 [1988] 2 Cr. App. Rep. (S) 95.
227 [1988] 2 Cr. App. Rep. (S) 100.
228 [1997] 2 Cr. App. R. (S) 167.
229 [1993] 14 Cr. App. R. (S) 372.
230 [2002] 1 Cr. App. R. (S) 12.

In addition to these judgments, and since 25 October 2009, sentencing guidelines have also existed and, in accordance with *R v Tongue (Ross)*, 'once guidelines have been issued it should be the exception rather than the rule to cite previous cases'.[231] The original 2009 guideline[232] was updated in 2014, with current information contained in the same guideline for Bribery and Money Laundering offences.[233] As is the same with the majority of offences, the first and primary consideration when sentencing fraud offences is the seriousness of the offending behaviour. This is step one. This is measured by looking at both the culpability of the offender and the level of harm caused or risked being caused. Culpability is measured by looking at the role of the particular offender, the extent to which the offence was planned and also how sophisticated the offence was. Factors which indicate a high level of culpability include 'a leading role where offending is part of a group activity' and where there is a 'large number of victims'.[234] Medium culpability is when the offender has played a significant role in a group activity and lesser culpability is where the offender was not 'motivated by personal gain' or the offender only had a 'peripheral role'.[235] Whilst, as discussed above, the primary offence of fraud does not require a result to have occurred, that is, a loss or gain was actually achieved, in terms of harm, the larger the loss or gain the more serious the offence will be considered to be. The guideline sets out five categories of harm, which are classified on the amount of money that has been lost or was intended to have been lost. For example a category 1 harm is where the loss was £500,000 or more; category 3 is where £20,000–£100,000 is lost; and category 5 is where less than £5,000 is lost. Interestingly, where the situation is loss intended rather than actual loss caused, the category will be lowered by one: so if the loss intended for example is £20,000–£100,000 then the harm category is that of 4 rather than 3.[236] The court will also take into consideration the harm that has been suffered by the victim. If it decides that there was a high impact of harm, such as it having a 'serious detrimental effect on the victim',[237] this can cause the harm category to be raised by one; a medium impact requires a move upwards within the category and a lesser impact requires no adjustment.

Having established the appropriate harm category the guideline provides starting points and sentencing ranges. Step two is therefore to use these ranges to reach an appropriate sentence. The guideline provides a starting point and range for each harm category and within that category for three levels of culpability. Examples can be seen in Table 4.1 below.[238]

---

231 [2007] EWCA Crim 561.

232 Sentencing Guidelines Council, *Sentencing for Fraud – Statutory Offences Definitive Guideline* (Sentencing Guidelines Secretariat: London, 2009).

233 Sentencing Council, *Fraud, Bribery and Money Laundering Offences Definitive Guideline* (Sentencing Guidelines Secretariat: London, 2014).

234 *Ibid.*, 6.

235 *Ibid.*

236 *Ibid.*

237 *Ibid.*

238 *Ibid.*, 8.

TABLE 4.1 Sentencing guidelines for section 1 Fraud Act 2006

Harm	Culpability A	Culpability B	Culpability C
Category 1 £500,000 or more Starting point based on £1 million	**Starting point** 7 years custody **Category range** 5–8 years custody	**Starting point** 5 years custody **Category range** 3–6 years custody	**Starting point** 3 years custody **Category range** 18 months–4 years custody
Category 3 £20,000–£100,000 Starting point based on £50,000	**Starting point** 3 years custody **Category range** 18 months–4 years custody	**Starting point** 18 months custody **Category range** 26 weeks–3 years custody	**Starting point** 26 weeks custody **Category range** Medium–level community order–1 year custody
Category 5 Less than £5,000 Starting point based on £2,500	**Starting point** 36 weeks custody **Category range** High level community order–1 year custody	**Starting point** Medium-level community order **Category range** Band B fine–26 weeks custody	**Starting point** Band B fine **Category range** Discharge–Medium-level community order

Bearing in mind that the Court of Appeal in *R v Clark* recommended five to nine years for amounts ranging from £250,000 to £1 million, the Guideline would thus appear to be more lenient than judicial suggestions. To establish where in the category range the most appropriate sentence sits, the court will then look at whether there are any aggravating or mitigating factors. Aggravating factors, such as previous convictions, a failure to comply with current court orders or attempts to prevent the victim from reporting or obtaining assistance,[239] will make the offence more serious. Mitigation, such as previous good character, mental disorder or learning disability, remorse or cooperation with the investigating authorities,[240] can result in a reduction in sentence. The court must then take the following steps:

- Step three: consider any other circumstances, such as whether the offender assisted the prosecution, which might reduce the sentence.[241]
- Step four: consider whether a further reduction should be given for a guilty plea.
- Step five: consider whether the total sentence for all offences committed is appropriate – known as the totality principle.
- Step six: consider the appropriateness of confiscation, compensation and other ancillary orders (as discussed above).

---

239   *Ibid.*, 10.
240   *Ibid.*
241   Serious Organised Crime and Police Act 2005, ss. 73–74.

- Step seven: give reasons as to why it is making the decision it is making.[242]
- Step eight: take into consideration any time that has been served in custody whilst held on remand.

Sentencing examples for fraud range from the infamous cases as cited above, to the more mundane. For instance, in the Independence Insurance fraud, Michael Bright was sentenced to two terms of seven years for two counts of conspiracy to defraud, with each term to run concurrently, and disqualified from being a director for 12 years. As the offences took place before the Fraud Act 2006 existed, the ten-year sentence, as mentioned above, was not open to the sentencing judge in terms of the fraud, although the maximum sentence available for conspiracy to defraud was, nevertheless, ten years.[243] Despite this term being available, and the fact that the sentencing judge said that the offence committed by Bright was 'so grave' and 'altogether beyond the scope that Parliament could have had in mind when fixing such a maximum' and 'if any offence should attract the maximum penalty, it is this one',[244] the maximum term was not given. This was because it was decided that whilst the conspiracy charge was the most appropriate for trial purposes, the lesser charge of fraudulent trading fully covered the substance of the offences in question, and thus it should only be this maxima (seven years[245]) that should be available. Notwithstanding the receipt of the lesser sentence, Bright appealed,[246] arguing that it was unjust to use the full maxima and that the mitigating factors of old age, good character and poor health had not been taken into account. The Court of Appeal dismissed the appeal, arguing that the crime had been one of 'utmost gravity',[247] and interestingly, also stated that the sentencing court had been wrong in limiting the original sentence to one of seven years. Whilst the court had the power to increase the sentence it remained unchanged and arguably Bright was lucky that this increase was not imposed; especially when as per the guidelines above, his crime was committed with a high level of culpability and caused a vast amount of harm. This leniency is further supported by *R v Clark*, which not only states that ten years imprisonment is appropriate where the case involves amounts of £1 million or more but also suggests that the use of consecutive sentencing may have been more appropriate than the use of concurrent sentences. A more just sentence, therefore, would arguably have been in the region of 14 to 20 years.

Dissimilar to money laundering, there would therefore appear to be a greater reluctance by the courts to impose the maximum available sentence. This is further

---

242 A duty imposed under Criminal Justice Act 2003, s. 174.

243 Criminal Justice Act 1987, s. 12(3).

244 M. Leroux, 'Michael Bright gets maximum seven years from Independent Insurance Fraud' (*The Times*, 25 October), available from http://business.timesonline.co.uk/tol/business/industry_sectors/banking_and_finance/article2733660.ece, accessed 10 June 2011.

245 Although this has now been increased to ten years – Companies Act 2006, s. 993.

246 *R v Bright* [2008] 2 Cr. App. R. (S) 102.

247 In October 2008, Michael Bright also paid £1,258,467.04 pursuit to a confiscation order – *R v Bright* [2008] EWCA Crim 462, para. 33.

supported by the fact that the perpetrators in the Guinness share-trading fraud received sentences of five years[248] (Ernest Saunders), 30 months[249] (Anthony Parnes), 12 months and a fine of £5 million (Gerald Ronson) and a fine of £4 million (Jack Lyons). Other cases include Carl Cusnie (former Chairman of Versailies) who, for a £150 million[250] fraud, was jailed for six years and disqualified for being a director for ten years; Fred Clough (Finance Director of Versailies) who received five years imprisonment[251] and a 15-year disqualification and Abbas Gokal (connected with the fall of the Bank of Credit and Commerce International (BCCI)[252]) who received 14 years. This leniency to large-scale fraud can however be compared to the USA where Jeffrey Skilling (Enron) was sentenced to 24 years and 4 months imprisonment and ordered to pay US$26 million towards restoring the Enron pension fund and Bernard Madoff received 150 years imprisonment and a criminal forfeiture order of US$100 million for his massive Ponzi scheme. Whilst this latter example is beyond extreme, it does at least show that the courts in the USA are dealing more seriously with the harm caused by fraud.

More mundane examples include Jacinta Kibunyi,[253] who in 2009 was sentenced to 12 months imprisonment following a plea of guilty to possessing a false identity document, having used a false passport to open a bank account. Whilst using false passports is obviously serious, the sentence here could be argued to be on the excessive side, especially when compared to the facts and amount of money involved in the Bright case and the court's acknowledgement that she may have been a victim of trafficking. Furthermore, there is the case of John and Anne Darwin, who were sentenced to six years three months and six years six months respectively, for six convictions of fraud and nine of money laundering. By faking John Darwin's death, the couple received nearly £680,000 in benefits. John Darwin was also convicted of dishonestly obtaining a passport.[254] Anne Darwin additionally agreed to pay £591,838.25 under the terms of the POCA 2002, and because he had no realisable financial assets, John Darwin agreed to pay a nominal sum of £1.[255] Finally, there is the case of Guy Pound,[256] whose initial sentence of

---

248 Although this was halved on appeal.
249 This was reduced on appeal to 21 months.
250 Although he was sentenced on the basis of a loss of £20 million.
251 He had cooperated with the authorities and pled guilty and had received a 50 per cent discount off his sentence.
252 For more information on the collapse of BCCI see N. Passas, 'The genesis of the BCCI Scandal' (1996) *Journal of Law and Society*, 23(1), 57; J. Beaty and S. C. Gwynne, *The Outlaw Bank: A Wild Ride to the Secrets of BCCI* (Beard Books: Frederick, MD, 2004).
253 *R v Jacinta Kibunyi*, Court of Appeal Criminal Division, 14 January 2009, unreported.
254 N. Bunyan and R. Edwards, 'Canoe wife trail: Darwin's jailed for more than six years' (*The Daily Telegraph*, 23 July 2008), available from http://www.telegraph.co.uk/news/2448044/Canoe-wife-trial-Darwins-jailed-for-more-than-six-years.html, accessed 10 June 2011.
255 The Times Online, 'Canoe fraudster Anne Darwin to repay nearly £600,000' (*The Times*, 11 November 2009), available from http://www.timesonline.co.uk/tol/news/uk/article6912213.ece, accessed 10 June 2010.
256 *R v Pound (Guy); Attorney General's Reference (No. 59 of 2004)*, [2004] EWCA 2488.

three years imprisonment was increased to six for defrauding a charitable trust over a period of 11 years and making a gain of £2 million. Bearing in mind his level of planning, breach of trust, abuse of power and high culpability, his sentence, even when increased, still appears to be on the low side. What is worth noting is that fraud cases, both by false representation and by abuse of a position of trust are plentiful. The courts are not shy to consistently sentence people to periods of custody in the five–six year range, even though they still appear reluctant to use the maxima of ten years, even in cases where amounts are over £1 million, the money is used to fund a lavish lifestyle and the offender is defrauding vulnerable victims. It does beg the question how bad the fraud needs to be to attract sentences of over six years.

The court also has the ability to use the ancillary orders of confiscation (see Chapter 2), compensation (the payment of monies to the victims involved), financial reporting and disqualification. A financial reporting order used to be found in sections 76–79 of the Serious Organised Crime and Police Act 2005, but these sections were repealed by section 50(1)(a) of the Serious Crime Act 2015 which came into force on 3 May 2015. Stand-alone financial reporting orders therefore no longer exist, although a financial reporting requirement can now be attached to a serious crime prevention order which is available under sections 1–41 of the Serious Crime Act 2007 and is discussed in Chapter 7. In accordance with section 79 of the Serious Organised Crime and Police Act 2005, which is still in force, the requirement requires the offender to make regular reports to the authorities about their financial affairs. Failure to provide the necessary reports or the inclusion of false or misleading information can lead to a separate criminal conviction and a further custodial term.[257]

Furthermore, if the offence was in connection with 'the promotion, formation, management, liquidation or striking off of a company, with the receivership of the company's property or with his being an administrative receiver of a company',[258] the court can disqualify the offender from acting as a director of a company for a specified period of time. The disqualification, provision for which is found in the Company Directors Disqualification Act 1986, prevents the offender from acting as a company director, even if the job title is different, or from instructing others to act on his behalf. Whilst the offender can work for a company, without the court's permission, they cannot be concerned in the promotion, formation or management of the company, act as an insolvency practitioner, act as a receiver of a company's property, or take part in the promotion, formation or management of a limited liability partnership. Disqualification can last for a maximum period of 15 years and is thus a clear example of incapacitating the offender to prevent further offending behaviour. Anyone found to be in contravention of the order is liable for an additional criminal offence with a maximum imprisonment period of two years.[259]

257 Serious Organised Crime and Police Act 2005, s. 79.
258 Company Directors Disqualification Act 1986, s. 2.
259 Company Directors Disqualification Act 1986, s. 13.

TABLE 4.2 Recent fraud by false representation cases

Offence: Fraud by false representation
Legislation: section 2 Fraud Act 2006
Maximum Penalty: ten years imprisonment

Name	Date	Sentence	Brief Details
Louis Eugene Dempsey	20.10.2015	nine months	Found guilty of falsely claiming that he had fallen on a wet surface at a supermarket in Brighton, East Sussex. His fraud was attempting to claim £11,000 in compensation.
Peter Barnett	20.9.2015	four months plus compensation worth £5,892.70 and 200 hours of unpaid work	Pleaded guilty of defrauding Chiltern Railways of £5,892.70 over a 31-month period by not having a valid train ticket. The judge said: 'You really had it all. It remains unclear why you acted so badly . . . the custody threshold has been passed for a sentence of 16 weeks . . . this is a serious case and people should know that failure to par fares is a criminal offence and if caught face criminal prosecution and also imprisonment. The sentence is not only to punish you but to deter others.'[260]
Michael Smith	22.9.2015	four years	Pleaded guilty to fraud by false representation, fraud by abuse of position and making a false statement with the intention to induce somebody to accept it as genuine. He duped a cavity wall insulation company into working on 43 homes believing that they would be paid. The company went into liquidation and nine people lost their jobs.[261]
Lindsey Stoneham	21.9.2015	three years six months	Pleaded guilty to fraud by false representation amounting to £428,409 and also the fraudulent evasion of VAT. The judge said: 'In any view what you did over a significant amount of time was a sophisticated type of offending which involved sophisticated planning.'[262]
Robinson Agbonifoayetan	13.8.2015	six years	Pleaded guilty to defrauding two women by posing as a U.S. general and telling stories of personal tragedy and loss. The fraud amounted to £42,000.
Samuel Oliver Cook	21.7.2015	two years	Pleaded guilty to defrauding £110,000 from six victims. He took the money supposedly to invest it in the stock market but spent it on a lavish lifestyle.

260 http://www.thelawpages.com/court-cases/Peter-Barnett-16171–1.law.
261 http://www.hartlepoolmail.co.uk/news/crime/hartlepool-man-jailed-after-causing-firm-to-go-out-of-business-in-cavity-wall-scam-1–7475149.
262 http://www.thelawpages.com/court-cases/Lindsey-Stoneham-16087–1.law.

TABLE 4.3 Recent fraud by abuse of position of trust cases

Offence: Fraud by abuse of a position of trust
Legislation: section 4 Fraud Act 2006
Maximum Penalty: ten years imprisonment

Name	Date	Sentence	Brief Details
Susan Elaine Rennie	5.11.2015	four years six months	Pleaded guilty to defrauding £587,471.24 from her employer. The judge said: 'You were entrusted with certain responsibilities for the company finances and you abused that. You chose not to stop your offending but continued it up to the point of resignation, increasing the amount you took.'[263]
Peter Charles Bottomley	18.8.2015	six years	Pleaded guilty to fraud by abuse of position of trust, by false representation, to making or supplying articles for use in frauds, false accounting and theft. Between 2008 and 2014 he defrauded £356,883.16 from four elderly and vulnerable victims.
Pauline Elfreda Cooper	14.8.2015	five years eight months	Pleaded guilty to defrauding her employers Saipem Ltd, to the amount of £1.3 million. She made 28 money transfers to her own account, purporting to be making payments to HMRC.[264]
Michael Everard Scott	18.6.2015	five years six months and disqualified from acting as a company director for ten years	Found guilty of deducting monies from staff salaries but not paying it to HM Revenue. Fraud amounted to £950,000. The judge said: 'I have formed the view that sadly you have an obstinate and stubborn side to you. You present yourself as a man who always believes himself to be right and everybody else wrong . . . You created a web of companies by changing the names of the companies and changing the names of the people who were supposed to be paying the staff . . . it is abundantly clear you are not a fit person to run a company.'[265]
Gaynor Elizabeth Casey	2.6.2015	one year	Pleaded guilty to theft and fraud, amounting to £12,450.73, from her mother. The judge said: 'This money was not to keep you above the bread line. It was for you to do, and buy, things that you wanted . . . I have to pass a sentence which makes it quite clear to people who have a power of attorney that they must act in a position of trust and that immediate custody will follow if they don't.'[266]
Guy Bruce Houghton	19.2.2015	three years four months	Pleaded guilty to defrauding £500,000 from his grandmother, who had dementia, whilst holding lasting power of attorney. Money used to fund a lavish lifestyle.

263 http://www.thelawpages.com/court-cases/Susan-Elaine-Rennie-16380–1.law.
264 http://www.kentonline.co.uk/ashford/news/calculated-fraudster-steals-13m-from-32326/.
265 http://www.thelawpages.com/court-cases/Michael-Everard-Scott-15531–1.law.
266 http://www.thelawpages.com/court-cases/Gaynor-Elizabeth-Casey-15439–1.law.

Future recommendations

The UK's fraud policy has gathered pace following the publication of the Fraud Review, the introduction of the Fraud Act 2006 and the creation of the NFA. However, the policy is now in a state of flux following a series of measures initially introduced by the Coalition government. The Fraud Act, seen by many as an improvement on the offences created by the Theft Acts (1968–1996), criminalised different types of fraudulent activities and provides prosecutors with new powers to tackle fraud. However, despite promises and reassurances from the Coalition government to create a single ECA, there are still too many agencies that perform the same function, a position that has deteriorated following the creation of the NCA. For example, HM Treasury has been charged with developing and implementing the UK's policies towards money laundering and terrorist financing, yet it has very little to do with the UK's fraud policy. Furthermore, the Home Office, which has been charged with tackling the problems associated with organised crime, now appears to manage the fraud policy. It is likely that during the lifetime of the current Conservative government that the Home Office will make another attempt to abolish the SFO after a number of unsuccessful efforts.

It is therefore recommended that a single government department be given the task of tackling all types of financial crime, with it seeming to be logical that this task is given to HM Treasury, given its experience with money laundering and terrorist financing. Additionally, it is strongly suggested that a single financial crime agency is created so as to avoid the current overlap between the SFO and the FCA. The UK government should develop a unitary financial crime agency that incorporates the functions of the agencies outlined above. The primary legislation that imposes reporting obligations is the POCA 2002, under which fraud is reported to the NCA. However, in some circumstances, allegations of fraud are reported to banks, the police and in the regulated sector such reports are made to the FCA. There is still no legal obligation to report instances of fraud, which can be contrasted with the approach adopted in the USA and with the approach to money laundering. It is therefore suggested that the UK should adopt a similar mandatory counterfraud reporting strategy, and that all suspicious transactions for fraud must be reported to the NCA.

Further reading

R. Bosworth-Davies, 'Investigating financial crime: The continuing evolution of the public fraud investigation role – a personal perspective' (2009) *Company Lawyer*, 30(7), 195–199.

J. de Grazia, *Review of the Serious Fraud Office – Final Report* (Serious Fraud Office: London, 2008).

A. Doig, *Fraud* (Willan Publishing: Cullompton, 2006).

Fraud Advisory Panel, *Roskill Revisited: Is There a Case for a Unified Fraud Prosecution Office?* (Fraud Advisory Panel: London, 2010).

P. Kiernan and G. Scanlan, 'Fraud and the law commission: The future of dishonesty' (2003) *Journal of Financial Crime*, 10(3), 199–208.

M. Levi, 'The Roskill Fraud Commission revisited: An assessment' (2003) *Journal of Financial Crime*, 11(1), 38–44.

J. Masters, 'Fraud and money laundering: The evolving criminalisation of corporate non-compliance' (2008) *Journal of Money Laundering Control*, 11(2), 103–122.

D. Ormerod, 'The Fraud Act 2006 – criminalising lying?' (2007) *Crim L.R.*, March, 193–219.

D. Ormerod and D. Williams, *Smith's Law of Theft* (Oxford University Press: Oxford, 2007).

B. Rider, 'A bold step?' (2009) *Company Lawyer*, 30(1), 1–2.

G. Scanlan, 'Offences concerning directors and officers of a company: Fraud and corruption in the United Kingdom – the present and the future' (2008) *Journal of Financial Crime*, 15(1), 22–37.

R. Wright, 'Fraud after Roskill: A view from the Serious Fraud Office' (2003) *Journal of Financial Crime*, 11(1), 10–16.

R. Wright, 'Developing effective tools to manage the risk of damage caused by economically motivated crime fraud' (2007) *Journal of Financial Crime*, 14(1), 17–27.

5

INSIDER DEALING

Introduction

Insider dealing is the illegal trading in shares or securities by someone, or at the instigation of someone, with inside knowledge of unpublished business data or information that would affect the price of shares being bought or sold.[1] It has been defined by Alexander as:

> trading in organised securities markets by persons in possession of material non-public information, and has been recognised as a widespread problem that is extremely difficult to eradicate. Some of the insider dealing is based on corporate information, that is, information about a company's finances or operations.[2]

Because of the desirability of having a clean market in the United Kingdom (UK), a policy of criminalising the activity with an additional civil recovery route has been introduced. The primary focus of this chapter will therefore be to analyse these initiatives, including an attempt to quantify the extent of the problem. The chapter will then consider background to the policy of criminalising and regulating insider dealing, plus an evaluation of the financial institutions and regulatory bodies involved. Finally, we look at the success of criminal and civil sentencing options and practices.

---

1 Serious Fraud Office, 'Insider dealing', 2010, available from http://www.sfo.gov.uk/media/99234/ insider%20dealing%20web%201.pdf, accessed 4 October 2011.

2 K. Alexander, *Insider dealing and market abuse, the Financial Services and Markets Act 2000* – ESRC Centre for Business Research, University of Cambridge, Working Paper No. 222 (University of Cambridge: Cambridge, UK, 2001, 4).

What is the offence of insider dealing?

The offence of insider dealing is contained in section 52 of the Criminal Justice Act 1993, which came into force on 1 March 1994.[3] This states that it is an offence for an individual who has information as an insider to deal in securities on a regulated market on the basis of such information. It is important to note that this criminal offence can *only* be committed by a person and not by a company. This position can be contrasted with the market abuse regime, which is discussed in Chapter 6. A regulated market is defined as any 'market, however operated, which, by an order made by the Treasury, is identified (whether by name or by reference to criteria prescribed by the order) as a regulated market'.[4] An individual who has inside information is also guilty of an offence if they encourage another person to deal in securities or, they disclose such inside information otherwise than in accordance with the proper functions of their employment.[5] The Insider Dealing Directive states that each Member State should ban a person who possesses inside information from 'disclosing that inside information to any third party unless such disclosure is made in the normal course of the exercise of his employment, profession or duties; [and] recommending or procuring a third party, on the basis of that inside information, to acquire or dispose of transferable securities admitted to trading on its securities markets'.[6] In short, these three offences are known as dealing, encouraging another to deal and disclosing information.[7] For all three offences it is important to prove that there is the existence of inside information. This is defined by section 56 of the Act as information which:

(a) relates to particular securities or to a particular issuer of securities or to particular issuers of securities and not to securities generally or to issuers of securities generally;
(b) is specific or precise;
(c) has not been made public; and
(d) if it were made public would be likely to have a significant effect on the price of any securities.[8]

This definition is largely based on that adopted by the Insider Dealing Directive which stated that inside information is that 'which has not been made public of a precise nature relating to one or several issuers of transferable securities or to one

---

3 For an excellent discussion of the offences under the Criminal Justice Act 1993, see E. Lomnicka, 'The new insider dealing provisions, Criminal Justice Act 1993, Part V' (1994) *Journal of Business Law*, March, 173–188.
4 Criminal Justice Act 1993, s. 60.
5 Criminal Justice Act 1993, s. 52(2).
6 Insider Dealing Directive, Council Directive 89/592/EEC, Article 3.
7 Serious Fraud Office, 'Insider dealing', 2010, available from http://www.sfo.gov.uk/media/99234/insider%20dealing%20web%201.pdf, accessed 4 October 2011.
8 Criminal Justice Act 1993, s. 56(1).

or several transferable securities, which, if it were made public, would be likely to have a significant effect on the price of the transferable security or securities in question'.[9] In this context it is therefore important to ascertain whether or not the said information has been made public. Made public, according to section 58 of the Act, is if the information has been:

- published for the purpose of informing investors and their professional advisers;
- contained in records which are open to inspection by the public;
- is readily acquired by those likely to deal in any securities; or,
- derived from information which has been made public.

The information in question does not have to have been communicated to the public at large, as long as a section of the public are made aware of it; does not have to have been published in the UK; can be acquired on an observation-only basis; can attract a fee; and, can be acquired only by those exercising expertise or diligence.[10] A person will be classed as being an insider, for the purposes of the Act, if the relevant information has been gained through them being a director, employee or shareholder or they have access to such information through the course of their office, profession or employment.[11] A person therefore has information as an insider 'if and only if it is, and he knows it is, inside information, and he has it, and knows that he has it, from an inside source'.[12] Once again, this definition is largely based on the definition adopted by the Directive which provided that a person can be identified as an insider if,

> by virtue of his membership of the administrative, management or supervisory bodies of the issuer, – by virtue of his holding in the capital of the issuer, or – because he has access to such information by virtue of the exercise of his employment, profession or duties, possesses inside information from taking advantage of that information with full knowledge of the facts by acquiring or disposing of for his own account or for the account of a third party, either directly or indirectly, transferable securities of the issuer or issuers to which that information relates.[13]

Welch *et al.* noted that

> Member States tended to divide into two camps, those which treated anyone holding inside information as an insider and those which required some link with the company or issuer before a person in possession of inside information

---

9 Insider Dealing Directive, Council Directive 89/592/EEC, Article 1(1).
10 Criminal Justice Act 1993, s. 58(3).
11 Criminal Justice Act 1993, s. 57(2).
12 Criminal Justice Act 1993, s. 57(1).
13 Insider Dealing Directive, Council Directive 89/592/EEC, Article 2(1).

became subject to the prohibition on insider dealing. The Insider Dealing Directive was a minimum harmonisation directive and required Member States to prohibit insider dealing only by insiders with a link to the company, known as primary insiders.[14]

In accordance with the Act, a person is therefore not deemed to have information as an insider just because it is inside information and gained from an inside source. Rather it must be proven that they had actual knowledge of both of these aspects.[15] Securities for the purpose of the offence relate to price-affected securities, with the inside information in question needing to have a 'significant effect on the price [or value] of the securities'[16] involved, thus making the inside information price sensitive. Examples of relevant securities include shares, debt securities, warrants, depositary receipts, options, futures and contracts for differences.[17] The Insider Dealing Directive stated that securities included:

> shares and debt securities, as well as securities equivalent to shares and debt securities; contracts or rights to subscribe for, acquire or dispose of securities referred to in (a) futures contracts, options and financial futures in respect of securities referred to in (a) when admitted to trading on a market which is regulated and supervised by authorities recognised by public bodies, operates regularly and is accessible directly or indirectly to the public.[18]

Furthermore, a regulated market is one that has been identified as such for the purposes of the Act by HM Treasury,[19] with one example being the London Stock Exchange.[20] For the offence to be made out the prosecuting authority also needs to show that the individual was within the UK at the time of the dealing; the regulated market is one which has been defined as regulated in the UK by HM Treasury; if the offence involved a professional intermediary, they too were within the UK at the time of the dealing; and, finally, if the offence involves encouraging another to deal, the discloser and recipient of the information and/or encouragement are within the UK when the information or encouragement is given and received.[21]

---

14 J. Welch, M. Pannier, E. Barrachino, J. Bernd and P. Ledeboer, *Comparative Implementation of EU Directives (I) – Insider Dealing and Market Abuse* (The British Institute of International and Comparative Law: London, 2005, 9).

15 Serious Fraud Office, 'Insider dealing', 2010, available from http://www.sfo.gov.uk/media/99234/insider%20dealing%20web%201.pdf, accessed 4 October 2011.

16 Criminal Justice Act 1993, s. 56(2).

17 Criminal Justice Act 1993, Schedule 2.

18 Insider Dealing Directive, Council Directive 89/592/EEC, Article 2(1).

19 Criminal Justice Act 1993, s. 60.

20 Serious Fraud Office, 'Insider dealing', 2010, available from http://www.sfo.gov.uk/media/99234/insider%20dealing%20web%201.pdf, accessed 4 October 2011.

21 Criminal Justice Act 1993, s. 62.

Dealing

As stated above, the first offence is committed if a person using inside information deals in price-affected securities on a regulated market. The person involved can either be relying on a professional intermediary or acting as a professional intermediary themselves.[22] Dealing in securities is defined by section 55 of the Act as either acquiring or disposing of securities or procuring (directly or indirectly) an acquisition or disposal of the securities by another person.[23] Acquiring includes entering into a contract to create a security or making an agreement that a security will be acquired.[24] Furthermore, disposing involves bringing to an end such a contract or entering into an agreement that a security will be disposed of.[25] Interestingly, there is no requirement to establish a causal link between the held information and the dealing, although, as detailed below, it is a defence if the trader can prove that they would have dealt in the same way regardless of the inside information. Examples of this behaviour include where the inside information is that a publicly listed company is about to be taken over, which would usually result in the price of its shares increasing. By buying shares before this information is made public the likely result is a large profit for the insider. Conversely, the inside information could be that a publicly listed company is about to issue a profit warning and before this information is widely known the insider sells their shares to avoid losses.[26]

Encouraging another to deal

This offence covers the situation whereby the person with the inside information encourages another to deal with securities on any regulated market on the basis of this information and the insider knows or has reasonable cause to believe that such dealing will take place. It is worth noting that the offence of encouraging another to deal is not a result crime and thus takes place as soon as the encouragement is given, even if no subsequent dealing occurs.

Disclosing information

The final offence is committed where an individual who has inside information discloses this to another person and they have reasonable cause to believe that they (the other person) will use this information to deal in price-affected securities on any regulated market or as a professional intermediary or through a professional intermediary. The offence is only carried out when the disclosure occurs outside

---

22 Criminal Justice Act 1993, s. 52(1) and (3).
23 Criminal Justice Act 1993, s. 55(1).
24 Criminal Justice Act 1993, s. 55(2).
25 Criminal Justice Act 1993, s. 55(3).
26 P. Barnes, 'Insider dealing and market abuse, the UK's record on enforcement' (2011) *International Journal of Law, Crime and Justice*, 39, 174–189, at 176.

of the individuals 'proper performance of the functions of his employment, office or profession'[27] and although it can be made in writing, is more likely to be made orally.[28]

Defences

There are, however, a number of defences to the three offences, and all are contained within section 53 and Schedule 1 of the Criminal Justice Act 1993.[29] For example, the offence will not have been committed if the person in question can show that at the time of the dealing they either did not expect to make a profit (which also includes the avoidance of a loss[30]); had reasonable grounds for believing that the information on which the dealing was based was widely known; or, that they would have acted in the way that they did even if they had not known about the insider information.[31] For this latter excuse, the defendant would have to prove that 'he had a compelling reason for dealing in the securities in question and that he would have done so on that basis regardless of the inside information'.[32] If the offence is based on an individual encouraging another to deal in securities using insider information, the same three defences, outlined above, also apply.[33] Furthermore, if a person discloses insider information, they are not guilty of an offence under section 52 Criminal Justice Act 1993, if they can show that either they did not expect anyone to deal in securities based on that information, or, if there was such an expectation, they did not expect the dealing to result in a profit.[34]

In addition to these defences, a number of so-called special defences also exist within Schedule 1 of the Act. The first of these is acting in good faith as a market maker, with a market maker described as 'a person who holds himself out at all normal times in compliance with the rules of a regulated market or an approved organisation as willing to acquire or dispose of securities; and is recognised as doing so under those rules'.[35] Furthermore, under paragraph 2, it is a defence if an individual can show that the inside information was 'market information' and it was 'reasonable for an individual in his position to have acted as he did despite having

---

27 Criminal Justice Act 1993, s. 52(2)(b).
28 Serious Fraud Office, 'Insider dealing', 2010, available from http://www.sfo.gov.uk/media/99234/insider%20dealing%20web%201.pdf, accessed 4 October 2011.
29 For a more detailed discussion of the defences under the Criminal Justice Act 1993 see M. Jain, 'Significance of mens rea in insider dealing' (2004) *Company Lawyer*, 25(5), 132–140.
30 Criminal Justice Act 1993 s. 53(6).
31 Criminal Justice Act 1993, s. 53(1).
32 Serious Fraud Office, 'Insider dealing', 2010, available from http://www.sfo.gov.uk/media/99234/insider%20dealing%20web%201.pdf, accessed 4 October 2011.
33 Criminal Justice Act 1993, s. 53(2).
34 Criminal Justice Act s. 53(3).
35 Criminal Justice Act 1993, Schedule 1, para. 1.

such information as an insider at the time'.[36] For this purpose, market information is information consisting of one or more of the following facts:

(a) that securities of a particular kind have been or are to be acquired or disposed of, or that their acquisition or disposal is under consideration or the subject of negotiation;

(b) that securities of a particular kind have not been or are not to be acquired or disposed of;

(c) the number of securities acquired or disposed of or to be acquired or disposed of or whose acquisition or disposal is under consideration or the subject of negotiation;

(d) the price (or range of prices) at which securities have been or are to be acquired or disposed of or the price (or range of prices) at which securities whose acquisition or disposal is under consideration or the subject of negotiation may be acquired or disposed of;

(e) the identity of the persons involved or likely to be involved in any capacity in an acquisition or disposal.[37]

Moreover, a person has not committed the offence of insider dealing if they can prove that they acted in connection with a disposal or acquisition which was already subject to negotiation or under consideration; did so with a view to facilitating this disposal or acquisition; and, that the insider information was market information and was acquired by their involvement in the disposal or acquisition.[38] The above meaning of market information also applies here. Finally, it is a defence if the person involved can show that they acted in accordance with 'price stabilisation rules'.[39] These are defined as rules made under section 144(1) of the Financial and Services and Markets Act 2000. Whichever defence is relied upon, the burden of proof, which is on the balance of probabilities, is on the defence to prove that such a situation existed.[40]

The extent of insider dealing

The difficulties of estimating the extent of financial crime have been noted throughout this book and such difficulties are even more apparent with insider dealing. This is largely for two reasons; one because a large amount of insider dealing is thought to take place on a relatively low-level basis. A person may obtain some inside information, and deals on this basis, but does not deal in a sufficient amount of securities

---

36 Criminal Justice Act 1993, Schedule 1, para. 2.
37 Criminal Justice Act 1993, Schedule 1, para. 4.
38 Criminal Justice Act 1993, Schedule 1, para. 3.
39 Criminal Justice Act 1993, Schedule 1, para. 5.
40 Serious Fraud Office, 'Insider dealing', 2010, available from http://www.sfo.gov.uk/media/99234/insider%20dealing%20web%201.pdf, accessed 4 October 2011.

to raise any alarm bells. Additionally, through the use of 'rings' there can be so many people involved and so many links between the dealer and the insider that it is almost impossible to link the two together. Barnes therefore explains how the only official estimate of insider dealing comes from a report to the House of Commons in May 1990 from the Trade and Industry Committee. This states that between May 1988 and 1990, 240 investigations were conducted into possible insider dealing cases. Moreover, between 1985 and 1990, 101 cases had been investigated and transferred to the Department of Trade and Industry, which resulted in 19 prosecutions and 10 convictions.[41] More recently, Dubow and Monteiro looked at market cleanliness by assessing the rise and fall of share prices two days before information was released to the public. Significant changes in share prices were seen as evidence of some level of insider dealing. Between 2000 and 2005, between 25 and 33 per cent of all merger bids involved statistically significant price changes in a two-day window prior to the information being publically known, thus indicating some insider dealing activity.[42] Barnes, however, claims that the figure is much higher than this. Taking two months prior to announcement as the measuring point, he found that in more than 90 per cent of cases there was some evidence of insider dealing.[43] Barnes therefore estimates, on the basis of 50 profit warnings and 150 takeover bid announcements per year, that there are approximately 1,000 instances of insider dealing each year. When this is compared to the low level of prosecution as outlined below, he argues that there is only a one in 500 chance of being caught.[44] The Financial Conduct Authority (FCA) reported in 2014 that there had been a considerable reduction in instances of insider dealing since the start of the 2007–08 financial crisis.[45] The FCA concluded that 'it is plausible that the prosecutions and the communication about the new regulatory stance acted as a credible deterrence to insider trading'.[46] Whether it is this that has caused the reduction or whether instead the black figure of insider dealing is still vast is obviously debatable.

Policy background

The UK's insider dealing policy, like its strategies towards money laundering and counter-terrorist financing, has been influenced by the measures introduced by

---

41 P. Barnes, 'Insider dealing and market abuse, the UK's record on enforcement' (2011) *International Journal of Law, Crime and Justice*, 39, 174–189, at 186.

42 B. Dubow and N. Monteiro, *Measuring Market Cleanliness*, FSA Occasional Paper, March 2006 (Financial Services Authority: London, 2006).

43 P. Barnes, *Stock Market Efficiency, Insider Dealing and Market Abuse* (Gower: Aldershot, 2009).

44 P. Barnes, 'Insider dealing and market abuse, the UK's record on enforcement' (2011) *International Journal of Law, Crime and Justice*, 39, 174–189, at 186.

45 For a more detailed discussion of the association between the 2007–08 financial crisis and financial crime, see N. Ryder, *The Financial Crisis and White Collar Crime, the Perfect Storm?* (Edward Elgar: Cheltenham, 2014).

46 Financial Conduct Authority, *Why has the FCAs Market Cleanliness Statistic for Takeover Announcements Decreased Since 2009?* (Financial Conduct Authority: London, 2014, 20).

the European Union (EU). However, it is important to note that the Cohen Committee,[47] which was established in 1943, did not consider the need to introduce a new criminal offence of insider dealing.[48] There is some uncertainty as to the commencement of the EU's policy towards insider dealing. For example, some commentators have suggested that the EU's regulation of insider dealing was influenced by insider trading regulations in the United States of America (USA) that were introduced as a result of the Wall Street Crash in 1929.[49] The origins of insider dealing can be found in the USA, which criminalised insider trading via the Securities Exchange Commission Act 1934. Furthermore, its insider dealing policy was also influenced by the fact that several European countries had already introduced laws to tackle insider dealing.[50] In 1987 the EU published its draft Insider Dealing Council Directive,[51] which was finally introduced in 1989.[52] The final draft, entitled the 'Directive Coordinating Regulations on Insider Dealing', was accepted in November 1989.[53] Duderstadt took the view:

> [t]hat this was at all possible in such a short time was due mainly to three factors, first, the suction arising from the programme for the completion of a Single Market, secondly, the annexing of the draft Directive with those measures which, since they served to complete the common market, could be adopted by a majority vote; and, thirdly, the fact that the German financial market, the main opposition to legislation, increasingly appeared in an unfavourable light internationally because of its supposedly inadequate insider dealing regulation.[54]

The aim of the proposal was to 'ensure equality of opportunity to all investors'.[55] Furthermore, the Directive sought to 'provide minimum standards for insider dealing laws throughout the Community'.[56] The first attempt to introduce insider dealing laws in the UK occurred in 1977 and 1978.[57] Finally, the then Conservative

---

47 *The Report of the Committee on Company Law Amendment Chaired by Justice Cohen* (Cohen Report) (HMSO: London, 1945), Cmnd 6659.

48 J. Davies, 'From gentlemanly expectations to regulatory principles, a history of insider dealing in the UK, Part 1' (2015) *Company Lawyer*, 36(5), 132–143, at 132.

49 J. Hansen, 'The new proposal for a European Union directive on market abuse' (2002) *University of Pennsylvania Journal of International Economic Law*, 23, 241–268, at 250.

50 This included, for example, France, Sweden, Denmark, Norway and the UK.

51 The original Directive was published in May 1987 (Directive 7310/87) and amended in October 1988 (Directive 8810/88).

52 Council Directive 89/592/EEC.

53 85/592. See I. Duderstadt, 'Implementation of the insider dealing directive in the UK and Germany' (1996) *Journal of Financial Crime*, 4(2), 105–116, at 107.

54 *Ibid.*

55 F. Cantos, 'EEC draft directive on insider dealing' (1989) *Journal of International Banking Law*, 4(4), N174–176, at 174.

56 M. Ashe, 'The directive on insider dealing' (1992) *Company Lawyer*, 13(1), 15–19, at 15.

57 J. Welch, M. Pannier, E. Barrachino, J. Bernd and P. Ledeboer, *Comparative Implementation of EU Directives (I) – Insider Dealing and Market Abuse* (The British Institute of International and Comparative Law: London, 2005, 18).

government introduced the Companies Act 1980, which created a criminal offence for certain persons to deal in 'securities when they had unpublished price sensitive information'.[58] These provisions were amended by the Company Securities (Insider Dealing) Act 1985.[59]

However, the provisions of the Company Securities (Insider Dealing) Act 1985 were very ineffective, a point clearly illustrated by the fact that no successful prosecutions were brought under the Act. Nonetheless, McVea stated that:

> The present British legislation, enshrined in the Company Securities (Insider Dealing) Act 1985 as supplemented by the Companies Act 1985 and the Financial Services Act 1986, is a much more advanced and thorough body of legislation than the proposed EEC [European Economic Community] measures. Consequently the UK Government will have little to do by way of compliance with its provisions.[60]

The Directive was implemented in the UK via the Criminal Justice Act 1993, and it contained a number of provisions that have influenced the UK's policy towards insider dealing. For example, Article 3 'requires a prohibition on insiders possessing inside information from (a) disclosing that information to any third person unless such disclosure is made in the normal course of the exercise of his employment, profession or duties; or (b) recommending or procuring a third party, on the basis of inside information, to acquire or dispose of transferable securities'. Additionally, the EU introduced the Market Abuse Directive in 2003,[61] which was instigated via the Financial Services and Markets Act.[62] The Market Abuse Directive 'prohibits abusive behaviour such as insider dealing and market manipulation. It creates obligations aimed at deterring abuses, such as insiders lists, suspicious transaction reporting, and disclosure of trades by managers of issuers. It also requires issuers to disclose inside information.'[63] Importantly, the Directive requires Member States to 'require that any person professionally arranging transactions in financial

---

58 Companies Act 1980, part V.

59 Company Securities (Insider Dealing) Act 1985, ss. 1–8.

60 H. McVea, 'Plans for compulsory insider dealing legislation by the EEC' (1987) *Company Lawyer*, 8(5), 223–224, at 223.

61 Market Abuse Directive 2003/6 ([2003] OJ L96/16). The 'European Commission published the proposed Directive on insider dealing and market manipulation (market abuse) on 30 May 2001'. See M. McKee, 'The proposed EU Market Abuse Directive' (2001) *Journal of International Financial Markets*, 3(4), 137–142, at 137. In 2009 the EU Commission instigated a call for evidence as part of its ongoing review of the effectiveness of the Market Abuse Directive. See European Commission, 'Call for evidence Review of Directive 2003/6/EC on insider dealing and market manipulation (Market Abuse Directive)', 2009, available from http://ec.europa.eu/internal_market/consultations/docs/2009/market_abuse/call_for_evidence.pdf, accessed 12 August 2010.

62 Financial Services and Markets Act 2000, ss.118–118C. For a more detailed discussion of the Market Abuse Directive and its impact in the United Kingdom see Chapter 6.

63 Ed., 'Commission seeks evidence in review of Market Abuse Directive' (2009) *Company Law Newsletter*, 252, 4–5, at 4.

instruments who reasonably suspects that a transaction might constitute insider dealing or market manipulation shall notify the competent authority without delay'.[64] The use of suspicions transaction reports has become an integral part of the UK's insider dealing policy and is managed by the FCA.

Financial institutions and regulatory bodies

The regulation of insider dealing, like the other types of financial crime discussed in this book, has been governed by a wide range of government departments, financial regulatory and law enforcement bodies. The principal or primary government department that manages the UK's insider dealing policy was the then Department of Trade and Industry (DTI). This has more recently being taken over by the FCA. Article 8 of the Insider Dealing Directive provides that each Member State shall nominate an authority to make certain that the provisions of the Directive are complied with. Hannigan noted that the 'appropriate competent authorities in the UK would be the DTI and the Stock Exchange which currently bear the brunt of insider dealing regulation although the Securities and Investments Board (SIB) might also be nominated as its role develops'.[65] Therefore the DTI was given a wide range of investigatory powers under the Financial Services Act 1986 to counter the threat posed by insider dealing.[66] In particular, the DTI was permitted to appoint investigators who would determine if an offence of insider dealing had been committed.[67] The Financial Services Act 1986 also provides the investigators with a broad range of investigatory powers.[68] This was a welcome addition to the arsenal of UK law enforcement agencies as these powers were unique and not contained in the previous legislative framework. The DTI delegated most of its insider dealing functions to the SIB, and was created following the publications of the seminal recommendations of Professor Gower in 1984.[69] The subsequent White Paper envisaged two practitioner bodies, the SIB covering the regulation of securities and investments and the Marketing of Investment Boards (MIB) covering the marketing of investments. After the publication of the White Paper the MIB was established in the form of an organising committee, but it was subsequently decided that it should merge to form a single body, the SIB. Lomnicka took the view that 'the SIB was incorporated in . . . anticipation of the FSA 1986'.[70] The SIB exercised both legislative and administrative functions, and was described as an

---

64 Market Abuse Directive 2003/6 ([2003] OJ L96/16), Article 6(9).
65 B. Hannigan, 'Regulating insider dealing – the EEC dimension' (1989) *Journal of International Banking Law*, 4(1), 11–14, at 14.
66 Financial Services Act 1986, s. 177.
67 Financial Services Act 1986, s. 177(1).
68 Financial Services Act 1986, s. 105.
69 *Financial Services in the UK, A New Framework for Investor Protection*, Cmnd. 9432.
70 E. Lomnicka, 'Making the Financial Services Authority accountable' (2000) *Journal of Business Law*, January, 65–81, at 66.

'umbrella organisation'.[71] The SIB's Core Rule 28 deals with insider dealing and 'prohibiting firms from knowingly effecting transactions that would contravene the statutory restrictions, whether for their own account or for a customer'.[72] Core Rule 28 provides that:

> a firm is prohibited from carrying out a transaction (either in the U.K. or elsewhere) for its own account (or on the account of an associate acting on its own account), when it knows of circumstances which mean that it, its associate, or an employee of either, is prohibited from effecting the transaction by virtue of the CJA [Criminal Justice Act] (Part V) 1993.[73]

If a firm breaches Core Rule 28, the Financial Services Act 1986 provides that the SIB could pursue a civil action for breach of a statutory duty where a business had 'failed to comply with the regulatory standards required of it under the FSA [1986]'.[74] Gray noted that:

> Section 62 conferred on an investor a right of action if he suffered loss as a result of an investment business's contravention of any of the matters mentioned in s 62(1), primarily any of the SIB rules and regulations governing the conduct of investment business or those of an SRO [Self-Regulating Organisation] or Recognised Professional Body where applicable to that investment business.[75]

It is important to note that the effectiveness of the enforcement measures contained in the Financial Services Act 1986, and the regulatory performance of the SIB and DTI have been questioned by several commentators. For example, Welch *et al.*, writing for the British Institute of International and Comparative Law concluded that:

> It proved extremely difficult to prosecute cases of insider dealing successfully under the criminal law. In addition, the powers of the regulatory bodies under the Financial Services Act 1986 in relation to activities which fell short of criminal behaviour extended only to authorised persons and, in some cases, key employees.[76]

---

71 *Ibid.*, 67.
72 M. White, 'The implications for securities regulation of new insider dealing provisions in the Criminal Justice Act 1993' (1995) *Company Lawyer*, 16(6), 163–171, at 169.
73 H. McVea, 'Fashioning a system of civil penalties for insider dealing, sections 61 and 62 of the Financial Services Act 1986' (1996) *Journal of Business Law*, July, 344–361, at 355.
74 J. Gray, 'Financial Services Act 1986 reforms, Part 2' (1991) *International Banking Law*, 9(9), 412–416, at 412.
75 *Ibid.*, 414.
76 J. Welch, M. Pannier, E. Barrachino, J. Bernd and P. Ledeboer, *Comparative Implementation of EU Directives (I) – Insider Dealing and Market Abuse* (The British Institute of International and Comparative Law, London, 2005, 20).

Following the 1997 General Election and victory for Labour, the SIB and the other self-regulating agencies were merged into the Financial Services Authority (FSA), which was appointed as the regulatory agency to tackle insider dealing. The FSA was given four statutory objectives under the Financial Services and Markets Act 2000, one of which was the reduction of financial crime.[77] Under the Act, financial crime was given a very broad definition that includes fraud, dishonesty, misconduct, or misuse of information relating to a financial market and handling the proceeds of crime.[78] The FSA perceived insider dealing as a significant threat to its statutory objectives and it is also viewed as being 'the highest profile aspect' of its market abuse regime.[79] Filby took the view that 'the FSA has now been responsible for enforcing the insider dealing regulations under both Acts since late 2001. This responsibility ranges from detecting insider dealing, through to investigating suspected instances, to applying sanctions.'[80] Therefore insider dealing fell within the regulatory remit of the FSA under its financial crime statutory objective. The FSA adopted a 'preventative' approach towards tacking insider dealing, which means that 'market participants' were expected to have in place the following mechanisms:

1   appropriate and effective systems and controls to prevent insider dealing;
2   an insider list that is as short as possible and based on a need-to-know;
3   a willingness to undertake a thorough internal review following a leak;
4   effective and targeted training of staff including support staff;
5   monitoring of staff personal account dealing;
6   robust controls when dealing with third parties;
7   effective information technology controls; and
8   an awareness of the limitation of code words as an effective tool to keep information confidential, especially if used in isolation.[81]

An essential part of this preventative stance is the use of suspicious transaction reports. As will be explained in the next chapter (market abuse), authorised firms are required to report suspicious transactions of insider dealing activity to the FCA, even if the transaction does not occur. This was one of the innovative parts introduced in the UK following the implementation of the Market Abuse Directive in 2005. The FCA Handbook provides that a regulated firm must report any suspicious activity to them and failure to comply with this requirement could result in

---

77   Financial Services and Markets Act 2000, s. 6.
78   Financial Services and Markets Act 2000, s. 6(3).
79   Financial Services Authority, 'Speech by Margaret Cole, Director of Enforcement, American Bar Association', 4 October 2007, available from http://www.fsa.gov.uk/pages/Library/Communication/Speeches/2007/1004_mc.shtml, accessed 9 November 2011.
80   M. Filby, 'The enforcement of insider dealing under the Financial Services and Markets Act 2000' (2003) *Company Lawyer*, 24(11), 334–341, at 334.
81   Financial Services Authority, 'Speech by Margaret Cole, Director of Enforcement, American Bar Association', 4 October 2007, available from http://www.fsa.gov.uk/pages/Library/Communication/Speeches/2007/1004_mc.shtml, accessed 9 November 2011.

a breach and punishment.[82] For example, in 2009 the FSA fined Mark Lockwood £20,000 for failing to identify a transaction and for not reporting the transaction to the FSA which allowed the firm to be used for the purpose of an insider dealing transaction.[83] Furthermore, in January 2012 the FSA fined Caspar Agnew £65,000 for failing to identify and act on a suspicious order that allowed his firm to be used to facilitate an insider dealing transaction.[84] The importance of the suspicious transaction reports was emphasised by the FSA who noted that 'some 95% of these [suspicious transaction reports] relate to potential insider dealing. We cannot overestimate the importance of these reports and the role of market participants in detecting and preventing market abuse.'[85] Additionally, there are three other ways in which the FCA becomes aware of allegations of insider dealing, namely through supervision, market surveillance, and whistle-blowing.

It is important to point out that one of the most important reforms relating to the regulation of the financial services sector in the UK was the enactment of the Financial Services Act 2012. This legislation resulted in the abolishment of the single regulatory model and the tripartite system of regulation that was managed by the FSA, HM Treasury and Bank of England. In its place, the system of regulation is managed by the Bank of England, which is supported by the Prudential Regulation Authority (PRA)[86] and the FCA.[87] What becomes clear after reviewing the legislative amendments introduced by the Financial Services Act 2012 is that the FCA has continued to use the same powers that were utilised by the FSA. For example, the most significant powers that the FCA has employed against insider dealing are its investigative and enforcement powers. The Financial Services and Markets Act (FSMA) 2000 provides the FCA with extensive investigatory powers. The FCA has the ability to require information from authorised persons,[88] to appoint investigators,[89] to obtain the assistance of overseas financial regulators[90] and

---

82 FSA Handbook, 'Supervision', SUP 15.10, available from http://fsahandbook.info/FSA/html/handbook/SUP/15/10, accessed 10 November 2011.

83 Financial Services Authority, 'FSA fines broker for failing to prevent insider dealing', 2 September 2009, available from http://www.fsa.gov.uk/pages/Library/Communication/PR/2009/115.shtml, accessed 9 November 2011.

84 Financial Services Authority, 'Former compliance officer at Greenlight Capital and JP Morgan Cazenove trader fined', 27 January 2012, available from http://www.fsa.gov.uk/library/communication/pr/2012/007.shtml, accessed 3 February 2012.

85 *Ibid.*

86 For a more detailed discussion see G. Baber, 'The Prudential Regulation Authority, special measures for special times' (2014) *Company Lawyer*, 35(12), 353–360 and G. Walker, 'Prudential Regulation Authority' (2011) *Financial Regulation International*, 7 October 2011.

87 For a brief discussion of the reform of the FSA and the Financial Services Act 2012 see A. Kokkins, 'The Financial Services Act 2012, the recent overhaul of the UK's financial regulatory structure' (2013) *International Company and Commercial Law Review*, 24(9), 325–328.

88 Financial Services and Markets Act 2000, s. 165. It is also important to note that the PRA also has the power to require information. See Financial Services and Markets Act 2000, s. 165A.

89 Financial Services and Markets Act 2000, s. 167.

90 Financial Services and Markets Act 2000, s. 169. The PRA also has the power to gain the support of overseas regulators with respect to financial stability. See Financial Services and Markets Act 2000, s. 169A.

to provide appointed investigators with additional powers.[91] Under FSMA 2000, the FCA is able to conduct a general investigation[92] and an investigation into particular cases.[93] Furthermore, the 2000 Act provides that the FCA is permitted to appoint more investigators 'where there are circumstances suggesting that insider dealing in the CJA sense has occurred'.[94] As will be discussed in the following section of this chapter, the FSA has begun to use its enforcement and investigative powers with greater frequency. For example, writing in its Financial Crime News Letter in 2010, Margaret Cole the then FSA's Director of Enforcement stated that:

> We are determined to deliver a strong deterrent message, and a year on from our first ever insider dealing criminal case, we have secured two further convictions. Last month also saw our largest ever fine on an individual, Simon Eagle for £2.8 million, for deliberate market abuse. Through such enforcement actions we aim to change behaviour so that markets are cleaner, fairer and more orderly, and retail customers get a fairer deal. We continue to work successfully in partnership with other key organisations and this has been highlighted in our recent enforcement successes. This year we carried out our largest ever operation against suspected insider dealing where we worked in joint operation with the Serious Organised Crime Agency.[95]

The FSA retained the power to bring criminal prosecutions for insider dealing under the CJA 1993; however, it is arguable that the authority has been slow in progressing down this route, attracting criticism, preferring to use financial penalties as its main enforcement mechanism, with some commentators wondering if the FSA would ever get around to commencing criminal prosecutions for insider dealing at all. In the early days of the FSA, after so long as a self-regulating club, there seemed to be a culture of reluctance on the part of the authority's senior management to acknowledge that one of its tasks was to reduce the incidence of financial crime and combat market abuse. There does, however, now seem to be some evidence that the FSA is beginning to get tougher with insider dealers and more criminal prosecutions are likely in the future. Alexander notes the increasing FSA intensity and refers to a speech by Margaret Cole, Director of the FSA's Enforcement Division, where she emphasised that the FSA would be seeking to increase the number of criminal prosecutions it brings,[96] with others within the FSA calling it 'one of the most significant changes in our approach' and that shortly after this speech the

91 Financial Services and Markets Act 2000, s. 172.
92 Financial Services and Markets Act 2000, s. 167.
93 Financial Services and Markets Act 2000, s. 168.
94 Financial Services and Markets Act 2000, s. 168(2)(a).
95 Financial Services Authority, 'Financial Crime News Letter' (2010) July Issue 14, at 1.
96 R. Alexander, 'Corporate crimes, are the gloves coming off?' (2009) *Company Lawyer*, 30(11), 321–322.

FSA obtained its first conviction for insider dealing.[97] This increase in intensity and focus towards criminal prosecutions has borne fruit with the first criminal conviction for insider dealing brought by the FSA in which a solicitor was sentenced to eight months for passing on information to his father-in-law about an impending takeover. Additionally, the courts have recently given a green light to the FSA to use their prosecutorial powers, confirming that the FSA is able to bring prosecutions under the CJA without recourse to the Secretary of State or Director of Public Prosecutions. It is also clear that the reach of the FSA is expanding as a result of its more aggressive approach to dealing with market abuse stretching out beyond traditional securities markets and into the debt markets. Despite this optimism, a freedom of information request in 2014 illustrates that the FSA only made four arrests in 2012, one in 2011, 17 in 2010, 16 in 2009 and 11 in 2008.[98] Following the realignment of financial regulation system, the spotlight has now turned onto the FCA and it is to them that we now look for better regulation and an increase in prosecution and conviction rates.

Sentencing and recovery

Criminal prosecutions

Although it is recognised by a number of prosecuting authorities that insider dealing exists, as outlined above, the number of cases that end in a successful prosecution are minimal. Barnes argues that on average there are only one or two criminal prosecutions per year.[99] And Filby took the view that 'prosecutions for insider dealing under s. 56 of the Criminal Justice Act 1993 ('CJA') for insider dealing have been few and far between. The legislation itself has been criticised for restricting what is a highly technical fraud to the criminal arena.'[100] This has, however, increased over the last few years, with the FSA having secured ten convictions of insider dealing by 2009, and in August 2011 were in the process of prosecuting another 13 individuals.[101] For the financial year of 2010–11 the FSA achieved 'five criminal convictions for insider dealing, with sentences ranging from 12 months to three years and four months [and] five confiscation orders against individuals totalling

---

97 See *R v Christopher McQuoid* [2009] EWCA Crim 1301 and Financial Services Authority, 'Solicitor and his father-in-law found guilty in FSA insider dealing case', 27 March 2009, available from http://www.fsa.gov.uk/pages/Library/Communication/PR/2009/042.shtml, accessed 4 November 2015.

98 Financial Conduct Authority, 'FOI3519 response', 21 November 2014, available from https://www.fca.org.uk/your-fca/documents/foi/foi3519-response, accessed 4 November 2015.

99 P. Barnes, 'Insider dealing and market abuse, the UK's record on enforcement' (2011) *International Journal of Law, Crime and Justice*, 39, 174–189, at 183.

100 M. Filby, 'The enforcement of insider dealing under the Financial Services and Markets Act 2000' (2003) *Company Lawyer*, 24(11), 334–341, at 336.

101 Financial Service Authority, 'Investment banker and two associates charged with insider dealing' (Press Release, 4 August 2011), available from http://www.fsa.gov.uk/pages/Library/Communication/PR/2011/069.shtml, accessed 6 October 2011.

£1,705,285.76'.[102] In July 2014 the FCA reported that it had obtained 23 convictions for insider dealing offences since 2004.[103] In March 2015 this figure had risen to 27 convictions with a further seven prosecutions awaiting trial in 2016.[104]

The maximum sentence on conviction on indictment for insider dealing in England and Wales is seven years imprisonment, an unlimited fine, or both.[105] Additionally, the Financial Services Act 1986 'provides a right of action for certain breaches of the regulatory framework established by the FSA'.[106] Furthermore, it is important to point out that there are two other grounds for liability for insider dealing under the common law – breach of fiduciary duty and breach of confidence.[107] Examples of the criminal prosecutions, noted above, include Christopher McQuoid[108] who was given an eight-month custodial term for using inside information to make a profit of almost £50,000. In addition to the term of imprisonment, a confiscation order was made to retrieve all of the benefit and he was ordered to pay £30,000 in prosecution costs. In an appeal against sentence, which was dismissed, the Court of Appeal confirmed that those involved in insider dealing were criminals,[109] that it was a species of fraud and hence was cheating.[110] Margaret Cole stated:

> By pursuing a criminal prosecution in this case, the FSA has shown that we will take tough action to achieve our aim of credible deterrence in the financial markets . . . Anyone engaging in similar acts should see this as a clear warning that the FSA intends to bring all its powers to bear to protect the integrity of our markets.[111]

Despite what some may have seen as a warning that insider dealing would be classed as a serious offence and commensurate with an immediate custodial term, in March 2009, Timothy Power, former executive of the Belgo Group, received an 18-month jail sentence, suspended for two years, for two counts of insider dealing amounting to a profit of £9.8 million.[112] Whilst it is accepted that Power

---

102 Financial Services Authority, *Annual Report 2010/11* (Financial Services Authority: London, 2011, 60).

103 Financial Conduct Authority, *Why Has the FCAs Market Cleanliness Statistic for Takeover Announcements Decreased Since 2009?* (Financial Conduct Authority: London, 2014, 20).

104 Financial Conduct Authority, 'Former senior trader sentenced for insider dealing', available from http://www.fca.org.uk/news/former-senior-trader-sentenced-for-insider-dealing, accessed 18 November 2015.

105 Criminal Justice Act 1993, s. 61.

106 Financial Services Act 1986, s. 62.

107 H. McVea, 'Fashioning a system of civil penalties for insider dealing, sections 61 and 62 of the Financial Services Act 1986' (1996) *Journal of Business Law*, July, 344–361, at 344.

108 Regina v Christopher McQuoid [2009] EWCA Crim 1301.

109 *Ibid.*, at para. 8.

110 *Ibid.*, at para. 9.

111 Financial Services Authority, 'An update from the Financial Crime and Intelligence Division' (2009) *Financial Crime News Letter*, (13), 1–7.

112 P. Cheston, 'Former Belgo chief spared prison for insider trading deal' (*London Evening Standard*, 2 March 2009), available from http://www.thisislondon.co.uk/standard/article-23656323-former-belgo-chief-is-spared-prison-for-insider-trading-deal.do;jsessionid=A890C0DFCC53652272A3B0EA79225CFE.

served 163 days in imprisonment whilst waiting for his trial, had pleaded guilty and his offences were old in nature (committed in 1997–98), his suspended sentence would still appear to be lenient, especially when the sentencing judge described the offences as:

> Serious because they are a grave breach of trust by someone at the centre of a company which is going to cause sensitive movement on the Stock Exchange and upon which other people are relying for honesty and transparency.[113]

In December of the same year, however, father and son team, Neel and Matthew Uberoi were sentenced to prison terms of 24 and 12 months respectively for insider dealing trades worth a benefit of £288,050.05. In passing sentence, Judge Tester argued:

> This offence is cheating and it is important for economic and social wellbeing to have clean markets. The public rightly recoils from the idea of people with inside information having a license to print money.[114]

Whilst this was more punitive than previous cases, it is still fairly lenient when compared to the 2006 case of Asif Butt.[115] He was initially sentenced to five years imprisonment for conspiracy to commit insider dealing. Using confidential information, over a period of three years and through 19 criminal transactions, Butt made £388,488 profit for his investment bank (Credit Suisse), equating to £237,000 in personal benefit (not too dissimilar to the £288,000 benefit mentioned above). Whilst describing his offence as serious, 'flagrant, calculated and deliberate',[116] the Court of Appeal still reduced the sentence to four years.

More recent cases include: Malcolm Calvert who in 2010 was sentenced to 21 months in prison for five counts of insider dealing amounting to a profit of £103,883;[117] Neil Rollins whose sentence of 27 months was reduced by the Court of Appeal to 18 months imprisonment for counts of insider dealing and money laundering;[118] and, Christian Littlewood who in 2011 received a sentence of three years and four months in custody for eight counts of dealing Alternative Investment

---

113 *Ibid.*

114 Financial Services Authority, 'Corporate broker intern and his father receive 12 and 24 month prison sentences respectively for insider dealing' (Press Release, 10 December 2010) 2009, available from http://www.fsa.gov.uk/pages/Library/Communication/PR/2009/170.shtml, accessed 6 October 2011.

115 *R v Butt (Asif Nazir)* [2006] 2 Cr. App. R. (S) 44.

116 *Ibid.*, at para. 25.

117 Financial Services Authority, 'Former Cazenove broker sentenced to 21 months in prison for insider dealing' (Press Release, 11 March 2010), available from http://www.fsa.gov.uk/pages/Library/Communication/PR/2010/043.shtml, accessed 6 October 2011.

118 Financial Service Authority, 'Neil Rollins update' (Press Release, 30 June 2011, available from http://www.fsa.gov.uk/pages/Library/Communication/Statements/2011/neil_rollins.shtm, accessed 6 October 2011.

Market (AIM) listed shares between 2000 and 2008. His co-defendant Helmy Omar Sa'aid received two years imprisonment and a confiscation order of £640,000.[119] Profits were thought to be in the region of £590,000 on trading of shares worth over £2 million.[120] More up-to-date cases are available in Table 5.1. There are no sentencing guidelines on insider dealing so nothing to measure these sentences against; but as with Fraud there appears to be a real reluctance to use or even get close to the maximum available sentence, even when the dealing is worth more than £1 million.

Civil recovery

In addition to criminal prosecutions there is also a civil recovery route that was initially carried out by the FSA and continues to be used by the FCA. When successful prosecutions have occurred in this arena, the FSA has been relatively harsh in terms of using its sentencing powers. For example, in 2006 the FSA issued the largest fine that had ever been issued against an individual, fining the hedge fund manager of GLG Partners LP (GLG) and Philippe Jabre (former Managing Director) £750,000 each for insider dealing and market abuse. Jabre was privy to confidential share information on 11 February 2003, which he agreed not to use until it had become public. The information was announced on 17 February, but on 12 and 13 February he breached the restriction by short selling approximately US$16 million of ordinary shares.[121] In 2009 the FSA fined Mark Lockwood, a trading desk manager, £20,000 for failing to prevent insider dealing. Whilst he had reason to believe that a transaction was being conducted on the basis of insider dealing he failed to either prevent the trade or alert the FSA through the submission of a Suspicious Activity Report.[122] What is interesting in this example is that Lockwood was fined for a failure to act rather than being positively involved in the offence. This was because it was acknowledged that given his job role he was under an obligation to notify the FSA of any suspicious behaviour, which in this case he obviously failed to do. More recently, in March 2015, the FCA fined Kenneth Carver £35,212 for insider dealing, where he had made a profit of £24,206.70. Georgina Philippou, acting director of enforcement at the FCA, said:

> Carver knew that there was a risk of market abuse and traded anyway. He used his own funds to place a trade on Willmott's [whom he got the information

119 Financial Services Authority, 'Investment banker, his wife and family friend sentenced for insider dealing' (Press Release, 2 February 2011), available from http://www.fsa.gov.uk/pages/Library/Communication/PR/2011/018.shtml, accessed 6 October 2011.

120 Financial Services Authority, *Annual Report 2010/11* (FSA, London, 2011, 60).

121 Financial Services Authority, 'FSA fines GLG Partners and Philippe Jabre £750,000 each for market abuse' (Press Release, 1 August 2006), available from http://www.fsa.gov.uk/pages/Library/Communication/PR/2006/077.shtml, accessed 6 October 2011.

122 Financial Services Authority, 'FSA fines broker for failing to prevent insider dealing' (Press Release, 2 September 2009), available from http://www.fsa.gov.uk/pages/Library/Communication/PR/2009/115.shtml, accessed 6 October 2011.

from] behalf and knew that Willmott had a financial incentive to persuade him to trade. Market abuse is a serious offence and today's fine reflects the fact that we will not hesitate in taking action against individuals who act on inside information. Carver gave significant co-operation and provided a detailed account of events at an early stage of the investigation alongside evidence of serious financial hardship to the FCA. Carver also settled at an early stage of the Authority's investigation. Had it not been for this, the Authority would have imposed a financial penalty of £122,212.[123]

These examples would suggest that recently the FCA and the courts are trying to project the deterrent image that insider dealing is a serious offence and is just as serious as other financial crimes. However, this is arguably not being mirrored in practice, with some serious and dishonest offences being met with fairly low-level or suspended sentences. When the maximum penalty for the offence is seven years imprisonment, how large must the benefit be before a reasonably serious sentence is passed, whether that be through the civil or criminal routes.

Market manipulation

It is also important to briefly deal with the concept of market manipulation, which can be defined as conduct that can misinform or deceive others into making misleading investment decisions.[124] Market manipulation is a term that has been used in the broader sense of including 'practices deemed harmful to the capital markets'.[125] It has also been defined as an 'unwarranted interference in the operation of ordinary market forces of supply and demand; an interference in the market's normal price-forming mechanism'.[126] The FSA asserted that market manipulation encompasses three elements. First, it includes financial dealings that provide fictitious indictors to obtain the price of a monetary tool at a synthetic level. Second, it involves a series of contracts or orders to utilise fabricated devices or products. Third, it incorporates the sharing and dispersal of information that provides false or misleading signals.[127] Examples of conduct that amounts to market manipulation include providing false statements or transactions that could result in price of shares fluctuating.[128]

123 Financial Conduct Authority, 'Kenneth Carver fined £35,212 for insider dealing', 2015, available from http://www.fca.org.uk/news/kenneth-carver-fined-for-insider-dealing, accessed 18 November 2015.
124 Action Fraud, 'Market manipulation', (n/d), available from http://www.actionfraud.police.uk/fraud-az-market-manipulation, accessed 28 May 2012.
125 W. Carrol, 'Market manipulation, an international comparison' (2002) *Journal of Financial Crime*, 9(4), 300–307, at 300.
126 E. Lomnicka, 'Preventing and controlling the manipulation of financial markets, towards a definition of market manipulation' (2001) *Journal of Financial Crime*, 8(4), 297–304, at 297.
127 Financial Services Authority, 'Market Abuse Directive'', (n/d), available from http://www.fsa.gov.uk/pages/about/what/international/pdf/mad%20(pl).pdf, accessed 27 May 2012.
128 Action Fraud, 'Market manipulation', (n/d), available from http://www.actionfraud.police.uk/fraud-az-market-manipulation, accessed 28 May 2012.

It can also include 'disseminating misleading information which moves the price of investments up or down', or 'improper use of market power'.[129] Other instances of market manipulation include a process called 'share romping' as illustrated during the Guinness fraud in the 1980s.[130] Wright stated that:

> Market manipulation is a general term covering a number of practices deemed harmful to the capital markets. Conduct that can lead to a violation of the market manipulation provisions extends from active trading to merely spreading information about a particular security or company. Market manipulation comes in many forms, whose number is limited only by human ingenuity.[131]

Market manipulation poses a significant threat to global financial markets,[132] a point also emphasised by Lomnicka.[133] It has been argued that market manipulation 'destroys investor confidence, leads to a reduction of trading activity, and reduces the overall prosperity and revenue generated by market activity'.[134] Market manipulation was criminalised by the Financial Services Act 1986 which states that:

> [if a person] makes a statement, promise or forecast which he knows to be misleading, false or deceptive or dishonestly conceals any material facts; or recklessly makes (dishonestly or otherwise) a statement, promise or forecast which is misleading, false or deceptive, [he] is guilty of an offence if he makes the statement, promise or forecast or conceals the facts for the purpose of inducing, or is reckless as to whether it may induce, another person (whether or not the person to whom the statement, promise or forecast is made, or from whom the facts are concealed) to enter or offer to enter into or to refrain from entering or offering to enter into an investment agreement or to exercise, or refrain from exercising, any rights conferred by an investment.[135]

Furthermore, the Financial Services Act 1986 provides that:

> Any person who does any act or engages in any course of conduct which creates a false or misleading impression as to the market in or the price or

129 E. Lomnicka, 'Preventing and controlling the manipulation of financial markets, towards a definition of market manipulation' (2001) *Journal of Financial Crime*, 8(4), 297–304, at 298.
130 R. Wright, 'Market abuse and market manipulation, the criminal, civil and regulatory interface' (2001) *Journal of International Financial Markets*, 3(1), 19–25, at 19.
131 W. Carroll, 'Market manipulation, an international comparison' (2002) *Journal of Financial Crime*, 9(4), 300–307, at 300.
132 A. Alkhamees, 'Private action as a remedy against market manipulation in the USA' (2012) *Journal of Financial Regulation and Compliance*, 20(1), 41–55, at 41.
133 Lomnicka, 'Preventing and controlling the manipulation of financial markets, towards a definition of market manipulation' at 297.
134 E. Swan, 'Derivatives market manipulation by 'wash sales' in violation of the US Commodity Exchange Act' (1995) *Journal of Financial Crime*, 3(1), 53–56, at 53.
135 Financial Services Act 1986, s. 47(1).

value of any investments is guilty of an offence if he does so for the purpose of creating that impression and of thereby inducing another person to acquire, dispose of, subscribe for or underwrite those investments or to refrain from doing so or to exercise, or to refrain from exercising, any rights conferred by those investments.[136]

These provisions were largely incorporated into the Financial Services and Markets Act 2000, which grants the FSA the ability to initiative criminal prosecutions for market manipulation.[137] The 2000 Act provides that a person commits an offence if they '(a) make a statement, promise or forecast which he knows to be misleading, false or deceptive in a material particular; (b) dishonestly conceals any material facts whether in connection with a statement, promise or forecast made by him or otherwise; or (c) recklessly makes (dishonestly or otherwise) a statement, promise or forecast which is misleading, false or deceptive in a material particular'.[138] This section states that a person is guilty of an offence if,

> he makes the statement, promise or forecast or conceals the facts for the purpose of inducing, or is reckless as to whether it may induce, another person (whether or not the person to whom the statement, promise or forecast is made) (a) to enter or offer to enter into, or to refrain from entering or offering to enter into, a relevant agreement; or (b) to exercise, or refrain from exercising, any rights conferred by a relevant investment.[139]

In 2011 the European Commission published its draft Directive on the 'criminal sanctions for insider dealing and market manipulation'.[140] The Directive provides that Member States 'shall take the necessary measures to ensure that the following conduct constitutes a criminal offence, when committed intentionally:

(a) giving false or misleading signals as to the supply of, demand for, or price of, a financial instrument or a related spot commodity contract;
(b) securing the price of one or several financial instruments or a related spot commodity contract at an abnormal or artificial level;
(c) entering into a transaction, placing an order to trade, or any other activity in financial markets affecting the price of one or several financial instruments or a related spot commodity contract, which employs a fictitious device or any other form of deception or contrivance;
(d) dissemination of information which gives false or misleading signals as to financial instruments or related spot commodity contracts, where those persons

---

136 Financial Services Act 1986, s. 47(2).
137 Financial Services and Markets Act 2000, s. 397.
138 Financial Services and Markets Act 2000, s. 397(1).
139 Financial Services and Markets Act 2000, s, 397(2).
140 Brussels, 20.10.2011, COM(2011) 654 final, 2011/0297 (COD).

derive, for themselves or another person, an advantage or profit from the dissemination of the information in question.[141]

However, the Coalition government confirmed that it would not be opting into the European Directive to criminalise market manipulation, something that the current Conservative government has also now confirmed. The Financial Secretary to the Treasury stated that 'the Government has decided at this time not to opt in to the European Commission's proposal for a criminal sanctions directive on insider dealing and market manipulation, although hopes to be in a position to do so in the future'.[142] One of the main reasons for opting out of the proposal is that 'the UK already covers all of the offences in its criminal law and also goes further'.[143] It is interesting to note that the government has decided against incorporating the Directive to criminalise market manipulation because they believe market manipulation is already a criminal offence. However, since market manipulation is covered by the Market Abuse Regime, it is not strictly a criminal offence, which will be further explored in the next chapter.

TABLE 5.1 Recent insider dealing cases

Offence: Insider Dealing
Legislation: section 52 Criminal Justice Act 1993
Maximum Penalty: seven years imprisonment

Name	Date	Sentence	Brief Details
Julian Rifat	19.3.2015	one year seven months and fined £100,000	Pleaded guilty to insider dealing having passed on secret information to a fellow trader allowing him to make more than £250,000
Paul Gerard Coyle	3.3.2015	one year and a confiscation order of £203,234	Pleaded guilty to insider dealing worth £79,000. He was the head of tax at WM Morrison Supermarkets Plc and used confidential price-sensitive information to make a profit by trading in Ocado shares.
Richard Anthony Joseph	11.3.2013	four years	Found guilty of conspiracy to commit insider dealing. He paid for insider information and made a profit of more than £590,000.

(*Continued*)

---

141 *Ibid.*, Article 4.
142 HM Treasury, 'Criminal Sanctions Directive on market abuse written ministerial statement', 20 February 2012, available from http://www.hm-treasury.gov.uk/d/wms_fst_200212.pdf, accessed 1 June 2012.
143 *Ibid.*

TABLE 5.1 (Continued)

Name	Date	Sentence	Brief Details
Paul Milson	7.3.2013	two years and a confiscation order of £245,000	Pleaded guilty to passing confidential information onto an independent stockbroker.
Thomas Ammann	12.12.2012	two years eight months	Pleaded guilty to dealing and encouraging insider dealing. The judge said: 'Your actions had significant impact on public confidence in the integrity of the market at a time that the City is held in increasingly low esteem. . . . Your activities not only cast a cloud over the particular business that employed you but potentially affects the perception of mergers and acquisitions business within the city as a whole. An honest shareholder who tries to read the market is offended by someone like you who can put aside skill and research by relying on information you are barred from using.'[144]
Neten Shah	27.7.2012	one year six months	Found guilty of being part of a criminal gang who were trading on inside information making a profit of £732,044.59. Convicted with five others – Ali Mustafa, Pardip Saini, Paresh Shah, Bijal Shah and Truptest Patel.
James Ernest Swallow	20.6.2012	ten months	Pleaded guilty to insider dealing worth £1.9 million. Swallow also made his clients approximately £10.2 million. Convicted with two others – James Sanders (see below) and Miranda Sanders.
James Paul Sanders	20.6.2012	four years	Involved in the above and seen as the main participant.

Future recommendations

The UK has adopted a very tough legislative stance towards preventing insider dealing. Its policy has been heavily influenced by the provision of the Insider Dealing Directive and the eagerness of US authorities to criminalise insider dealing activities in Europe. Despite the laudable intentions of the early insider dealing legislative provisions, their ineffectiveness was illustrated by the small number of successful prosecutions brought during the 1980s. It was hoped that the civil enforcement provisions in the Financial Services Act 1986 would be effective weapons against insider dealing. However, these provisions were heavily underused by the SIB, which

---

144 http://www.thelawpages.com/court-cases/Thomas-Ammann-10544–1.law.

subsequently influenced the Labour government in 1997 to announce the creation of the FSA, which would become the new financial regulatory agency to tackle insider dealing. The criminalisation of insider dealing in the UK is largely seen as a failure as a result of the high burden of proof required in such difficult evidentiary cases. The attempt to address this perceived failure has come in the form of a civil regime enacted as part of FSMA 2000. The FSA and the FCA are now being more aggressive, particularly in respect of criminal prosecutions for insider dealing, which should allow it to claim success, at least in respect of market abuse; although it can still be argued that in terms of criminal sentences the length of custodial sentences imposed are generally low.

Further reading

M. Ashe, 'The directive on insider dealing' (1992) *Company Lawyer*, 13(1), 15–19, at 15.

P. Barnes, 'Insider dealing and market abuse: The UK's record on enforcement' (2011) *International Journal of Law, Crime and Justice*, 39, 174–189.

P. Barnes, *Stock Market Efficiency, Insider Dealing and Market Abuse* (Gower: Aldershot, 2009).

R. Cheung, 'Insider trading sentencing, an Anglo-American comparison' (2014) *Journal of Business Law*, 7, 564–584.

B. Dubow and N. Monteiro, *Measuring Market Cleanliness, FSA Occasional Paper* (Financial Services Authority: London, March, 2006).

M. Filby, 'The enforcement of insider dealing under the Financial Services and Markets Act 2000' (2003) *Company Lawyer*, 24(11), 334–341.

J. Gray, 'Financial Services Act 1986 reforms, Part 2' (1991) *International Banking Law*, 9(9), 412–416.

B. Hannigan, 'Regulating insider dealing – the EEC dimension' (1989) *Journal of International Banking Law*, 4(1), 11–14.

J. Hansen, 'The new proposal for a European Union directive on market abuse' (2002) *University of Pennsylvania Journal of International Economic Law*, 23, 241–268, at 250.

E. Lomnicka, 'The new insider dealing provisions, Criminal Justice Act 1993, Part V' (1994) *Journal of Business Law*, March, 173–188.

H. McVea, 'Fashioning a system of civil penalties for insider dealing, sections 61 and 62 of the Financial Services Act 1986' (1996) *Journal of Business Law*, July, 344–361, at 355.

H. McVea, 'Plans for compulsory insider dealing legislation by the EEC' (1987) *Company Lawyer*, 8(5), 223–224, at 223.

M. White, 'The implications for securities regulation of new insider dealing provisions in the Criminal Justice Act 1993' (1995) *Company Lawyer*, 16(6), 163–171, at 169.

6

MARKET ABUSE

Introduction

The term market abuse covers both the use of inside information and market manipulation. Conduct which can amount to market abuse therefore includes insider dealing, improper disclosure, market manipulation, behaviour giving rise to false and misleading impressions, misuse of information, and behaviour that is likely to give rise to market distortion.[1] Policy in the United Kingdom (UK) was largely managed by the Financial Service Authority (FSA), but, following the 2007–08 financial crisis, the FSA was replaced by the Financial Conduct Authority (FCA) by virtue of the Financial Services Act 2012. The policy is threefold: the market abuse regime, the enforcement powers of the FCA and the reporting of suspicious transactions. The primary focus of this chapter will therefore be to analyse these initiatives and will include an attempt to quantify the extent of the problem. The chapter will then consider background to the policy of criminalising and regulating market abuse with particular emphasis on the civil market abuse regime brought in by the Code of Market Conduct, plus an evaluation of the financial institutions and regulatory bodies involved. Finally, we look at the success of criminal and civil sentencing options and practices.

What are the civil and criminal offences of market abuse?

Market abuse is defined both in statute and in the European Union (EU) Market Abuse Directive (MAD).[2] Section 118 of the Financial Services and Markets Act

---

1 S. Sheikh, 'FSMA market abuse regime: A review of the sunset clauses International' (2008) *Company and Commercial Law Review*, 19(7), 234–236.

2 Directive 2003/6/EC of the European Parliament and of the Council of 28 January 2003 on insider dealing and market manipulation (market abuse). For a brief discussion on the Market Abuse Directive see M. McKee, 'The proposed E.U. Market Abuse Directive' (2001) *Journal of International*

(FSMA) 2000, defines the behaviour as including trading on the basis of inside information; disclosing inside information otherwise than in the proper course of employment; trading which gives misleading or false impressions; trading which uses deception or fictitious devices; the disclosing of information which leads to a misleading or false impression; and, behaviour that is likely to distort the market.[3] In short, as outlined in the introduction, the abuse is made up of insider dealing and market manipulation. In a similar vein, the MAD[4] also splits the behaviour into these two areas. Inside information is defined as 'information that is precise, non-public and likely to have a significant impact on the price of a financial instrument',[5] whilst market manipulation is said to be comprised of three forms:

- transactions and orders to trade that give false or misleading signals or secure the price of a financial instrument at an artificial level;
- transactions or orders to trade that employ fictitious devices; and
- distribution of information likely to give false or misleading signals.

Under such definitions market abuse is not a criminal offence, although offences do exist, both within the FSMA 2000 and the Financial Services Act 2012. Offences within the FSMA 2000 include misleading the FCA or the Prudential Regulation Authority (PRA)[6] and misleading the Competition and Markets Authority (CMA).[7] The FSMA 2000 also used to include an offence of misleading statements and practices,[8] but the offence was repealed on 1 April 2013 by the Financial Services Act 2012, which also creates three further offences: misleading statements,[9] misleading impressions[10] and misleading statements/impressions in relation to benchmarks.[11] On the basis that insider dealing has already been dealt with in Chapter 5, only market abuse will be discussed here.

Misleading the authorities

As outlined above, the FSMA 2000 contains two misleading offences. The first is in relation to any dealings with the FCA or PRA under the Act and is made out where a person who is required to comply with an obligation under the Act recklessly or knowingly 'gives a regulator information which is false or misleading in a material

---

Financial Markets, 3(4), 137–142 and G. Ferrarini, 'The European Market Abuse Directive' (2004) *Common Market Law Review*, 41(3), 711–741.

3 Financial Services and Markets Act 2000, s. 118.

4 'The Market Abuse Directive 2003/6/EC', available from http://www.fsa.gov.uk/pages/About/What/International/pdf/MAD.pdf, accessed 18 October 2011.

5 *Ibid.*

6 Financial Services and Markets Act 2000, s. 398.

7 Financial Services and Markets Act 2000, s. 399.

8 Financial Services and Markets Act 2000, s. 397.

9 Financial Services Act 2012, s. 89.

10 Financial Services Act 2012, s. 90.

11 Financial Services Act 2012, s. 91.

particular'.[12] This requirement to comply with an obligation can also be imposed under the Alternative Investment Fund Managers Regulations 2013, the short selling regulation and EU Regulations Nos. 345/2013, 346/2013 and 2015/760.[13] In many respects this is a loophole offence, in the sense that it includes all those situations where 'no other provision'[14] applies. The second misleading offence refers to any action which misleads the CMA, although rather than creating a new offence, in essence all section 399 of the Act does is to bring into the FSMA 2000, section 44 of the Competition Act 1998. This states that a person is guilty of an offence if they knowingly or recklessly provide the CMA with information which is either misleading or false.[15]

Misleading statements and impressions

The first of the three new offences under the Financial Service Act 2012 is found in section 89. This involves the situation where a person knowingly or recklessly makes a misleading statement or where they dishonestly conceal material facts when a statement is made,[16] with the intention to induce (or being reckless as to whether this may induce) another person to enter into market activity. This could be that the other person either enters into or does not enter into any agreement or exercises, or does not exercise 'any rights conferred by a relevant investment'.[17]

The second offence contained in section 90 relates to misleading impressions. Under this section an offence can be committed where a person intentionally creates a misleading impression as to the price or value of a relevant investment or as to the market in general, and the situation falls within either or both of subsections (2) and (3).[18] Section 90(2) covers the event where a person has intentionally created the misleading impression so as to induce another person into market activity. This can include acquiring, disposing of, subscribing for or underwriting investments or refraining from undertaking these activities or exercising or refraining from exercising rights conferred by the investments.[19] Section 90(3) is relevant where the person knowingly or recklessly makes a false or misleading impression and through creating this impression intends to either make a gain (for themselves or for another person) or cause loss to another person.[20] The offence can also be committed where the person doesn't necessarily intend the aforementioned results, but is aware that by

---

12 Financial Services and Markets Act 2000, s. 398(1).
13 Financial Services and Markets Act 2000, s. 398(1A).
14 Financial Services and Markets Act 2000, s. 398(2). For a more detailed discussion see A. Haynes, 'Market abuse, fraud and misleading communications' (2012) *Journal of Financial Crime*, 19(3), 234–254.
15 Competition Act 1998, s. 44(1).
16 Financial Services Act 2012, s. 89(1)(a)–(c).
17 Financial Services Act 2012, s. 89(2)(a) and (b).
18 Financial Services Act 2012, s. 90(1).
19 Financial Services Act 2012, s. 90(2).
20 Financial Services Act 2012, s. 90(4).

creating the false or misleading impression it is likely that such results will occur.[21] For the purposes of this offence, gain can include 'getting what one does not have'[22] in addition to 'keeping what one [does] have'.[23] Likewise, loss includes 'parting with what one has'[24] in addition to 'not getting what one might get'.[25]

The final offence is legislated for under section 91. This relates to the creation of a false or misleading impression or the making of a false or misleading statement in connection with the setting of a specified benchmark. In terms of a false or misleading statement, an offence is made out where a person makes such a statement in the course of setting a benchmark, they intend that the statement is used for that purpose, and know or are reckless to the fact that the statement is false or misleading.[26] For false and/or misleading impressions, a person commits a criminal offence where they intend to create the impression, knowing or being reckless as to the fact that it is false or misleading, knowing that impression may affect the setting of a benchmark, and the person is aware that the impression may affect the setting of that benchmark.[27] A benchmark in this context is defined under section 93 of the Act as 'a benchmark of a kind specified in an order made by the Treasury'.[28] Definitions relevant to other phrases used within these three offences can also be found in section 93. In relation to the offence found under section 91, some academics have suggested that its creation was a 'direct result of the [Wheatley] Review's recommendations in respect of LIBOR [London Interbank Offered Rate] and addresses the fact that it was not open to the FSA to bring criminal prosecutions against individuals who were involved in the manipulation of LIBOR'.[29] It is interesting to note that in early 2016, the LIBOR-related prosecutions have *not* used any of these criminal offences, but have rather concentrated on the common law offence of conspiracy to defraud.[30]

For all market abuse offences, irrelevant of where they are defined, the activity must occur within the UK. For the purposes of market manipulation under section 118 of the FSMA 2000, it must be in relation to qualifying investments which are either 'admitted to trading on a prescribed market'[31] operating in the UK or 'which a request for admission to trading on such a prescribed market has been made'.[32]

---

21 Financial Services Act 2012, s. 90(3).
22 Financial Services Act 2012, s. 90(7).
23 Financial Services Act 2012, s. 90(7).
24 Financial Services Act 2012, s. 90(8).
25 Financial Services Act 2012, s. 90(8).
26 Financial Services Act 2012, s. 91(1).
27 Financial Services Act 2012, s. 91(2).
28 Financial Services Act 2012, s. 93(4).
29 V. Callaghan and Z. Ullah, 'The LIBOR scandal – the UK's legislative response' (2013) *Journal of International Banking Law and Regulation*, 28(4), 160–165, at 163. Also see M. Sandler, M. Brown, P. Willis and E. Clay, 'Market abuse' (2014) *Compliance Officer Bulletin*, 118(Aug), 1–37.
30 See for example the successful prosecution of Tom Hayes for the manipulation of LIBOR: *R v Hayes (Tom Alexander)* [2015] EWCA Crim 1944, Southwark Crown Court, 3 August 2015.
31 Financial Services and Markets Act 2000, s. 118A(1)(b)(i).
32 Financial Services and Markets Act 2000, s. 118A(1)(b)(ii).

For these purposes, investments that are 'related investments' in such a prescribed market will also fall under such behaviour.[33] In this context, behaviour is defined as 'action or inaction'[34] and so includes the situation where either the trader should have alerted the market to a problem and neglected to do so, or created a reasonable expectation that they would act in a particular way and again failed to do so. In relation to the criminal offences under the Financial Services Act 2012, the person making the statement or creating the impression must be within the UK and either the person who is induced must also be within the UK or the intended agreement would have been exercised within the UK.[35]

Defences

Defences for market abuse in the main rely on the suspected market manipulator proving a number of elements. First they must show that they believed that they were not engaging in market abuse and that this belief was objectively reasonable, for which there must be sufficient evidence. The next stage is to convince the FCA that they took all reasonable precautions and exercised all due diligence in performing the transactions in question. Because of the fact that the test is *all* reasonable precautions and *all* due diligence, this sets a fairly high standard and *any* lack of care may be sufficient grounds for the FCA to disallow the defence. A defence can also be relied upon if it can be proven that the disclosure in question was protected. A protected disclosure must satisfy three conditions and if proven will 'not be taken to breach any restriction on the disclosure of information',[36] misleading or otherwise. The first condition is where the discloser knows or suspects 'that another person has engaged in market abuse';[37] the information in question came to the discloser in the course of their profession, employment, trade or profession;[38] and, the disclosure is made to either the FCA or to a nominated officer as soon as practicable after the information came to light.[39]

Defences also exist under the Financial Services Act 2012. For the offence of misleading statements, it is a defence if a person can show that the statement was made in conformity with control of information rules, price stabilising rule or 'the relevant provisions of Commission Regulation (EC) No 2273/2003 of 22 December 2003 implementing Directive 2003/6/EC of the European Parliament and of the Council as regards exemptions for buy-back programmes and stabilisation of financial instruments'.[40] Section 93 confirms that the definitions for both price stabilising and control of information rules are that which are found in the FSMA

---

33 Financial Services and Markets Act 2000, s. 118A(1)(b)(iii).
34 Financial Services and Markets Act 2000, s. 130A(3).
35 Financial Services Act 2012, ss. 89(4) and 90(10).
36 Financial Services and Markets Act 2000, s. 131A(1).
37 Financial Services and Markets Act 2000, s. 131A(2).
38 Financial Services and Markets Act 2000, s. 131A(3).
39 Financial Services and Markets Act 2000, s. 131A(4).
40 Financial Services Act 2012, s. 89(3).

2000.[41] Price-stabilising rules relate to provisions put in place by the FCA which grant a defence or 'safe harbour'[42] against market manipulation, whilst control of information rules are those which are put in place by either the FCA or the PRA and which relate to the 'disclosure and use of information held by an authorised person'.[43] These three defences are also available for the offences criminalised under sections 90 and 91 of the Financial Services Act 2012. The only additional alternative available for misleading impressions, under section 90, is where the abuser is able to show that they reasonably believed that their conduct would not create a false or misleading impression that would result in market abuse activity.[44]

The civil market abuse regime

As stated above, market abuse under section 118 of the FSMA 2000 and the MAD is not a criminal offence. Rather, a civil market abuse regime has been developed under these instruments. This is largely to bypass the high burden of evidential proof that is needed in a criminal case, which arguably in the past has led to a small numbers of prosecutions. The government's answer to the problem of the lack of convictions for insider dealing was to 'fill the regulatory gap'.[45] The approach to tackling such abuse is therefore the Market Abuse Regime, which arguably reflects that the focus was not merely on insider dealing but the whole ambit of activities that could affect the probity of the financial market. Indeed, one of the key aims of the Market Abuse regime is to give the FCA maximum flexibility in its task by requiring a lower standard of proof than needed to secure a criminal conviction.[46] Additionally, unlike the criminal provisions of the Criminal Justice Act 1993 for insider dealing, the market abuse regime does not require the prosecuting authority to show intent on the part of the market participant,[47] a cause for initial concern explained by the government on the basis that the market abuse regime was not primarily about catching errant individuals but about providing clean and efficient financial markets.[48] As Swan notes, this leads to the potential of market abuse being committed by 'mistake' and therefore it is clearly possible that the offence can be

---

41 Financial Services and Markets Act 2000, ss. 137P and 137Q.

42 'Financial Conduct Authority Handbook Mar 2.1.4', available from https://www.handbook.fca.org.uk/handbook/MAR/2/1.html, accessed 21 January 2015.

43 Financial Services and Markets Act 2000, s. 137P.

44 Financial Services Act 2012, s. 90(9)(a).

45 See M. Filby, 'Part VIII Financial Services and Markets Act: Filling insider dealing's regulatory gaps' (2004) *Company Lawyer*, 23(12), 363–370. However, it is important to report that there has been a decrease in the number of convictions obtained by the regulators for insider dealing since the 2007–08 financial crisis. See J. Titcomb, 'Insider trading has plummeted since the financial crisis: Here's why', 11 July 2014, available from http://www.telegraph.co.uk/finance/financial-crime/10960400/Insider-trading-has-plummeted-since-the-financial-crisis.-Heres-why.html, accessed 13 January 2016.

46 E. Swan, 'Market abuse: A new duty of fairness' (2004) *Company Lawyer*, 25(3), 67–68.

47 MAR1.2.6G.

48 A. Alcock, 'Market abuse-the new witchcraft' (2001) *New Law Journal*, 151, 1398.

committed negligently,[49] although in a response to the Joint Committee on Financial Services and Markets the FSA did note that they did not 'propose to prosecute people for accidental offences'.[50] This lack of intent requirement has now been confirmed by the Court of Appeal.[51]

The concept of a civil regime in the UK itself is not new and was a hotly debated topic during the passage of the Criminal Justice Act 1993, but was obviously felt to be a step too far at that time.[52] However, the obvious lack of success of the criminal provision within the Criminal Justice Act 1993 put civil enforcement squarely back on the agenda. The overall aim of the FSMA 2000 was therefore to provide a comprehensive regulatory structure to oversee all financial services operations. To enable this to happen, it gives considerable power to the FCA to make rules in pursuit of its statutory objectives. The five objectives are maintaining market confidence,[53] ensuring financial stability,[54] promoting public awareness,[55] protecting consumers[56] and reducing financial crime.[57] Arguably, tackling market abuse covers three of the stated objectives, and if used innovatively can also help to promote public awareness. Therefore it is important not to read it in isolation, but to also include reference to the wider role of the FCA in keeping markets clean and efficient for investor confidence to blossom. This additionally protects individual consumers against mis-selling and reduces the incidence of financial crime, in particular that of fraud on investors.[58]

Under the civil regime the FCA is required to publish a code of conduct outlining what the FCA's responsibilities are in respect of guarding against market abuse.[59] The Code of Market Conduct (hereafter known as 'the Code') of the FCA Handbook is 'central'[60] to the operation of the Market Abuse Regime, described by others as the 'backbone' of the regime.[61] The original version only stated what

---

49 E. Swan, 'Market abuse: A new duty of fairness' (2004) *Company Lawyer*, 25(3), 67–68.
50 Joint Committee on Financial Services and Markets, 'First Report, para 265', available from http://www.publications.parliament.uk/pa/jt199899/jtselect/jtfinser/328/32809.htm, accessed 8 July 2010.
51 *Winterflood Securities Ltd and others v Financial Services Authority* [2010] EWCA Civ 423; [2010] WLR (D) 101.
52 See Ed., 'Insiders beware!' (1993) *Company Lawyer*, 14(11), 202.
53 Financial Services and Markets Act 2000, s. 3.
54 Financial Services and Markets Act 2000, s. 3A. This section was inserted by the Financial Services Act 2010 in response to the global financial crisis.
55 Financial Services and Markets Act 2000, s. 4.
56 Financial Services and Markets Act 2000, s. 5.
57 Financial Services and Markets Act 2000, s. 6.
58 Note that during the preparation of this amended chapter the Conservative government has implemented a series of major reforms to bank and financial services regulation. These have been implemented by the Financial Services Act 2012.
59 Financial Services and Markets Act 2000, s. 119.
60 L. Linklater, 'The market abuse regime: Setting standards in the twenty-first century' (2001) *Company Lawyer*, 22(9), 267–272, at 269.
61 D. Sabalot and R. Everett, *Financial Services and Markets Act 2000* (Butterworths New Law Guide LexisNexis: London, 2004, 270).

behaviour did *not* amount to market abuse.[62] However later versions have included examples of what does amount to market abuse, thus giving clear guidelines to market participants of the types of behaviour to avoid. The Code is thus designed to provide assistance and guidance in ascertaining whether certain behaviour amounts to market abuse. Despite this design the Code is nevertheless quick to point out that it is not an exhaustive description of all types of behaviour amounting to market abuse, nor is it an exhaustive description of all factors to be taken into account in the determination of whether or not behaviour is to be regarded as market abuse. The Code also contains two so-called safe harbours, outlining behaviour that will not amount to market abuse, these being share buy-back schemes and price-stabilisation programmes associated with new issues.[63] Whilst the Code plays a central role in controlling market abuse, reference must also be made to the Handbook generally, in particular the High-Level Standards such as Principles of Business, and Senior Management Arrangement, Systems and Controls, and the specific Handbooks such as Supervision, Decision Procedures and Penalties Manual, Disclosure Rules and Transparency Rules and the Listing Rules.

The fundamental question is therefore what actually amounts to behaviour that would be regarded as market abuse under this civil regime. In determining this it is necessary to look at both the FSMA 2000 and the Code. A brief description of what is covered in section 118 FSMA 2000 has already been outlined above, but here we will offer a little more detail. Perhaps unsurprisingly, the first of the seven listed behaviours is the offence of insider dealing,[64] which requires an insider to deal, or try to deal on the basis of inside information. The second form of behaviour caught by the regime is where 'an insider discloses inside information to another person otherwise than in the proper course of the exercise of his employment, profession or duties'.[65] The third behaviour that was outlined in the first edition of this book was abolished in 2014 and the fourth type of conduct concerns trades or transactions that '(a) give, or are likely to give, a false or misleading impression as to the supply of, or demand for, or as to the price of, one or more qualifying investments, or (b) secure the price of one or more such investments at an abnormal or artificial level'.[66] The fifth behaviour covered by section 118 'consists of effecting transactions or orders to trade which employ fictitious devices or any other form of deception or contrivance';[67] the sixth 'behaviour consists of the dissemination of information by any means which gives, or is likely to give, a false or misleading impression as to a qualifying investment by a person who knew or could reasonably be expected to have known that the information was false or misleading'[68] and the

---

62 These are termed 'safe harbours' in which the activity is not subject to the prohibition.
63 MAR 1.10 and Annex 1.
64 Financial Services and Markets Act 2000, s. 118(2).
65 Financial Services and Markets Act 2000, s. 118(3).
66 Financial Services and Markets Act 2000, s. 118(5).
67 Financial Services and Markets Act 2000, s. 118(6).
68 Financial Services and Markets Act 2000, s. 118(7).

seventh behaviour is that it is '(a) is likely to give a regular user of the market a false or misleading impression as to the supply of, demand for or price or value of, qualifying investments, or (b) would be, or would be likely to be, regarded by a regular user of the market as behaviour that would distort, or would be likely to distort, the market in such an investment'.[69]

With reference to insider dealing and similar to criminal provisions, to be caught by the civil regime the information must be 'inside information' and be held by an 'insider'.[70] Simply having inside information is not of itself sufficient. One clear improvement as a result of the MAD is that issuers of securities are now required to produce insider lists of people with access to 'inside information'.[71] What constitutes an insider is considered in Chapter 5. The Code provides additional information on what an insider would look like,[72] and lays out a set of criteria where if a person, such as a senior manager in an organisation that is the target of takeover, is in possession of inside information, then they will be classified as being an insider for the purpose of the market abuse provisions. It is quite transparent that the definition of insider primarily relates to a person in possession of inside information, and therefore it is arguable that the definition of inside information is key to being able to bring about a successful action for market abuse against that insider. What amounts to inside information is thus contained in section 118C(2) and (3) of the FSMA 2000 (see Chapter 5) with guidance again provided in the Code.[73] Information is precise under section 118C(5) of the FSMA if it indicates circumstances that exist or may reasonably be expected to come into existence or an event that has occurred or may reasonably be expected to occur,[74] and is specific enough to enable a conclusion to be drawn as to the possible effect of those circumstances or that event on the price of qualifying investments or related investments.[75] This is not a particularly well-defined section and could conceivably lead to some debate. The question remains of how precise or how specific the inside information needs to be. If too specific then the FCA will struggle to bring successful enforcement actions. It is submitted that this is the correct approach in that the requirement for inside information should not be overly restricted by a requirement of too great a specificity. Many issues have an impact on the price of securities and such a broad approach is thus to be welcomed.[76]

In addition to the need to be precise, the information needs to be 'likely to have a significant effect on the price of those qualifying investments or related

---

69 Financial Services and Markets Act 2000, s. 118(8).
70 For a more detailed discussion of the Market Abuse Directive and insider dealing see Chapter 5.
71 See now DTR 2.8 FSA Handbook.
72 MAR 1.2.7, 1.2.8E and 1.2.9G.
73 MAR 1.2.10.
74 Financial Services and Markets Act 2000, s. 118(C)(5)(a).
75 Financial Services and Markets Act 2000, s. 118(C)(5)(b).
76 For a look at Finnish case law on the issue of what is precise see J. Hayrynen, 'The precise definition of inside information?' (2008) *Journal of International Banking Law and Regulation*, 23(2), 64–70.

investments'.[77] In similar fashion to the older criminal provisions this requirement leads to the conclusion that for the prohibition to apply, the action on the part of the person accused of market abuse must be more than trivial, as minor movements in the prices of qualifying investments will not amount to market abuse. Exactly what will amount is a matter for the FCA to determine, and a trawl through the authorities' enforcement actions list will give some idea as to what 'significant' will mean in practice.[78] Thus, the FCA will consider what the reasonable investor would be likely to do. For example, the more significant the price movement gained from the inside information, the more likely that the FCA will see it as significant within the meaning of the provision.[79]

A further key issue is whether or not the information has been made public. Information is only inside information if it 'is not generally available',[80] and once it is regarded as generally available it ceases to be information for the purposes of market abuse. Helpfully, both section 118C(8) of the FSMA 2000 and the Code provide assistance and examples to determine whether or not information is to be regarded as generally available.[81] The example given in the Code is of a passenger on a train who sees a burning factory during his journey. If he calls his broker and tells him to sell shares in that company, this will not amount to market abuse as the information will be deemed to have been generally available.[82] Information is however available in many forms today and so it can be a difficult question as to whether information is no longer to be regarded as inside information or whether it is generally available, with this being a matter of evidence. What does come through however is that the professional and talented market analyst and broker are protected against accusations of market misconduct, providing of course that the source of their information is not regarded as inside information. The broker's professional and thorough analysis of the broker will not fall foul of the regime, even if the information is paid for and if the information is not generally available to the market as a whole, unless of course they have done the same research. One of the new and innovative features required by the MAD is the introduction of more proactive measures to prevent market abuse. In this the MAD requires a system of suspicious transaction reporting,[83] and whilst not a new phenomenon by any means to the financial sector, in respect of money laundering it was new requirement for suspected market abuse.[84]

---

77 Financial Services and Markets Act 2000, s. 118C(6).
78 See Financial Services Authority, 'Enforcement Notices, Financial Services Authority', n/d, available from. http://www.fsa.gov.uk/pages/About/What/financial_crime/market_abuse/library/notices/index.shtml, accessed 1 July 2010.
79 W. Hudson, *The Law of Finance* (Oxford University Press: Oxford, 2009, 284).
80 Financial Services and Markets Act 2000, s. 118C(2)(a), 118C(3)(a) and 118C(4)(b).
81 MAR1.2.12E and see chapter 5.
82 MAR1.2.14G.
83 Article 6.9 MAD.
84 Detailed suspicious transaction reporting requirements a contained in the Supervision Handbook SUP at SUP 15.10.

The new market abuse regime has been described as 'novel',[85] 'controversial'[86] and the 'new witchcraft'.[87] These comments arguably stem from the civil enforcement mechanisms contained within the provisions. The new regime is designed to complement the criminal provisions of the Criminal Justice Act 1993 by running parallel and in addition to them rather than replacing and substituting them.[88] The original UK regime came into force in 2001 but was soon subject to a major revision by virtue of the MAD, which, as discussed above, aimed to set a minimum standard across EU markets.[89] The MAD was the first of the provisions to be brought through using the Lamfalussy process[90] designed to speed up the implementation of provisions forming part of the EUs Financial Services Action Plan. The process was designed to bring a level of uniformity to the EU approach to tackling market misuse, which had reported that the existing regulatory regime was slow and rigid and unevenly implemented.[91] The UK Market Abuse Regime, incorporating the Directive, has been in force since 1 July 2005.[92]

Market abuse regulation

A series of important amendments as to how market abuse is regulated in the UK are due to take place. For example, the Market Abuse Regulation (MAR) will apply in the UK from 3 July 2016.[93] It has been suggested by the FCA that the objective of MAR is to 'increase market integrity and investor protection, while ensuring a single rulebook and level playing field across the EU; [while] increasing the attractiveness of securities markets for capital raising'.[94] The scope of the MAR is extensive and applies to:

a. Financial instruments admitted to trading on a regulated market or for which a request for admission to trading on a regulated market has been made,

---

85 L. Linklater. 'The market abuse regime: setting standards in the twenty-first century' (2001) *Company Lawyer*, 22(9), 267–272.

86 A. Alcock, 'Market abuse' (2002) *Company Lawyer*, 23(5) 142–150, at 143.

87 Alcock, A. 'Market abuse-the new witchcraft' (2001) *New Law Journal*, 151, 1398.

88 A. Sykes, 'Market abuse: A civil revolution' (1999) *Journal of International Financial Markets*, 1(2), 59–67.

89 2003/6/EC.

90 The Lamfalussy Process is a method towards the expansion of and development of EU regulations that apply to the financial services sector. For a more detailed discussion see J. Coffey and J. Overett Somnier, 'The Market Abuse Directive – the first use of the Lamfalussy process' (2003) *Journal of International Banking Law and Regulation*, 18(9), 370 and D. Vitkova, 'Level 3 of the Lamfalussy process: An effective tool for achieving pan-European regulatory consistency?' (2008) *Law & Financial Markets Review*, 2(2), 158.

91 J. Hansen, 'MAD in a hurry: The swift and promising adoption of the EU Market Abuse Directive' (2007) *European Business Law Review*, 15(2), 183–221.

92 Amendments made to FSMA 2000 by the Financial Services and Markets Act 2000 (Market Abuse) Regulations 2005, S.I. 2005/381.

93 Financial Conduct Authority, 'Market Abuse Regulation (MAR)', 6 May 2015, available from http://www.fca.org.uk/firms/markets/market-abuse/mar, accessed 1 January 2016.

94 *Ibid.*

b.   Financial instruments traded on a multilateral trading facility,
c.   Financial instruments traded on an organised trading facility and financial instruments not covered by point (a), (b) or (c).[95]

The MAR also contains several important requirements that include inside information and disclosure, insider dealing and unlawful disclosure, market manipulation, market soundings, buy-back programmes and stabilisation measures, accepted market practices, insider lists, suspicious transaction and order reports, managers' transactions, investment recommendations and whistle-blowing.[96]

The extent of market abuse

The extent of market abuse, like the other types of financial crime addressed throughout this book, is extremely difficult to determine. Efforts to accurately determine its level are flawed with methodological difficulties. However, several attempts have been made to measure the extent of market abuse in the UK. For example, in 2006 the FSA published its 'measure for the scale of market abuse'.[97] Whilst it was unable to illustrate the exact level of market abuse, it did 'suggest that some informed trading may have taken place prior to 28.9% of the takeover announcements and 21.7% of the FTSE350 trading announcements which were identified as being most likely to contain information of use to an insider trader'.[98] The informed trading, according to the FSA, could therefore amount to instances of market abuse. In 2007 the FSA published an update on its 2006 report.[99] The 2007 report indicated that there was a 'significant decrease in the level of possible informed trading ahead of FTSE 350 companies' trading announcements, with only 2% of significant announcements being preceded by informed price movements compared to 11.1% in the period 2002/03 and 19.6% in 1998–2000'.[100] Furthermore, in its 2010 Annual Report the FSA stated that the abnormal pre-announcement price movement's data set declined to the lowest figure since 2003.[101] However, the FSA admitted that 'this fall has taken place against the backdrop of increasing focus on market abuse, due to the nature of the statistic, the reason behind this decline cannot be determined with

---

95   *Ibid.*
96   *Ibid.*
97   FSA, 'FSA publishes measure of scale of market abuse', 17 March 2006, available from http://www.fsa.gov.uk/pages/Library/Communication/PR/2006/020.shtml, accessed 10 November 2011.
98   Financial Services Authority, *Measuring market cleanliness FSA Occasional Paper Series 23* (Financial Services Authority: London, 2006, 24).
99   Financial Services Authority, *Updated measurement of market cleanliness FSA Occasional Paper Series 25* (Financial Services Authority: London, 2007).
100 Financial Services Authority, 'FSA publishes updated measure of UK market cleanliness', 7 March 2007, available from http://www.fsa.gov.uk/library/communication/pr/2007/031.shtmlm, accessed 9 December 2011. Also see A. Hayes, 'Market abuse' (2010) *Compliance Officer Bulletin*, 75(Apr), 1–31.
101 Financial Services Authority, *Annual Report 2010/2011* (Financial Services Authority: London, 2011, 62).

certainty'.[102] Nonetheless, Hector Sants, the former Chief Executive of the FSA, stated that the levels of market abuse were still at an 'unacceptably high level'.[103] He added:

> There's no evidence that the UK marketplace is worse than other major financial centres but I don't think that should be our benchmark. Our benchmark should seek to have a market that participants really believe to be clean and fair and, as a general test, I think that if you were to ask the market participants, they would share my view that there is too much market abuse.[104]

Financial institutions and regulatory bodies

The civil market abuse regime is primarily enforced by the FCA as a result of its statutory objective to reduce financial crime under the FSMA 2000. Under this Act the FCA has been given an extensive array of enforcement powers to ensure that firms comply with the regime and it imposes sanctions for those firms that breach that regime. Therefore it is arguable that the primary function of the market abuse regime is to punish market abusers, and to that end Part VIII FSMA 2000 is actually entitled 'Penalties for Market Abuse'. Whilst this was the position of the original intention of the Act, this has been emphasised by the MAD, which requires Member States' regulatory authorities to attempt to prevent market abuse occurring. As outlined above, this can be shown by the Code and the many examples within the Code of what amounts to market abuse and who commits it. Therefore, market participants should be able to ascertain when they are coming dangerously close to committing the prohibited activities contained in Part VIII of the FSMA 2000 and the offences contained with the Financial Services Act 2012. Despite this help the market abuse regime still plays a vital role in bringing market abusers to account and in support of this aim the FCA has considerable power, as discussed below, to undertake investigations into alleged market abusers and issue financial penalties.

Reporting of suspicious transactions

The final part of UK policy towards market abuse is the reporting of suspicious transactions through the use of suspicious transactions reports.[105] However, it is very important to note that the use of and reporting of suspicious transactions in the market abuse regime are different from those managed by the Terrorism Act 2000

---

102 *Ibid.*

103 BBC News, 'UK market abuse unacceptably high' (*Says FSA Boss* Sunday 14 March 2010), available from http://news.bbc.co.uk/1/hi/8566904.stm, accessed 20 October 2011.

104 Andrew Cave, 'Market abuse is unacceptably high' (13 March 2011) 2010, available from http://www.telegraph.co.uk/finance/newsbysector/banksandfinance/7436104/Market-abuse-is-unacceptably-high-says-FSA-boss.html, accessed 14 December 2011.

105 For a brief commentary see E. Herlin-Karnell, 'White-collar crime and European financial crises: Getting tough on EU market abuse' (2012) *European Law Review*, 37(4), 481–494, at 489.

and the Proceeds of Crime Act 2002. The obligation to report suspected dealings of market abuse exists as a result of the MAD, which was implemented in the UK on 1 July 2005.[106] The reporting obligations apply to firms that:

> arrange or execute transactions for clients in qualifying investments (as defined in the Financial Services and Markets Act 2000 (Prescribed Markets and Qualifying Investments) Order 2001); are admitted to trading on a prescribed market; and which have reasonable grounds to suspect that the transaction might constitute market abuse.[107]

In determining whether or not to report the transaction, the firm or individual must have reasonable grounds of suspicion, which is the same test utilised by the Proceeds of Crime Act 2002. Furthermore, the FCA has its own rules for the reporting of suspicious transactions and they provide that:

> a firm which arranges or executes a transaction with or for a client in a qualifying investment admitted to trading on a prescribed market and which has reasonable grounds to suspect that the transaction might constitute market abuse must notify the FCA without delay.[108]

Hayes recommended that 'all staff that are likely to encounter suspicious transactions (and therefore expose the firm to the requirements to submit STRs [suspicious transaction reports]) should be made aware of these obligations'.[109] If a firm or individual does not file a suspicious transaction report the FCA has the power to impose a financial penalty. For example, in 2009 the FSA fined Mark Lockwood £20,000 for failing to 'identify and act on a suspicious client order that allowed the firm to be used to facilitate insider dealing. As a result of his failings the firm failed to identify the trade as suspicious and report it to the FSA.'[110] The FSA stated:

> This fine emphasises the importance of the Suspicious Transaction Reporting [STR] regime. Tackling market abuse and insider dealing is not just an issue for the regulator. Broking firms are the front line of defence against people who seek to misuse and profit from their possession of privileged information. STRs are a key tool for the FSA in detecting market abuse. Lockwood's

---

106 A. Hayes, 'Market abuse' (2010) *Compliance Officer Bulleting*, 75(Apr), 1–31, at 30.
107 *Ibid.*
108 Financial Services Authority, *FSA Handbook – SUP (Supervision)* (Financial Services Authority: London, 2008) at SUP 15.10.2.
109 A. Hayes, 'Market abuse' (2010) *Compliance Officer Bulleting*, 75(Apr), 1–31, at 30.
110 Financial Services Authority, 'FSA fines broker for failing to prevent insider dealing', 2 September 2009, available from http://www.fsa.gov.uk/library/communication/pr/2009/115.shtml, accessed 14 January 2016. For a summary of this see Travers Smith Regulatory Investigations Group, 'FSA enforcement action: Themes and trends' (2010) *Compliance Officer Bulletin*, 76(May), 1–32 and R. Peat and S. Bazley, 'Enforcement briefing' (2009) *Company Lawyer*, 30(12), 380–381.

failure could have meant that this incident went undetected and unpunished. Approved persons should be in no doubt as to their responsibilities in this area and the FSA will not hesitate to take action where they fall down on these.[111]

As previously outlined, the FSA was replaced by the FCA following the enactment of the Financial Services Act 2012. Therefore it is necessary to outline the FCA's policy towards reporting allegations of market abuse. The FCA has stated that:

> Firms arranging or executing transactions in certain financial instruments are required to report suspicious transactions to the FCA without delay. A suspicious transaction is one in which there are *reasonable grounds* to suspect it might constitute market abuse, such as insider dealing or market manipulation.[112]

As outlined in Chapter 2, the interpretation of the term suspicion has caused significant problems to reporting entities and in order to assist authorised firms the FCA has provided several examples of conduct that could amount to market abuse. The following examples provided by the FCA are merely indicative of what could amount to a suspicious transaction:

- A client opens an account and immediately gives an order to conduct a significant transaction or, in the case of a wholesale client, an unexpectedly large or unusual order, in a particular security – especially if the client is insistent that the order is carried out very urgently or must be conducted before a particular time specified by the client,
- A transaction is significantly out of line with the client's previous investment behaviour (e.g. type of security; amount invested; size of order; time security held),
- A client specifically requests immediate execution of an order regardless of the price at which the order would be executed (assuming more than a mere placing of 'at market' order by the client),
- There is unusual trading in the shares of a company before the announcement of price-sensitive information relating to the company,
- An employee's own account transaction is timed just before clients' transactions and related orders in the same financial instrument,
- An order will, because of its size in relation to the market in that security, clearly have a significant impact on the supply of or demand for or the price

---

111 Financial Services Authority, 'FSA fines broker for failing to prevent insider dealing', 2 September 2009, available from http://www.fsa.gov.uk/library/communication/pr/2009/115.shtml, accessed 14 January 2016.
112 Financial Conduct Authority, 'Obligation to report suspicious transactions', 17 March 2015, available from http://www.fca.org.uk/firms/markets/market-abuse/suspicious-transaction-reporting, accessed 14 January 2016.

or value of the security, especially an order of this kind to be executed near to a reference point during the trading day – e.g. near the close,

- A transaction appears to be seeking to modify the valuation of a position while not decreasing/increasing the size of that position, and
- A transaction appears to be seeking to bypass the trading safeguards of the market (e.g. as regards volume limits; bid/offer spread parameters; etc.).[113]

What will happen if such reports are not made is discussed below.

Sentencing and recovery

A person found guilty of any of the new criminal offences under the Financial Service Act 2012 is liable to a term of imprisonment not exceeding seven years, an unlimited fine or both.[114] For misleading the FCA or PRA the maximum penalty is a fine,[115] whilst for misleading the CMA the maximum penalty is increased to a term of custody not exceeding two years and/or a financial penalty.[116] Even though market abuse is defined as a criminal offence under the FSMA 2000, as detailed above the majority of market abusers are dealt with using financial penalties under the civil market abuse regime rather than through a criminal route. These enforcement powers are contained in Part XI of the FSMA 2000 and allow the investigating authorities to appoint professionals to undertake 'general'[117] or 'particular'[118] investigations. For the purpose of this part of the Act, 'investigating authorities' refers to the FCA, the PRA and in some limited circumstances the Secretary of State.[119] Investigations into particular cases include instances of suspected insider dealing[120] and market abuse.[121] To bring a disciplinary action the FCA must be satisfied that a person has either engaged in market abuse[122] or has encouraged or required another person to undertake behaviour which, if they had engaged in such action, would amount to market abuse.[123] The outcome of such investigations is sent to the Regulatory Decisions Committee, an administrative decision maker, to decide whether or not to bring disciplinary actions against an individual.

---

113 FCA Handbook, *Supervision: SUP 15 Ann 5 Indications of Possible Suspicious Transactions* (Financial Conduct Authority, London, 2015).
114 Financial Services Act 2012, s. 92.
115 Financial Services and Markets Act 2000, s. 398(3).
116 Competition Act 1998, s. 44(3).
117 Financial Services and Markets Act 2000, s. 167.
118 Financial Services and Markets Act 2000, s.168.
119 Financial Services and Markets Act 2000, s. 168(6).
120 Financial Services and Markets Act 2000, s. 168(2)(a).
121 Financial Services and Markets Act 2000, s. 168(2)(d).
122 Financial Services and Markets Act 2000, s. 123(1)(a).
123 Financial Services and Markets Act 2000, s. 123(1)(b).

Before a fine can be imposed the FCA must prepare and issue a statement of its intention to fine, which is known as a statement of policy.[124] Before this is issued a draft version is published and the public are invited to make representations.[125] Such statements will be taken into account when setting the level of fine. When the level has been decided upon the FCA must then issue a warning notice which will state the amount involved.[126] It is at this point that the named individual or company will be able to argue any relevant defences. If having taken any representations into account, a financial penalty is still deemed appropriate the FCA will finally issue a decision notice which will contain the final decision regarding the level of fine.[127] An important check and balance here is that if the FCA decides to take action against a person, that person may refer the matter to the Financial Services and Markets Tribunal, an independent tribunal set up to hear appeals against FCA decisions and, if necessary, can appeal this decision to the Court of Appeal, as long as this appeal is on a point of law.

Where market abuse has been proved, the FCA has a number of options that are dependent on the severity of the abuse. For instance, by virtue of the FSMA 2000, the FSA is authorised to impose 'a penalty of such amount as it considers appropriate'.[128] In determining what this amount should be, the Authority must have regard to:

(a) whether the behaviour in respect of which the penalty is to be imposed had an adverse effect on the market in question and, if it did, how serious that effect was;
(b) the extent to which that behaviour was deliberate or reckless; and
(c) whether the person on whom the penalty is to be imposed is an individual.[129]

In addition to these guidelines the FCA also has a financial penalties policy that provides a framework for calculating the size of fines; it is contained within its Handbook. This penalty setting regime is based on three principles:

1   Disgorgement – a firm or individual should not benefit from any breach;
2   Discipline – a firm or individual should be penalised for wrongdoing; and,
3   Deterrence – any penalty imposed should deter the firm or individual who committed the breach, and others, from committing further or similar breaches.[130]

Under this framework the amount that an individual pays is made up of two elements: disgorgement of the benefit and a fine that reflects the seriousness of the

---

124 Financial Services and Markets Act 2000, s. 124.
125 Financial Services and Markets Act 2000, s. 125.
126 Financial Services and Markets Act 2000, s. 126(3).
127 Financial Services and Markets Act 2000, s. 127.
128 Financial Services and Markets Act 2000, s. 123(1).
129 Financial Services and Markets Act 2000, s. 124(2).
130 Financial Conduct Authority, 'FCA Handbook', available from https://www.handbook.fca.org.uk/handbook/DEPP/6/5.html, accessed 26 January 2016.

breach. This is incorporated into a five-step framework. In terms of market abuse the five steps are:

(a) Step 1: the removal of any financial benefit derived directly from the market abuse (this can be a profit or a loss avoided);

(b) Step 2: the determination of a figure which reflects the seriousness of the market abuse and whether or not it was referable to the individual's employment. The figure may therefore be based on a percentage of the individual's income (0–40%) or be a multiple (0–4) of the profit made or loss avoided;

(c) Step 3: an adjustment can be made to the Step 2 figure to take into account any aggravating and mitigating circumstances;

(d) Step 4: an upwards adjustment can also be made to the amount arrived at after Steps 2 and 3 are concluded, where it is thought appropriate, to ensure that the penalty has the appropriate deterrent effect; and

(e) Step 5: if applicable, a settlement discount will be applied. This discount does not apply to disgorgement of any financial benefit derived directly from the market abuse.[131]

Fines made against firms follow a similar structure. Instead of individual income however, the FCA will take into account the amount of revenue generated by the firm, with the fine representing a percentage of this revenue. Depending on the seriousness of the abuse this fine can range from 0–20 per cent.[132]

The above framework has led to quite sizeable penalties being imposed, many of which have been in relation to incidences whereby individuals or companies have failed to submit accurate and/or timely suspicious transaction reports. For example, in 2010 the FSA fined the London branch of Societe Generale (SocGen) £1,575,000, the London branch of Commerzbank AG £595,000, Credit Suisse £1.75 million, Getco Europe Limited £1.4 million and Instinet Europe Limited £1.05 million for market abuse offences. Similarly in 2009, Barclays Capital Securities Limited and Barclays Bank PLC were fined £2.45 million.[133] In February 2012 the FSA imposed a financial penalty of £3.63 million on David Einhorn for engaging in market abuse;[134] his firm Greenlight Capital Inc was also fined £3.65 million.[135]

131 Financial Conduct Authority, 'FCA Handbook, DEPP 6.5 and 6.5C', available from https://www.handbook.fca.org.uk/handbook/DEPP/6/5.html and https://www.handbook.fca.org.uk/handbook/DEPP/6/5C.html#DES548, accessed 26 January 2016.

132 Financial Conduct Authority, 'FCA Handbook, DEPP 6.5A', available from https://www.handbook.fca.org.uk/handbook/DEPP/6/5A.html, accessed 26 January 2016.

133 Financial Services Authority, 'Transaction reporting cases', available from http://www.fsa.gov.uk/pages/About/What/financial_crime/market_abuse/library/index.shtml, accessed 18 October 2011.

134 FSA, 'Final Notice: David Einhorn', 15 February 2012, available from http://webarchive.nationalarchives.gov.uk/20130301170532/ and http://www.fsa.gov.uk/static/pubs/final/david-einhorn.pdf, accessed 13 January 2016.

135 FSA, 'Final Notice: Greenlight Capital Inc', 15 February 2012, available from http://webarchive.nationalarchives.gov.uk/20130301170532/ and http://www.fsa.gov.uk/static/pubs/final/greenlight-capital.pdf, accessed 13 January 2016.

When the FCA took over in 2013, it continued in using the civil regime and imposed three financial penalties for market abuse, under the heading of market manipulation.[136] Michael Coscia was fined £597,993,[137] Stefan Chaligne £900,000 and ordered to pay a disgorgement of €362,950[138] and Patrick Sejean £650,000.[139] Furthermore in 2014, Ian Hannam was fined £450,000 by the FCA for engaging in two instances of market abuse[140] and '7722656 Canada Inc' formerly trading as Swift Trade Inc was fined £8 million for engaging in market abuse to create a false or misleading impression in order to achieve a profit.[141] In 2015 the FCA imposed six financial penalties for breaches of its market abuse regime, including Da Vinci Invest Ltd £1.46 million;[142] Mineworld Ltd £5 million;[143] Gyorgy Szabolcs £290,000;[144] Szabolcs Banya £410,000;[145] Tamas Pornye £410,000;[146] and, Kenneth George Carver £35,212.[147]

In addition to issuing financial penalties the FCA also has the power to publicly censure market participants by publishing a statement that a person has engaged in market abuse;[148] which is presumably to damage their reputation and standing. In some cases this 'naming and shaming' will be sufficient punishment and deterrence. Additionally, the FCA can either apply to the courts for restitution or it can order restitution itself.[149] Furthermore, the FCA can also suspend or restrict the

---

136 For a more detailed discussion of market manipulation see Chapter 5.
137 FCA, 'Final Notice: Michael Coscia', 3 July 2013, available from http://www.fca.org.uk/your-fca/documents/final-notices/2013/michael-coscia, accessed 13 January 2016.
138 FCA, 'Final Notice: Stefan Chaligne', 21 January 2013, available from http://www.fca.org.uk/your-fca/documents/final-notices/2013/fsa-final-notice-2013-stefan-chaligne, accessed 13 January 2016.
139 FCA, 'Final Notice: Patrick Sejean', 24 January 2013, available from http://www.fca.org.uk/your-fca/documents/final-notices/2013/fsa-final-notice-2013-stefan-chaligne, accessed 13 January 2016.
140 FCA, 'Final Notice: Ian Hannam', 22 July 2014, available from https://www.fca.org.uk/news/fca-publishes-final-notice-for-ian-hannam, accessed 13 January 2016.
141 FCA, 'Final Notice: 7722656 Canada Inc', 24 January 2014, available from https://www.fca.org.uk/your-fca/documents/final-notices/2014/7722656-canada-inc, accessed 13 January 2016.
142 FCA, 'Final Notice: Da Vinci Invest Ltd', 12 August 2015, available from http://www.fca.org.uk/news/fca-secures-high-court-judgment-awarding-injunction-and-over-7-million-in-penalties, accessed 13 January 2016.
143 FCA, 'Final Notice: Mineworld Ltd', 12 August 2015, available from http://www.fca.org.uk/news/fca-secures-high-court-judgment-awarding-injunction-and-over-7-million-in-penalties, accessed 13 January 2016.
144 FCA, 'Final Notice: Gyorgy Szabolcs Brad', 12 August 2015, available from http://www.fca.org.uk/news/fca-secures-high-court-judgment-awarding-injunction-and-over-7-million-in-penalties, accessed 13 January 2016.
145 FCA, 'Final Notice: Szabolcs Banya', 12 August 2015, available from http://www.fca.org.uk/news/fca-secures-high-court-judgment-awarding-injunction-and-over-7-million-in-penalties, accessed 13 January 2016.
146 FCA, 'Final Notice: Tamas Pornye', 12 August 2015, available from http://www.fca.org.uk/news/fca-secures-high-court-judgment-awarding-injunction-and-over-7-million-in-penalties, accessed 13 January 2016.
147 FCA, 'Final Notice: Kenneth George Carver', 20 March 2015, available from http://www.fca.org.uk/news/kenneth-carver-fined-for-insider-dealing, accessed 13 January 2016.
148 Financial Services and Markets Act 2000, s. 123.
149 Financial Services and Markets Act 2000, s. 384.

future business activities of individuals who it has found guilty of market abuse. This option is seen as an additional disciplinary measure and may include a limit on a regulated activity or a restriction on a person's 'performance of their controlled functions'.[150]

One of the most controversial and initially confusing elements of the market abuse regime has surrounded the nature of the civil offence. As already noted, the intention of Part VIII of the FSMA 2000 was to introduce a civil enforcement regime parallel to the criminal provision contained in the Criminal Justice Act 1993. The confusion is not helped by the terms used to describe the regime, such as 'offence' and 'prosecute',[151] words normally associated with criminal sanctions. The introduction of the civil enforcement mechanisms forced the FCA to consult,[152] beyond its original intention, due to the volume of comments on their original consultation.[153] The key issue here is whether or not the so-called civil sanctions are compatible with the European Convention on Human Rights (ECHR) as incorporated into English law by the Human Rights Act 1998, which is a relevant question when a decision of the FCA has been referred to the Financial Services and Markets Tribunal.[154] Section 123 of the FSMA 2000 merely states that the FCA has to be 'satisfied' that market abuse or encouraging such activity has occurred, which does not create a particularly high standard. This argument relates to whether the civil penalties in the regime can accurately be described as civil or whether in reality they are more akin to criminal sanctions. The controversy has centred on the two key issues of the reduced burden of proof required to prove market abuse as opposed to the criminal standard required by the criminal provisions of the Criminal Justice Act 1993, and whether or not the allegation of market abuse is a criminal charge, which should then be subject to the usual due process protections.[155]

Despite the popularity of the civil regime the FSA can still commence a criminal prosecution. Factors that are taken into account when deciding whether or not to criminally prosecute include:

1   the seriousness of the misconduct: if the misconduct is serious and prosecution is likely to result in a significant sentence, criminal prosecution may be more likely to be appropriate

150 Financial Conduct Authority, 'FCA Handbook DEPP ^A.1.3', available from https://www.hand-book.fca.org.uk/handbook/DEPP/6A/1.html, accessed 26 January 2016.

151 M. Filby, 'The enforcement of insider dealing under the Financial Services and Markets Act 2000' (2003) *Company Lawyer*, 24(11), 334–341.

152 Financial Service Authority, 'Feedback statement on responses to Consultation Paper 10: Market Abuse', 1999, available from http://www.fsa.gov.uk/pubs/cp/cp10_response.pdf, accessed 5 July 2010.

153 Financial Services Authority, 'Consultation Paper 10 Market Abuse Part 1: Consultation on a draft Code of Market Conduct', 1998, available from http://www.fsa.gov.uk/pubs/cp/cp10.pdf, accessed 5 July 2010.

154 C. Conceicao, 'The FSA's approach to taking action against market abuse' (2007) *Company Lawyer*, 29(2), 43–45.

155 Additionally there have been concerns that the market abuse regime lacks certainty required by Article 7 ECHR.

2 whether there are victims who have suffered loss as a result of the misconduct: where there are no victims a criminal prosecution is less likely to be appropriate;

3 the extent and nature of the loss suffered: where the misconduct has resulted in substantial loss and/or loss has been suffered by a substantial number of victims, criminal prosecution may be more likely to be appropriate;

4 the effect of the misconduct on the market: where the misconduct has resulted in significant distortion or disruption to the market and/or has significantly damaged market confidence, a criminal prosecution may be more likely to be appropriate;

5 the extent of any profits accrued or loss avoided as a result of the misconduct: where substantial profits have accrued or loss avoided as a result of the misconduct, criminal prosecution may be more likely to be appropriate;

6 whether there are grounds for believing that the misconduct is likely to be continued or repeated: if it appears that the misconduct may be continued or repeated and the imposition of a financial penalty is unlikely to deter further misconduct, a criminal prosecution may be more appropriate than a financial penalty;

7 whether the person has previously been cautioned or convicted in relation to market misconduct or has been subject to civil or regulatory action in respect of market misconduct;

8 the extent to which redress has been provided to those who have suffered loss as a result of the misconduct and/or whether steps have been taken to remedy any failures in systems or controls which gave rise to the misconduct: where such steps are taken promptly and voluntarily, criminal prosecution may not be appropriate; however, potential defendants will not avoid prosecution simply because they are able to pay compensation;

9 the effect that a criminal prosecution may have on the prospects of securing redress for those who have suffered loss: where a criminal prosecution will have adverse effects on the solvency of a *firm* or individual in circumstances where loss has been suffered by *consumers*, the FSA may decide that criminal proceedings are not appropriate;

10 whether the *person* is being or has been voluntarily cooperative with the FSA in taking corrective measures; however, potential defendants will not avoid prosecution merely by fulfilling a statutory duty to take those measures;

11 whether an individual's misconduct involves dishonesty or an abuse of a position of authority or trust;

12 where the misconduct in question was carried out by a group, and a particular individual has played a leading role in the commission of the misconduct: in these circumstances, criminal prosecution may be appropriate in relation to that individual;

13 where the misconduct in question was carried out by two or more individuals acting together and one of the individuals provides information and gives full assistance in the FSA's prosecution of the other(s), the FSA will take this co-operation into account when deciding whether to prosecute the individual who has assisted the FSA or bring market abuse proceedings against him;

14 the personal circumstances of an individual may be relevant to a decision whether to commence a criminal prosecution.[156]

As already discussed, however, such incidences are rare. Since 2013, when the FCA took over, criminal prosecutions have only taken place in insider dealing cases.

Future recommendations

As discussed in Chapter 5, the criminalisation of insider dealing in the UK is in the main seen as a failure, largely because of the high burden of proof required in such difficult evidentiary cases. There has therefore been an attempt to address this in the form of a civil regime, enacted as part of the FSMA 2000, which covers not just insider dealing but all forms of market abuse. Whether or not this regime has been more successful is difficult to judge, even though some considerable time has elapsed since its initial enactment. This is partly because of the requirements of the MAD, which altered UK policy within only four years of it coming into force. It is certainly evident however that the level of fines issued for market abuse remain high and this coupled with a more aggressive approach taken by the FCA, particularly in respect of criminal prosecutions for insider dealing, should allow it to claim success in its mission to combat insider dealing and market manipulation. Despite this, challenges will undoubtedly still remain. The perception of the victimless crime and the ongoing difficulties in proving the offence will remain problematic, especially if the Financial Services and Markets Tribunal apply a criminal standard of proof to the more important cases, an issue which could bring the civil regime to a halt. As Rider notes, the compromises seen in respect of civil liberties issues have resulted in civil offences becoming as difficult to prove as the criminal ones they were designed to remedy and replace.[157]

Further reading

A. Alcock, 'Five years of market abuse' (2007) *Company Lawyer*, 28(6), 163–171.

A. Alcock, 'Market abuse' (2002) *Company Lawyer*, 23(5), 142–150.

A. Alcock, 'Market abuse – the new witchcraft' (2001) *New Law Journal*, 151, 1398.

R. Alexander, 'Corporate crimes: Are the gloves coming off?' (2009) *Company Lawyer*, 30(11), 321–322.

P. Barnes, 'Insider dealing and market abuse: The UK's record on enforcement' (2011) *International Journal of Law Crime and Justice*, 39(3), 174–189.

R. Burger, 'A principled front in the war against market abuse' (2007) *Journal of Financial Regulation and Compliance*, 15(3), 331–336.

---

156 Financial Conduct Authority, *The Enforcement Guide* (FCA, London, 12.7) available from https:// www.handbook.fca.org.uk/handbook/document/EG_FCRMAML_20110701.pdf, accessed 26 January 2016.

157 B. Rider, 'An abominable fraud?' (2010) *Company Lawyer*, 31(7), 197–198.

R. Burger and G. Davies, 'What's new in market abuse – Part 2' (2005) *New Law Journal*, 155, 964.

C. Conceicao, 'The FSA's approach to taking action against market abuse' (2007) *Company Lawyer*, 29(2), 43–45.

Ed., 'Insiders beware!' (1993) *Company Lawyer*, 14(11), 202.

M. Filby, 'Part VIII Financial Services and Markets Act: Filling insider dealing's regulatory gaps' (2004) *Company Lawyer*, 23(12), 363–370.

J. Haines, 'FSA determined to improve the cleanliness of markets: Custodial sentences continue to be a real threat' (2008) *Company Lawyer*, 29(12), 370.

J. Hansen, 'MAD in a hurry: The swift and promising adoption of the EU Market Abuse Directive' (2007) *European Business Law Review*, 15(2), 183–221.

A. Hayes, 'Market abuse' (2010) *Compliance Officer Bulletin*, 75(Apr), 1–31.

A. Haynes, 'Market abuse: An analysis of its nature and regulation' (2007) *Company Lawyer*, 28(11), 323–335.

A. Haynes, 'Market abuse, Northern Rock and bank rescues' (2009) *Journal of Banking Regulation*, 10(4), 321–334.

A. Haynes, 'The burden of proof in market abuse cases' (2013) *Journal of Financial Crime*, 20(4), 365–392.

J. Hayrynen, 'The precise definition of inside information?' (2008) *Journal of International Banking Law and Regulation*, 23(2), 64–70.

E. Herlin-Karnell, 'White-collar crime and European financial crises: Getting tough on EU market abuse' (2012) *European Law Review*, 37(4), 481–494.

L. Linklater, 'The market abuse regime: Setting standards in the twenty-first century' (2001) *Company Lawyer*, 22(9), 267–272.

B. Rider, 'Where angels fear!' (2008) *Company Lawyer*, 29(9), 257–258.

M. Sandler, M. Brown, P. Willis, and E. Clay, 'Market abuse' (2014) *Compliance Officer Bulletin*, 118(Aug), 1–37.

S. Sheikh, 'FSMA market abuse regime: A review of the sunset clauses' (2008) *International Company and Commercial Law Review*, 19(7), 237–236.

E. Swan, 'Market abuse: A new duty of fairness' (2004) *Company Lawyer*, 25(3), 67–68.

A. Sykes, 'Market abuse: A civil revolution' (1999) *Journal of International Financial Markets*, 1(2), 59–67.

C. Willey, 'Market abuse update' (2012) *Compliance Officer Bulletin*, 93(Feb), 1–28.

7

BRIBERY AND CORRUPTION

Introduction

Bribery and corruption have received a considerable amount of attention since the introduction and implementation of the Bribery Act 2010 and the extension of the remit of the Serious Fraud Office (SFO). Bribery has been referred to as an illegal gratuity, extortion, conflict of interest, kickback, corporate espionage and a commission or fee. According to the Organisation for Economic Co-operation and Development (OECD), bribery is defined as 'the offering, promising or giving [of] something in order to influence a public official in the execution of his/her official duties'.[1] However, perhaps one of the simplest definitions is offered by the SFO, which argues that bribery is the 'giving or receiving [of] something of value to influence a transaction'.[2] A bribe can therefore include:

> money, other pecuniary advantages, such as [a] scholarship for a child's college education, or non-pecuniary benefits, such as favourable publicity. In the international context, bribery involves a business firm from country A offering financial or non-financial inducements to officials of country B to obtain a commercial benefit.[3]

1 OECD Observer, *The Fight against Bribery and Corruption* (OECD, 2000) as cited in R. Sanyal, and S. Samanta, 'Trends in international bribe-giving: do anti-bribery laws matter?' (2011) *Journal of International Trade Law & Policy*, 10(2), 151–164, at 152.
2 Serious Fraud Office, 'Bribery and corruption', available from http://www.sfo.gov.uk/bribery—corruption/bribery—corruption.aspx, accessed 23 November 2011.
3 R. Sanyal, and S. Samanta, 'Trends in international bribe-giving: Do anti-bribery laws matter?' (2011) *Journal of International Trade Law & Policy*, 10(2), 151–164, at 153.

It has been argued that bribery can be divided into two categories – direct and indirect.[4] The more common of these two types is indirect, and this is usually conducted via an agent or a go-between. This type of conduct traditionally arises where the respective parties agree to meet to try to gain a competitive advantage, for example. The agent is normally paid a commission from the additional revenue generated by the resultant work or trade.[5] Beale and Esposito offer the following useful example of what constitutes a direct bribe:

> A company commences arbitration against the government of a country and the government's defence is that it has recently learned that the company paid bribes to government employees or officials in connection with the project; that is an allegation of direct bribery.[6]

Denning, citing Latymer, stated that bribery was 'a princely kind of thieving',[7] yet despite these simple definitions it is still a very difficult term to define.[8] This point is illustrated by the different statutory definitions of bribery offered by the Public Bodies Corrupt Practices Act 1889, the Prevention of Corruption Act 1906 and the Prevention of Corruption Act 1916. The uncertainty over its definition was clarified by the Bribery Act 2010. To aid with this clarity, this chapter begins by outlining the relevant offences created by the Bribery Act and then goes on to look at the United Kingdom's (UK) bribery policy, which is administered by the Ministry of Justice and enforced by the SFO in conjunction with the Financial Conduct Authority (FCA). The policy, which has been adopted, is very similar to that outlined in the previous chapters of this book and can be divided into three parts: criminalisation, regulatory agencies and the use of suspicious transactions reports. The primary focus of this chapter will therefore be to analyse these initiatives including an attempt to quantify the extent of the problem. The final part of the chapter reviews the available criminal and civil sentencing options and practices.

What is the offence of bribery?

Prior to the Bribery Act 2010, the criminal offence of bribery was housed in the provisions of the Public Bodies Corrupt Practices Act 1889, the Prevention of Corruption Acts 1906 and the Prevention of Corruption Act 1916.[9] These laws

---

4 K. Beale, and P. Esposito, 'Emergent international attitudes towards bribery, corruption and money laundering' (2009) *Arbitration*, 75(3), 360–373, at 362.

5 *Ibid.*

6 *Ibid.* For other examples of conduct that amounts to a bribe see J. Horder, 'Bribery as a form of criminal wrongdoing' (2011) *Law Quarterly Review*, 127(Jan), 37–54, at 37–38.

7 A. Denning, 'Independence and impartiality of the judges' (1954) *South African Law Journal*, 71, 345.

8 The Law Commission, *Reforming Bribery* (HMSO, 2008).

9 OECD, 'Steps taken to implement and enforce the OECD Convention on Combating Bribery of Foreign Public Officials in International Business Transactions: UNITED KINGDOM', 28 May 2010, available from http://www.oecd.org/dataoecd/17/30/48362318.pdf, accessed 27 March 2012.

were described as an 'untidy and unsatisfactory jumble',[10] which needed replacing with a 'concise modern mini-code, which should ensure rather more effective compliance with the United Kingdom's international obligations to curb bribery and corruption'.[11] Furthermore, these statutory provisions were described as being 'inconsistent, anachronistic and inadequate'[12] in terms of complying with international anti-corruption obligations.

The impetus for the reform of the law of bribery was undoubtedly sparked by the recommendation of the Committee on Standards in Public Life that the government should clarify the law on bribery.[13] As a result, the Law Commission published its proposals in 1998, although it wasn't until the Bribery Act 2010 that its recommendations were finally implemented.[14] Other relevant statutory measures included the Anti-terrorism, Crime and Security Act 2001 and the Criminal Justice and Immigration Act 2008 which both extended the scope of the UK's bribery and corruption laws, although it was not until the implementation of the Bribery Act on 1 July 2011 that the four current bribery offences were actually introduced.

Offences of bribing another person

Section 1 of the Bribery Act 2010 states that a person is guilty of an offence if they offer, promise or give a financial or other advantage to another person in one of two possible circumstances. These circumstances are set out in the Act as separate 'cases' and include:

> Case 1 is where –
> (a) P offers, promises or gives a financial or other advantage to another person, and
> (b) P intends the advantage: –
> > (i)   to induce a person to perform improperly a relevant function or activity, or
> > (ii) to reward a person for the improper performance of such a function or activity.[15]

> Case 2 is where –
> (a) P offers, promises or gives a financial or other advantage to another person, and
> (b) P knows or believes that the acceptance of the advantage would itself constitute the improper performance of a relevant function or activity.[16]

---

10 Ed., 'The Bribery Act 2010' (2010) *Criminal Law Review*, 6, 439–440, at 439.

11 *Ibid.*

12 D. Aaronberg, and N. Higgins, 'Legislative comment the bribery act 2010: All bark and no bite . . . ?' (2010) *Archbold Review*, 5, 6–9, at 6.

13 Committee on Standards in Public Life, *First Report 'Standards in Public Life'* (Cm 2850–1, HMSO: London, 1995, 43).

14 Law Commission, *Legislating the Criminal Code: Corruption No. 248* (Law Commission, 1998).

15 Bribery Act 2010, s. 1(2).

16 Bribery Act 2010, s. 1(3).

For the purposes of the Act, a function or activity is defined as either,

(a) any function of a public nature,
(b) any activity connected with a business,
(c) any activity performed in the course of a person's employment, [or]
(d) any activity performed by or on behalf of a body of persons (whether corporate or unincorporate).[17]

It must also meet one or more of three set conditions, that is that a person performing the function or activity is expected to perform it in 'good faith', 'impartially' or 'is in a position of trust by virtue of performing it'.[18] Furthermore, there is no requirement that the activity or function is either performed in the UK or even has any connection with the UK.[19]

A further definitional term given by the Act is that of 'improper performance'. This is taken to relate to the situation whereby either the activity or function has been 'performed in breach of a relevant expectation', or the failure to carry out the said activity or function is in 'itself a breach of a relevant expectation'.[20] What is to be expected is decided by implementing what is known as the 'expectation test'. This is defined as 'a test of what a reasonable person in the United Kingdom would expect in relation to the performance of the type of function or activity concerned'.[21] This is therefore a question for jurors to decide.

A person is therefore guilty of an offence under section 1 if they pledge, promise or provide a monetary, pecuniary or other benefit to another person with the purpose that there should be an illicit or shady performance of a function or activity, or knowing that approval would amount to this unlawful conduct. Arguably, it is this offence that 'targets those who offer or pay bribes'.[22] It is also important to note that the improper performance is rewarded by the 'advantage'.[23] The Act stipulates that it is irrelevant if the advantage was offered, assured or directly given between the participants or whether a third party was utilised. Furthermore, it is immaterial if the person receiving the offer is the same person due to perform the activity.[24] According to the City of London Police a person commits an offence under section 1 of the Bribery Act 2010 if they offer, promise or give a 'financial or other advantage to another person, intending to induce them to perform improperly a relevant function or activity or to reward a person for such improper

17 Bribery Act 2010, s. 3(2).
18 Bribery Act 2010, s. 3(3)–(5).
19 Bribery Act 2010, s. 3(6).
20 Bribery Act 2010, s. 4(1).
21 Bribery Act 2010, s. 5.
22 D. Aaronberg, and N. Higgins, 'Legislative comment the Bribery Act 2010: All bark and no bite . . . ?' (2010) *Archbold Review*, 5, 6–9, at 6.
23 Bribery Act 2010, s. 1.
24 Bribery Act 2010, s. 1(4 &5).

performance'.[25] Similarly, Gentle notes that an offence is committed under section 1 where 'a person offers, promises or gives an advantage to another, intending that the advantage should induce him to perform improperly a function which he is expected to carry out impartially, in good faith or as a consequence of his being in a position of trust'.[26]

Offences relating to being bribed

Section 2 of the Bribery Act 2010 provides that a person ('R') commits an offence if the following cases apply,

> Case 3 is where R requests, agrees to receive or accepts a financial or other advantage intending that, in consequence, a relevant function or activity should be performed improperly (whether by R or another person).[27]

> Case 4 is where –
> (a) R requests, agrees to receive or accepts a financial or other advantage, and
> (b) the request, agreement or acceptance itself constitutes the improper performance by R of a relevant function or activity.[28]

> Case 5 is where R requests, agrees to receive or accepts a financial or other advantage as a reward for the improper performance (whether by R or another person) of a relevant function or activity.[29]

> Case 6 is where, in anticipation of or in consequence of R requesting, agreeing to receive or accepting a financial or other advantage, a relevant function or activity is performed improperly –
> (a) by R, or
> (b) by another person at R's request or with R's assent or acquiescence.[30]

Therefore a person is guilty of an offence under this section if they wish, consent to, or accept an advantage with the specific purpose that they will perform a relative function or activity improperly either by themselves or by another person, or as a reward for such a performance.[31] Arguably, this section of the Act 'targets

---

25 City of London Police, 'Bribery Act 2010 summary', available from http://www.cityoflondon.police. uk/CityPolice/Departments/ECD/anticorruptionunit/briberyact2010summary.htm, accessed 24 November 2011.

26 S. Gentle, 'The Bribery Act 2010: Part 2: The corporate offence' (2011) *Criminal Law Review*, 2, 101–110, at 102.

27 Bribery Act 2010, s. 2(2).

28 Bribery Act 2010, s. 2(3).

29 Bribery Act 2010, s. 2(4).

30 Bribery Act 2010, s. 2(5).

31 Bribery Act 2010, s. 2.

those who accept or solicit bribes'.[32] The mere request, agreement or acceptance of a benefit constitutes improper performance and it neither matter whether the advantage is received directly or through a third party nor whether the benefit is to those same parties or another.[33] This applies to instances where the improper performance has either been done or is yet to be done by the person or someone acting under their instruction or acquiescence. It is also irrelevant whether the person performing the function or activity knows that it is improper. This is therefore the counter-part of the first offence. The City of London Police have noted that a person is guilty of an offence under this section of the Act where they request, agree to receive or accept:

> a financial or other advantage intending that, in consequence, a relevant function or activity should be performed improperly by themselves or another. In the above it does not matter whether the advantage is direct or through a third party, nor whether the benefit is for that person or another.[34]

Similarly, Gentle notes that 'in broad terms, the criminal conduct consists of a person requesting, agreeing to receive or accepting an advantage or prospective advantage to perform improperly a relevant function'.[35]

Bribing a foreign public official

By virtue of section 6 of the Bribery Act 2010, a person ('P') commits the offence of bribing a foreign public official ('F') if 'P's intention is to influence F in F's capacity as a foreign public official'.[36] P must also 'intend to obtain or retain (a) business, or (b) an advantage in the conduct of business'.[37] In relation to section 6, the Ministry of Justice has noted that this:

> creates a standalone offence of bribery of a foreign public official. The offence is committed where a person offers, promises or gives a financial or other advantage to a foreign public official with the intention of influencing the official in the performance of his or her official functions. The person offering, promising or giving the advantage must also intend to obtain or retain business or an advantage in the conduct of business by doing so. However, the

32 D. Aaronberg, and N. Higgins, 'Legislative comment The Bribery Act 2010: All bark and no bite . . . ?' (2010) *Archbold Review*, 5, 6–9, at 7.
33 Bribery Act 2010, s. 2(4)–(6).
34 City of London Police, 'Bribery Act 2010 summary', available from http://www.cityoflondon.police.uk/CityPolice/Departments/ECD/anticorruptionunit/briberyact2010summary.htm, accessed 24 November 2011.
35 S. Gentle, 'The Bribery Act 2010: Part 2: The corporate offence' (2011) *Criminal Law Review*, 2, 101–110, at 102.
36 Bribery Act 2010, s. 6(1).
37 Bribery Act 2010, s. 6(2).

offence is not committed where the official is permitted or required by the applicable written law to be influenced by the advantage.[38]

A person is, therefore, guilty of the offence if they aim to manipulate or induce the official in the performance of their role as a public official with the intention of obtaining or retaining business or a business advantage.[39] The City of London Police have taken the view that the offence has been committed:

> Where a person in the act of intending to obtain or retain business, or an advantage in the conduct of business, bribes a foreign public official with the intent to influence them in their capacity . . . This only applies if they directly, or through a third party, offer, promise or give any financial or other advantage to the foreign official or to another at the officials request or with their assent or acquiescence and the official is neither permitted nor required by the applicable local written law to be influenced in their capacity by the offer, promise or gift.[40]

Failure of commercial organisations to prevent bribery

In addition to individual liability, the Bribery Act 2010 also introduces a new form of corporate criminal liability. Therefore under section 7 of the Act, a commercial organisation can also be found guilty of an offence if a person associated with the organisation bribes another, intending to obtain or retain business or a business advantage for that organisation.[41] In essence it creates an additional direct rather than alternative vicarious liability, when the commission of a section 1 or section 6 bribery offence has taken place on behalf of an organisation. For there to be any liability, however, the organisation in question must be stipulated as a 'relevant commercial organisation'. This is defined as,

(a) a body which is incorporated under the law of any part of the United Kingdom and which carries on a business (whether there or elsewhere),
(b) any other body corporate (wherever incorporated) which carries on a business, or part of a business, in any part of the United Kingdom,
(c) a partnership which is formed under the law of any part of the United Kingdom and which carries on a business (whether there or elsewhere), or
(d) any other partnership (wherever formed) which carries on a business, or part of a business, in any part of the United Kingdom.[42]

---

38 Ministry of Justice, *The Bribery Act 2010 – Guidance* (Ministry of Justice, 2011, 11).
39 Bribery Act 2010, s. 6.
40 City of London Police, 'Bribery Act 2010 summary', available from http://www.cityoflondon. police.uk/CityPolice/Departments/ECD/anticorruptionunit/briberyact2010summary.htm, accessed 24 November 2011.
41 Bribery Act 2010, s. 7.
42 Bribery Act 2010, s. 7(5).

For the purposes of this section, an 'associated person' is seen as an individual who 'performs services for or on behalf of' the organisation',[43] with the person being, for example, the organisation's agent, subsidiary or employee.[44] This has been stated to be a 'matter of substance rather than form',[45] with it being necessary for all surrounding circumstances to be taken into account, although a presumption will exist if the associated person is an employee of the organisation. The scope of section 7 is intentionally broad, so as to encompass the whole range of individuals who may be committing bribery on behalf of a third-party organisation. To be held as an 'associated person', however, 'the perpetrator of the bribery must be performing services for the organisation in question and must also intend to obtain or retain business or an advantage in the conduct of business for that organisation'.[46]

Because of this introduction of corporate criminal liability, section 7 of the Bribery Act 2010 has been described as a significant move 'away from the current approach',[47] with the Ministry of Justice providing that under section 7:

> A commercial organisation will be liable to prosecution if a person associated with it bribes another person intending to obtain or retain business or an advantage in the conduct of business for that organisation.[48]

It is also worth noting that for the offence to be made out there is no requirement to prove that the activity was committed in the UK or elsewhere. Indeed, there is no need to even show a close connection to the UK as is needed for the other bribery offences under the Act.[49]

Moreover, the existence of section 7 does not affect the common law principle that governs the liability of corporate bodies for criminal offences. Under this provision, prosecuting bodies must prove a mens rea or fault element in addition to the actus reus or conduct element. This common law principle, also known as the identification principle, should still be used instead of section 7 of the Bribery Act 2010 where it is possible to prove 'that a person who is properly regarded as representing the "directing mind" of the body in question possessed the necessary fault element required for the offence'.[50]

Defences

Applicable only to section 7 offences, it is a defence if the relevant commercial organisation can prove that it had in place 'adequate procedures' designed

---

43 Bribery Act 2010, s. 8(1).
44 Bribery Act 2010, s. 8(3).
45 Ministry of Justice, *Bribery Act 2010, Circular 2011/05* (Ministry of Justice, 2011), para. 23.
46 *Ibid.*
47 T. Pope, and T. Webb, 'Legislative comment–the Bribery Act 2010' (2010) *Journal of International Banking Law and Regulation*, 25(10), 480–483, at 482.
48 Ministry of Justice, *The Bribery Act 2010 – Guidance* (Ministry of Justice, 2011, 15).
49 Ministry of Justice, *Bribery Act 2010, Circular 2011/05* (Ministry of Justice, 2011) para. 22.
50 *Ibid.*, at para. 18.

to prevent persons associated with the commercial organisation from bribing another person.[51] 'In accordance with established case law, the standard of proof which the commercial organisation would need to discharge in order to prove the defence, in the event it was prosecuted, is the balance of probabilities.'[52] The expression 'adequate procedures' has generated much debate. The Ministry of Justice, as required by the Act, published guidance to assist commercial organisations to comply with the Act. This guidance sets out the six general principles of adequate procedures namely:

1 Proportionality;
2 Top-level commitment to anti-bribery measures;
3 Risk assessment;
4 Due diligence regarding business partners;
5 Communication; and,
6 Monitoring and review.[53]

The Serious Fraud Office (SFO) is keen to underline that section 7 does not provide an offence of strict liability, because of the availability of the defence of adequate procedures. Thus, if there are adequate procedures, then no offence has been committed. This is a complete defence and not just mitigation.[54]

In addition to the section 7 defence, the Bribery Act 2010 also details a general defence that is available to the bribery offences contained in sections 1 and 2 of the Act. It is also applicable to attempting, aiding, abetting, counselling, procuring, conspiring to commit or inciting the commission of these offences.[55] The defence is contained within section 13 of the Act which states that:

> It is a defence for a person charged with a relevant bribery offence to prove that the person's conduct was necessary for –
> (a) the proper exercise of any function of an intelligence service, or
> (b) the proper exercise of any function of the armed forces when engaged on active service.[56]

The aim of the defence is to enable the intelligence services, or the armed forces to undertake legitimate functions that may 'require the use of a financial or other advantage to accomplish the relevant function'.[57] It has therefore been introduced

51 Bribery Act 2010, s.7.
52 Ministry of Justice, *The Bribery Act 2010 – Guidance* (Ministry of Justice, 2011, 15).
53 *Ibid.*
54 Serious Fraud Office, 'Richard Alderman, speech the Bribery Act 2010–The SFO's approach and international compliance', 9 February 2011, available from http://www.sfo.gov.uk/about-us/our-views/director's-speeches/speeches-2011/the-bribery-act-2010-the-sfo's-approach-and-international-compliance.aspx, accessed 13 November 2011.
55 Bribery Act 2010, s. 13(6).
56 Bribery Act 2010, s. 13(1).
57 The Government's Explanatory Notes to s. 13 Bribery Act 2010.

to allow for operational necessities. To rely on the defence, the defendant needs to prove, on the balance of probabilities, that their conduct was necessary. As explained by Lord Bach, the Parliamentary Under-Secretary of State for the Ministry of Justice:

> The police and other law enforcement agencies have an important role to play in protecting and defending the public from the threat caused by serious crime. Our objective is to ensure that these law enforcement agencies are not hindered in tackling serious crime.[58]

The extent of bribery

The threat posed by bribery cannot be underestimated and is graphically illustrated by the following quote from Pope and Webb:

> Such practices damage businesses through market distortion, prevention of fair competition, and by undermining confidence and business ethics. However, it is the human tragedy of corrupt business cultures that highlights the need for action in particular: where bribes and embezzlement of public funds are commonplace, citizens of that state suffer the most. Money meant to be used to improve schools, hospitals, roads, water supply and the like is instead transferred to a limited group of corrupt individuals.[59]

Whilst this threat has far-ranging consequences, as with all forms of financial crime, any attempt to measure the full extent of bribery and corruption is fraught with methodological difficulties, with it being virtually impossible to determine the exact extent. It has been estimated by some commentators, nevertheless, that approximately US$1 trillion is paid in bribes on a worldwide basis each year.[60] This is also backed up by the World Bank.[61] Sanyal and Samanta take the view that:

> The enormous growth in international commerce over the past 60 years has been accompanied by an increase in bribery. The World Bank estimates that more than USD1 trillion in bribes are paid each year out of a world economy of USD30 trillion – 3 per cent of the world's economy. And, the impact is particularly severe on foreign investment. In fact, the World Bank estimates that corruption serves, essentially, as a 20 per cent tax.[62]

---

58 Hansard, HL Vol 716, col.GC89, 13 January 2010.
59 T. Pope and T. Webb. 'Legislative comment – the Bribery Act 2010' (2010) *Journal of International Banking Law and Regulation*, 25(10), 480–483, at 480.
60 *Ibid.*
61 C. William, 'Trillion Dollar Bribery' (2011) *New Law Journal*, 161(7447), 25–26, at 25.
62 R. Sanyal and S. Samanta, 'Trends in international bribe-giving: Do anti-bribery laws matter?' (2011) *Journal of International Trade Law & Policy*, 10(2), 151–164, at 151.

The World Economic Forum estimated the extent of corruption at 5 per cent of the global gross domestic product, approximately US$2.6 trillion;[63] and that it increases the cost of conducting business by approximately 10 per cent.[64] The World Bank estimated that bribes in excess of US$1 trillion are paid each year.[65] Similarly, in 2014 the EU announced that annual losses attributed to corruption totalled €120 million.[66]

There are two organisations, in particular, which study global bribery and corruption: the World Bank and Transparency International. The World Bank believes that 'corruption is a product of bad governance and the weaknesses inherent in public sector institutions'.[67] Similarly, Transparency International defines corruption as the 'abuse of entrusted power for private gain. It hurts everyone whose life, livelihood or happiness depends on the integrity of people in a position of authority.'[68] In this context, the Bribery Act 2010, by overhauling the UK's patchwork of archaic corruption laws,[69] is regarded in the industry as 'the single most important development' in combating white collar crime.[70] Other commentators, including Aaronberg and Higgins, state that the Act 'provides the United Kingdom with some of the most draconian and far-reaching anti-corruption legislation in the world',[71] with Salens commenting that it has the potential to 'propel the UK to the forefront' in the international fight against bribery and corruption.[72] On a scale of 1–10, where 10 is very clean, Transparency International in 2010 gave the UK a rating of 7.6, placing it in 20th position out of 178. Whilst this may appear

63 'Clean business is good business – the businesss case against corruption' (2008) (A joint publication by the International Chamber of Commerce, Transparency International, the United Nations Global Compact and the World Economic Forum Partnering against Corruption Initiative (PACI), available from http://www.weforum.org/pdf/paci/BusinessCaseAgainstCorruption.pdf, accessed 18 August 2013.

64 'Global Agenda Council on Anti-Corruption & Transparancy 2012–2014' (World Economic Forum, 2012), available from http://www.weforum.org/content/global-agenda-council-anti-corruption-transparency-2012–2014, accessed 17 February 2014.

65 OECD 'The rationale for fighting corruption', n/d, available from https://www.oecd.org/cleang-ovbiz/49693613.pdf, accessed 13 June 2016.

66 James Fontanella-Khan, 'Corruption in the EU costs business €120bn a year, study finds' (*Financial Times*, 3 February 2014), available from http://www.ft.com/cms/s/0/28f11862–8cf9–11e3-ad57–00144feab7de.html?siteedition=uk#axzz2sLiCCodw, accessed 4 February 2013.

67 I. Carr, 'Fighting corruption through the United Nations convention on corruption 2003: A global solution to a global problem?' (2005) *International Trade Law and Regulation*, 11(1), 24–29, at 28.

68 Transparency International, 'Corruption Perceptions Index 2010', available from http://www.transparency.org/policy_research/surveys_indices/cpi/2010, accessed 28 June 2011.

69 J. Benstead, 'Biting the bullet' (2010) *New Law Journal*, 160(7434), 1291–1292, at 1291.

70 Salens, 'Anti-bribery and corruption: The UK propels itself to the forefront of global enforcement' available from http://www.salans.com/~/media/Assets/Salans/Publications/Salans%20Client%20Alert%20UK%20Bribery%20Act%20Implementation%20Date.ashx, accessed 24 July 2010.

71 D. Aaronberg and N. Higgins, 'Legislative comment the bribery act 2010: All bark and no bite . . . ?' (2010) *Archbold Review*, 5, 6–9, at 6.

72 Salens, 'Anti-bribery and corruption: The UK propels itself to the forefront of global enforcement', available from http://www.salans.com/~/media/Assets/Salans/Publications/Salans%20Client%20Alert%20UK%20Bribery%20Act%20Implementation%20Date.ashx, accessed 24 July 2010.

satisfactory, the UK was still behind Denmark, New Zealand, Ireland, Barbados and Qatar, with the leading nation being Singapore with a 9.3 rating. This would therefore indicate that there is still some work to do. The USA, in 23rd place, had a rating of 7.1, whereas the bottom place was reserved for Somalia with a 1.1 rating. When a score of zero amounts to a labelling of a country as being 'highly corrupt', this is not an enviable position for Somalia to be in.[73]

Policy background

The UK's policy towards bribery, like the other types of financial crime discussed in this book, has been influenced by a series of international legislative measures introduced by the United Nations (UN), the European Union (EU) and the Organisation for Economic Co-operation and Development (OECD). One of the first international measures, introduced in 1994, was when the OECD accepted a recommendation that required member states to 'take effective measures to deter, prevent and combat the bribery of foreign public officials in connection with international business transactions'.[74] This requirement was strengthened by the OECD Convention on Combating Bribery of Foreign Public Officials in International Business Transactions.[75] In response to this, the EU introduced its first bribery-related provisions in 1995 in its Convention of the European Union on the Fight against Corruption involving Officials of the European Communities or Officials of Member States.[76] In 1997 it approved a Convention on the Fight against Corruption involving Officials of the European Communities or Officials of Member States.[77] Furthermore, in 2003 the UN introduced its Convention against Corruption, which is administered by the UN Office on Drugs and Crime.[78]

The OECD Convention, which the UK signed in 1997,[79] has 37 other countries as signatories[80] and 'establishes legally binding standards to criminalise bribery

73 Transparency International, 'Corruption Perceptions Index 2010', available from http://www.transparency.org/policy_research/surveys_indices/cpi/2010, accessed 28 June 2011.
74 S. Sheikh, 'The Bribery Act 2010: Commercial organisations beware!' (2011) *International Company and Commercial Law Review*, 22(1), 1–16, at 3.
75 See G. Sacerdoti, 'The 1997 OECD convention on combating bribery of foreign public officials in international business transactions' (1999) *International Business Law Journal*, 1, 3–18.
76 S. Sheikh, 'The Bribery Act 2010: Commercial organisations beware!' (2011) *International Company and Commercial Law Review*, 22(1), 1–16, at 3.
77 Convention on the Fight Against Corruption involving Officials of the European Communities or Officials of Member States, done at Brussels, 26 May 1997, 37 I.L.M. 12; OJ 1997 C 195.
78 For a more detailed and critical commentary on the provision of the 2003 Convention see P. Webb, 'The United Nations convention against corruption: Global achievement or missed opportunity?' (2005) *Journal of International Economic Law*, 8(1), 191–229 and M. Kubiciel, 'Core criminal law provisions in the United Nations convention against corruption' (2009) *International Criminal Law Review*, 9(1), 139–155.
79 OECD Convention on Combating Bribery of Foreign Public Officials in International Business Transactions, 1997, available from http://www.oecd.org/dataoecd/4/18/38028044.pdf, accessed 13 December 2011.
80 *Ibid.*

of foreign public officials in international business transactions'.[81] It is the only international anti-corruption instrument focused on the supply side of the bribery transaction, that is, the person making the bribe rather than the recipient.[82] The OECD argues that its Convention is working and reports that 'more than 135 individuals and companies have been convicted of foreign bribery'. This occurred in the first ten years of the Convention's existence, with fines during this period of time amounting to €1.24 billion.[83] Interestingly, there is no collective enforcement governance, and enforcement action is carried out by individual countries. The OECD does not therefore act as global policemen. The UK's initial response to these conventions was the passing of the Anti-terrorism, Crime and Security Act 2001. This was only ever meant to be a transient and temporary instrument until more comprehensive corruption legislation could be introduced.[84] This has obviously now taken place through the Bribery Act 2010.

The UK's reform of its bribery laws began with the publication of a Law Commission Report in 1998.[85] The Law Commission recommended that 'the common law offence of bribery and the statutory offences of corruption should be replaced by a modern statute'.[86] The then Labour government responded by publishing a Corruption Bill, which after being subjected to pre-legislative scrutiny by the Joint Committee,[87] was rejected, resulting in a revised version which was published in 2005.[88] This was followed by another consultation exercise by the Law Commission in 2007,[89] which subsequently led to the publication of its 2008 Report.[90] In response to this Report, and to emphasise the impetus to address the threat posed by bribery, the then Justice Secretary, Jack Straw stated:

> Bribery is a cancer which destroys the integrity, accountability and honesty that underpins ethical standards both in public life and in the business community. The fight against bribery is not an optional extra or a luxury to be dispensed with in testing economic times. Our current law is old, complex

---

81 *Ibid.*

82 *Ibid.*

83 OECD, *OECD Working Group on Bribery 'Annual report 2008'* (OCED, 2008, 2).

84 M. Raphael, *Blackstone's Guide to the Bribery Act 2010* (OUP, 2010, 116).

85 Law Commission, *Legislating the Criminal Code: Corruption No. 248* (Law Commission, 1998). For a more detailed discussion of this report see G. Sullivan, 'Proscribing corruption – some comments on the Law Commission's report' (1998) *Criminal Law Review*, August, 547–555.

86 S. Sheikh, 'The Bribery Act 2010: Commercial organisations beware!' (2011) *International Company and Commercial Law Review*, 22(1), 1–16, at 4.

87 For an excellent discussion of the scrutiny of the Corruption Bill see A. Kennon, 'Pre-legislative scrutiny of draft Bills' (2004) *Public Law*, Autumn, 477–494.

88 Home Office, *Reform of the Prevention of Corruption Acts and SFO Powers in Cases of Bribery against Foreign Officials* (Home Office: London, 2005).

89 Law Commission, *Reforming Bribery: A Consultation* (Law Commission, 2007). For a more detailed discussion see P. Alldridge, 'Reforming bribery: Law Commission consultation paper 185: (1) Bribery reform and the law–again' (2008) *Criminal Law Review*, 9, 671–686.

90 Law Commission, *Reforming Bribery: A Consultation* (Law Commission, 2007).

and fragmented . . . A new law will provide our investigators and prosecutors with the tools they need to deal with bribery much more effectively.[91]

The Report was followed by the publication of a White Paper in 2009 that finally resulted in the enactment of the Bribery Act 2010.[92] Prior to its introduction, Kenneth Clarke, then the Secretary of State for Justice, stated that the Act would:

> reinforce its [the UK's] reputation as a leader in the global fight against corruption . . . The Act will ensure that the UK is at the forefront of the battle against bribery allowing the country to clamp down on corruption without being burdensome to business.[93]

The provisions of the Bribery Act 2010 have received a mixture of responses from commentators. For example, some writers have suggested that the provisions 'go too far and fear [that] the new "gold standard" legislation poses a threat to UK competitiveness'.[94] Other concerns have been raised in relation to the increased prosecutorial powers under the Act and the compliance costs that firms in the UK are expected to meet.[95] Conversely, it has also been described as a 'major piece of legislation, of immense practical importance to the conduct of business, whether in the public or private sphere'.[96] Alexander further argues that the Act is desperately needed because 'corruption is not merely a regrettable evil; it kills',[97] and identifies examples including children dying from unsafe medication which was approved by corrupt health officials.

Financial institutions and regulatory bodies

As mentioned above, there are two main regulatory bodies that enforce the provisions of the Bribery Act 2010, namely the SFO and the FCA. In addition to these agencies, the City of London Police have also begun to investigate allegations of bribery and corruption.[98] As part of its efforts to reduce this type of financial

---

91 Ministry of Justice, 'Government welcomes new bribery law recommendations', 20 November 2008, available from http://www.wired-gov.net/wg/wg-news-1.nsf/0/329BD09E4E75E813802575070 0478C2E?OpenDocument, accessed 25 November 2011.

92 The Ministry of Justice, *Bribery: Draft Legislation* (The Stationery Office, 2009). For an excellent commentary on the draft law see C. Well, 'Bribery: Corporate liability under the draft bill' (2009) *Criminal Law Review*, 7, 479–487.

93 Ministry of Justice, press release 'UK clamps down on corruption with new Bribery Act', available from http://www.justice.gov.uk/news/press-release-300311a.htm, accessed 29 November 2011.

94 T. Pope, and T. Webb. 'Legislative comment–the Bribery Act 2010' (2010) *Journal of International Banking Law and Regulation*, 25(10), 480–483, at 480.

95 *Ibid.*

96 Ed., 'The Bribery Act 2010' (2010) *Criminal Law Review*, 6, 439–440, at 439.

97 R. Alexander, 'The Bribery Act 2010: Time to stand firm', (2011) *Journal of Financial Crime*, 18(2), Editorial.

98 T. Duthie, and D. Lawler, 'Legislative comment the United Kingdom bribery bill' (2010) *Construction Law Journal*, 26(2), 146–152, at 147.

crime, the SFO has placed 'huge emphasis on raising awareness, education, persuasion, and ultimately prevention'.[99] Moreover, as outlined in earlier chapters of this book, the FCA has a statutory obligation to reduce financial crime under the Financial Services and Markets Act 2000.[100] Clearly, bribery falls within the definition of financial crime under this statutory objective, with bribery also being relevant to its secondary statutory objective of maintaining market confidence. Bribery affects the latter statutory aim because 'bribery and corruption distort natural competition and could affect the UK's reputation, making it a less attractive place for firms to conduct insurance or other business'.[101] The Financial Services Authority (FSA), therefore, pinpointed the threat posed by bribery in its 2008 Financial Risk Outlook, stating that:

> International efforts to combat corruption combined with the continuing development of the UK's legal framework on corruption may increase the level of interest in the financial services sector's efforts to combat corruption and bribery. There is a risk that firms could come under pressure to pay bribes, especially if they are operating in jurisdictions where paying bribes is widely expected. In addition, financial services firms may launder the proceeds of corruption or be used to transmit bribes.[102]

It is important to note here, however, that the FCA does not actually enforce the provisions of the Bribery Act 2010, with its role only applying where 'authorised firms fail adequately to address corruption and bribery risk, including where these risks arise in relation to third parties acting on behalf of the firm'. The FSA has previously argued that it does 'not need to obtain evidence of corrupt conduct to take regulatory action against a firm'.[103] Therefore firms that are regulated by the FCA are bound to comply with its anti-bribery provisions as set out in its Handbook and, in particular, its 11 Principles for Business. These include:

1 Integrity
2 Skill, care and diligence
3 Management and control
4 Financial prudence

---

99 C. Monteity, 'The Bribery Act 2010: Part 3: Enforcement' (2011) *Criminal Law Review*, 2, 111–121, at 114.
100 Financial Service and Markets Act 2000, s. 6(3).
101 Financial Services Authority, *Anti-bribery and Corruption in Commercial Insurance Broking Reducing the Risk of Illicit Payments or Inducements to Third Parties* (Financial Services Authority: London, 2010, 6).
102 Financial Services Authority, *Financial Risk Outlook 2008* (Financial Services Authority: London, 2008, 35).
103 Financial Services Authority, 'One-minute guide – Anti-bribery and corruption in commercial insurance broking', available from http://www.fsa.gov.uk/smallfirms/resources/one_minute_ guides/insurance_intermed/anti_bribery.shtml, accessed 24 November 2011.

5 Market conduct
6 Customer's interest
7 Communications with clients
8 Conflict of interest
9 Customers: relationships of trust
10 Client assets
11 Relationships with regulators.

Of particular relevance to bribery and corruption are Principles 1, 2 and 3. Principle 1 provides that a firm is obliged to 'conduct business with integrity'. This is especially relevant as 'broker firms and their employees may themselves be engaged in corrupt practices'. Principle 2 states that a firm must 'conduct its business with due skill, care and diligence', whilst Principle 3 sets out an obligation that 'a firm must take reasonable care to organise and control its affairs responsibly and effectively, with adequate risk management systems'. In addition to adhering to the FCA's Principles of Business, a firm's senior management team are also 'responsible for making an appropriate assessment of financial crime risks, including those relating to bribery and corruption'.[104] Furthermore, Rule Systems and Controls (SYSC)[105] 3.2.6R states that firms are required to 'establish and maintain effective systems and controls . . . for countering the risk that the firm might be used to further financial crime'.[106] This means that firms have the responsibility to assess the risks of becoming involved in, or facilitating, bribery and corruption and are obliged to take all reasonable steps in preventing such risks from crystallising. Authorised firms therefore have an additional regulatory obligation. This makes them responsible for putting in place and maintaining relevant policies and processes which can be utilised in preventing corruption and bribery and thus allows them to conduct their businesses with integrity.[107] Gentle notes that:

> the FSA has shown itself ready to take action against authorised firms for breaches of principle 3 (of the Principles for Business) when firms fail to comply with systems and controls designed to prevent criminal activity such as bribery.[108]

---

104 Financial Services Authority, *Anti-bribery and Corruption in Commercial Insurance Broking Reducing the Risk of Illicit Payments or Inducements to Third Parties* (Financial Services Authority: London, 2010, 10).
105 Senior Management Arrangements, Systems and Controls.
106 Financial Services Authority, *The Full Handbook – SYSC Senior Management Arrangements, Systems and Controls* (Financial Services Authority: London, 2011) at Rule SYSC 3.2.6R.
107 Financial Services Authority, 'One-minute guide – Anti-bribery and corruption in commercial insurance broking', available from http://www.fsa.gov.uk/smallfirms/resources/one_minute_guides/insurance_intermed/anti_bribery.shtml, accessed 24 November 2011.
108 S. Gentle, 'The Bribery Act 2010: Part 2: The corporate offence' (2011) *Criminal Law Review*, 2, 101–110, at 110.

If a firm breaches any of these 11 Principles, the FCA has an extensive array of enforcement powers that it can use. These will be discussed in the sentencing and recovery section below.

Financial intelligence

In addition to the creation of criminal offences designed to capture individuals intimately involved in bribery and corruption, it is also the intention of the Bribery Act 2010 to extend the responsibility for bribery to those who are involved on a peripheral basis. Therefore it additionally includes those who could be described as the controlling minds and all those organisations involved or on whose behalf bribery took place or was even contemplated. This can include individuals and organisations that are many steps away from the organisation itself. Any peripheral involvement can be subject to a financial penalty in addition to any action taken against individuals intimately involved. The wide scope of the Act therefore significantly increases the responsibility of commercial organisations to manage such risk issues. The ambit of the law thus covers any commercial organisation with a business presence in the UK. This brings into consideration any part of that organisation, even if the controlling body was overseas and the alleged bribery was also offshore.[109] Consequently, this should encourage businesses to review their existing anti-bribery policies and procedures and ensure that their associates are similarly complaint.

Internationally, the OECD Guidelines for Multinational Enterprises[110] and the OECD Business Approaches to Combating Corrupt Practices[111] provide guidance, as do United States of America (USA) Federal Sentencing Guidelines.[112] In the UK, the SFO has been designated as the national reporting point for allegations of bribery of foreign public officials by British nationals or companies incorporated in the UK, even if the matter occurred overseas. This should be helpful because a key element in combating bribery and corruption is the requirement to report such instances to the authorities. However, in the UK the obligation to report is not that well established. This is largely because there is no actual statutory obligation to report bribery, corruption or fraud, unlike that which exists for money laundering where reporting is required by the Proceeds of Crime Act 2002.[113] This omission is demonstrated in the fraud arena, where 'not having a centralised body to

---

109 Ministry of Justice, 'Bribery Act implementation', 20 July 2010, available from http://www.justice. gov.uk/news/newsrelease200710a.htm, accessed 15 December 2011.

110 OECD, 'Guidelines for Multinational Enterprises', available from http://www.oecd.org/documen t/28/0,3343,en_2649_34889_2397532_1_1_1_1,00.html, accessed 24 July 2010.

111 OECD, 'Business Approaches to Combating Bribery', available from http://www.oecd.org/datao-ecd/45/32/1922830.pdf, accessed 24 July 2010.

112 US Federal Sentencing Guidelines, 'Chapter eight – part b – remedying harm from criminal conduct, and effective compliance and ethics program', available from http://www.ussc. gov/2007guid/8b2_1.html, accessed 24 July 2010.

113 Proceeds of Crime Act 2002, ss. 327–340.

co-ordinate fraud intelligence across the public and private sectors has made it easier for criminals to operate undetected and free to re-offend'.[114] The National Fraud Intelligence Bureau (NFIB) thus seems to rely on 'best endeavours' and 'encouragement' to report[115] although such crimes *should*, nevertheless, still be reported to the police.[116]

By contrast, the other significant actor in the UK, namely the FCA, which is responsible for regulating financial services, does have the ability to *impose* reporting obligations.[117] Regulated firms are obliged to inform the FCA, 'promptly, of anything relating to the firm of which the FCA would reasonably expect prompt notice' (SYSC 6.3 Financial Crime).[118] The outcome is that the SFO, which is tasked with taking the lead in bribery matters and which is designated as the reporting centre, lacks statutory backing to compel reporting, whereas the FCA, in the sector it regulates, can instil bribery reporting obligations. The relationship between the SFO and the FCA therefore lies at the heart of the UK's efforts to control economic crime and this inconsistency in designation and power needs to be addressed to enable the situation whereby the agency that is responsible for dealing with cases of bribery, corruption and fraud also has the power to make the reporting of it a statutory obligation.

In an attempt to try to control such crime the SFO has published its 'Approach to Dealing with Overseas Corruption'.[119] This provides guidance and industry-specific codes of practice including, for example, advice that 'a negotiated settlement rather than a criminal prosecution' would give protection against a mandatory EU procurement.[120] Corporate hospitality is also covered, with the government recognising that the provision of corporate hospitality is a part of business life. In the past the government has not been prescriptive in establishing sufficient protective parameters in this regard, preferring rather to leave the issue to prosecutorial discretion and common sense.[121] The ultimate consequence of this, however, is fundamental uncertainty, which is likely to remain until test cases are brought to

---

114 NFA, 'National Fraud Intelligence Bureau', available from http://www.lslo.gov.uk/nfa/WhoWe-WorkWith/Pages/NFIB.aspx, accessed 22 April 2010.

115 *Ibid.*

116 Home Office, 'Counting rules for recorded crime', available from http://rds.homeoffice.gov.uk/rds/pdfs10/countgeneral10.pdf, accessed 29 April 2010.

117 Financial Services Authority, 'What we do: who we regulate' 'We regulate most financial services markets, exchanges and firms. We set the standards that they must meet and can take action against firms if they fail to meet the required standards', available from http://www.fsa.gov.uk/pages/About/What/Who/index.shtml, accessed 27 September 2011.

118 FSA, 'Principles for business', available from http://www.fsa.gov.uk/Pages/Library/Communication/PR/1999/099.shtml, accessed 29 April 2010.

119 SFO, 'Approach of the Serious Fraud Office to dealing with overseas corruption', available from http://www.sfo.gov.uk/media/107247/approach%20of%20the%20serious%20fraud%20office%20v3.pdf, accessed 24 July 2010.

120 EU Public Services Procurement Directive 2004/18/EC Art. 45.

121 Wragge & Co., 'Bribery Act to come into force April 2011: Time to take action', 23 July 2010, available from http://www.wragge.com/analysis_6175.asp, accessed 24 July 2010.

trial. For example, whilst lavish corporate hospitality, such as taking clients to, say, a Rugby World Cup match in New Zealand or the Rio de Janeiro Olympic Games, would clearly be open to scrutiny for proportionality, the Justice Secretary has nevertheless stated that the government does not want 'to stop firms getting to know their clients by taking them to events like Wimbledon or the Grand Prix'.[122] The guidance, therefore, whilst it recognises that corporate hospitality and promotional expenditure is an everyday part of business life, does not provide detail on when that boundary is crossed, even though the government additionally states that 'it is, however, clear that hospitality and promotional or similar business expenditure *can* be employed as bribes' (emphasis added).[123] This means that commercial organisations are obliged to put in place clear procedures and give directions to their employees to ensure that, at best, their motives are not misinterpreted.

Sentencing and recovery

A person found guilty of any of the offences contained in sections 1, 2 and 6 of the Bribery Act 2010 is liable to a maximum custodial sentence of ten years imprisonment and/or an unlimited fine. For the offence found in section 7, the maximum penalty is an unlimited fine.[124] Although the SFO is arguably the lead agency in prosecuting cases of bribery and corruption, proceedings under the Act require the personal consent of not just the Director of the SFO but also, either the Director of Public Prosecutions (DPP) or the Director of Revenue and Customs Prosecutions.[125] The Crown Prosecution Service (CPS) has stated that not only is bribery a serious offence, but that 'there is an inherent public interest in bribery being prosecuted'.[126] In determining whether or not to prosecute, the CPS will take into account both aggravating and mitigating factors. These might include the amount of money involved; whether there has been a breach of a position of trust; whether it involved a vulnerable or elderly victim; the period over which the offence was carried out; whether any voluntary repayments had been made; and whether there were any personal factors such as disability, illness or family difficulties.[127]

Historically, however, and particularly with reference to the situation prior to the Bribery Act 2010, there have been few criminal cases taken to trial,[128] with this

122 Ministry of Justice. 'The Bribery Act: Guidance', March 2011, Available from http://www.justice. gov.uk/downloads/guidance/making-reviewing-law/bribery-act-2010-guidance.pdf, accessed 5 May 2011.

123 *Ibid.*

124 Bribery Act 2010, s. 11(3).

125 Bribery Act 2010, s. 10.

126 The Crown Prosecution Service, 'Bribery Act 2010: Joint Prosecution Guidance of the Director of the Serious Fraud Office and the Director of Public Prosecutions', available from http://www. cps.gov.uk/legal/a_to_c/bribery_act_2010/, accessed 9 February 2016.

127 The Crown Prosecution Service, *'Bribery', Legal Guidance* (Crown Prosecution Service: London, 2008).

128 D. Aaronberg, and N. Higgins, 'Legislative comment the Bribery Act 2010: All bark and no bite . . . ?' (2010) *Archbold Review*, 5, 6–9, at 6.

situation continuing even after the de Grazia Review in 2008.[129] The few examples that do exist include one case from September 2009, where a British construction company, Mabey and Johnson, was held liable for bribing foreign officials in order to win business contracts. The company pleaded guilty to overseas corruption charges, for paying €1 million in bribes through middlemen with reference to £60–£70 million contracts, and to the breaching of UN Iraq sanctions relating to Saddam Hussein's 'Oil for Food Programme'. The case concluded with a plea bargain, which led to a financial penalty of £3.5 million, in addition to compensation payable to the countries of Ghana, Jamaica and Iraq and legal costs totalling £3.1 million. Interestingly, this was the first conviction in the UK of a company for such offences, with the SFO deciding to prosecute the company rather than the actual individuals involved.[130]

More recently however the number of convictions has begun to slowly increase and perhaps due to this there are now sentencing guidelines to help judges determine the most appropriate sentence. Initially, the only available aid came in the form of two Court of Appeal cases, both of which were decided prior to 2010. The first, *R v Anderson (Malcolm John)*,[131] involved the appeal of a sentence of 12 months imprisonment for accepting a bribe in return for contracts that were beneficial to the appellant's business. On the basis that the appellant was of previous good character and that the financial gain was relatively small, a sentence of six months was held to be more appropriate. The second is that of *R v Francis Hurell*.[132] The sentence in question was again for 12 months, but this time was for attempting to bribe a police officer, through the offering of £2,000 so that the officer would not carry out a breath test. Even though the Court held that any attempt to bribe a police officer in the execution of their duty was serious, it nevertheless substituted the sentence of one of three months.

Such guidance may have been useful in the case of Mark Jessop, who in April 2011 was sentenced to a two-year custodial sentence and ordered to pay £150,000 in compensation and £25,000 in prosecution costs. The orders were in relation to ten counts of engaging in activities that made funds available to the Iraqi government in contravention of UN Iraq sanctions, again in relation to the 'Oil for Food Programme'.[133] Other criminal prosecutions include Dennis Kerrison, Paul Jennings, Militiades Papachristos and David Turner, all former executives of Innospec Ltd, who in October 2011 were charged with corruption in relation to making and conspiring to make corrupt payments to public officials in Indonesia and Iraq in

---

129 J. de Grazia, *Review of the Serious Fraud Office–Final Report* (Serious Fraud Office: London, 2008).

130 Case Comment, 'First UK company convicted for overseas corruption' (2010) *Company Lawyer*, 31(1), 16.

131 [2003] 2 Cr. App. R. (S) 28.

132 [2004] 2 Cr. App. R. (S) 23.

133 Serious Fraud Office, 'Medical goods to Iraq supplier jailed for paying kick-backs' (Press Release 13 April 2011) available from http://www.sfo.gov.uk/press-room/latest-press-releases/press-releases-2011/medical-goods-to-iraq-supplier-jailed-for-paying-kick-backs.aspx, accessed 29 November 2011.

order to secure contracts for the business.[134] In January 2012, Turner pleaded guilty to three counts of conspiracy to corrupt, and in June and July 2012, Jennings also pleaded guilty to three counts of conspiracy. Both Kerrison and Papachristos were convicted of one count of conspiracy each in June 2014.[135] Turner was sentenced to 16 months in custody, suspended for two years with 300 hours of unpaid work. Kerrison, Jennings and Papchristos were sentenced to four years, two years and 18 months in custody respectively, although Kerrison's sentenced was later reduced to three years by the Court of Appeal. Innospec Ltd pleaded guilty to bribing state officials in Indonesia and was fined US$12.7 million.[136]

The first criminal conviction of a corporation for offences involving the bribery of foreign public officials took place in December 2014. Smith & Ouzman Ltd, a company that specialised in printing security documents, was convicted of offences of corruptly agreeing to make payments totalling nearly £500,000.[137] The payments were used to influence who was awarded business contracts in both Mauritania and Kenya. Nicholas Smith (Sales and Marketing Manager) and Christopher Smith (Chairman) were also convicted. Smith and Ouzman Ltd was ordered to pay £2.2 million, Nicholas Smith received a custodial sentence of three years and Christopher Smith a sentenced of 18 months, suspended for two years, 250 hours of unpaid work and a three-month curfew.[138]

The amounts of money involved can be quite large and in recognition of this and the increase in criminal convictions, there is now a definitive guideline[139] from the Sentencing Council, which covers the three bribery offences under sections 1, 2 and 6 of the Bribery Act 2010. The way in which this guideline works is explained in detail in Chapter 4, but as with all guidelines from the Sentencing Council the judge must first determine how serious the offence is by considering the level of the offender's culpability and then the level of harm that was either caused or was risked being caused. Examples of high culpability include where the intended corruption is of a senior official who performs a public function or where the offending takes place over a substantial period of time. Medium culpability is where the offender takes a significant role in a group activity and lesser culpability is where the offender is not motivated by personal gain.[140] Harm is divided into four categories, with the

---

134 Serious Fraud Office, 'Innospec Ltd: Two more executives charged with corruption' (Press Release, 27 October 2011), available from http://www.sfo.gov.uk/press-room/latest-press-releases/press-releases-2011/innospec-ltd-two-more-executives-charged-with-corruption.aspx, accessed 29 November 2011.
135 It is worth noting that these were not offences under the Bribery Act 2010 but under section 1 of the Criminal Law Act 1977.
136 Serious Fraud Office, 'Innospec Ltd', (Case Information), available from https://www.sfo.gov.uk/cases/innospec-ltd/, accessed 10 February 2016.
137 The offences were contrary to s. 1 of the Prevention of Corruption Act 1906.
138 Serious Fraud Office, 'Smith and Ouzman Ltd', (Case information), available from https://www.sfo.gov.uk/cases/smith-ouzman-ltd/, accessed 10 February 2016.
139 Sentencing Council, *Fraud, Bribery and Money Laundering Offences Definitive Guideline* (Sentencing Guidelines Secretariat: London, 2014).
140 *Ibid.*

factors listed in a category one offence deemed to be the most serious. This includes 'serious detrimental effect on individuals'[141] and the 'serious undermining of the proper function of local or national government, business or public services'.[142] Once the judge has determined the level of culpability and the category of harm, they can then refer to the guideline, which provides starting points in terms of appropriate penalties and also a category range.[143] For example, where culpability is medium and the level of harm is classified as being at category three the starting point is 18 months in custody with a category range of 26 weeks to three years in custody. The judge will increase or decrease from the starting point taking into account aggravating or mitigating factors, whether the offender aided the prosecution and the timely entry of a guilty plea. Once all of these factors are considered the most appropriate sentence is reached.

The convictions covered so far in this chapter have been for offences under the old pieces of legislation, namely the Prevention of Corruption Act 1906 and the Criminal Law Act 1977. In December 2014, however, the SFO secured its first convictions under the Bribery Act 2010 against Gary West and Stuart Stone. Both men were executives of Sustainable Growth Group and/or its subsidiary companies. The men, with James Whale, were involved in a scam to induce people to invest via a pension plan in green biofuel products.[144] For the bribery offences West received four years imprisonment and Stone six years.[145] Furthermore, in February 2016, Sweett Group Plc was convicted under section 7 of the Bribery Act 2010 for 'failing to prevent an act of bribery intended to secure and retain a contract'.[146] Sweett Group Plc was ordered to pay £2.25 million: a £1.4 million fine, £851,152.23 as a confiscation order and the remainder covering the SFO's costs. The SFO stated:

> Acts of bribery by UK companies significantly damage this country's commercial reputation. This conviction and punishment, the SFO's first under section 7 of the Bribery Act, sends a strong message that UK companies must take full responsibility for the actions of their employees and in their commercial activities act in accordance with the law.[147]

---

141 *Ibid.*, at 42.
142 *Ibid.*, at 42.
143 *Ibid.*, at 43.
144 Serious Fraud Office, 'City directors convicted in £23m 'Green biofuel' trial' (*News Release* 5 December 2014) available from https://www.sfo.gov.uk/2014/12/05/city-directors-convicted-23m-green-biofuel-trial/, accessed 10 February 2016.
145 Serious Fraud Office, 'City directors sentenced to 28 years in total for £23 million green bio fuel fraud', (*News Release*, 8 December 2014) available from https://www.sfo.gov.uk/2014/12/08/city-directors-sentenced-28-years-total-23m-green-biofuel-fraud/, accessed 10 February 2016.
146 Bribery Act 2010, s. 7(1)(b).
147 Serious Fraud Office, 'Sweett Group PLC sentenced and ordered to pay £2.25 million after Bribery Act conviction', 19 February 2016, available from https://www.sfo.gov.uk/2016/02/19/sweett-group-plc-sentenced-and-ordered-to-pay-2-3-million-after-bribery-act-conviction/, accessed 26 February 2016.

Judge Beddoe, when sentencing, stated:

> The whole point of section 7 is to impose a duty on those running such com-
> panies throughout the world properly to supervise them. Rogue elements
> can only operate in this way – and operate for so long – because of a failure
> properly to supervise what they are doing and the way they are doing it.[148]

In February 2016, the SFO had a number of other pending cases concerning brib-
ery and corruption, including investigations into the following companies: ENRC
Ltd; Alstom Network UL Ltd and Alstom Power Ltd; Innovia Securency PTY Ltd;
Rolls-Royce Plc and Soma Oil & Gas; and, Standard Bank Plc.[149]

Since the implementation of the Bribery Act 2010 there have also been a very
small number of successful prosecutions brought by the CPS. For example, in *R v
Patel* the defendant was a clerk at a magistrates' court, who was bribed £500 for
not inputting information about a traffic violation onto a court database. Patel later
pleaded guilty and was sentenced to a total of nine years imprisonment for bribery
and misconduct offences although this was reduced to four years on appeal. The
next successful prosecution under the Bribery Act was *R v Mushtaq*. The defendant
offered a bribe to a licensing officer from Oldman Council to pass him on a driv-
ing test that he had failed. In December 2012, Mushtaq was given a two-month
custodial sentence, suspended for 12 months and a two-month curfew order.[150]
Finally, in April 2013, Li Yang, a postgraduate student was convicted of attempting
to bribe his university professor after he had failed his dissertation. The defendant
pleaded guilty to bribery and possessing an imitation firearm and was sentenced to
a custodial sentence of 12 months.[151]

In addition, and perhaps instead of, criminal liability, the FCA also has the power
to impose civil fines under section 206(1) of the Financial Services and Markets Act
2000.[152] The use of this was seen, for example, in July 2011 when the FSA (as it was
then) fined Willis Limited £6.895 million for weaknesses in its anti-bribery and
corruption systems and controls.[153] As a result of an extensive investigation, the FSA
determined that Willis Limited had failed to:

1   Guarantee that it established and recorded an adequate commercial rationale to
     support its payments to overseas third parties;

---

148 *Ibid.*
149 Serious Fraud Office, 'Our cases', available from https://www.sfo.gov.uk/our-cases/#aza, accessed
     10 February 2016.
150 http://www.thelawpages.com/court-cases/Mawia-Mushtaq-11023–1.law.
151 http://www.thelawpages.com/court-cases/Yang-Li-10957–1.law.
152 J. Horder, 'Bribery as a form of criminal wrongdoing' (2011) *Law Quarterly Review*, 127(Jan), 37–54,
     at 43.
153 Financial Services Authority, 'FSA fines Willis Limited 6.895m for anti-bribery and corruption
     systems and controls failings', 21 July 2011, available from http://www.fsa.gov.uk/pages/Library/
     Communication/PR/2011/066.shtml, accessed 24 November 2011.

2 ensure that adequate due diligence was carried out on overseas third parties to evaluate the risk involved in doing business with them; and,

3 adequately review its relationships on a regular basis to confirm whether it was still necessary and appropriate for Willis Limited to continue with the relationship.[154]

In this particular instance the FSA concluded that Willis Limited had:

> failed to take the appropriate steps to ensure that payments it was making to overseas third parties were not being used for corrupt purposes. This is particularly disappointing as we have repeatedly communicated with the industry on this issue and have previously taken enforcement action for failings in this area. The involvement of UK financial institutions in corrupt or potentially corrupt practices overseas undermines the integrity of the UK financial services sector. The action we have taken against Willis Limited shows that we believe that it is vital for firms not only to put in place appropriate anti-bribery and corruption systems and controls, but also to ensure that those systems and controls are adequately implemented and monitored.[155]

The FSA, in 2011, also fined Aon Limited £5.25 million for 'failing to take reasonable care to establish and maintain effective systems and controls to counter the risks of bribery and corruption associated with making payments to overseas firms and individuals'.[156] Here, the FSA determined that Aon Ltd had 'failed to properly assess the risks involved in its dealings with overseas firms and individuals who helped it win business and failed to implement effective controls to mitigate those risks'.[157]

More recently, in 2013, the FCA fined JLT Speciality Limited £1.8 million for an 'unacceptable approach to bribery and corruption risks from overseas payments'.[158] The FCA concluded that the company 'was found to have failed to conduct proper due diligence before entering into a relationship with partners in other countries who helped JLT Speciality Limited secure new business, known as overseas introducers. JLT Speciality Limited also did not adequately assess the potential risk of new insurance business secured through its existing overseas introducers.'[159] Furthermore, in 2014, the FCA fined Besso Limited £315,000 for 'failing to take reasonable care to establish and maintain effective systems and controls for countering the risks

---

154 *Ibid.*

155 *Ibid.*

156 *Ibid.*

157 *Ibid.*

158 Financial Conduct Authority, 'Firm fined £1.8million for "unacceptable" approach to bribery & corruption risks from overseas payments', 19 December 2013, available from https://www.fca.org. uk/news/firm-fined-18million-for-unacceptable-approach-to-bribery-corruption-risks-from-overseas-payments, accessed 8 February 2016.

159 *Ibid.*

of bribery and corruption'.[160] The FCA concluded:'Besso failed to ensure that they had proper systems and controls in place to counter the risks of bribery and corruption in their business activities.'[161]

Deferred prosecution agreements

In addition to the usual criminal options, the Crime and Courts Act 2013 also provides the SFO with another important weapon in its armoury against those companies that fail to prevent bribery under section 7 of the Bribery Act 2010. Under section 45 of the 2013 Act,[162] the SFO or the DPP is permitted to use a Deferred Prosecution Agreement (DPA).[163] The Crime and Courts Act 2013 states that 'persons who may enter into a DPA with a prosecutor' can be divided into three categories: a company, a partnership or an unregistered organisation.[164] It is important to note that DPAs are *not* available to individuals. The first DPA used was seen in *Serious Fraud Office v Standard Bank Plc* in November 2015. Here, Standard Bank Plc was accused of breaching section 7 of the Bribery Act 2010 and the proceedings were stopped once the use of the DPA was approved by the court. As a result of this decision, Standard Bank agreed to pay financial orders totalling $25.2 million, an additional $7 million to the Tanzanian government and SFO's costs of £330,000. David Green, the then Chairman of the SFO, stated:

> This landmark DPA will serve as a template for future agreements. The judgment from Lord Justice Leveson provides very helpful guidance to those advising corporates. It also endorses the SFO's contention that the DPA in this case was in the interests of justice and its terms fair, reasonable and proportionate. I applaud Standard Bank for their frankness with the SFO and their prompt and early engagement with us.[165]

It is worth noting that Standard Bank Plc was not criminally convicted of bribery or corruption offences.[166]

---

160 Financial Conduct Authority, 'Besso Limited fined for anti-bribery and corruption systems failings', 19 March 2014, available from https://www.fca.org.uk/news/besso-limited-fined-for-antibribery-and-corruption-systems-failings, accessed 8 February 2016.

161 *Ibid.*

162 Crime and Courts Act 2013, s. 45.

163 Crime and Courts Act 2013, s. 45 Schedule, 17.3. For an early commentary from the SFO on why it would use DPAs, see The Serious Fraud Office, 'David Green CB QC, Director, at the 10th Annual Corporate Accountability Conference, PricewaterhouseCoopers, London', 14 June 2012, available from https://www.sfo.gov.uk/2012/06/14/10th-annual-corporate-accountability-conference-held-pricewaterhousecoopers/, accessed 26 February 2012.

164 Crime and Courts Act 2013, s. 45, Schedule 4(1).

165 Serious Fraud Office, 'SFO agrees first UK DPA with Standard Bank', 30 November 2015, available from https://www.sfo.gov.uk/2015/11/30/sfo-agrees-first-uk-dpa-with-standard-bank/, accessed 26 February 2016.

166 For an excellent commentary on DPAs see M. Bisgrove and M. Weekes, 'Deferred prosecution agreements: A practical consideration' (2014) *Criminal Law Review*, 6, 416–438 and F. Mazzacuva,

The civil recovery order

As well as criminal and civil financial penalties, the court can also make a civil recovery order under section 243 of the Proceeds of Crime Act 2002. The order is applicable when on the balance of probabilities it can be established that the individual or company in question is in possession of property that was obtained through unlawful conduct. The order allows for the recovery of such property and, interestingly, does not require a criminal conviction for it to be made. Examples of when this has been used include Balfour Beatty, which was ordered to pay £2.25 million for 'payment irregularities' by an African subsidiary on an Egyptian construction contract, and AMEC plc, which faced an order for almost £5 million for making irregular payments in connection with a bridge building contract in South Korea.[167] Likewise, in February 2011, the SFO recovered £7 million from the engineering group M. W. Kellogg, which pleaded guilty to the payment of bribes amounting to more than £100 million to Nigerian government officials by its parent company. Commenting on the case, the Director of the SFO stated:

> in cases such as this a prosecution is not appropriate. Our goal is to prevent bribery and corruption or remove any of the benefits generated by such activities. This case demonstrates the range of tools we are prepared to use.[168]

Other civil recover orders include that against Oxford Publishing Ltd, which in 2013 were ordered to pay £1,895,435 in recognition of sums that it had received through bribery and corruption practices. They were also ordered to pay the SFO's costs of £12,500.[169]

The Serious Crime Prevention Order

Furthermore, the court has the option of making a Serious Crime Prevention Order (SCPO) under Part 1 of the Serious Crime Act 2007, which came into force on 6 April 2008. A SCPO is a civil order which is intended to restrict, discipline and prevent future involvement in serious crime and which can be made either by the High Court or by application to the Crown Court. For an order to be made, the

---

'Justifications and purposes of negotiated justice for corporate offenders: Deferred and non-prosecution agreements in the UK and US systems of criminal justice' (2014) *Journal of Criminal Law*, 78(3), 249–262.

167 T. Duthie, and D. Lawler, 'Legislative comment the United Kingdom Bribery Bill' (2010) *Construction Law Journal*, 26(2), 146–152, at 146.

168 J. Russell, 'SFO settles Nigeria Bribery case for £7m' (*The Telegraph*, 2011), available from http://www.telegraph.co.uk/finance/newsbysector/industry/8329298/SFO-settles-Nigeria-bribery-case-for-7m.html, accessed 29 November 2011.

169 Serious Fraud Office, 'Oxford Publishing Ltd to pay almost £1.9 million as settlement after admitting unlawful conduct in its East African operations' (News Release, 3 July 2012), available from https://www.sfo.gov.uk/2012/07/03/oxford-publishing-ltd-pay-almost-1-9-million-settlement-admitting-unlawful-conduct-east-african-operations/, accessed 10 February 2016.

court must be satisfied, on the balance of probabilities, that the person has been involved in serious crime, and it has reasonable grounds for believing that the making of the order would protect the public from further such crime.[170] This can be easily established if the person in question has been convicted of such an offence. For the purposes of the order, serious crime is defined in Part 1 of Schedule 1 of the Act, and includes money laundering, fraud, corruption and bribery. The order can contain a number of requirements, prohibitions, restrictions and other terms that are considered by the court to be appropriate in protecting the public from future offending.[171] Examples of such requirements are detailed in section 5(3) of the Act including, for example, restrictions on working arrangements, travel both abroad and within the UK, the means of communication and association with named individuals and access to certain premises. An order can also require a person to answer questions, provide information and/or provide documents at a time or place specified in the order.[172] When such requirements are made, the court must ensure that their prohibitive effect is proportionate to the purpose of protecting the public against future serious crime. Interestingly, however, a SCPO cannot require a person to:

- provide oral answers to questions or requirements to provide information (section 11);
- answer questions, or provide information or documents which are covered by legal professional privilege (section 12);
- produce excluded material as defined by section 11 of the Police and Criminal Evidence Act (section 13(1)(a));
- disclose any information or produce any document held by him in confidence as part of a banking business unless there is consent from the person to whom confidence is owed; or
- the order specifically required disclosure of information or documents of this kind, or it required disclosure of specified information or documents of this kind (section 13 (2)–(4)); or,
- provide information or documents or answer questions if it would involve a disclosure prohibited by another enactment (section 14).[173]

A SCPO can last for a maximum of five years, although the commencement can be delayed to coincide with release from custody. The court can also set different start and end dates for specific requirements, prohibitions or restrictions.[174] In addition

---

170 Serious Crime Act 2007, s. 1(1).
171 Serious Crime Act 2007, s. 1(3).
172 Serious Crime Act 2007, s. 5(5).
173 Crown Prosecution Service, 'Serious Crime Prevention Orders' available from http://www.cps.gov. uk/legal/s_to_u/serious_crime_prevention_orders_%28scpo%29_guidance/, accessed 29 November 2011.
174 Serious Crime Act 2007, s. 16.

to orders being made against named individuals, a SCPO can also be issued against a body corporate, a partnership or an unincorporated association.[175] In a speech given on 26 February 2009, the then Director of the SFO, Richard Alderman, explained how SCPOs:

> enable prosecutors to obtain court orders regulating the future conduct of those who have been engaged in serious crime. SCPOs can be obtained before or after a conviction. The conditions that can attach to such orders are almost limitless. A company might, for example, be asked to submit its trading accounts for scrutiny every six months. I am very interested in these orders. An SCPO obtained from the High Court quickly without prosecution is a very important weapon for us.[176]

Perhaps controversially, on the basis that a SCPO is a civil order, breach of it, without reasonable excuse, amounts to a criminal offence. On summary conviction this can make the individual liable for up to 12 months imprisonment, which can be extended on conviction on indictment by up to five years.[177]

Future recommendations

The Bribery Act 2010 is a significant improvement on the existing offences under the Public Bodies Corrupt Practices Act 1889, the Prevention of Corruption Act 1906 and the Prevention of Corruption Act 1916. Interestingly, the Bribery Act 2010 requires companies to have in place adequate procedures to prevent people associated with them from being bribed. If a commercial entity fails to prevent an associated person from committing bribery on their behalf, it has committed an offence. However, provided the commercial entity is able to demonstrate that it has in place 'adequate procedures to prevent persons associated with the commercial entity from undertaking such conduct' it will avoid prosecution. It is clear that this is an extension of the anti-money laundering system used by the FCA to include bribery and corruption. Importantly, the Bribery Act 2010 extended the remit of the SFO to prosecute allegations of bribery, which is also a welcome development. Even so, the effectiveness of the SFO will depend on it being granted the appropriate levels of funding by the UK government. The introduction of the Bribery Act 2010 has resulted in a small number of what could be called minor instances of bribery convictions and the most significant development has been the use of DPAs. It is likely that the SFO will continue to use DPAs and seek to impose financial penalties as opposed to instigating criminal proceedings, thus following a similar pattern as that outlined in the money laundering and fraud chapters of this book.

---

175 Serious Crimes Act 2007, ss. 30–32.
176 Cameron McKenna, 'The Serious Fraud Office', available from http://www.law-now.com/law-now/2009/anticorruptionthesfo?cmckreg=true, accessed 29 November 2011.
177 Serious Crime Act 2007, s. 25.

When bribery and corruption are so vast however, we would recommend that all avenues of prevention, recovery and prosecution are regularly used.

Further reading

D. Aaronberg and N. Higgins, 'The Bribery Act 2010: All bark and no bite . . . ?' (2010) *Archbold Review*, 5, 6–9.

D. Aaronberg and N. Higgins, 'Legislative comment the Bribery Act 2010: All bark and no bite . . . ?' (2010) *Archbold Review*, 5, 6–9.

P. Alldridge, 'Reforming bribery: Law Commission consultation paper 185: (1) Bribery reform and the law – again' (2008) *Criminal Law Review*, 9, 671–686.

K. Beale and P. Esposito, 'Emergent international attitudes towards bribery, corruption and money laundering' (2009) *Arbitration*, 75(3), 360–373.

Ed., 'The Bribery Act 2010' (2010) *Criminal Law Review*, 6, 439–440.

S. Gentle, 'Legislative comment – the Bribery Act 2010: Part 2: The corporate offence' (2011) *Criminal Law Review*, 2, 101–110.

Law Commission, *Reforming Bribery, Law Com No.313* (Law Commission: London, 2007).

Ministry of Justice, *The Bribery Act 2010 – Guidance* (Ministry of Justice: London, 2011).

T. Pope and T. Webb, 'Legislative comment – the Bribery Act 2010' (2010) *Journal of International Banking Law and Regulation*, 25(10), 480–483.

M. Raphael, *Blackstone's Guide to the Bribery Act 2010* (Oxford University Press: Oxford, 2010).

R. Sanyal and S. Samanta, 'Trends in international bribe-giving: Do anti-bribery laws matter?' (2011) *Journal of International Trade Law & Policy*, 10(2), 151–164.

S. Sheikh, 'The Bribery Act 2010: Commercial organisations beware!' (2011) *International Company and Commercial Law Review*, 22(1), 1–16.

C. Well, 'Bribery: Corporate liability under the draft bill' (2009) *Criminal Law Review*, 7, 479–487.

8

THE AVOIDANCE AND EVASION OF TAX

Introduction

Taxation in the United Kingdom (UK) can largely be divided into the taxes that are paid to central government and those paid to local government. Examples of the former include income tax, stamp duty, inheritance tax, capital gains tax, corporation tax, national insurance and taxes due on goods such as fuel, alcohol and tobacco; whereas for the latter there are council tax and business rates. No one likes paying tax and many will take steps to reduce their liability, but as Green explains, whilst 'we recognise that taxes are the fuel on which society runs . . . we resent it when others fail to pay their fair share'.[1] For clarity purposes, from the outset a distinction needs to be made between tax avoidance and tax evasion. Tax avoidance is either where legitimate means are used to reduce a tax liability, such as saving in a tax-free individual saving account (ISA) or by paying into a pension scheme, or where a tax avoidance scheme is used. Whilst the latter is not illegal per se it often exploits loopholes in the tax system and as such flouts the spirit of the law. In essence, tax avoidance schemes often involve 'bending the rules of the tax system to gain a tax advantage that Parliament never intended'.[2] Tax evasion, however, is the avoidance of paying taxes through illegal means. This may be achieved by a company misrepresenting its income, by it inflating the deductions that it can offset or by hiding money away in offshore accounts.

Taxation law is both vast and complicated and there is simply not the space here to deal with all forms of tax evasion. This chapter will therefore focus on the behaviours involved in evading and avoiding income tax, value added tax (VAT) and corporation tax. These three areas have been chosen as they significantly contribute

---

1 S. P. Green, *Lying, Cheating, and Stealing: A Moral Theory of White-Collar Crime* (Oxford University Press: Oxford, 2007, 1).
2 HL Deb, 25 February 2015, cW.

to the tax receipts collected by Her Majesty's Revenue and Customs (HMRC). For example between 2004 and 2015, income tax, capital gains tax and national insurance contributions made up on average 56 per cent of the total amount of money collected by HMRC. VAT contributed on average 19 per cent of the total receipts and corporation tax another 10 per cent.[3] Mirroring other chapters, this chapter will begin by looking at the criminal offences that exist to cover those types of tax evasion mentioned above. Next we will consider the background to the policy of criminalising and regulating both tax evasion and avoidance and then will evaluate the financial institutions and regulatory bodies that are involved in this enforcement. Next we look at sentencing policy and practices and, finally, offer some concluding thoughts on this particularly difficult area.

What are the offences?

Evasion of income tax

The offence of fraudulent evasion of income tax is found in section 106A of the Taxes Management Act 1970 (as amended by the Taxation (International and Other Provisions) Act 2010) which has been in force since 1 April 2010. The offence is committed if a person is 'knowingly concerned in the fraudulent evasion of income tax by that or any other person'.[4] A common denominator in many evasion offences is the necessity for the individual to be knowingly involved. This equates to having both knowledge[5] (which is more than mere suspicion) and being actually involved in the evasion. The conduct must also be dishonest which is defined under the two-stage test in *Ghosh*.[6] First the jury must ask whether according to the ordinary standards of reasonable and honest people what was done was dishonest and then, if it was, whether the defendant realised that what they had done was dishonest by these standards. The first part of the test is objective and the second subjective. For the purposes of tax evasion, therefore, the jury will ask whether according to ordinary standards the reasonable and honest person would have been involved in the type of behaviour that the defendant was involved in and second whether the defendant appreciated that what they were doing was dishonest by those standards.

Evasion of value added tax

The offences that relate to the fraudulent evasion of VAT are found in section 72 of the Value Added Tax Act 1994, with the current version being in force since 12 March 2015. In effect there are four offences under the legislation. The first,

---

3   HM Revenue & Customs, *HMRC Tax & NI Receipts, Monthly and Annual Historical Record* (HMRC: London, 19 June 2015), available from https://www.gov.uk/government/uploads/system/uploads/attachment_data/file/435404/May15_Receipts_Bulletin_v1.pdf.

4   Taxes Management Act 1970, s. 106A(1).

5   The concept of knowledge was defined by the Supreme Court, see Chapter 4.

6   [1982] Q.B. 1053.

found under section 72(1), is committed if a person 'is knowingly concerned in . . . the fraudulent evasion of VAT by him or any other person'.[7] This includes the situation where for example a person knows that money is owed but deliberately fails to submit a tax return or alternatively produces false accounts.[8] The offence is also made out if the person takes 'steps with a view to'[9] fraudulently evade VAT, which could occur where an individual fails to keep proper accounts or has not registered with HMRC for VAT purposes.[10] The second offence, known as false statement for VAT purposes,[11] relates to the provision of false particulars. This can be committed either where an individual has produced or sends to HMRC a document 'which is false in a material particular'[12] and intends to deceive or where that person has made a statement which either they know to be false or they are reckless as to whether or not it is true. This would be the case if a person suppresses sales or inflates the cost of purchases.[13] The third offence is available under section 72(10) and is committed when an individual 'acquires possession of or deals with any goods, or accepts the supply of any services, having reason to believe that VAT on the supply of the goods or services . . . has been or will be evaded'.[14] Furthermore, under section 72(8) there is a rather bizarre catch-all offence that effectively criminalises any conduct that amounts to an offence. Referred to as conduct amounting to an offence, the section reads: 'Where a person's conduct during any specified period must have involved the commission by him of one or more offences under the preceding provisions of this section, then, whether or not the particulars of that offence or those offences are known, he shall, by virtue of this subsection, be guilty of an offence.'[15]

Corporation tax

Following on from the above sections the reader's expectation is probably that this segment will outline the offence of fraudulently evading corporation tax. Despite the amount of corporation tax which is thought is evaded (see below), it is somewhat surprising that such an offence does not exist. The only criminal offence that is relevant here is the common law offence of cheating the public revenue. Because

---

7 Value Added Tax Act 1994, s. 72(1).
8 Lexis Nexis, 'Tax evasion offences – overview', available from http://www.lexisnexis.com/uk/lex-ispsl/corporatecrime/document/391421/55KB-9471-F188-N1BB-00000–00/Tax%20evasion%20offences%E2%80%94overview, accessed 12 July 2015.
9 Value Added Tax Act 1994, s. 72(1).
10 Lexis Nexis, 'Tax evasion offences – overview', available from http://www.lexisnexis.com/uk/lex-ispsl/corporatecrime/document/391421/55KB-9471-F188-N1BB-00000–00/Tax%20evasion%20offences%E2%80%94overview, accessed 12 July 2015.
11 Crown Prosecution Service, 'Fraud, False accounting, fraudulent evasion of VAT, False statement for VAT purposes, Conduct amounting to an offence', available from http://www.cps.gov.uk/legal/s_to_u/sentencing_manual/fraud/, accessed 12 July 2015.
12 Value Added Tax Act 1994, s. 72(3).
13 Lexis Nexis, 'Tax evasion offences – overview', available from http://www.lexisnexis.com/uk/lex-ispsl/corporatecrime/document/391421/55KB-9471-F188-N1BB-00000–00/Tax%20evasion%20offences%E2%80%94overview, accessed 12 July 2015.
14 Value Added Tax Act 1994, s. 72(10).
15 Value Added Tax Act 1994, s. 72(8).

it is based in the common law there is no statutory definition, although that given in Stephen's *Criminal Digest* does appear to have a certain amount of authority. He states that cheating is when someone 'fraudulently obtains the property of another by any deceitful practice . . . which is of such a nature that it directly affects, or may directly affect, the public at large'.[16] Cheating the public revenue has also been defined in *R v Less and Depalo*:

> The common law offence of cheating the Public Revenue does not necessarily require a false representation either by words or conduct. Cheating can include any form of fraudulent conduct which results in diverting money from the Revenue and in depriving the Revenue of the money to which it is entitled. It has, of course, to be fraudulent conduct. That is to say, deliberate conduct by the defendant to prejudice, or take the risk of prejudicing, the Revenue's right to the tax in question knowing that it has no right to do so.[17]

The offence has not been used to any great extent for corporation tax, perhaps allowing us to reach the conclusion that there is no real criminal offence for those who choose to evade paying this form of tax. In July 2015 the Conservative government gave its first budget, much of which dealt with issues of tax. However, despite the recognition that all must pay their taxes and introducing several methods to ensure this, there was nothing regarding making evading paying corporation tax a criminal offence. It seems somewhat unfair then that individuals are being treated vastly differently to companies and corporations, especially when it is the latter that arguably owe more money to HMRC.

The extent of tax evasion

As with all financial crimes there is a large black figure of crime, in the sense that it is extremely difficult to know how many people and companies are evading their tax liabilities. Menkes stated that 'the phenomena of hiding income can be traced back to 13th century sea piracy and the sale of stolen goods, creatively developed in response to the Catholic Church's war on usury, which compelled merchants and money-lenders taking interest on their activity to hide the profit'.[18] It has also been suggested that tax evasion is frequently associated with the shadow economy. This led Khil and Achek to state that:

> Given that tax evasion cannot be directly observed and it is linked to shadow economy, it is difficult for researchers to measure this variable. International reports conduct surveys to evaluate individuals' perceptions about tax evasion

16 James Fitzjames Stephen, *A Digest of the Criminal Law* 9th ed. (Sweet & Maxwell: London, 1950, 362).

17 Unreported, 2 March 1993 – summary available from http://swarb.co.uk/regina-v-less-and-depalo-cacd-2-mar-1993/.

18 M. Menkes, 'The divine comedy of governance in tax evasion matters: Or not?' (2015) *Journal of International Banking Law and Regulation*, 30(6), 325–329, at 326.

as a proxy for a country's tax evasion score. Accordingly, several empirical studies use the estimates provided in these reports.[19]

Picur and Riahi-Belkaoui stated that 'tax evasion is a crucial problem for countries, as economic development can be severely hampered by lower public revenues due to the lack of tax compliance'.[20] Even though there are measurement difficulties, HMRC nevertheless attempts to measure what it calls the tax gap, that is:

> the difference between the amount of tax that should, in theory, be collected by HMRC, against what is actually collected. The theoretical liability represents the tax that would be paid if all individuals and companies complied with both the letter of the law and our interpretation of Parliament's intention in setting law (referred to as the spirit of the law).[21]

This therefore includes tax lost through deliberate evasion, but also through tax avoidance schemes. In 2012–13, HMRC estimated that the tax gap in the UK was £34 billion, which equated to 6.8 per cent of all tax liabilities.[22] This appears to be a fairly steady figure with previous annual results including: £36 billion in 2008–09; £31 billion in 2009–10 and £33 billion in 2010–11 and 2011–12.[23] Of the £34 billion lost in 2012–13, £12.4 billion (36 per cent) was absent from VAT, £14.2 billion (41 per cent) from income tax, national insurance contributions and capital gains tax, and £3.9 billion (11 per cent) from corporation tax.[24] Interestingly, HMRC acknowledge that the tax gap is not just caused by criminal behaviour with it estimating that only £4.1 billion is lost because of tax evasion and £5.4 billion because of criminal attacks.[25] The remaining £24.5 billion, it estimates, is lost to the economy because of the behaviours of avoidance (£3.1 billion), legal interpretation (£4.5 billion), non-payment (£4.4 billion), the hidden economy (£5.9 billion), failure to take reasonable care (£4.2 billion), and error (£2.9 billion).[26] Tax evasion is also a significant problem in other jurisdictions and it has been suggested

---

19 H. Khil, and I. Achek, 'The determinants of tax evasion: A literature review' (2015) *International Journal of Law & Management*, 57(5), 486–497, at 490. For a detailed commentary on efforts to calculate the extent of tax evasion see F. Schneider, 'The size of the shadow economies of 145 countries all over the world: First results over the period 1999–2003', IZA Discussion Paper No. 143, *Forschungsiinstitut zur Zukunft der Arbeit* (Institute for the Study of Labor (IZA): Bonn, 2004).

20 R. D. Picur, and A. Riahi-Belkaoui, 'The impact of bureaucracy, corruption and tax compliance' (2006) Review of Accounting and Finance, 5(2), 174–180, at 174.

21 HM Revenue & Customs, *Measuring Tax Gaps 2014* (HMRC Corporate Communications, 2014, 16).

22 *Ibid.*, 3.

23 *Ibid.*, 4.

24 *Ibid.*, 11.

25 *Ibid.*, 13.

26 *Ibid.*

that the United States of America (USA) could be annually losing between $30 and $70 billion.[27]

These might however be conservative estimates. The Public and Commercial Services Union (PCSU) (the union for most staff at HMRC) claim that for the financial year 2011–12, and when looking at fewer items to those considered in the above calculations, the tax gap was not the £22.3 billion as estimated by HMRC but was in fact £73.4 billion. This significant increase is because of additionally including offshore tax abuse (£6.5 billion) and untaxed proceeds of fraud and other crime (£4.3 million), and also by significantly increasing the estimate of trading in the shadow economy from £9.9 billion to £40.3 billion.[28] This divergence was also seen for the tax year 2013–14 when HMRC estimated the tax gap to be £34 billion[29] whilst PCSU claimed that it was £119.4 billion.[30] Furthermore, in relation to corporation tax, research undertaken by MSCI between 2008 and 2012 suggests that when looking at 995 companies in the MSCI World Index, approximately 4 per cent paid on average less than 10 per cent in tax and 21.4 per cent paid taxes that were significantly lower than the average tax rate of the country in which revenue was generated.[31] Many of the companies involved are able to do this by basing their company in a tax haven country, so they commit tax avoidance rather than actual tax evasion, but such practices, as mentioned above, still breach the spirit of the law and perhaps more importantly cost countries vast amounts of lost revenue.

Policy background

The UK's policy towards tackling tax evasion and avoidance is primarily administered by HM Treasury and HMRC. Rhodes and Jones took the view that 'in 1997 the government made clear its view that "tax crime is a crime as much as any other" so that benefits enjoyed as a result of tax evasion amount to the proceeds of crime'.[32] Between 2010 and 2015, the Coalition government attempted to tackle tax avoidance by implementing a number of important policy initiatives. For example, in May 2010 the Coalition government proclaimed that it would 'make

27 J. Simser, 'Tax evasion and avoidance typologies' (2008) *Journal of Money Laundering Control*, 11(2), 123–134, at 124.

28 Richard Murphy, *The Tax Gap: Tax Evasion in 2014 – and What Can Be Done About It* (Public and Commercial Services Union: London, 2015).

29 HM Revenue & Customs, *Measuring Tax Gaps 2015* (HMRC Corporate Communications: London, 2015, 3).

30 Richard Murphy, *The Tax Gap: Tax Evasion in 2014 – and What Can Be Done About It* (Public and Commercial Services Union: London, 2015).

31 MSCI, *The 'Tax Gap' in the MSCI World* (MSCI ESG Research, London, December 2013), available from https://www.msci.com/resources/factsheets/MSCI_ESG_Research_Issue_Brief_The_Tax_Gap_in_the_MSCI_World.pdf.

32 J. Rhodes, and S. Jones, 'The Proceeds of Crime Act 2002 and tax evasion' (2004) *Private Client Business*, 1, 51–59, at 51.

every effort to prevent tax avoidance'.[33] This announcement was followed by the publication of 'Tackling tax avoidance', which, interestingly, outlined the Coalition government's strategy towards avoidance.[34] In this policy document, HM Treasury announced that its anti-avoidance strategy was based on three principles:

1   preventing avoidance at the outset;
2   detecting it early where it persists; and,
3   counteracting it through legislative change and challenge through litigation.[35]

Not content with these measures, HM Treasury stated in December 2012 that 'there are still too many people who illegally evade their taxes, or use aggressive tax avoidance in order not to pay their fair share', and consequently set out the government's commitment to taking action against such people.[36] This statement was followed by the publication of how the HMRC would tackle tax evasion in December 2012,[37] and a report entitled 'Levelling the tax playing field', which illustrated the success stories of how HMRC had tackled tax evasion and avoidance since 2010.[38] Additionally, HMRC published its offshore evasion strategy, 'No safe havens', which sets out HMRC's approach to tackling offshore evasion.[39] HMRC has stated that the aims of this strategy are to ensure that:

1   there are no jurisdictions where UK taxpayers feel safe to hide their income and assets from HMRC;
2   would-be offshore evaders realise that the balance of risk is against them;
3   offshore evaders voluntarily pay the tax due and remain compliant;
4   those who do not come forward are detected and face vigorously enforced sanctions; and,
5   there will be no place for facilitators of offshore evasion.[40]

Between 2010 and 2015 the Coalition government provided HMRC with an additional £917 million funding with a view to 'generating additional compliance revenues of £7 billion a year by 2015'.[41] This was followed by the announcement in 2012 that HMRC would be granted an additional £77 million to reduce tax

---

33 HM Government, *The Coalition: Our Programme for Government* (HM Government: London, 2010, 10).
34 HM Treasury, *Tackling Tax Avoidance* (HM Treasury: London, 2011).
35 *Ibid.*
36 HM Treasury, 'The Chancellor of the exchequer delivered the autumn statement to Parliament on 5 December 2012', available from https://www.gov.uk/government/speeches/autumn-statement-2012-chancellors-statement, accessed 15 March 2016.
37 HMRC, *Closing in on Tax Evasion: HMRC's Approach* (HMRC: London, 2012).
38 HMRC, *Levelling the Tax Playing Field Compliance Progress Report – March 2013* (HMRC: London, 2013).
39 HMRC, *No Safe Havens 2014* (HMRC: London, 2014).
40 HM Revenue and Customs, *No Safe Havens 2014* (HM Revenue and Customs: London, 2014, 3).
41 HM Government *Policy Paper 2010 to 2015 Government Policy: Tax Evasion and Avoidance* (HM Government: London, 2015).

evasion and avoidance. This was soon followed by a G8 summit in June 2013, which announced the introduction of a number of measures that were aimed at improving international tax transparency on tax evasion and tax avoidance.[42] In particular, the G8 leaders asked the Organisation for Economic Co-operation and Development (OECD) to create a template so that global corporations could report to the relevant tax authorities where they make their profits and how much tax they had paid around the world. This therefore gives tax authorities a new tool against tax avoidance by multinationals.[43] As a result of this G8 summit the government developed a new action plan. This implemented a number of strategies, including:

1   conducting and sharing more information relating to money laundering and terrorist financing risks;
2   ensuring that the Companies Act 2006 and the 2007 Money Laundering Regulations compelled companies to revel who actually owned them;
3   ensuring that competent authorities were able to access important information on trusts and that this information was shared;
4   reviewing corporate transparency;
5   assisting Overseas Territories and Crown Dependencies to implement the Recommendations of the Financial Action Task Force; and,
6   improving levels of international co-operation in the exchange of information.[44]

Additionally, HMRC attempted to encourage people to pay their tax liabilities by informing them how much money they owed before they launched an investigation. The Coalition government announced that this voluntary declaration scheme had resulted in HMRC raising £610 million. Another important part of the UK's policy towards tax evasion was the ability to prosecute people for breaches of tax legislation. Between 2010 and 2015, HMRC stated that the number of people who had been prosecuted for tax evasion had steadily increased from 165 in 2010–11, to 565 in 2012–13, and to 1,165 in 2014–15, thus representing a 58% increase in convictions.[45]

Furthermore, the Coalition government made some headway in preventing and limiting tax avoidance by large multinational companies. It argued that several multinational companies 'avoid paying some taxes by shifting profits away from the location' where the profits originate through a process called base erosion and profit

---

42   *Ibid.*
43   *Ibid.*
44   Ed., 'Plan released to combat tax evasion and money laundering' (2013) *Company Lawyer*, 34(9), 281.
45   See P. Berwick, and R. McCann, 'HMRC gets tough with tax evaders', 30 January 2013, available from http://www.ftadviser.com/2013/01/30/regulation/regulators/hmrc-gets-tough-with-tax-evaders-Q91OcHU1vzMC1Zfl7UKFjN/article.html, accessed 17 March 2016 and V. Holder, 'HMRC steps up tax evasion drive after 58% rise in convictions', 14 December 2015, available from http://www.ft.com/cms/s/0/4ff76fa0-a030–11e5–8613–08e211ea5317.html#axzz439zaVfkO, accessed 17 March 2016.

shifting' (BEPS).[46] It added that 'the international corporate tax standards have struggled to keep pace with changes in global business practices, with an increasing share of trade taking place online'.[47] The use of BEPS was highlighted by the OECD, which stated in February 2016 that it had 'agreed a new framework that would allow all interested countries and jurisdictions to join in efforts to update international tax rules'.[48] Furthermore, another important measure introduced by the Coalition government was the creation and subsequent expansion of HMRC's Affluent Unit.[49] The Affluent Unit seeks to target wealthy individuals who use tax avoidance schemes, have a low effective rate of tax against their total income, fail to file self-assessment returns on time, avoid paying stamp duty, have bank accounts in Switzerland, and/or have offshore property portfolios.[50] The Unit has proven to be an extremely effective entity with it netting 60 per cent more money in 2014 than in 2013.[51] The report, published by Pinsent Masons, concluded that it had collected £137.2 million in additional tax from investigations in 2013–14, up from £85.7 million in 2012–13.[52] As a direct result of this success, the government has provided the Unit with more funding which has enabled the recruitment of 100 additional tax inspectors.[53] The prevention of and reclamation of lost tax therefore appears to be high on the government's agenda and can therefore be sharply contrasted with the UK's counter-fraud strategy, where funding for the Serious Fraud Office (SFO) has continued to fall since 2010. Whilst we are not saying that the current government's focus on tax evasion is not per se a bad thing, we do wonder why this focus is not centred on all financial crime.

Another important development in the UK's policy towards tax evasion has been the extension of its remit to include tackling offshore tax evasion and

---

46 HM Government, *Policy Paper 2010 to 2015 Government Policy: Tax evasion and Avoidance* (HM Government: London, 2015).

47 *Ibid.*

48 OECD, 'All interested countries and jurisdictions to be invited to join global efforts led by the OECD and G20 to close international tax loopholes', 23 February 2016, available from http://www.oecd.org/tax/all-interested-countries-and-jurisdictions-to-be-invited-to-join-global-efforts-led-by-the-oecd-and-g20-to-close-international-tax-loopholes.htm, accessed 15 March 2016. For a more detailed discussion of the steps undertaken by the OECD to tackle BEPS see OECD, *Action Plan on Base Erosion and Profit Shifting* (OECD, 2013).

49 See HMRC, 'HMRC's affluent unit recruits 100 new inspectors', 16 January 2013, available from https://www.gov.uk/government/news/hmrc-s-affluent-unit-recruits-100-new-inspectors, accessed 15 March 2016.

50 *Ibid.*

51 BBC News, 'Tax crackdown by HMRC unit nets 60% more money, report says' 20 January 2015, available from http://www.bbc.co.uk/news/business-30973191, accessed 16 March 2015.

52 Pinsent Masons, 'Amount of extra tax collected via HMRC investigations into "mass affluent" jumps 60% to £137.2 Million', n/d, available from http://www.pinsentmasons.com/en/media/press-releases/2015/amount-of-extra-tax-collected-via-hmrc-investigations-into-mass-affluent-jumps-60-to-1372-million-1/, accessed 16 March 2015.

53 See HMRC, 'HMRC's affluent unit recruits 100 new inspectors', 16 January 2013, available from https://www.gov.uk/government/news/hmrc-s-affluent-unit-recruits-100-new-inspectors, accessed 15 March 2016.

avoidance. For example, in February 2012, HM Treasury announced a Joint Statement regarding an Intergovernmental Approach to Improving International Tax Compliance and Implementing the US Foreign Account Tax Compliance Act 2010.[54] The 2010 Act seeks to target non-compliance by USA taxpayers who hold foreign accounts. It focuses on the reporting by USA taxpayers about some foreign financial accounts and offshore assets and financial accounts held by USA taxpayers in which they hold a substantial ownership interest.[55] This measure was initially undertaken by the UK, France, Germany, Italy and Spain, which in July 2012 announced the publication of a new agreement to implement the Foreign Account Tax Compliance Act 2010.[56] In 2013, HMRC were given more than £150 million in funding to tackle tax avoidance and evasion, as well as reducing fraud, error and debt in the tax credits system.[57] Therefore it can be argued that the UK's tax evasion policy is based on a number of key concepts, including high-level international cooperation with other nation states and the provision of advice and guidance for UK territories. The policy is largely administered by HM Treasury but enforced by HMRC, which have developed a number of innovative mechanisms towards the collection of revenue, such as the creation of its Affluent Unit.

Financial institutions and regulatory bodies

The main agency that tackles tax evasion and tax avoidance is HMRC. The main function of HMRC according to the National Audit Office is to 'administer the tax system, including the management and reduction of risks to tax revenue'.[58] In addition it measures the tax gap (as explained above) and assesses what behaviour led to that gap. HMRC seeks to collect tax payments and to act as a customs authority. Its jurisdiction covers, but is not limited to, income tax, customs duty,

---

54 HM Treasury, 'Joint statement regarding an intergovernmental approach to improving international tax compliance and implementing FATCA', 8 February 2012, available from https://www.gov.uk/government/news/joint-statement-regarding-an-intergovernmental-approach-to-improving-international-tax-compliance-and-implementing-fatca, accessed 15 March 2016. For a more detailed discussion see HM Government, *Model Intergovernmental Agreement to Improve Tax Compliance and to Implement FATCA: Agreement between the [Government of the] United States of America and [the Government of] [FATCA Partner] to Improve International Tax Compliance and to Implement FATCA* (HM Government: London, 2012).

55 IRS, 'Foreign Account Tax Compliance Act', n/d, available from https://www.irs.gov/Businesses/Corporations/Foreign-Account-Tax-Compliance-Act-FATCA, accessed 16 March 2016.

56 HM Treasury, 'G5 FATCA agreement strengthens UK ability to tackle tax evasion', 26 July 2012, available from https://www.gov.uk/government/news/g5-fatca-agreement-strengthens-uk-ability-to-tackle-tax-evasion, accessed 15 March 2016.

57 HM Government, *Policy Paper 2010 to 2015 Government Policy: Tax Evasion and Avoidance* (HM Government: London, 2015).

58 National Audit Office, *Tackling Tax Fraud: How HMRC Responds to Tax Evasion, the Hidden Economy and Criminal Attacks* (National Audit Office: London, 2015, 6).

VAT and national insurance.[59] Furthermore, it is responsible for 'safeguarding the flow of money to the Exchequer through collection, compliance and enforcement activities'.[60] HMRC was established by virtue of the Commissioners for Revenue and Customs Act 2005,[61] which saw the merger of the Inland Revenue and HM Customs and Excise. It has been described as the lead strategic tax policy and policy development agency and leads on policy maintenance and implementation. This arrangement for policymaking is known as the policy partnership.[62]

HMRC has a number of strategic objectives, including: maximising the collection of tax revenues; clamping down on avoidance and evasion; transforming tax and payments for its customers; and, designing and delivering a professional, efficient and engaged organisation.[63] Consequently, HMRC has adopted a threefold approach towards tackling non-compliance with the UK's taxation laws. First, it promotes compliance with tax law. Second, it aims to prevent people and businesses from getting their tax affairs wrong. Third, it responds when people and businesses get their tax calculations wrong.[64] As outlined in the second chapter of this book, one of the most important pieces of legislation introduced to tackle financial crime was the Proceeds of Crime Act (POCA) 2002. In addition to codifying the criminalisation of money laundering, the 2002 Act also modified the anti-money laundering (AML) reporting obligation imposed on the regulated sector. POCA 2002 is ably supported by the 2007 Money Laundering Regulations, which provide that HMRC is the supervisory authority for money services businesses, high-value dealers, trust or company service providers, accountancy service providers and estate agency businesses.[65]

Sentencing and recovery

A person who is found guilty on indictment of the fraudulent evasion of income tax is liable to a maximum sentence of seven years in custody and/or to an unlimited

59 HMRC, 'About Us', n/d, available from https://www.gov.uk/government/organisations/hm-revenue-customs/about, accessed 17 March 2016.

60 *Ibid.*

61 Commissioners for Revenue and Customs Act 2005, s. 4. For a brief discussion see J. Jones, 'HMRC' (2005) *British Tax Review*, 3, 270–271.

62 HMRC, 'About Us', n/d, available from https://www.gov.uk/government/organisations/hm-revenue-customs/about, accessed 17 March 2016.

63 For a more detailed discussion see HMRC, *Single departmental plan 2015–2020* (HMRC, 2016).

64 National Audit Office, *Tackling Tax Fraud: How HMRC Responds to Tax Evasion, the Hidden Economy and Criminal Attacks* (National Audit Office: London, 2015, 5). For a more detailed discussion of the powers used by HMRC see J. Collins, and M. Piggin, 'Finance Act notes: Criminal investigations and HMRC powers – sections 82–87 and Schedule 22' (2007) *British Tax Review*, 5, 562–570.

65 The Money Laundering Regulations 2007, S.I. 2007/2157. For a more detailed discussion see J. Fisher, 'The anti-money laundering disclosure regime and the collection of revenue in the United Kingdom' (2010) *British Tax Review*, 3, 235–266, M. Goldby, 'Anti-money laundering reporting requirements imposed by English law: Measuring effectiveness and gauging the need for reform' (2013) *Journal of Business Law*, 4, 367–397.

fine.[66] This is the same penalty for the fraudulent evasion of VAT.[67] Because it is a common law offence cheating the public revenue does not have its sentence enshrined in statute. Out of kilter with the other offences, the Court has unlimited sentencing powers including up to life in custody.[68] When comparing the two statutory offences to the maximum penalties for the other criminal offences considered in this book it would appear that the government has set a hierarchy of seriousness in terms of financial crimes – if we take the maximum penalties as an indicator of gravity. The ranking is thus: money laundering and terrorist financing at the top (14 years); fraud and bribery and corruption in the middle (ten years); and insider dealing, market abuse and tax evasion at the bottom (seven years).

Whilst tax evasion and indeed tax avoidance schemes have been in existence since time immemorial, the desire to prosecute and sentence such 'criminals' has only really gathered pace in the last few years. As outlined above, in 2010 and as part of the Spending Review settlement, HMRC was allocated over £900 million to be spent over four years to tackle the problems of both tax avoidance and evasion, with the intention being that HMRC would 'increase the number of criminal prosecutions fivefold'.[69] Statistics for all tax offences show a steady increase in convictions since 2010–11, from 280 in that year to 401 in 2011–12, 522 in 2012–13, and 682 in 2013–14.[70] As the starting point under the previous Labour government was 107,[71] the fivefold goal has not only been achieved in terms of prosecutions, but also in terms of actual convictions. Unfortunately, HMRC do not keep records on the amount of money that has been recovered following successful prosecutions[72] but we can only imagine that this is in the millions. As the government continues to emphasise the importance of keeping within the spirit of the law in terms of taxation, it is predictable that these conviction rates will continue to rise, especially when in the 2015 July budget, George Osborne boosted HMRC's capacity by providing them with three-quarters of a billion pounds to tackle tax fraud, offshore trusts and the hidden economy. It is thought that such investment will yield up to £7.2 billion in extra tax.[73]

Despite there only being a fairly recent emphasis on prosecuting tax evaders, sentencing guidelines on the subject have existed for some time. In Attorney General's Reference (Nos. 86 and 87 of 1999)[74] the Attorney General identified

---

66 Taxes Management Act 1970, s. 106A(2).
67 Value Added Tax Act 1994, s. 72(1).
68 Crown Prosecution Service, 'Cheating the revenue (contrary to common law)', available from http://www.cps.gov.uk/legal/s_to_u/sentencing_manual/cheating_the_revenue_(contrary_to_common_law)/, accessed 16 March 2016.
69 Crown Prosecution Service, 'Prosecuting tax evasion' speech by Kier Starmer, available from http://www.cps.gov.uk/news/articles/prosecuting_tax_evasion/, accessed 16 March 2016.
70 HC Deb, 14 May 2014, c681W.
71 HC Deb, 26 March 2013, c1466.
72 HC Deb, 14 May 2014, c681W.
73 G. Osborne, 'Summer budget 2015 speech', available from https://www.gov.uk/government/speeches/chancellor-george-osbornes-summer-budget-2015-speech, accessed 16 March 2016.
74 [2001] 1 Cr. App. R. (S) 141 (CA (Crim Div)).

seven aggravating factors of tax and excise evasion. These were 'the sophisticated nature of the fraud which continued over three years, the exploitation of a scheme designed to promote vocational training, the breach of trust, the fraudulent obtaining of money, the amount of the loss to the Revenue, the personal benefit to each defendant, and the concealment of the fraud in documentation subject to audits'.[75] Relying on a number of other authorities, including Thornhill,[76] Alibhai[77] and Aziz,[78] the Court of Appeal held that where tax had been evaded for a period of time such defendants should expect not just to pay the owed tax and a financial penalty, but also to serve a term of custody. Length of sentence would be determined on 'a number of factors including the amount of tax evaded, the period of time during which the evasion took place, the effort made to conceal the fraud, whether others were drawn in and corrupted, the character of the defendant, the extent if known of his or her personal gain, whether there was a plea of guilty, and what was recovered'.[79]

In addition to case law, there is also a definitive guideline from the Sentencing Council, which covers fraud, bribery and money laundering offences and which has been effective since 1 October 2014. As mentioned in Chapters 2, 4 and 7, the Sentencing Council produce sentencing guidelines that must be followed by all courts and, furthermore, 'once guidelines have been issued it should be the exception rather than the rule to cite previous cases'.[80] In relation to revenue fraud and relevant to this chapter, the guidelines cover the fraudulent evasion of income tax and the VAT offences. As with all guidelines issued by the Council, the first step for any sentencer is to consider the culpability of the offender and the level of harm that was either caused or risked being caused. The latter also includes the intended loss or actual loss that was caused to HMRC. There are three levels of culpability: high, medium and lesser. Examples of high culpability include a leading role where it is a group activity, abuse of power or position of trust and significant planning; whilst lesser culpability could be evidenced where it was a one-off crime or the individual had limited awareness of the extent of the revenue fraud.[81] Harm is divided into seven categories, with category one detailing crimes worth £50 million or more, category four dealing with crimes between £5000,000 and £2 million and category seven with less than £20,000. When culpability and harm are assessed, the sentencer then uses a table[82] to work out the most appropriate sentence. For example if there was a category four offence and the culpability was considered to be high, the starting point would be five years and six months

---

75 *Attorney General's Reference (Nos. 86 and 87 of 1999)* Crim. L.R. 58.
76 (1980) 2 Cr. App. R. (S) 320.
77 (1992) 13 CR. App. R. (S) 682.
78 [1996] 1 Cr. App. R. (S) 265.
79 *Attorney General's Reference (Nos. 86 and 87 of 1999)* Crim. L.R. 59.
80 *Tongue (Ross)* [2007] EWCA Crim 561.
81 Sentencing Council Fraud, *Bribery and Money Laundering Offences, Definitive Guideline* (Sentencing Council: London, 2014).
82 *Ibid.*, at 23.

in custody with a range of four years to six years and six months in custody. How many high culpability factors were present in the offence and the level of the fraud in terms of financial gain/loss would determine whether the judge would go below, at, or above the starting point. This can also be influenced by the presence of other aggravating factors such as previous convictions, offence committed whilst on bail, multiple frauds, attempts to conceal or dispose of the evidence and wrongly placing the blame on others. Mitigation, used to lower the sentence, can also affect sentence length and may include a serious medical condition, age or lack of maturity, being a primary carer, remorse and having a learning disability or mental disorder.[83] The sentencer would then consider whether there were any other factors that would reduce the sentence, such as assisting in a prosecution and/or pleading guilty, and finally, it would look at the totality of the sentence if there were more than one offence to consider.

Guidelines for cheating the public revenue are sparse, largely because the offence is so infrequently charged. There used to be mention of the offence in the 2009 Definitive Guideline on Sentencing for Fraud,[84] but this has since been revoked by the guideline on Fraud, Bribery and Money Laundering as mentioned above. The most recent guideline does not cover cheating the public revenue at all. Sentencers therefore have to rely on a list of aggravating and mitigating factors as supplied by the Crown Prosecution Service (CPS) and a handful of appeal cases.[85]

Examples of sentencing for evading VAT include Rohan Pershad, a Queen's Counsel who was convicted in 2013 for cheating the public revenue by his failure to pay VAT for a period of 12 years. This amounted to an additional income of £624,579, which should have been paid to HMRC.[86] In February 2013, Pershad received three and a half years imprisonment. His was the first prosecution by the CPS/HMRC following the setting up of a special task force by HMRC, which specifically looked at lawyers who were evading tax.[87] In September 2014, John

83 *Ibid.*, at 25.
84 'This guideline does not cover the common law offence of creating the public revenue . . . (which) is generally reserved for the most serious and unusual offences and where a sentence 'in excess of the statutory maximum for other offences . . . would be . . . proper'. As such cases are unusual, no proposals are made for sentencing offenders convicted of this offences. It would be open to a court to have regard to the principles expressed in the guideline for fraud against HMRC when sentencing an offender convicted of cheating the public revenue but it should be used only as a point of reference as higher starting points are likely to be necessary.
85 For more details see: Crown Prosecution Service, 'Cheating the revenue (contrary to common law)' available from http://www.cps.gov.uk/legal/s_to_u/sentencing_manual/cheating_the_revenue_(contrary_to_common_law)/, accessed 16 March 2016.
86 Crown Prosecution Service, 'Queen's Counsel convicted of £600,000 VAT fraud', available from http://www.cps.gov.uk/news/latest_news/qc_convicted_of_gbp_600k_vat_fraud/index.html, accessed 16 March 2016.
87 R. Murray-West, 'Barrister sentenced for £600,000 tax fraud' (*The Telegraph*, 26 February 2013), available from http://www.telegraph.co.uk/finance/personalfinance/9895308/Barrister-sentenced-for-600000-tax-fraud.html, accessed 16 March 2016.

Woolfenden was sentenced to two years in custody for VAT evasion and failing to declare monies from online trading. Woolfenden was an eBay trader and failed to declare the income that he was acquiring through these online sales. Over a period of six years and with an annual turnover of approximately £1.4 million, he had evaded paying £299,752.93.[88] The above guideline was not operational in either of these cases, although when looking at the relevant tables the court does not appear to have been that far from it. Details are limited in terms of the defendants' culpability, but a sentence of three and a half years would put Pershad in the medium culpability range of a category four offence, and two years for Woolfenden would similarly put him in the medium culpability range of a category five offence.

In terms of evading income tax, examples include Melvyn Careswell, a plumber, who in July 2012 was sentenced to 12 months in custody for evading approximately £50,000 in tax. He had been running his own plumbing company for five years without registering his earnings with HMRC.[89] Plumbers appeared to be a priority for HMRC in 2011, as in August of that year five plumbers were arrested and another 600 were under investigation by HMRC, with some owing up to £150,000 in unpaid taxes.[90] Launching taskforces for particular areas and particular professions is something that HMRC are regularly doing, with other examples including investigations into the Midlands' haulage industry[91] and the restaurant trade in Yorkshire and Humber in July 2013.[92] Returning to sentencing, in January 2015, Zaher Somani was sentenced to three and a half years in custody for income tax evasion. For a period of seven years he had been underestimating his income on his tax returns and owed HMRC approximately £250,000.[93] During this period, Somani was serving as a magistrate and thus, as the sentencing judge, James Sampson, commented on, pretended 'to be a man

---

88 Crown Prosecution Service, 'Man sentenced for eBay tax evasion totalling almost £300,000', available from http://www.cps.gov.uk/news/latest_news/man_sentenced_for_ebay_tax_evasion_totalling_almost_gbp300000/index.html, accessed 16 March 2016.

89 I. Cowie, 'Plumber jailed for tax evasion as HMRC receipts rise' (*The Telegraph*, 27 July 2012), available from http://blogs.telegraph.co.uk/finance/ianmcowie/100019166/plumber-jailed-for-tax-evasion-as-hmrc-receipts-rise/, accessed 12 March 2016.

90 I. Cowie, 'Time to come clean as HMRC flushes out tax evasion?' (*The Telegraph*, 17 August 2011), available from http://blogs.telegraph.co.uk/finance/ianmcowie/100011592/time-to-come-clean-as-hmrc-flushes-out-tax-evasion/, accessed 13 March 2016.

91 HMRC, 'Crackdown in hauliers in the Midlands', available from https://www.gov.uk/government/news/crackdown-on-hauliers-in-the-midlands, accessed 11 March 2016.

92 HMRC, 'Tax taskforce to crack down on restaurants in the North East', available from https://www.gov.uk/government/news/tax-taskforce-to-crack-down-on-restaurants-in-the-north-east, accessed 16 March 2016.

93 http://www.dailymail.co.uk/news/article-2934295/Former-magistrate-fiddled-tax-returns-evade-250–000-income-tax-send-children-private-schools-gamble-casinos.html.

of integrity and honesty'[94] – a factor which most definitely would have been viewed as an aggravating factor and when looking at the Sentencing Council's guidance[95] quite rightly puts him as having high culpability. Moreover in May 2015, Anthony Lewis, a self-employed salesman who had failed to register with HMRC for tax and national insurance purposes, was sentenced to 18 months for five counts of fraudulently evading income tax. Between November 2008 and May 2014, Lewis had failed to pay £87,148 to HMRC.[96] What is interesting about all of these sentencing examples is that they follow very closely the guidance provided by the Sentencing Council, even those that were given prior to the guideline being issued.

As previously mentioned, HMRC and the CPS have not traditionally used the offence of cheating the public revenue to any great extent. When it is used it is generally reserved for high-profile scams or a high-profile person where the maximum penalty of seven years is deemed to be insufficient. One example was a VAT fraud where the loss suffered to HMRC was estimated at £107 million. The defendant, who was deemed to be the ringleader, was sentenced to 17 years.[97]

As mentioned throughout this chapter the government of late has been 'cracking down' on those tax avoidance schemes that breach the spirit of the law. One example, known as rate-booster schemes, is designed to allow groups to artificially move money around different companies within the group in order to claim tax relief on what they claim are overseas profits. Corporation tax on profits is thus avoided as these companies claim that tax has already been paid on overseas profits.[98] Two large companies that have recently been issued with tax demands because of their involvement in such schemes are Next Brand Ltd and Peninsular & Oriental Steam Navigation Company (P&O). In May 2015, the First-Tier Tribunal[99] (FTT) upheld the HMRC's demand from the Next group for £22.4 million in unpaid taxes. Furthermore, in June 2015 the Upper Tribunal[100] upheld

---

94 Mail Online, 'Former magistrate fiddled his tax returns to evade £250,000 in income tax so he could send his children to private schools and gamble in casinos', available from http://www.dailymail. co.uk/news/article-2934295/Former-magistrate-fiddled-tax-returns-evade-250–000-income-tax-send-children-private-schools-gamble-casinos.html, accessed 13 March 2016.

95 Sentencing Council Fraud, *Bribery and Money Laundering Offences, Definitive Guideline* (Sentencing Council: London, 2014, 23).

96 HMRC, 'Nottingham salesman jailed for tax fraud', available from http://www.mynewsdesk.com/ uk/hm-revenue-customs-hmrc/pressreleases/nottingham-salesman-jailed-for-tax-fraud-1159766, accessed 13 March 2016.

97 Spears, 'Cheating HMRC could lead to life in jail', available from http://www.spearswms.com/ news/cheating-hmrc-could-lead-to-life-in-jail/#.VZ4oO03bK70, accessed 12 March 2016.

98 HMRC, 'Clothing giant Next loses tax avoidance case', available from https://www.gov.uk/ government/news/clothing-giant-next-loses-tax-avoidance-case, accessed 12 March 2016.

99 *Next Brand Limited* [2015] TC 04368.

100 *Peninsular & Oriental Steam Navigation Company v R & C Commrs* (2015) UKUT 0312.

the FTT's earlier ruling that HMRC were correct to issues P&O with a demand for £14 million. Both of these cases are incredibly important as it is thought that HMRC will now be able to recover £140 million from another 20 companies, all of which were involved in similar behaviour.[101] Moreover, when P&O and Next were initially issued with the demands approximately 70 other rate-booster schemes were conceded by other companies, rather than face court proceedings. HMRC have claimed that this has resulted in the collection of a further £500 million.[102] These two cases thus have the potential to secure over £676 million in unpaid taxes, which does not include any amount that will now be paid because of the deterrent effects of the judgments. Other companies that have lost appeals regarding tax avoidance schemes include Bristol and West (worth £30 million),[103] Land Securities plc (£60 million),[104] Vocalspruce Ltd (£88 million), Abbeyland (£50 million) and WHA (£600 million). In 2013, HMRC recovered nearly £1.2 billion in unpaid corporation tax.[105]

Individuals have also been focused upon in terms of tax avoidance, with celebrities such as Jimmy Carr,[106] Chris Moyles[107] and Davina McCall[108] being in the headlines. Gary Barlow, Howard Donald and Mark Owen of Take That lost an appeal to the FTT in 2014 where a tax avoidance scheme known as 'Icebreaker' was discredited. With their manager, Jonathan Wild, the men were members of a partnership called Larkdale LLP that invested in Icebreaker and used the scheme to hide £63 million from HMRC. In his decision on 9 May 2014, Judge Bishopp said that the scheme 'is, and was known and understood by all concerned to be, a tax avoidance scheme'.[109] Colin Jackson, the Olympic hurdler, is also said to have invested in

101 CCH Daily, 'P&O loses £14m double tax relief 'rate-booster' case', available from https://www.accountancylive.com/po-loses-%C2%A314m-double-tax-relief-rate-booster-case, accessed 11 March 2016.
102 HMRC, 'Clothing giant Next loses tax avoidance case', available from https://www.gov.uk/government/news/clothing-giant-next-loses-tax-avoidance-case, accessed 12 March 2016.
103 HMRC, 'Bristol and West loses Corporation Tax avoidance case', available from https://www.gov.uk/government/news/bristol-and-west-loses-corporation-tax-avoidance-case, accessed 16 March 2016.
104 HMRC, 'Morgan Stanley's £60m tax avoidance scheme beaten in court', available from https://www.gov.uk/government/news/morgan-stanley-s-60m-tax-avoidance-scheme-beaten-in-court, accessed 16 March 2016.
105 HMRC, 'HMRC wins in court have protected over £1 billion', available from https://www.gov.uk/government/news/hmrc-wins-in-court-have-protected-over-1-billion, accessed 16 March 2016.
106 BBC News, 'Jimmy Carr and the morality of tax avoidance', available from http://www.bbc.co.uk/news/magazine-18537051, accessed 16 March 2016.
107 E. Alexander, 'Chris Moyles could face 'huge tax bill' after tax avoidance appeal fails', (Independent, 1 October 2014), available from http://www.independent.co.uk/news/people/chris-moyles-could-face-huge-tax-bill-after-tax-avoidance-appeal-fails-9766651.html, accessed 16 March 2016.
108 The Sunday Times, 'Stars face heft bill over film tax breaks', available from http://www.thesundaytimes.co.uk/sto/news/uk_news/People/article1513839.ece, accessed 16 March 2016.
109 Independent, 'Celebrities hid £340m in icebreaker tax avoidance scheme used by Gary Barlow', available from http://www.independent.co.uk/news/uk/home-news/celebrities-hid-340m-in-icebreaker-tax-avoidance-scheme-used-by-gary-barlow-9367454.html, accessed 12 March 2016.

Icebreaker through a partnership called Sparkdale LLP. Sparkdale claimed losses of £9,399,878, which members of the partnership could then use to offset their own personal tax liabilities.[110]

In addition to criminal proceedings, HMRC have also taken the decision to 'name and shame' tax evaders through its 'most-wanted' gallery. Available through flickr,[111] in March 2016 the gallery 33 photos of HMRC's most-wanted tax fugitives and seven photos of those who had been caught and jailed. Behind each photo there is a profile of the individual, including name, age range, nationality, estimated cost to the taxpayer and brief details of the offence.[112] The gallery has been in operation since 2012 and contains people who owe HMRC more than £25,000.[113] Moreover, since April 2010, HMRC also publish details of those who they define as deliberate tax defaulters. These are people who have received penalties either for 'deliberate errors in their tax returns [or for] deliberately failing to comply with their tax obligations'.[114] The minimum threshold is again £25,000 and can be used for those who have deliberately defaulted in certain VAT and excise duties.[115] In March 2016 the list had 19 entries (although there were 37 entries in May 2015) and included the name of the company or individual, the business, trade or occupation, an address, default dates, penalty amounts and the total amount of tax due.[116] The publication of such details is allowed under section 94 Finance Act 2009 and 'aims to deter deliberate tax defaulters; reassure those who do pay the right tax; and encourage those who do not, to come forward and bring their tax affairs up to date'.[117]

As with the other financial crimes considered in this book, when sentencing, the judge must also consider whether it is appropriate to make ancillary orders that assist in the recovery of the losses caused. If appropriate the court can make a confiscation order (see Chapter 2), a compensation order (the payment of monies to the victims involved), a financial reporting order (see Chapter 4) and disqualify the offender from acting as a company director (see Chapter 4). If appropriate the court can also consider deportation.[118]

---

110 BBC News, 'Colin Jackson involved in tax avoidance scheme', available from http://www.bbc.co.uk/news/uk-wales-27411490, accessed 16 March 2016.

111 See https://www.flickr.com/photos/hmrcgovuk/sets/72157631087785530/.

112 For an example see: https://www.flickr.com/photos/hmrcgovuk/14854540497/in/album-72157631087785530/.

113 HMRC, 'Tax cheats named by HMRC', available from https://www.gov.uk/government/news/tax-cheats-named-by-hmrc, accessed 16 March 2016.

114 HMRC, 'Published details of deliberate tax defaulters', available from https://www.gov.uk/government/publications/publishing-details-of-deliberate-tax-defaulters-pddd#history, accessed 16 March 2016.

115 The government's explanatory note to Finance Act 2009, s. 94.

116 *Ibid.*

117 The government's explanatory note to Finance Act 2009, s. 94.

118 Crown Prosecution Service, 'Fraudulent evasion of income tax', available from http://www.cps.gov.uk/legal/s_to_u/sentencing_manual/revenue_offences_fraudulent_evasion_of_income_tax/index.html, accessed 16 March 2016.

TABLE 8.1 Recent fraudulent evasion of income tax cases

Offence: fraudulent evasion of income tax
Legislation: section 106A of the Taxes Management Act 1970
Maximum Penalty: seven years imprisonment

Name	Date	Sentence	Brief Details
Fredo Guedes	19.1.2016	two years eight months	Pleaded guilty to evading £131,359.99 of income tax, £18,968.84 of national insurance and £96,699.78 of VAT between 2006 and 2013. He charged his clients VAT but was using a VAT number that no longer existed. The judge said: 'You fraudulently received public money meant for the administration of public services. You knew that the harder you worked, the more money you would receive and the more you could dishonestly retain.'[119]
Andrew Thomas Henry Jenkins	17.8.2015	one year suspended	Pleaded guilty to the evasion of income tax and national insurance. Explaining the sentence the judge said: 'There must be a penalty in a case like this which will deter others. You defrauded the revenue of a very large sum of money and knew perfectly well what you were doing . . . You suggest you believe you were receiving your income net of tax and national insurance . . . I find that explanation completely incredible. You paid no tax at all even when any intelligent person would have appreciated that was dishonest.'[120]
Jason Andrew Smith	16.10.14	nine months	Pleaded guilty to failing to pay tax for a period of five years during a period when he was a self-employed salesman. He had set up a service company and had displayed knowledge of tax liabilities and so was held to be dishonest.

119 http://www.thelawpages.com/court-cases/Fredo-Guedes-16752–1.law.
120 http://www.thelawpages.com/court-cases/Anthony-Thomas-Henry-Jenkins-15866–1.law.

Name	Date	Sentence	Brief Details
Khan Mohammed Suleman	4.4.2014	four years	Pleaded guilty to evading income tax and cheating the public revenue for a nine-year period. His liabilities amounted to more than £445,000.
Mark Hawthorn	22.8.2013	six months	Pleaded guilty to two counts of evading income tax and national insurance amounting to £3,759. He was claiming a number of benefits and failed to pay any tax on his earnings.
Balbir Baden	28.7.2010	one year three months	He fraudulently underpaid tax amounting to £270,000. The judge said: 'Everyone who is self-employed has to be trusted and it strikes at the core of that accountability.'[121]

TABLE 8.2 Recent fraudulent evasion of VAT cases

Offence: fraudulent evasion of VAT
Legislation: section 72 Value Added Tax Act 1994
Maximum Penalty: seven years imprisonment

Name	Date	Sentence	Brief Details
Lindsey Stoneham	21.9.2015	three years six months	Pleaded guilty to evading VAT and defrauding amounts of money totalling £428,409 for an 18-month period. The judge said: 'In any view what you did over a significant amount of time was a sophisticated type of offending which involved sophisticated planning.'[122]
Terence Robert John Perdue	31.7.2015	one year six months and banned from acting as a company director for seven years	Pleaded guilty to evading VAT and also failing to comply with environmental regulations. On payments that he had received amounting more than £3.3 million he had failed to pay £327,000 in tax liabilities. The judge said: 'You knew what you were doing and I consider, in these circumstances, the sentence I should impose is one of immediate imprisonment.'[123]

(Continued)

121 http://www.thelawpages.com/court-cases/Balbir-Baden-5391-1.law.
122 http://www.thelawpages.com/court-cases/Lindsey-Stoneham-16087-1.law.
123 http://www.thelawpages.com/court-cases/Terrance-Robert-John-Perdue-15750-1.law.

TABLE 8.2 (Continued)

Name	Date	Sentence	Brief Details
Paresh Vyas	17.6.2015	five years	Pleaded guilty to evading VAT liabilities worth £1,313,500.
Sarju Popat	17.6.2015	five years six months and banned from acting as a company director for eight years	Involved in the above offence. Popat, with Paresh Vyas and Manoj Vyas (below), worked at a car company in Harrow. They sold more than 160 luxury vehicles, charging the customers the relevant VAT, but only paid VAT on their profits.
Manoj Vyas	17.6.2015	four years and banned from acting as a company director for eight years	As above
Neil Anthony Lesfrance	8.5.2015	three years	Pleaded guilty to submitting false VAT repayment returns. He claimed that he had received nearly £47,000 more than he actually had done.
Omar Farooq Mayet	17.11.2014	one year six months and a victim surcharge of £100	Pleaded guilty to obtaining VAT repayments. He registered a fake taxi business and claimed quarterly VAT repayments totalling £35,771. The judge said: 'It was clearly a fraudulent enterprise right from the outset . . . You became embroiled in greed through this fraud.'[124]

Future recommendations

The UK's taxation regime has been heavily criticised, not least since the revelations in February 2015 made by the whistle-blower Herve Falciani who claimed that HSBC reassured its international clients that details of accounts held would not be disclosed to national authorities in numerous jurisdictions, regardless of indications of undeclared assets.[125] As a result of these allegations the enforcement performance of HMRC has come under a greater level of scrutiny.[126] This is not surprising since

---

124 http://www.thelawpages.com/court-cases/Omar-Farooq-Mayet-14397-1.law.

125 The International Consortium for Investigative Journalists, 'Banking giant HSBC sheltered murky cash linked to dictators and arms dealers', 8 February 2015, available from http://www.icij.org/project/swiss-leaks/banking-giant-hsbc-sheltered-murky-cash-linked-dictators-and-arms-dealers, accessed 20 June 2015.

126 For an interesting commentary on the tax position and liability of banks see R. Collier, 'Intentions, banks, politics and the law: The UK Code of Practice on Taxation for Banks' (2014) *British Tax Review*, 4, 478–508.

HMRC has only offered one referral to the CPS for prosecution out of approximately 7,000 of HSBC's clients and the bank has not faced any sanctions. In order to address such problems the government announced a set of proposals to create a new corporate offence of failure to prevent the facilitation of evasion.[127] In July 2015, the government proposed:

- A new criminal offence for corporations that fail to take adequate steps to prevent the facilitation of tax evasion by their agents;
- Tougher financial penalties for offshore evaders, including the possibility of a penalty based on the value of the asset on which tax was evaded as well as wider public naming of offshore evaders;
- A new penalty regime for those who enable tax evasion, based on the tax they have helped taxpayers to evade and the naming of such enablers; and,
- A new simpler criminal offence to make the prosecution of offshore evaders easier.[128]

Several commentators have called on the government to quickly introduce this new criminal offence following the publication of the proposals. However, the Chairman of the Chartered Institute of Taxation (CIOT) has stated:

> The CIOT supports targeted measures to stamp out tax evasion and believes that tax professionals play an important part in assisting people to comply with their tax obligations. In our view, the Government and HMRC really need to make it clear what the public policy rationale is for the corporate evasion criminal offence in light of the recent ministerial statement. We have been saying that there is enough law in this area already and the ministerial statement seems to support that view.[129]

However, at the time of writing the book, in early 2016, there have been no further developments in this area. Therefore it is likely that HMRC will continue to exercise its criminal and civil enforcement powers until the introduction of the new corporate offence of failure to prevent the facilitation of evasion. Once this proposal has been introduced it will hopefully place tax evasion on the same level as money laundering and bribery and may finally lead to it being taken as seriously as these other types of financial crime.

---

127 Ed., 'Call for clarity on future of law on corporate tax evasion' (2016) *Company Lawyer*, 37(1), 8.

128 HM Revenue and Customs, *Tackling Offshore Tax Evasion: A New Corporate Criminal Offence of Failure to Prevent the Facilitation of Evasion* (HM Revenue and Customs: London, 2015).

129 Chartered Institute of Taxation, 'Press Release: The Chartered Institute of Taxation Wants Clarity on Future of Law on Corporate Tax Evasion', n/d, available from http://www.tax.org.uk/media-centre/press-releases/press-release-chartered-institute-taxation-wants-clarity-future-law, accessed 13 March 2016.

Further reading

P. Alldridge and A. Mumford, 'Tax evasion and the Proceeds of Crime Act 2002' (2005) *Legal Studies*, 25(3), 353–373.

Anon, 'Fighting tax evasion: Commission proposes wider exchanges of information within EU' (2013) *EC Focus*, 309, 1–3.

A. Barry, 'Examining tax evasion and money laundering' (1999) *Journal of Money Laundering Control*, 2(4), 326–330.

M. Beare, 'Searching for wayward dollars: Money laundering or tax evasion – which dollars are we really after?' (2002) *Journal of Financial Crime*, 9(3), 259–267.

M. Beare, 'Searching for wayward dollars: Money laundering or tax evasion – which dollars are we really after?' (2002) *Journal of Financial Crime*, 9(3), 259–267.

M. Boyrie, S. Pak, and J. Zdanowicz, 'Money laundering and income tax evasion: The determination of optimal audits and inspections to detect abnormal prices in international trade' (2004) *Journal of Financial Crime*, 12(2), 123–130.

M. Bridges, 'Tax evasion: A crime in itself – the relationship with money laundering' (1996) *Journal of Financial Crime*, 4(2), 161–168

M. Bridges and P. Green, 'Tax evasion and money laundering – an open and shut case?' (1999) *Journal of Money Laundering Control*, 3(1), 51–56

M. Bridges and P. Green, 'Tax evasion: Update on the proceeds of crime debate' (2000) *Journal of Money Laundering Control*, 3(4), 371–372

P. Burrell, 'Preventing tax evasion through money-laundering legislation' (2000) *Journal of Money Laundering*, 3(4), 304–308.

Ed., 'Call for clarity on future of law on corporate tax evasion' (2016) *Company Lawyer*, 37(1), 8.

Ed., 'Plan released to combat tax evasion and money laundering' (2013) *Company Lawyer*, 34(9), 281.

M. Menkes, 'The divine comedy of governance in tax evasion matters: Or not?' (2015) *Journal of International Banking Law and Regulation*, 30(6), 325–329.

K. Oliver, 'International taxation: Tax evasion as a predicate offence to money laundering' (2002) *International Legal Practitioner*, 27(2), 55–63.

J. Rhodes and S. Jones, 'The Proceeds of Crime Act 2002 and tax evasion' (2004) *Private Client Business*, 1, 51–59.

N. Ryder and S. Bourton, 'HSBC and tax evasion scandal: The prosecution of white-collar criminals and the legacy of the coalition government' (2015) *Criminal Lawyer*, 226, 3–4.

J. Simser, 'Tax evasion and avoidance typologies' (2008) *Journal of Money Laundering Control*, 11(2), 123–134.

A. Watters, 'The mission creep of tax evasion' (2016) *Solicitors Journal*, 160(1), 32.

9

CONCLUSIONS AND RECOMMENDATIONS

This book has identified and provided a detailed and critical review of the United Kingdom's (UK) policies and legislative attempts to tackle financial crime. The UK has to a large extent attempted to implement all of the financial crime conventions of the United Nations (UN) and the legislative measures of the European Union (EU). Therefore the UK has created a generally robust and at times aggressive legislative slant towards financial crime. This has been reflected in the creation of several regulatory and law enforcement agencies that been given the difficult task of enforcing the extensive legislative frameworks. The first chapter of the book began by illustrating how difficult it has been to not only define financial crime, but also how impossible it has been to accurately identify the extent of each of the financial crimes considered in this book. We highlighted the importance of the seminal definition of white collar crime provided by Professor Edwin Sutherland and how this definition has attracted a great deal of criticism. Furthermore, the first chapter provided a summary of research and reports that have attempted to estimate the extent of each of the financial crimes considered in this book. It is important to note that there is still not an internationally agreed definition of financial crime despite the multitude of international legislative instruments introduced by the UN and EU.

Money laundering

The second chapter of the book dealt with the threats posed by money laundering and illustrated how the UK has fully implemented both the UN and EU anti-money laundering (AML) measures. The UK has fully complied with its international obligations under the Vienna and Palermo conventions and its requirements under the Money Laundering Directives. In fact, the UK's measures go beyond its international obligations. Furthermore, it has even been suggested that the UK has implemented the EU AML Directives to only 'gold plate' its domestic legislation. The origins of the criminalisation of money laundering can be traced from the Drug Trafficking Offences Act 1986, since when the legislative framework has been updated and codified by the Proceeds of Crime Act (POCA) 2002. The criminal offences contained in Part 7 of POCA 2002 have been more frequently used and we have seen an increase in the number of prosecutions and convictions for money laundering. The 2002 Act introduced a new era in the UK towards the criminalisation of money laundering – a single codified law. The ambit of the offences is extremely wide and meets the benchmarks of the Financial Action Task Force (FATF) and the international measures of the UN and EU. The involvement of the Financial Services Authority (FSA), now the Financial Conduct Authority (FCA), is an innovative attempt to reduce the impact of money laundering. It is the first time that a financial regulatory body in the UK has been given such a specific role. However, the city regulator has implemented a costly and at times unnecessarily complicated regime, yet it has at least attempted to lessen the AML obligations by implementing a more flexible regime. For example, the Systems and Controls or SYSC part of the Handbook have imposed a wide range of what can be referred to as 'pre-placement' strategy. If an authorised firm breached the FCA regulations it can be subjected to punishment from the City regulator. For example, the FCA has continued to impose record financial penalties on firms that have weak levels of AML compliance. The financial sanctions are imposed on firms even where there is no evidence of money laundering. The FCA has continued the 'credible deterrence' policy that was initially used by the FSA on Money Laundering Reporting Officers (MLRO). Here, the City regulator imposed a financial penalty on both the firm and MLRO, which can have a detrimental impact on both parties. However, there is a clear weakness in the enforcement response of the FCA towards money laundering, and that is the lack of criminal prosecutions. This is somewhat surprising as the ability of the FCA to instigate criminal proceedings is not only permitted by the Financial Services and Markets Act 2000 (FSMA 2000), but also the Supreme Court decision in *R v Rollins*. The most significant development in the area of money laundering has been the creation of the National Crime Agency (NCA) since the introduction of the Crime and Courts Act 2013. The NCA continues to act as the UK's financial intelligence unit (FIU) and manage its confiscation regime.

However, the effectiveness of these measures can be compared unfavourably with those in the United States of America (USA) because of the small number of successful convictions for money laundering. The UK's mutual legal assistance mechanisms are generally broad and adhere to the majority of the international legal instruments and relevant recommendations of the FATF. The preventative measures are epitomised by pre-placement policy adopted by the FCA and the extensive requirements of the Money Laundering Regulations (2007). However, these measures are costly and, as previously mentioned, at times it is an unnecessarily complicated regime, yet they have at least attempted to lessen the AML obligations by adopting a risk-based approach. The Suspicious Activity Report (SAR) reporting requirements have imposed significant administrative burdens on financial institutions. They have led to an increased level of record-keeping, report filing and internal policing requirements. The imposition of even more mandatory reporting requirements was inevitable, given the government's tough stance towards money laundering. It is questionable however whether the filing of an SAR will make any difference given the difficulties in securing prosecutions in money laundering offences. It is also possible to argue that the reporting requirements have created a 'needle-in-the-haystack' problem, especially given the large number of SARs annually submitted. It is likely that the next significant development in the AML arena will be the implementation of the EU's Fourth Money Laundering Directive. All member states are required to fully implement this by June 2017.

Terrorist financing

The third chapter of the book investigated the financing of terrorism and it outlined how the UK has attempted to tackle this type of financial crime. The UK, unlike the many other nation states, had introduced a plethora of counter-terrorist related legislation prior to the terrorist attacks in September 2001. For example, the UK has had specific counter-terrorist legislation since the early part of the twentieth century. The Prevention of Terrorism (Temporary Provisions) Act 1989 introduced a series of measures related to counter-terrorist financing (CTF) that predated the international convention by nearly a decade. These measures were intended to counteract the threat posed by the Irish Republican Army (IRA) and other domestic terrorist-related entities. However, a detailed review of the effectiveness of these provisions by the Home Office determined that they were not fit for purpose and should be reformed. This resulted in the introduction of the Terrorism Act 2000 that repealed the terrorist financing provisions of the Prevention of Terrorism (Temporary Provisions) Act 1989. The Terrorism Act 2000 was amended by the Anti-terrorism, Crime and Security Act 2001 and several related statutory instruments that were introduced following the terrorist attacks in September 2001. These legislative measures expanded the criminal offence of the financing of terrorism, required reporting entities to submit reports to the NCA that related to allegations of suspicious transactions for the purposes of supporting or funding terrorism, and introduced the UN sanctions regime and measures that allowed for the freezing of terrorist assets. The UK government has fully implemented UN resolutions and EU regulations and it must be commended for going beyond the scope of its international obligations.

The Terrorism Act 2000 overhauled the terrorist financing offences that yielded a derisory four convictions over a ten-year period and the legislation now applies to international acts of terrorism in addition to acts of domestic terrorism. This area has undergone a significant development since the first edition of the book was published in 2013. The threat posed by the financing of terrorism has been graphically illustrated by the continued use of a growing vast array of financial instruments that have been used by terrorist groups. This has been clearly illustrated by the continuing threat posed by such terrorist groups as al-Qaeda, Boko

Haram, Al Shabaab and Islamic State of Iraq and the Levant (ISIL). The UK has extended the scope of its legislative measures that criminalise the financing of terrorism. However, the use of these criminal provisions is still subject to a great deal of criticism because of their underwhelming use. The ability to freeze the assets of suspected terrorist organisations has been available since 1964, yet it was not until the fall of the Taliban that HM Treasury froze assets of over £80 million. The ability of the government to freeze the assets of terrorist organisations initially appeared to be an effective weapon against terrorist finance. Subsequently, HM Treasury has only frozen a further £10 million of suspected terrorist assets. However, the ability to freeze the assets of suspected terrorists has been limited because of the decision in *A v HM Treasury*. The ability of the UK to counter the threat posed by terrorist financing has been limited by several important judicial opinions that have not only criticised the UK's CTF measures, but also declared them as unconstitutional. Therefore this part of the policy must be criticised because it is a short-term solution to a long-term problem. The effectiveness of the reporting requirements under the Terrorism Act 2000 and the Anti-terrorism, Crime and Security Act 2001 must also be queried because of the extensive sources of funding options available to terrorists. The effectiveness of the UK's stance towards the financing of terrorism has also been limited by political infighting within the government over the creation of a single Economic Crime Agency (ECA). This was proposed by Fisher before the general election in 2010 and was subsequently adopted by the Coalition government as part of their Coalition agreement.[1] However, the idea was rejected by the Home Secretary, Theresa May MP, who opted to prioritise the creation of the NCA following the introduction and enactment of the Courts and Crime Act 2013. The role of the NCA is divided into four 'Commands', one of which tackles 'Economic Crime'. This disjointed approach towards establishing a single ECA that exclusively deals with all aspects of financial crime has adversely affected the UK's ability to tackle the financing of terrorism. For example, the Home Affairs Select Committee stated that the effectiveness of the UK's CTF strategy is also adversely affected by 'the fact that in the UK, the responsibility for countering terrorism finance is spread across a number of departmental departments and agencies with no department in charge of overseeing the policy'.[2] This was supported by Anderson who noted:

> the fact that asset-freezing is administered by a different department from other counter-terrorism powers means however that extra effort may be required if asset-freezing is always to be considered as an alternative to or in conjunction with other possible disposals for those believed to be engaged in terrorism.[3]

---

1 Policy Exchange, *Fighting Fraud and Financial Crime* (Policy Exchange: London, 2010).
2 Home Affairs Select Committee *Counter-terrorism Seventeenth Report of Session 2013–14* (Home Affairs Select Committee: London, 2014) 40.
3 Anderson, D. *Third report on the operation of the Terrorist Asset-Freezing Etc. Act 2010* (HM Government: 2013) at 13.

Fraud

The UK fraud policy has gathered pace following the publication of the Fraud Review in 2006, but is still in a state of flux. The UK has a single Fraud Act (2006), which criminalises different types of fraudulent activities and provides prosecutors with new powers to tackle fraud. The second part of its anti-fraud policy concerns primary and secondary agencies, and it is this part that is in need of fundamental reform. There is no single agency that takes a lead role in tackling fraud; there are simply too many agencies performing the same function, a position that is worsened by the fact that there is not one government department that manages all this. For example, HM Treasury has been charged with developing and implementing the UK's policies towards money laundering and terrorist financing, yet it has very little to do with the UK's fraud policy. Furthermore the Home Office has been charged with tackling the problems associated with organised crime, but does little to tackle fraud. Therefore it is recommended that a single government department is given the task of tackling all types of financial crime; it seems logical that this task is given to HM Treasury, given its experience with money laundering and terror-ist financing. Another example of the overlap between anti- fraud agencies relates to the fact that both the Serious Fraud Office (SFO) and FCA have the ability to conduct investigations and initiate prosecutions. The National Fraud Authority (NFA) has been given a three-year budget of £29 million to tackle an industry that is worth £30 billion. Therefore it faces an improbable mission to reduce the extent of fraud with a very small budget. This makes little to no sense. The UK government should develop a unitary financial crime agency that incorporates the functions of the agencies outlined above. It is possible to argue that this process has already started with the merger of several agencies, including the National Crime Squad, the National Criminal Intelligence Service, the Assets Recovery Agency and the Serious Organised Crime Agency into the NCA. The primary legislation that imposes reporting obligations is the POCA 2002, under which fraud is reported to NCA. However, in some circumstances allegations of fraud are reported to banks and the police, and the regulated sector reports to the FCA, and not the NCA. The system needs clarification.

The SFO has come under an increased level of scrutiny since its announcement in 2009 that it is seeking permission from the Attorney General to bring corrup-tion charges against BAE Systems Plc. Its performance since its creation in the 1980s has been criticised because of a number of high-profile failed prosecutions. However, it is important to note that the performance and effectiveness of the SFO will undoubtedly improve now that the UK has a single Fraud Act. The creation of the Fraud Prosecution Service is a welcome addition to the UK's armoury and early signs are promising in relation to its conviction rate. The creation of the NFA must however be questioned as it often duplicates the functions of both the FCA and the SFO. It is merely another level of unwanted bureaucracy. It is strongly rec-ommended and advisable that the function of administering suspected instances of fraud therefore lie with the NCA.

Insider dealing

The criminalisation of insider dealing in the UK is largely seen as a failure as a result of the high burden of proof required in such difficult evidentiary cases. The attempt to address this perceived failure has come in the form of a civil regime enacted as part of the FSMA 2000. Whether or not this regime has been more successful is difficult to judge, even nine years after enactment, partly because of the requirements of the Market Abuse Directive (MAD) making alterations only four years after it first came into force. It is certainly evident that the level of fines remains high and this, coupled with a more aggressive approach taken by the FCA, particularly in respect of criminal prosecutions for insider dealing, should allow it to claim success in its mission, at least in respect of market abuse. However, it is possible to argue that this is largely because of the decision by the Coalition government to abolish the FSA in 2012. Challenges will undoubtedly remain. The perception of the victimless crime and the ongoing difficulties in proving the offence will remain problematic, especially if the Financial Services and Markets Tribunal applies a criminal standard of proof to the more important cases, an issue that could bring the market abuse regime to a halt.

Market abuse

The market abuse regime can be considered to have operated efficiently since its introduction to financial regulatory system in the UK. It was administered by the FSA and now the FCA which have continued to pursue a credible deterrence strategy. However, what we have seen is a decline in the number of financial penalties imposed by the regulator since the onset of the 2007–2008 financial crisis. This could be explained by the record financial penalties imposed by the regulator for market manipulation and the manipulation of foreign currencies. The market abuse regime has been used alongside the insider dealing provisions of the Criminal Justice Act 1993, which has resulted in the creation of a generally effective market abuse regime. It is important to note that there is an element of uncertainty over the future direction of the UK's market abuse regime at the time of writing the book, because of the introduction of the Market Abuse Regulations in July 2016.

Bribery and corruption

The prevention of bribery has recently gained significant political attention by virtue of the introduction of the Bribery Act 2010. It is accepted that this legislation represented a significant improvement on the existing offences under the Public Bodies Corrupt Practices Act 1889, the Prevention of Corruption Act 1906 and the Prevention of Corruption Act 1916. Interestingly, the Bribery Act 2010 requires companies to have in place adequate procedures to prevent people associated with them from being bribed. If a commercial entity fails to prevent an associated person from committing bribery on their behalf, it has committed an offence. However, provided the commercial entity is able to demonstrate that it has in place 'adequate procedures to prevent persons associated with the commercial entity from undertaking such conduct' it will avoid prosecution. It is clear that this is an extension of the anti-money laundering system used by the FCA to incorporate bribery and corruption. Importantly, the Bribery Act 2010 extended the remit of the SFO to prosecute allegations of bribery, which is also a welcome development. Even so, the effectiveness of the SFO will depend on it being granted the appropriate levels of funding by the UK government. However, since the 2010 general election, the SFO has had its budget cut as part of a glut of extensive austerity measures. For example, the annual budget of the SFO in 2008–09 was £53.2 million, £32.1 million in 2013–14 and £30.8 million in 2014–15. The decision to reduce the budget of the SFO, at a time when instances of financial crime have increased and the duties of the SFO have been expanded to incorporate the enforcement of the Bribery Act 2010, must be questioned and criticised. However, the SFO has been given a new power against bribery and corruption by virtue of the Crime and Courts Act 2013: the deferred prosecution agreement. It is extremely likely that the SFO will continue to use this and it is hoped that through this mechanism this type of financial crime will lessen.

Tax evasion/avoidance

This, like the other types of financial crime discussed in this chapter, has attracted a great deal of attention and coverage in the last five years. This has partly been fuelled by media coverage of the perceived lack of tax revenue collected by HM Revenue and Customs (HMRC) and the lack of tax paid by large multinational companies, including Google, Uber and Amazon. The penultimate chapter of this book clearly illustrated how the lack of revenue collection has limited the effectiveness of the UK's policy towards tax evasion/avoidance. For example, in November 2015 a report by the National Audit Office concluded that an estimated £16 billion of taxable revenue was lost because of tax fraud.[4] The UK's response to tax evasion and tax avoidance could be considered to be rather lacklustre when compared to the other types of financial crime referred to in this book. For example, the revelations that HSBC Private Bank has aided numerous clients to avoid paying taxes was revealed by whistle-blower, Herve Falciani. In response to these strong accusations, HMRC has submitted a derisory one case to the Crown Prosecution Service for prosecution. This has also contributed towards a perception that this type of financial crime is not considered a high priority in the UK. However, a new criminal offence of corporate offence of failure to prevent the facilitation of evasion has been proposed and it is hoped that this might make a difference.[5] However, it is important to note that this is not an innovative response as similar offences already

---

4 National Audit Office, *Tackling Tax Fraud: How HMRC Responds to Tax Evasion, the Hidden Economy and Criminal Attacks* (National Audit Office: London, 2015).
5 Ed., 'Call for clarity on future of law on corporate tax evasion' (2016) *Company Lawyer*, 37(1), 8.

exist for money laundering and bribery. Furthermore, as we have seen throughout this book with other financial crimes, it is one thing to have the necessary criminal offences, but it appears another for the prosecuting authorities to actually use them. It remains to be seen therefore if this new criminal offence will be enacted so that is mirrors the UK's approach towards money laundering and bribery and then, even if it is, whether HMRC will target 'easy businesses' as opposed to the large multinational corporations that really deprive the UK of tax revenue.

Final thoughts

The UK's stance towards financial crime continues to evolve and develop at a very fast pace. The most significant alteration that will take place in the area of money laundering will be the implementation of the Fourth Money Laundering Directive, where the UK will once again state that it is merely gold plating its existing regime. The area of terrorist financing will continue to see a rise in the number of prosecutions under the Terrorism Act 2000 as more people are seen to provide financial support for terrorist groups in Syria. The UK is likely to be subjected to a new Mutual Evaluation Report of its AML and CTF legislation over the next several years. This will provide a new and detailed review of the effectiveness of the UK's financial crime agenda. Since the first edition of this book we have seen UK regulatory agencies pursue an enforcement strategy that either favours the imposition of financial penalties or deferred prosecution agreements. Nonetheless, the SFO has managed to successfully convict Tom Hayes for the manipulation of the London Interbank Offered Rate, even though eight other defendants were acquitted by a jury. We ended the first edition of the book by providing our support for the creation of a single agency that dealt with all aspects of financial crime. This issue has still not been resolved and if media reports are reliable the Conservative government will either try to encompass the current agencies into the NCA under the management of the Home Office rather than HM Treasury. It will be interesting to see which of these ministries will continue to manage the UK's financial crime agenda and indeed we await this future decision with much anticipation.

BIBLIOGRAPHY

D. Aaronberg and N. Higgins, 'Legislative comment the Bribery Act 2010: All bark and no bite . . . ?' (2010) *Archbold Review*, 5, 6–9.

M. Abarca, 'The need for substantive regulation on investor protection and corporate governance in Europe: Does Europe need a Sarbanes-Oxley?' (2004) *Journal of International Banking Law and Regulation*, 19(11), 419–431.

Action Fraud, 'Market manipulation' (n/d), available from http://www.actionfraud.police. uk/fraud-az-market-manipulation, accessed 28 May 2012.

Action Fraud, 'Online fraud' (2016), available from http://www.actionfraud.police.uk/ fraud-az-online-fraud, accessed 9 February 2016.

Action Fraud, 'Types of fraud' (2015), available from http://www.actionfraud.police.uk/ fraud-az-online-fraud, accessed 1 December 2015.

A. Alcock, 'Market abuse' (2002) *Company Lawyer*, 23(5), 142–150.

A. Alcock, 'Market abuse – the new witchcraft' (2001) *New Law Journal*, 151, 1398.

E. Alexander, 'Chris Moyles could face "huge tax bill" after tax avoidance appeal fails', *Independent* (1 October 2014), available from http://www.independent.co.uk/news/people/ chris-moyles-could-face-huge-tax-bill-after-tax-avoidance-appeal-fails-9766651.html, accessed 16 March 2016.

K. Alexander, *Insider dealing and market abuse: The Financial Services and Markets Act 2000—* ESRC Centre for Business Research, University of Cambridge, Working Paper No. 222 (Cambridge, 2001).

K. Alexander, 'The international anti-money laundering regime: The role of the Financial Action Task Force' (2001) *Journal of Money Laundering Control*, 4(3), 231.

R. Alexander, 'The Bribery Act 2010: Time to stand firm' (2011) *Journal of Financial Crime*, 18(2), Editorial.

R. Alexander, 'Corporate crimes: Are the gloves coming off?' (2009) *Company Lawyer*, 30(11), 321–322.

R. Alexander, 'Corruption as a financial crime' (2009) *Company Lawyer*, 30(4), 98.

R. Alexander, 'Money laundering and terrorist financing: Time for a combined offence', (2009) *Company Lawyer*, 30(7), 202.

A. O. Alkaabi, G. Mohay, A. Mccullagh, and N. A. Chantler, 'Comparative analysis of the extent of money laundering in Australia, UAE, UK and the USA' (20 January 2010)

Finance and Corporate Governance Conference 2010 paper. available from http://ssrn.com/abstract=1539843, accessed 6 July 2011.

A. Alkhamees, 'Private action as a remedy against market manipulation in the USA' (2012) *Journal of Financial Regulation and Compliance*, 20(1), 41–55.

P. Alldridge, 'Reforming bribery: Law Commission consultation paper 185: (1) Bribery reform and the law – again' (2008) *Criminal Law Review*, 9, 671–686.

P. Alldridge, *Money Laundering Law* (Hart: Oxford, 2003).

D. Anderson, *Third Report on the Operation of the Terrorist Asset-Freezing Etc. Act 2010* (HM Government: London, 2013).

T. Anderson, H. Lane, and M. Fox, 'Consequences and responses to the Madoff fraud' (2009) *Journal of International Banking and Regulation*, 24(11), 548–555.

A. Arora, 'The statutory system of the bank supervision and the failure of BCCI' (2006) *Journal of Business Law*, August, 487–510.

M. Ashe, 'The directive on insider dealing' (1992) *Company Lawyer*, 13(1), 15–19.

The Attorney General's Office, *Extending the Powers of the Crown Court to Prevent Fraud and Compensate Victims: A Consultation* (Attorney General's Office: London, 2008).

Attorney General's Office, *Fraud Review–Final Report* (Attorney General's Office: London, 2006).

Australian Government and Australian Institute of Criminology, *Charges and Offences of Money Laundering*, Transnational Crime Brief No. 4 (Australian Institute of Criminology: Canberra, 2008).

G. Baber, 'The Prudential Regulation Authority, special measures for special times' (2014) *Company Lawyer*, 35(12), 353–360.

J. Bagge, 'The future for enforcement under the new Financial Services Authority' (1998) *The Company Lawyer*, 19(7), 194–197, at 195.

I. Bantekas, 'The international law of terrorist financing' (2003) *American Journal of International Law*, 315–333.

P. Barnes, 'Insider dealing and market abuse: the UK's record on enforcement' (2011) *International Journal of Law, Crime and Justice*, 39, 174–189.

P. Barnes, *Stock Market Efficiency, Insider Dealing and Market Abuse* (Gower: Aldershot, 2009).

M. Basile, 'Going to the source: Why al-Qaeda's financial network is likely to withstand the current war on terrorist financing' (2004) *Studies in Conflict & Terrorism*, 27, 183.

BBC News, 'Arrogant Muslim preacher jailed' (18 April 2008), available from http://news.bbc.co.uk/1/hi/uk/7354397.stm, accessed 28 June 2011.

BBC News, 'Colin Jackson involved in tax avoidance scheme' (14 May 2014), available from http://www.bbc.co.uk/news/uk-wales-27411490, accessed 16 March 2016.

BBC News, 'Jimmy Carr and the morality of tax avoidance' (19 June 2012), available from http://www.bbc.co.uk/news/magazine-18537051, accessed 16 March 2016.

BBC News, 'Lee Rigby murder: Adebolajo and Adebowale jailed' (26 February 2014), available from http://www.bbc.co.uk/news/uk-26357007, accessed 10 August 2015.

BBC News, 'Tax crackdown by HMRC unit nets 60% more money, report says' (20 January 2015), available from http://www.bbc.co.uk/news/business-30973191, accessed 16 March 2015.

BBC News, 'Tunisia beach massacre 'linked' to museum killings' (5 August 2015), available from http://www.bbc.co.uk/news/uk-33791293, accessed 10 August 2015.

BBC News, 'UK market abuse unacceptably high' (*Says FSA Boss*) (14 March 2010), available from http://news.bbc.co.uk/1/hi/8566904.stm, accessed 20 October 2011.

BBC News, 'UK Maximum sentence for money launder' (25 February 1999) available from http://news.bbc.co.uk/1/hi/uk/285759.stm, accessed 6 June 2011.

K. Beale and P. Esposito, 'Emergent international attitudes towards bribery, corruption and money laundering' (2009) *Arbitration*, 75(3), 360–373.

J. Beaty and S. C. Gwynne, *The Outlaw Bank: A Wild Ride to the Secrets of BCCI* (Beard Books: Frederick, MD, 2004).

R. Bell, 'The confiscation, forfeiture and disruption of terrorist finances' (2003) *Journal of Money Laundering Control*, 7(2), 113.

M. Benson and S. Simpson, *White-Collar Crime: An Opportunity Perspective, Criminology and Justice Series* (Routledge: London, 2009).

J. Benstead, 'Biting the bullet' (2010) *New Law Journal*, 160(7434), 1291–1292, at 1291.

D. Bentley and R. Fisher, 'Criminal property under PCOA 2002 – time to clean up the law?' (2009) *Archbold News*, 2, 7–9.

P. Bergen and D. Sterman, 'Al-Shabaab backed by money from US' (29 September 2013), available from http://www.cnn.com/2013/09/29/opinion/bergen-shabaab-fundraising/, accessed 27 June 2014.

P. Berwick and R. McCann, 'HMRC gets tough with tax evaders' (30 January 2013), available from http://www.ftadviser.com/2013/01/30/regulation/regulators/hmrc-gets-tough-with-tax-evaders-Q91OcHU1vzMC1Zfl7UKFjN/article.html, accessed 17 March 2016 and Holder, V. 'HMRC steps up tax evasion drive after 58% rise in convictions', 14 December 2015, available from http://www.ft.com/cms/s/0/4ff76fa0-a030–11e5–8613–08e211ea5317.html#axzz439zaVfkO, accessed 17 March 2016.

C. Binham and H. Warrell, 'Theresa May revives attempt to abolish SFO' (5 October 2014), available from http://www.ft.com/cms/s/0/e15dc7c0–4ae9–11e4-b1be-00144feab7de.html#axzz3jLhJ8iis, accessed 21 August 2015.

P. Binning, 'In safe hands? Striking the balance between privacy and security – anti-terrorist finance measures' (2002) *European Human Rights Law Review*, 6, 737.

M. Bisgrove and M. Weekes, 'Deferred prosecution agreements: A practical consideration' (2014) *Criminal Law Review*, 6, 416–438.

Z. Bookman, 'Convergences and omissions in reporting corporate and white collar crime' (2008) *DePaul Business & Commercial Law Journal*, 6, 347–392.

R. Booth, S. Farrell, G. Bastable, and N. Yeo, *Money Laundering Law and Regulation a Practical Guide* (Oxford University Press: Oxford, 2011).

R. Bosworth-Davies, 'Investigating financial crime: The continuing evolution of the public fraud investigation role – a personal perspective' (2009) *Company Lawyer*, 30(7), 195–199.

G. Brown and T. Evans, 'The impact: The breadth and depth of the anti-money laundering provisions requiring reporting of suspicious activities' (2008) *Journal of International Banking Law and Regulation*, 23(5), 274–277.

Building Societies Association, 'Financial crime prevention', (n/d), available from http://www.bsa.org.uk/policy/policyissues/fcpandphysec/financialcrime.htm, accessed 1 July 2011.

N. Bunyan and R. Edwards, 'Canoe wife trail: Darwin's jailed for more than six years' (*The Daily Telegraph* 23 July 2008) available from http://www.telegraph.co.uk/news/2448044/Canoe-wife-trial-Darwins-jailed-for-more-than-six-years.html, accessed 10 June 2011.

Cabinet Office, *Recovering the Proceeds of Crime – A Performance and Innovation Unit Report* (Cabinet Office: London, 2000).

Cabinet Office, *The UK and the Campaign against International Terrorism – Progress Report* (Cabinet Office: London, 2002).

F. Cantos, 'EEC draft directive on insider dealing' (1989) *Journal of International Banking Law*, 4(4), N174–176.

E. Cape, 'The counter-terrorism provisions of the Protection of Freedoms Act 2012: Preventing misuse or a case of smoke and mirrors?' (2013) *Criminal Law Review*, 5, 385.

I. Carr, 'Fighting corruption through the United Nations Convention on Corruption 2003: A global solution to a global problem?' (2005) *International Trade Law and Regulation*, 11(1), 24–29.

W. Carroll, 'Market manipulation, an international comparison' (2002) *Journal of Financial Crime*, 9(4), 300–307.

S. Cassella, 'Reverse money laundering' (2003) *Journal of Money Laundering Control*, 7(1), 92.

A. Cave, 'Market abuse is unacceptably high' (2010) 13 March 2010, available from http://www.telegraph.co.uk/finance/newsbysector/banksandfinance/7436104/Market-abuse-is-unacceptably-high-says-FSA-boss.html, accessed 14 December 2011.

CCH Daily, 'P&O loses £14m double tax relief "rate-booster" case' (n/d), available from https://www.accountancylive.com/po-loses-%C2%A314m-double-tax-relief-rate-booster-case, accessed 11 March 2016.

M. Chamberlain, 'The Justice and Security Bill' (2012) *Civil Justice Quarterly*, 31(4), 424.

Charity Commission, 'Compliance toolkit: Protecting charities from harm' (2009) Module 7, page 1, available from http://www.charity-commission.gov.uk/Library/tkch1mod7.pdf, accessed 17 June 2011.

Chartered Institute of Taxation, 'Press release: The chartered institute of taxation wants clarity on future of law on corporate tax evasion' (n/d), available from http://www.tax.org.uk/media-centre/press-releases/press-release-chartered-institute-taxation-wants-clarity-future-law, accessed 13 March 2016.

A. Chase, 'Legal mechanisms of the international community and the United States concerning the state sponsorship of terrorism' (2004) *Virginia Journal of International Law*, 41.

P. Cheston, 'Former Belgo chief spared prison for insider trading deal' (*London Evening Standard* 2 March 2009) available from http://www.standard.co.uk/news/former-belgo-chief-is-spared-prison-for-insider-trading-deal-6821785.html, accessed 7 June 2016.

CIFAS, 'Fraud decrease serves as vindication and warning says Cifas' (21 January 2014), available from https://www.cifas.org.uk/twentythirteen_fraudtrends, accessed 20 August 2015.

City of London Police, *Assessment: Financial Crime against Vulnerable Adults* (Social Care Institute for Excellence: London, November 2011).

City of London Police, 'Bribery Act 2010 summary' (n/d), available from http://www.cityoflondon.police.uk/CityPolice/Departments/ECD/anticorruptionunit/briberyact2010summary.htm, accessed 24 November 2011.

CNN News, 'A timeline of the Charlie Hebdo terror attack' (9 January 2015), available from http://edition.cnn.com/2015/01/08/europe/charlie-hebdo-attack-timeline/, accessed 10 August 2015.

J. Coffey and J. Overett Somnier, 'The Market Abuse Directive – the first use of the Lamfalussy process' (2003) *Journal of International Banking Law and Regulation*, 18(9), 370.

R. Collier, 'Intentions, banks, politics and the law: The UK code of practice on taxation for banks' (2014) *British Tax Review*, 4, 478–508.

J. Collins and A. Kennedy, 'The cheat, his wife and her lawyer' (2003), Taxation November 136.

J. Collins and M. Piggin, 'Finance Act notes: Criminal investigations and HMRC powers – sections 82–87 and schedule 22' (2007) *British Tax Review*, 5, 562–570.

Committee on Standards in Public Life, *First Report 'Standards in Public Life'* (HMSO: London, 1995, Cm 2850–2851).

C. Conceicao, 'The FSA's approach to taking action against market abuse' (2007) *Company Lawyer*, 29(2), 43–45.

The Consultative Committee of Accountancy Boards, *Anti-Money Laundering Guidance for the Accountancy Sector* (Consultative Committee of Accountancy Boards: London, 2007).

CoreLogic, *2011 Mortgage Fraud Trends Report* (Irvine, California 2011).

I. Cowie, 'Plumber jailed for tax evasion as HMRC receipts rise' (*The Telegraph* 27 July 2012) available from http://blogs.telegraph.co.uk/finance/ianmcowie/100019166/plumber-jailed-for-tax-evasion-as-hmrc-receipts-rise/, accessed 12 March 2016.

I. Cowie, 'Time to come clean as HMRC flushes out tax evasion?' (*The Telegraph* 17 August 2011) available from http://blogs.telegraph.co.uk/finance/ianmcowie/100011592/time-to-come-clean-as-hmrc-flushes-out-tax-evasion/, accessed 13 March 2016.

H. Croall, 'Who is the white-collar criminal?' (1989) *British Journal of Criminology*, 29(2), 157.

Crown Prosecution Service, 'Bribery Act 2010: Joint prosecution guidance of the director of the serious fraud office and the director of public prosecutions' (n/d), available from http://www.cps.gov.uk/legal/a_to_c/bribery_act_2010/, accessed 9 February 2016.

Crown Prosecution Service, *'Bribery', Legal Guidance* (Crown Prosecution Service: London, 2008).

Crown Prosecution Service, 'Cheating the revenue (contrary to common law)' (n/d), available from http://www.cps.gov.uk/legal/s_to_u/sentencing_manual/cheating_the_revenue_(contrary_to_common_law)/, accessed 16 March 2016.

Crown Prosecution Service, 'DPP announces new head of fraud prosecution division' (2009), available from http://www.cps.gov.uk/news/press_releases/136_09/, accessed 22 January 2010.

Crown Prosecution Service, 'The Fraud Act 2006' (2008), available from http://www.cps.gov.uk/legal/d_to_g/fraud_act/, accessed 8 June 2011.

Crown Prosecution Service, 'Fraud, false accounting, fraudulent evasion of VAT, false statement for VAT purposes, conduct amounting to an offence' (n/d), available from http://www.cps.gov.uk/legal/s_to_u/sentencing_manual/fraud/, accessed 12 July 2015.

Crown Prosecution Service, 'Fraudulent evasion of income tax' (n/d), available from http://www.cps.gov.uk/legal/s_to_u/sentencing_manual/revenue_offences_fraudulent_evasion_of_income_tax/index.html, accessed 16 March 2016.

Crown Prosecution Service, 'Man sentenced for eBay tax evasion totalling almost £300,000' (n/d), available from http://www.cps.gov.uk/news/latest_news/man_sentenced_for_ebay_tax_evasion_totalling_almost_gbp300000/index.html, accessed 16 March 2016.

Crown Prosecution Service, 'Proceeds of Crime Act 2002 part 7–Money laundering offences' (n/d), available from http://www.cps.gov.uk/legal/p_to_r/proceeds_of_crime_money_laundering/, accessed 6 July 2011.

Crown Prosecution Service, 'Prosecuting tax evasion' (n/d), speech by Kier Starmer, available from http://www.cps.gov.uk/news/articles/prosecuting_tax_evasion/, accessed 16 March 2016.

Crown Prosecution Service, 'Queen's counsel convicted of £600,000 VAT fraud' (n/d), available from http://www.cps.gov.uk/news/latest_news/qc_convicted_of_gbp_600k_vat_fraud/index.html, accessed 16 March 2016.

Crown Prosecution Service, 'Serious crime prevention orders' (n/d), available from http://www.cps.gov.uk/legal/s_to_u/serious_crime_prevention_orders_%28scpo%29_guidance/, accessed 29 November 2011.

J. Davies, 'From gentlemanly expectations to regulatory principles, a history of insider dealing in the UK, Part 1' (2015) *Company Lawyer*, 36(5), 132–143, at 132.

D. Deem, 'Notes from the field: Observations in working with the forgotten victims of personal financial crimes' (2000) *Journal of Elder Abuse & Neglect*, 12(2), 33.

J. de Grazia, *Review of the Serious Fraud Office – Final Report* (Serious Fraud Office: London, 2008).

A. Denning, 'Independence and Impartiality of the Judges' (1954) *South African Law Journal*, 71, 345.

I. Dennis, 'Fraud Act 2006' (2007) *Criminal Law Review*, January, 1–2.

Department of Justice, 'Bank of America to pay $16.65bn in historic Justice Department settlement for financial fraud leading up to and during the financial crisis' (21 August

2014), available from http://www.justice.gov/opa/pr/bank-america-pay-1665-billion-historic-justice-department-settlement-financial-fraud-leading, accessed 20 August 2015.

Department of State, *Country Reports on Terrorism 2013* (Department of State, 2014).

B. Dickson, 'Northern Ireland emergency legislation – the wrong medicine?' (1992) *Public Law*, Winter, 592.

A. Doig, *Fraud* (Willan Publishing: Cullompton, 2006).

L. Donohue, *The Cost of Counterterrorism – Power, Politics and Liberty* (Cambridge University Press: Cambridge, UK, 2008).

V. Doshi, 'Elephant campaign: How Africa's "white gold" funds the al-Shabaab militants' (2 February 2014), available from http://www.independent.co.uk/voices/campaigns/elephant-campaign/elephant-campaign-how-africas-white-gold-funds-the-alshabaab-militants-9102862.html, accessed 27 June 2014.

B. Dubow and N. Monteiro, *'Measuring Market Cleanliness', FSA Occasional Paper* (Financial Services Authority: London, March, 2006).

I. Duderstadt, 'Implementation of the Insider Dealing Directive in the UK and Germany' (1996) *Journal of Financial Crime*, 4(2), 105–116.

T. Duthie and D. Lawler, 'Legislative comment the United Kingdom Bribery Bill' (2010) *Construction Law Journal*, 26(2), 146–152, at 147.

Ed., 'Insiders beware!' (1993) *Company Lawyer*, 14(11), 202.

Ed., 'Commission seeks evidence in review of Market Abuse Directive' (2009) *Company Law Newsletter*, 252, 4–5.

Ed., 'Call for clarity on future of law on corporate tax evasion' (2016) *Company Lawyer*, 37(1), 8.

Ed., 'Plan released to combat tax evasion and money laundering' (2013) *Company Lawyer*, 34(9), 281.

Ed., 'The Bribery Act 2010' (2010) *Criminal Law Review*, 6, 439–440.

O. Elagab, 'Control of terrorist funds and the banking system' (2006) *Journal of International Banking Law and Regulation*, 21(1), 40.

European Commission, 'Call for evidence review of directive 2003/6/EC on insider dealing and market manipulation (Market Abuse Directive)' (2009), available from http://ec.europa.eu/internal_market/consultations/docs/2009/market_abuse/call_for_evidence.pdf, accessed 12 August 2010.

European Commission, 'Financial Crime' (n/d), available from http://ec.europa.eu/internal_market/company/financial-crime/index_en.htm, accessed 21 March 2012.

M. Evans, 'Judge blasts National Crime Agency after blunders cause case to collapse' (2 December 2014), available from http://www.telegraph.co.uk/news/uknews/crime/11268097/Judge-blasts-National-Crime-Agency-after-blunders-cause-case-to-collapse.html, accessed 21 August 2015.

Federal Bureau of Investigation, '2009 Mortgage fraud report year in review' (n/d), available from http://www.fbi.gov/stats-services/publications/mortgage-fraud-2009, accessed 17 June 2013.

Federal Bureau of Investigation, 'Mortgage fraud report 2006' (May 2007), available from http://www.fbi.gov/stats-services/publications/mortgage-fraud-2006/2006-mortgage-fraud-report, accessed 23 May 2013.

Federal Bureau of Investigation, 'Mortgage fraud report 2007' (April 2008), available from http://www.fbi.gov/stats-services/publications/mortgage-fraud-2007, accessed 18 October 2013.

Federal Bureau of Investigation, 'Mortgage fraud report 2008' (2009), available from http://www.fbi.gov/stats-services/publications/mortgage-fraud-2008/2008-mortgage-fraud-report, accessed 17 June 2013.

Federal Bureau of Investigation, 'San Diego jury convicts four Somali immigrants of providing support to foreign terrorists' (2013), available from http://www.fbi.gov/sandiego/press-releases/2013/san-diego-jury-convicts-four-somali-immigrants-of-providing-support-to-foreign-terrorists, accessed 15 October 2014.

Federal Bureau of Investigation, 'Financial crimes report to the public' (n/d), available from http://www.fbi.gov/stats-services/publications/financial-crimes-report-2010-2011/financial-crimes-report-2010-2011#Financial, accessed 21 March 2012.

Federal Bureau of Investigation, 'Two Minnesota women convicted of providing material support to al Shabaab' (2011), available from http://www.fbi.gov/minneapolis/press-releases/2011/two-minnesota-women-convicted-of-providing-material-support-to-al-shabaab, accessed 15 October 2014.

G. Ferrarini, 'The European Market Abuse Directive' (2004) *Common Market Law Review*, 41(3), 711–741.

M. Filby, 'The enforcement of insider dealing under the Financial Services and Markets Act 2000' (2003) *Company Lawyer*, 24(11), 334–341.

M. Filby, 'Part VIII Financial Services and Markets Act: Filling insider dealing's regulatory gaps' (2004) *Company Lawyer*, 23(12), 363–370.

Financial Action Task Force, *FATF Report – Terrorist Financing in West Africa* (Financial Action Task Force: Paris, 2013).

Financial Action Task Force, *International Standards on Combating Money Laundering and the Financing of Terrorism & Proliferation* (Financial Action Task Force: Paris, 2012).

Financial Action Task Force, *Methodology for Assessing Technical Compliance with the FATF Recommendations and the Effectiveness of AML/CFT Systems* (Financial Action Task Force: Paris, 2013).

Financial Action Task Force, *Report on Money Laundering and Terrorist Financing Typologies 2003–2004* (Financial Action Task Force: Paris, 2004).

Financial Action Task Force, *Third Mutual Evaluation Report Anti-Money Laundering and Combating the Financing of Terrorism – United Kingdom* (Financial Action Task Force: Paris, 2007).

Financial Conduct Authority, 'Anti-money laundering' (14 November 2011), available from https://www.fca.org.uk/firms/being-regulated/meeting-your-obligations/firm-guides/systems/aml, accessed 24 June 2015.

Financial Conduct Authority, *Anti-Money Laundering Annual Report 2012/13* (Financial Conduct Authority: London, 2013).

Financial Conduct Authority, 'Besso Limited fined for anti-bribery and corruption systems failings' (19 March 2014), available from https://www.fca.org.uk/news/besso-limited-fined-for-antibribery-and-corruption-systems-failings, accessed 8 February 2016.

Financial Conduct Authority, 'The changing face of financial crime' (1 July 2013), available from http://www.fca.org.uk/news/speeches/the-changing-face-of-financial-crime, accessed 8 July 2013.

Financial Conduct Authority, 'Data security' (28 January 2015), available from https://www.fca.org.uk/about/what/enforcing/data-security, accessed 20 August 2015.

Financial Conduct Authority, *The Enforcement Guide* (London: FCA, 12.7), available from https://www.handbook.fca.org.uk/handbook/document/EG_FCRMAML_20110701.pdf, accessed 26 January 2016.

Financial Conduct Authority, 'Enforcing our rules and fighting financial crime' (28 January 2015), available from https://www.fca.org.uk/about/what/enforcing/, accessed 21 August 2015.

Financial Conduct Authority, 'FCA Handbook' (n/d), available from https://www.handbook.fca.org.uk/handbook/DEPP/6/5.html, accessed 26 January 2016.

Financial Conduct Authority, 'FCA Handbook DEPP A.1.3' (n/d), available from https://www.handbook.fca.org.uk/handbook/DEPP/6A/1.html, accessed 26 January 2016.

Financial Conduct Authority, 'FCA Handbook, DEPP 6.5 and 6.5C' (n/d), available from https://www.handbook.fca.org.uk/handbook/DEPP/6/5.html and https://www.handbook.fca.org.uk/handbook/DEPP/6/5C.html#DES548, accessed 26 January 2016.

Financial Conduct Authority, 'FCA Handbook, DEPP 6.5A' (n/d), available from https://www.handbook.fca.org.uk/handbook/DEPP/6/5A.html, accessed 26 January 2016.

Financial Conduct Authority, 'Fighting mortgage fraud' (1 May 2015), available from https://www.fca.org.uk/about/what/enforcing/fraud/mortgage, accessed 20 August 2015.

Financial Conduct Authority, 'Final notice on Guaranty First Bank (UK) Ltd' (8 August 2013), available from http://www.fca.org.uk/your-fca/documents/final-notices/2013/guaranty-trust-bank-uk-limited, accessed 3 July 2015.

Financial Conduct Authority, 'Final notice: 7722656 Canada Inc.' (24 January 2014), available from https://www.fca.org.uk/your-fca/documents/final-notices/2014/7722656-canada-inc, accessed 13 January 2016.

Financial Conduct Authority, 'Final notice: Da Vinci Invest Ltd.' (12 August 2015), available from http://www.fca.org.uk/news/fca-secures-high-court-judgment-awarding-injunction-and-over-7-million-in-penalties, accessed 13 January 2016.

Financial Conduct Authority, 'Final notice: Gyorgy szabolcs brad' (12 August 2015), available from http://www.fca.org.uk/news/fca-secures-high-court-judgment-awarding-injunction-and-over-7-million-in-penalties, accessed 13 January 2016.

Financial Conduct Authority, 'Final notice: Ian Hannam' (22 July 2014), available from https://www.fca.org.uk/news/fca-publishes-final-notice-for-ian-hannam, accessed 13 January 2016.

Financial Conduct Authority, 'Final notice: Kenneth George Carver' (20 March 2015), available from http://www.fca.org.uk/news/kenneth-carver-fined-for-insider-dealing, accessed 13 January 2016.

Financial Conduct Authority, 'Final notice: Michael Coscia' (3 July 2013), available from http://www.fca.org.uk/your-fca/documents/final-notices/2013/michael-coscia, accessed 13 January 2016.

Financial Conduct Authority, 'Final notice: Mineworld Ltd.' (12 August 2015), available from http://www.fca.org.uk/news/fca-secures-high-court-judgment-awarding-injunction-and-over-7-million-in-penalties, accessed 13 January 2016.

Financial Conduct Authority, 'Final notice: Patrick Sejean' (24 January 2013), available from http://www.fca.org.uk/your-fca/documents/final-notices/2013/fsa-final-notice-2013-stefan-chaligne, accessed 13 January 2016.

Financial Conduct Authority, 'Final notice: Stefan Chaligne' (21 January 2013), available from http://www.fca.org.uk/your-fca/documents/final-notices/2013/fsa-final-notice-2013-stefan-chaligne, accessed 13 January 2016.

Financial Conduct Authority, 'Final notice: Szabolcs Banya' (12 August 2015), available from http://www.fca.org.uk/news/fca-secures-high-court-judgment-awarding-injunction-and-over-7-million-in-penalties, accessed 13 January 2016.

Financial Conduct Authority, 'Final notice: Tamas Pornye' (12 August 2015), available from http://www.fca.org.uk/news/fca-secures-high-court-judgment-awarding-injunction-and-over-7-million-in-penalties, accessed 13 January 2016.

Financial Conduct Authority, 'Fine table – 2013' (18 November 2013), available from http://www.fca.org.uk/firms/being-regulated/enforcement/fines/2013, accessed 3 July 2015.

Financial Conduct Authority, 'Fine table – 2014' (7 January 2015), available from http://www.fca.org.uk/firms/being-regulated/enforcement/fines/2014, accessed 3 July 2015.

Financial Conduct Authority, 'Firm fined £1.8million for "unacceptable" approach to bribery & corruption risks from overseas payments' (19 December 2013), available from https://www.fca.org.uk/news/firm-fined-18million-for-unacceptable-approach-to-bribery-corruption-risks-from-overseas-payments, accessed 8 February 2016.

Financial Conduct Authority, 'FOI3519 response' (21 November 2014), available from https://www.fca.org.uk/your-fca/documents/foi/foi3519-response, accessed 4 November 2015.

Financial Conduct Authority, 'Former senior trader sentenced for insider dealing', available from http://www.fca.org.uk/news/former-senior-trader-sentenced-for-insider-dealing, accessed 18 November 2015.

Financial Conduct Authority, 'FSA fines Alpari and its former money laundering reporting officer, Sudipto Chattopadhyay for anti-money laundering failings' (5 May 2010), available from http://www.fsa.gov.uk/pages/library/communication/pr/2010/077.shtml, accessed 3 July 2015.

Financial Conduct Authority, 'How to avoid investment scams' (27 November 2014), available from https://www.fca.org.uk/consumers/scams/how-to-avoid-scams, accessed 21 August 2015.

Financial Conduct Authority, 'Kenneth Carver fined £35,212 for insider dealing' (2015), available from http://www.fca.org.uk/news/kenneth-carver-fined-for-insider-dealing, accessed 18 November 2015.

Financial Conduct Authority, 'Market Abuse Regulation (MAR)' (6 May 2015), available from http://www.fca.org.uk/firms/markets/market-abuse/mar, accessed 1 January 2016.

Financial Conduct Authority, 'Obligation to report suspicious transactions' (17 March 2015), available from http://www.fca.org.uk/firms/markets/market-abuse/suspicious-transaction-reporting, accessed 14 January 2016.

Financial Conduct Authority, 'Standard Bank PLC fined £7.6m for failures in its anti-money laundering controls' (23 January 2014), available from https://www.fca.org.uk/news/standard-bank-plc-fined-for-failures-in-its-antimoney-laundering-controls, accessed 3 July 2015.

Financial Conduct Authority, 'Unauthorised firms and individuals to avoid' (n/d), available from https://www.fca.org.uk/consumers/protect-yourself/unauthorised-firms/unauthorised-firms-to-avoid, accessed 21 August 2015.

Financial Conduct Authority, *Why Has the FCAs Market Cleanliness Statistic for Takeover Announcements Decreased Since 2009?* (Financial Conduct Authority: London, 2014).

Financial Conduct Authority Handbook, Mar 2.1.4 available from https://www.handbook.fca.org.uk/handbook/MAR/2/1.html, accessed 21 January 2015.

Financial Conduct Authority Handbook, *Supervision: SUP 15 Ann 5 Indications of Possible Suspicious Transactions* (Financial Conduct Authority: London, 2015).

Financial Reporting Council, *Money Laundering Guidance for Auditors on UK Legislation: Practice Note 12 (Revised)* (Financial Reporting Council: London, 2010).

Financial Services Authority, *Annual Report 2010/11* (Financial Services Authority: London, 2011).

Financial Services Authority, *Anti-Bribery and Corruption in Commercial Insurance Broking Reducing the Risk of Illicit Payments or Inducements to Third Parties* (Financial Services Authority: London, 2010).

Financial Services Authority, *Consultation paper 10 market abuse part 1: Consultation on a draft code of market conduct* (1998), available from http://www.fsa.gov.uk/pubs/cp/cp10.pdf, accessed 5 July 2010.

Financial Services Authority, 'Corporate broker intern and his father receive 12 and 24 month prison sentences respectively for insider dealing' (Press Release, 10 December 2010), 2009, available from http://www.fsa.gov.uk/pages/Library/Communication/PR/2009/170. shtml, accessed 6 October 2011.

Financial Services Authority, 'Coutts fined £8.75 million for anti-money laundering control failings' (26 March 2012), available from http://www.fsa.gov.uk/library/communication/pr/2012/032.shtml, accessed 3 July 2015.

Financial Services Authority, 'Delivering credible deterrence', speech by Margaret Cole, Director of Enforcement, FSA, Annual Financial Crime Conference, 27 April 2009, available from http://www.fsa.gov.uk/library/communication/speeches/2009/0427_mc.shtml, accessed 8 March 2013.

Financial Services Authority, *Developing our policy on fraud and dishonesty – discussion paper 26* (Financial Services Authority: London, 2003).

Financial Services Authority, 'Fake stockbroker sentenced to 15 months' (13 February 2008), available from http://www.fsa.gov.uk/library/communication/pr/2008/011.shtml, accessed 12 November 2012.

Financial Services Authority, 'Fake stockbroker sentenced to 15 months' (2008), available from http://www.fsa.gov.uk/pages/Library/Communication/PR/2008/011.shtml, accessed 28 March 2010.

Financial Services Authority, 'Feedback statement on responses to consultation paper 10: Market abuse' (1999), available from http://www.fsa.gov.uk/pubs/cp/cp10_response. pdf, accessed 5 July 2010.

Financial Services Authority, 'Fighting financial crime', available from http://www.fsa.gov. uk/about/what/financial_crime, accessed 21 March 2012.

Financial Services Authority, 'Final notice: Nationwide building society' (14 February 2007), available from http://www.fsa.gov.uk/pubs/final/nbs.pdf, accessed 20 August 2015.

Financial Services Authority, 'Final notice: Zurich insurance plc' (19 August 2010), available from http://www.fsa.gov.uk/pubs/final/zurich_plc.pdf, accessed 20 August 2015.

Financial Services Authority, *Financial Risk Outlook 2008* (Financial Services Authority: London, 2008).

Financial Services Authority, *Financial Services Authority Annual Report 2007/2008* (Financial Services Authority: London, 2008).

Financial Services Authority, 'Former Cazenove broker sentenced to 21 months in prison for insider dealing' (Press Release, 11 March 2010) available from http://www.fsa.gov.uk/pages/Library/Communication/PR/2010/043.shtml, accessed 6 October 2011.

Financial Services Authority, 'Former compliance officer at Greenlight Capital and JP Morgan Cazenove trader fined' (27 January 2012), available from http://www.fsa.gov.uk/library/communication/pr/2012/007.shtml, accessed 3 February 2012.

Financial Services Authority, 'Frequently asked questions' (Financial Services Authority 2011), available from http://www.fsa.gov.uk/pages/About/What/financial_crime/money_laundering/faqs/index.shtml, accessed 6 June 2011.

Financial Services Authority, 'FSA final notice 2013: EFG Private Bank Ltd' (31 May 2013), available from http://www.fca.org.uk/your-fca/documents/final-notices/2013/fsa-final-notice-2013-efg-private-bank-ltd, accessed 3 July 2015.

Financial Services Authority, 'FSA fines broker for failing to prevent insider dealing' (2 September 2009), available from http://www.fsa.gov.uk/pages/Library/Communication/PR/2009/115.shtml, accessed 9 November 2011.

Financial Services Authority, 'FSA fines broker for failing to prevent insider dealing' (2 September 2009), available from http://www.fsa.gov.uk/library/communication/pr/2009/115.shtml, accessed 14 January 2016.

Financial Services Authority, 'FSA fines broker for failing to prevent insider dealing' (Press Release, 2 September 2009), available from http://www.fsa.gov.uk/pages/Library/Communication/PR/2009/115.shtml, accessed 6 October 2011.

Financial Services Authority, 'FSA fines capita financial administrators limited £300,000 in first anti-fraud controls case', available from http://www.fsa.gov.uk/pages/Library/Communication/PR/2006/019.shtml, accessed 16 March 2006.

Financial Services Authority, 'FSA fines firm and MLRO for money laundering controls failings' (29 October 2009), available from http://www.fsa.gov.uk/pages/library/communication/pr/2008/125.shtml, accessed 3 July 2015.

Financial Services Authority, 'FSA fines GLG Partners and Philippe Jabre £750,000 each for market abuse' (Press Release, 1 August 2006), available from http://www.fsa.gov.uk/pages/Library/Communication/PR/2006/077.shtml, accessed 6 October 2011.

Financial Services Authority, 'FSA fines Habib Bank AG Zurich £525,000 and money laundering reporting officer £17,500 for anti-money laundering control failings' (15 May 2012), available from http://www.fsa.gov.uk/library/communication/pr/2012/055.shtml, accessed 3 July 2015.

Financial Services Authority, 'FSA fines Nationwide £980 000 for information security lapses', available from http://www.fsa.gov.uk/pages/Library/Communication/PR/2007/021.shtml, accessed 14 February 2007.

Financial Services Authority, 'FSA fines Norwich Union Life £1.26m', available from http://www.fsa.gov.uk/pages/Library/Communication/PR/2007/130.shtml, accessed 4 November 2009.

Financial Services Authority, 'FSA fines table 2007' (n/d), available from http://www.fsa.gov.uk/about/press/facts/fines/2007, accessed 8 March 2013.

Financial Services Authority, 'FSA fines table 2008' (n/d), available from http://www.fsa.gov.uk/about/press/facts/fines/2008, accessed 8 March 2013.

Financial Services Authority, 'FSA fines table 2009' (n/d), available from http://www.fsa.gov.uk/about/press/facts/fines/2009, accessed 8 March 2013.

Financial Services Authority, 'FSA fines table 2010' (n/d), available from http://www.fsa.gov.uk/about/press/facts/fines/2010, accessed 8 March 2013.

Financial Services Authority, 'FSA fines table 2011' (n/d), available from http://www.fsa.gov.uk/about/press/facts/fines/2011, accessed 8 March 2013.

Financial Services Authority, 'FSA fines table 2012' (n/d), available from http://www.fsa.gov.uk/about/press/facts/fines/2012, accessed 8 March 2013.

Financial Services Authority, 'FSA fines Willis Limited 6.895m for anti-bribery and corruption systems and controls failings' (21 July 2011), available from http://www.fsa.gov.uk/pages/Library/Communication/PR/2011/066.shtml, accessed 24 November 2011.

Financial Services Authority, *FSA Handbook* (Financial Services Authority: London, 2006).

Financial Services Authority, *FSA Handbook – SUP (Supervision)* (Financial Services Authority: London, 2008).

Financial Services Authority, 'FSA publishes updated measure of UK market cleanliness', 7 March 2007, available from http://www.fsa.gov.uk/library/communication/pr/2007/031.shtmlm, accessed 9 December 2011.

Financial Services Authority, 'FSA returns £270 000 to victims of share fraud' (n/d), available from http://www.fsa.gov.uk/pages/Library/Communication/PR/2010/032.shtml, accessed 21 March 2010.

Financial Services Authority, 'The FSA's new approach to fraud – Fighting fraud in partnership' (speech by Philip Robinson, 26 October 2004), available from http://www.fsa.gov.uk/Pages/Library/Communication/Speeches/2004/SP208.shtml accessed 3 August 2011.

Financial Services Authority, 'Investment banker, his wife and family friend sentenced for insider dealing' (Press Release, 2 February 2011), available from http://www.fsa.gov.uk/pages/Library/Communication/PR/2011/018.shtml, accessed 6 October 2011.

Financial Service Authority, 'Investment banker and two associates charged with insider dealing' (Press Release, 4 August 2011) available from http://www.fsa.gov.uk/pages/Library/Communication/PR/2011/069.shtml, accessed 6 October 2011.

Financial Services Authority, 'Market Abuse Directive' (n/d), available from http://www.fsa.gov.uk/pages/about/what/international/pdf/mad%20(pl).pdf, accessed 27 May 2012.

Financial Services Authority, *Measuring Market Cleanliness FSA Occasional Paper Series 23* (Financial Services Authority: London, 2006).

Financial Services Authority, *Money Laundering Handbook* (Financial Services Authority: London, 2006).

Financial Services Authority, *Neil Rollins update* (Press Release, 30 June 2011), available from http://www.fsa.gov.uk/pages/Library/Communication/Statements/2011/neil_rollins.shtml, accessed 6 October 2011.

Financial Services Authority, 'One-minute guide – Anti-bribery and corruption in commercial insurance broking' (21 July 2011), available from http://www.fsa.gov.uk/smallfirms/resources/one_minute_guides/insurance_intermed/anti_bribery.shtml, accessed 24 November 2011.

Financial Services Authority, 'Solicitor and his father-in-law found guilty in FSA insider dealing case' (27 March 2009), available from http://www.fsa.gov.uk/pages/Library/Communication/PR/2009/042.shtml, accessed 4 November 2015.

Financial Services Authority, 'Speech by Margaret Cole, Director of Enforcement, American Bar Association' (4 October 2007), available from http://www.fsa.gov.uk/pages/Library/Communication/Speeches/2007/1004_mc.shtml, accessed 9 November 2011.

Financial Services Authority, 'Transaction reporting cases' (2011), available from http://www.fsa.gov.uk/pages/About/What/financial_crime/market_abuse/library/index.shtml, accessed 18 October 2011.

Financial Services Authority, *Updated Measurement of Market Cleanliness FSA Occasional Paper Series 25* (Financial Services Authority: London, 2007).

Financial Services Authority, 'What is financial crime?' (n/d), available from http://www.fsa.gov.uk/pages/About/What/financial_crime/money_laundering/faqs/index.shtml, accessed 2 June 2010.

Financial Services Authority, 'What we do: who we regulate' 'We regulate most financial services markets, exchanges and firms. We set the standards that they must meet and can take action against firms if they fail to meet the required standards' (n/d), available from http://www.fsa.gov.uk/pages/About/What/Who/index.shtml, accessed 27 September 2011.

Financial Services Authority towards Imposing Financial Sanctions see Financial Services Authority, *Financial Services Firms' Approach to UK Financial Sanctions* (Financial Services Authority: London, 2009).

Financial Services Commission, *Guidance Notes – Systems of Control to Prevent the Financial System from Being Used for Money Laundering or Terrorist Financing Activities* (Financial Services Commission: London, 2011).

J. Fisher, 'The anti-money laundering disclosure regime and the collection of revenue in the United Kingdom' (2010) *British Tax Review*, 3, 235–266.

J. Fisher, *Fighting Fraud and Financial Crime: A New Architecture for the Investigation and Prosecution of Serious Fraud, Corruption and Financial Market Crimes* (Policy Exchange, London, 2010).

J. Fisher, 'Recent development in the fight against money laundering' (2002) *Journal of International Banking Law*, 17(3), 67–72, at 67.

J. Fisher and T. Sumpster, *Fighting Fraud and Financial Crime* (Policy Exchange, 2010, 12).

J. F. Stephen, *A Digest of the Criminal Law* 9th ed. (Sweet & Maxwell: London, 1950, 362).

J. Fontanella-Khan, 'Corruption in the EU costs business €120bn a year, study finds' (*Financial Times* 3 February 2014) available from http://www.ft.com/cms/s/0/28f11862–8cf9–11e3-ad57–00144feab7de.html?siteedition=uk#axzz2sLiCCodw, accessed 4 February 2013.

R. Forston, 'Money laundering offences under POCA 2002' in W. Blair and R. Brent (eds.), *Banks and Financial Crime: The International Law of Tainted Money* (Oxford University Press: Oxford, 2010).

C. Foster, 'Developments in accountability for the money laundering reporting officer in the United Kingdom' (2001) *Journal of International Financial Markets*, 3(3), 113–117.

E. Foster-Bowser and A. Sanders, 'Security threats in the Sahel and beyond: AQIM, Boko Haram and al Shabaab' (n/d), available from http://reliefweb.int/sites/reliefweb.int/files/resources/Full_Report_3818.pdf, accessed 30 September 2014.

Fox News, 'Extortion, bank robbery fuel ISIS bloody drive to establish Sharia caliphate' (14 June 2014), available from http://www.foxnews.com/world/2014/06/14/extortion-bank-robbery-fuel-isis-bloody-drive-to-establish-sharia-caliphate/, accessed 27 June 2014.

Fraud Advisory Panel, 'About us' (n/d), available from https://www.fraudadvisorypanel.org/about-us/, accessed 21 August 2015.

Fraud Advisory Panel, *Roskill Revisited: Is There a Case for a Unified Fraud Prosecution Office?* (Fraud Advisory Panel: London, 2010).

FSA, 'Final notice: David Einhorn' (15 February 2012), available from http://webarchive.nationalarchives.gov.uk/20130301170532/http://www.fsa.gov.uk/static/pubs/final/david-einhorn.pdf, accessed 13 January 2016.

FSA, 'Final notice: Greenlight Capital Inc.' (15 February 2012), available from http://webarchive.nationalarchives.gov.uk/20130301170532/http://www.fsa.gov.uk/static/pubs/final/greenlight-capital.pdf, accessed 13 January 2016.

FSA, 'FSA publishes measure of scale of market abuse' (17 March 2006), available from http://www.fsa.gov.uk/pages/Library/Communication/PR/2006/020.shtml, accessed 10 November 2011.

FSA, 'Principles for business' (12 October 1999), available from http://www.fsa.gov.uk/Pages/Library/Communication/PR/1999/099.shtml, accessed 29 April 2010.

FSA Handbook, 'Supervision', SUP 15.10 (n/d), available from http://fsahandbook.info/FSA/html/handbook/SUP/15/10, accessed 10 November 2011.

FSA Press Release, 'FSA fines Alpari and its former money laundering reporting officer, Sudipto Chattopadhyay for anti-money laundering failings' (5 May 2010), http://www.fsa.gov.uk/pages/Library/Communication/PR/2010/077.shtml, accessed 6 July 2011.

S. Furnell, *Cybercrime: Vandalizing the Information Society* (Addison-Wesley: London, 2002, 22).

J. Gaddis, 'And now this: Lessons from the old era for the new one', in S. Talbott and N. Chander (eds.), *The Age of Terror: America and the World After September 11* (Basic Books: New York, 2001) 1.

J. Gallagher, J. Lauchlan, and M. Steven, 'Polly Peck: The breaking of an entrepreneur?' (1996) *Journal of Small Business and Enterprise Development*, 3(1), 3–12.

Gambling Commission, *Money Laundering: The Prevention of Money Laundering and Combating the Financing of Terrorism Guidance for Remote and Non-Remote Casinos Second Edition* (The Gambling Commission: London, 2013).

S. Gentle, 'The Bribery Act 2010: Part 2: The corporate offence' (2011) *Criminal Law Review*, 2, 101–110, at 110.

S. Gentle, 'Proceeds of Crime Act 2002: Update' (2008) *Compliance Officer Bulletin*, 56(May), 31.

G. Gilligan, 'The problem of, and with, financial crime' (2012) *Northern Ireland Legal Quarterly*, 63(4), 495–508.

Global Witness, *Broken Vows – Exposing the Loupe Holes in the Diamond Industry's Efforts to Prevent the Trade in Conflict Diamonds* (Global Witness Publishing Inc., London, 2003).

M. Goldby, 'Anti-money laundering reporting requirements imposed by English law: Measuring effectiveness and gauging the need for reform' (2013) *Journal of Business Law*, 4, 367–397.

M. Goldby 'The impact of schedule 7 of the Counter-Terrorism Act 2008 on banks and their customers' (2010) *Journal of Money Laundering Control*, 13(4), 352.

P. Gottschalk, 'Categories of financial crime' (2010) *Journal of Financial Crime*, 17(4), 441–458.

P. Gottschalk, 'Executive positions involved in white-collar crime' (2011) *Journal of Money Laundering Control*, 14(4), 300–312.

J. Gray, 'Financial Services Act 1986 reforms, Part 2' (1991) *International Banking Law*, 9(9), 412–416.

K. Griffiths, 'Fraudulent broker gets 15 months' (14 February 2008), available from http://www.telegraph.co.uk/finance/markets/2784369/Fraudulent-broker-gets-15-months.html, accessed 12 November 2012.

J. Gurung, M. Wijaya, and A. Rao, 'AMLCTF compliance and SMEs in Australia: A case study of the prepaid card industry' (2010) *Journal of Money Laundering Control*, 13(3), 199.

J. Haines, 'The National Fraud Strategy: New rules to crack down on fraud' (2009) *Company Lawyer*, 30(7), 213.

B. Hannigan, 'Regulating insider dealing – the EEC dimension' (1989) *Journal of International Banking Law*, 4(1), 11–14.

J. Hansen, 'MAD in a hurry: The swift and promising adoption of the EU Market Abuse Directive' (2007) *European Business Law Review*, 15(2), 183–221.

J. Hansen, 'The new proposal for a European Union directive on market abuse' (2002) *University of Pennsylvania Journal of International Economic Law*, 23, 241–268, at 250.

P. Hardouin, 'Banks governance and public-private partnership in preventing and confronting organized crime, corruption and terrorism financing' (2009) *Journal of Financial Crime*, 16(3), 206.

C. Harnish, *The Terror Threat from Somalia – The Internationalization of Al Shabaab – A Report of the Critical Threats Project of the American Enterprise Institute* (American Enterprise Institute, Washington, DC, 2010).

J. Harvey, 'Compliance and reporting issues arising for financial institutions from money laundering regulations: A preliminary cost benefit study' (2004) *Journal of Money Laundering Control*, 7(4), 333–346.

J. Harvey, 'An evaluation of money laundering policies' (2005) *Journal of Money Laundering Control*, 8(4), 339–345, at 340.

A. Hauslohner, 'Jihadist expansion in Iraq puts Persian Gulf states in a tight spot' available from http://m.washingtonpost.com/world/jihadist-expansion-in-iraq-puts-persian-gulf-states-in-a-tight-spot/2014/06/13/e52e90ac-f317-11e3-bf76-447a5df6411f_story.html, accessed 27 June 2014.

A. Haynes, 'Market abuse' (2010) *Compliance Officer Bulletin*, 75(Apr), 1–31.

A. Haynes, 'Market abuse, fraud and misleading communications' (2012) *Journal of Financial Crime*, 19(3), 234–254.

J. Hayrynen, 'The precise definition of inside information?' (2008) *Journal of International Banking Law and Regulation*, 23(2), 64–70.

E. Herlin-Karnell, 'White-collar crime and European financial crises: Getting tough on EU market abuse' (2012) *European Law Review*, 37(4), 481–494.

HM Crown Prosecution Service, Inspectorate, *Review of the Fraud Prosecution Service* (HM Crown Prosecution Service Inspectorate: London, 2008).

HM Government, *The Coalition: Our Programme for Government* (HM Government: London, 2010).

HM Government, *CONTEST – The United Kingdom's Strategy for Countering Terrorism* (HM Government: London, 2011).

HM Government, *Countering International Terrorism: The United Kingdom's Strategy* (HM Government: London, 2006).

HM Government, *Policy Paper 2010 to 2015 Government Policy: Tax Evasion and Avoidance* (HM Government: London, 2015).

HM Government, *Report of the Official Account of the Bombings in London on 7th July 2005* (HM Government: London: London, 2006, 23).

HM Government, *Securing Britain in an Age of Uncertainty: The Strategic Defence and Security Review* (HM Government: London, 2010).

HM Government, *A Strong Britain in an Age of Uncertainty: The National Security Strategy* (HM Government: London, 2010).

HM Government, *The United Kingdom's Strategy for Countering International Terrorism* (HM Government: London, 2009).

HM Revenue and Customs, 'About us', n/d, available from https://www.gov.uk/government/organisations/hm-revenue-customs/about, accessed 17 March 2016.

HM Revenue and Customs, *Anti-Money Laundering Guidance for Trust or Company Service Providers* (HMRC: London, 2010).

HM Revenue and Customs, 'Bristol and West loses Corporation Tax avoidance case' (11 May 2016), available from https://www.gov.uk/government/news/bristol-and-west-loses-corporation-tax-avoidance-case, accessed 16 March 2016.

HM Revenue and Customs, *Closing in on Tax Evasion: HMRC's Approach* (HMRC: London, 2012).

HM Revenue and Customs, 'Clothing giant next loses tax avoidance case' (19 May 2015), available from https://www.gov.uk/government/news/clothing-giant-next-loses-tax-avoidance-case, accessed 12 March 2016.

HM Revenue and Customs, 'Crackdown in hauliers in the Midlands' (10 July 2013), available from https://www.gov.uk/government/news/crackdown-on-hauliers-in-the-midlands, accessed 11 March 2016

HM Revenue and Customs, 'HMRC's affluent unit recruits 100 new inspectors' (16 January 2013), available from https://www.gov.uk/government/news/hmrc-s-affluent-unit-recruits-100-new-inspectors, accessed 15 March 2016.

HM Revenue and Customs, HMRC Tax & NI Receipts, Monthly and Annual Historical Record (HMRC: London, 19 June 2015), available from https://www.gov.uk/government/uploads/system/uploads/attachment_data/file/435404/May15_Receipts_Bulletin_v1.pdf.

HM Revenue and Customs, 'HMRC wins in court have protected over £1 billion' (18 July 2013), available from https://www.gov.uk/government/news/hmrc-wins-in-court-have-protected-over-1-billion, accessed 16 March 2016.

HM Revenue and Customs, *Levelling the Tax Playing Field Compliance Progress Report – March 2013* (HMRC: London, 2013).

HM Revenue and Customs, *Measuring Tax Gaps 2014* (HMRC Corporate Communications: London, 2014).

HM Revenue and Customs, *Measuring Tax Gaps 2015* (HMRC Corporate Communications: London, 2015).

HM Revenue and Customs, 'Morgan Stanley's £60m tax avoidance scheme beaten in court', available from https://www.gov.uk/government/news/morgan-stanley-s-60m-tax-avoidance-scheme-beaten-in-court, accessed 16 March 2016.

HM Revenue and Customs, *No Safe Havens 2014* (HMRC: London, 2014).

HM Revenue and Customs, 'Notice MLR9b: Money Laundering Regulations registration guide for High Value Dealers' (13 September 2013), available from https://www.gov.uk/government/publications/notice-mlr9b-money-laundering-regulations-registration-guide-for-high-value-dealers/notice-mlr9b-money-laundering-regulations-registration-guide-for-high-value-dealers, accessed 1 July 2015.

HM Revenue and Customs, 'Nottingham salesman jailed for tax fraud' (12 May 2015), available from http://www.mynewsdesk.com/uk/hm-revenue-customs-hmrc/pressreleases/nottingham-salesman-jailed-for-tax-fraud-1159766, accessed 13 March 2016.

HM Revenue and Customs, 'Published details of deliberate tax defaulters' (1 April 2016), available from https://www.gov.uk/government/publications/publishing-details-of-deliberate-tax-defaulters-pddd#history, accessed 16 March 2016.

HM Revenue and Customs, *Single Departmental Plan 2015–2020* (HMRC: London, 2016).

HM Revenue and Customs, *Tackling Offshore Tax Evasion: A New Corporate Criminal Offence of Failure to Prevent the Facilitation of Evasion* (HMRC: London, 2015).

HM Revenue and Customs, 'Tax cheats named by HMRC' (12 November 2013), available from https://www.gov.uk/government/news/tax-cheats-named-by-hmrc, accessed 16 March 2016.

HM Revenue and Customs, 'Tax taskforce to crack down on restaurants in the North East' (10 July 2013), available from https://www.gov.uk/government/news/tax-taskforce-to-crack-down-on-restaurants-in-the-north-east, accessed 16 March 2016.

HM Treasury, *Advisory Notice on Money Laundering and Terrorist Financing Controls in Overseas Jurisdictions* (HM Treasury: London, 2015).

HM Treasury, *Anti-Money Laundering and Counter Terrorist Finance Supervision Report 2010–11* (HM Treasury: London, 2011).

HM Treasury, *Anti-Money Laundering and Counter Terrorist Finance Supervision Report 2011–12* (HM Treasury: London, 2012).

HM Treasury, *Anti-Money Laundering and Counter Terrorist Finance Supervision Report 2012–13* (HM Treasury: London, 2012).

HM Treasury, *Anti-Money Laundering and Counter Terrorist Finance Supervision Report 2013–14* (HM Treasury: London, 2013).

HM Treasury, 'Appointment of the UK President of the Financial Action Task Force' (n/d), available from http://www.gov-news.org/gov/uk/news/appointment_uk_president_financial_action/36083.html, accessed 3 July 2011.

HM Treasury, 'Asset Freezing Unit' (n/d), available from http://www.hm-treasury.gov.uk/fin_sanctions_afu.htm, accessed 14 March 2015.

HM Treasury, 'The Chancellor of the Exchequer delivered the autumn statement to Parliament on 5 December 2012' (5 December 2012), available from https://www.gov.uk/government/speeches/autumn-statement-2012-chancellors-statement, accessed 15 March 2016.

HM Treasury, *Combating the Financing of Terrorism: A Report on UK Action* (HM Treasury: London, 2002).

HM Treasury, 'Criminal Sanctions Directive on Market Abuse written ministerial statement' (20 February 2012), available from http://www.hm-treasury.gov.uk/d/wms_fst_200212.pdf, accessed 1 June 2012.

HM Treasury, *The Financial Challenge of Terrorism and Crime* (HM Treasury: London, 2007).

HM Treasury, 'Financial services policy agenda' (2010), available from http://www.hm-treasury.
gov.uk/fin_policy_agenda_index.htm, accessed 19 July 2011.

HM Treasury, 'G5 FATCA agreement strengthens UK ability to tackle tax evasion' (26 July
2012), available from https://www.gov.uk/government/news/g5-fatca-agreement-
strengthens-uk-ability-to-tackle-tax-evasion, accessed 15 March 2016.

HM Treasury, 'George Osborne, Chancellor of the Exchequer: Speech at the Lord Mayor's
dinner for bankers & merchants of the city of London, at Mansion House 16 June 2010'
(16 June 2010), available from www.hm-treasury.gov.uk/press_12_10.htm, accessed 26
June 2010.

HM Treasury, 'The Landsbanki Freezing Order' (2011), available from http://www.hm-
treasury.gov.uk/fin_stability_landsbanki.htm, accessed 24 June 2011.

HM Treasury, *A New Approach to Financial Regulation: Consultation on Reforming the Consumer
Credit Regime* (HM Treasury: London, 2010).

HM Treasury, 'Policy paper: Preventing money laundering', 5 June 2013, available from
https://www.gov.uk/government/publications/preventing-money-laundering/prevent
ing-money-laundering#financial-action-task-force-fatf, accessed 1 July 2015.

HM Treasury, *Tackling Tax Avoidance* (HM Treasury: London, 2011).

HM Treasury Select Committee, *Fixing LIBOR: Some Preliminary Findings* (HM Treasury:
London, 2012).

Home Affairs Select Committee, *Counter-Terrorism Seventeenth Report of Session 2013–14*
(Home Affairs Select Committee: London, 2014).

Home Office, 'Counter terrorist finance strategy' (5 June 2013), available from https://www.
gov.uk/government/publications/counter-terrorist-finance-strategy, accessed 15 July
2014.

Home Office, 'Counting rules for recorded crime' (4 July 2013), available from http://rds.
homeoffice.gov.uk/rds/pdfs10/countgeneral10.pdf, accessed 29 April 2010.

Home Office, *Cyber Crime Strategy, Cm 7842* (HMSO: London, 2010).

Home Office, 'Economic crime press release' (17 January 2011), available from http://www.
homeoffice.gov.uk/media-centre/news/economic-crime, accessed 22 January 2011.

Home Office, *Financial Orders under Part 8 of the Proceeds of Crime Act 2002* (Home Office:
London, 2015).

Home Office, *The National Crime Agency – A Plan for the Creation of a National Crime-Fighting
Capability* (Home Office: London, 2011).

Home Office, *Reform of the Prevention of Corruption Acts and SFO Powers in Cases of Bribery
against Foreign Officials* (Home Office: London, 2005).

Home Office, *Report on the Operation in 2004 of the Terrorism Act 2000* (Home Office: London,
2004).

Home Office, *The United Kingdom's Strategy for Countering Terrorism* (Home Office: London,
2011).

D. Hopton, *Money Laundering a Concise Guide for All Business* (Gower: Farnham, 2009).

J. Horder, 'Bribery as a form of criminal wrongdoing' (2011) *Law Quarterly Review*, 127(Jan),
37–54.

House of Commons, *Report of the Official Account of the Bombings in London on 7th July 2005*
(House of Commons: London, 2005, 23).

House of Lords, 'Money Laundering and the Financing of Terrorism: European Union Committee' (2009), available from http://www.publications.parliament.uk/pa/ld200809/
ldselect/ldeucom/132/9031811.htm, accessed 24 June 2011.

House of Representatives Committee on Homeland Security Subcommittee on Counterterrorism and Intelligence, *Boko Haram Emerging Threat to the U.S.* (Homeland U.S. House

of Representatives Committee on Homeland Security Subcommittee on Counterterrorism and Intelligence, 2011), available from http://www.fsa.gov.uk/pages/About/What/financial_crime/market_abuse/library/notices/index.shtml, accessed 1 July 2011.

A. Hudson, *The Law of Finance* (Sweet and Maxwell: Hebden Bridge, 2009).

T. Hurst, 'A post-Enron examination of corporate governance problems in the investment company industry' (2006) *The Company Lawyer*, 27(2), 41–49.

Independent, 'Celebrities hid £340m in icebreaker tax avoidance scheme used by Gary Barlow' (14 May 2014), available from http://www.independent.co.uk/news/uk/home-news/celebrities-hid-340m-in-icebreaker-tax-avoidance-scheme-used-by-gary-barlow-9367454.html, accessed 12 March 2016.

Inter-governmental Action Group Against Money Laundering in West Africa, *Threat Assessment of Money Laundering and Terrorist Financing in West Africa* (Inter-governmental Action Group Against Money Laundering in West Africa, 2010).

International Bar Association, the American Bar Association and the Council of Bars and Law Societies of Europe, *A Lawyer's Guide to Detecting and Preventing Money Laundering* (International Bar Association, the American Bar Association and the Council of Bars and Law Societies of Europe: London, 2014).

International Consortium for Investigative Journalists, 'Banking giant HSBC sheltered murky cash linked to dictators and arms dealers' (8 February 2015), available from http://www.icij.org/project/swiss-leaks/banking-giant-hsbc-sheltered-murky-cash-linked-dictators-and-arms-dealers, accessed 20 June 2015.

International Monetary Fund, 'Anti-money laundering/combating the financing of terrorism – topics' (n/d), available from http://www.imf.org/external/np/leg/amlcft/eng/aml1.htm#financingterrorism, accessed 26 June 2014.

International Monetary Fund, *Financial system abuse, financial crime and money laundering – background paper* (International Monetary Fund: Washington, DC, 12 February 2001).

International Monetary Fund, 'Money laundering: The importance of international countermeasures – address by Michel Camdessus, Managing Director of the International Monetary Fund' (10 February 1998), available from http://www.imf.org/external/np/speeches/1998/021098.HTM, accessed 19 March 2015.

IRS, 'Foreign Account Tax Compliance Act' (n/d), available from https://www.irs.gov/Businesses/Corporations/Foreign-Account-Tax-Compliance-Act-FATCA, accessed 16 March 2016.

M. Jain, 'Significance of mens rea in insider dealing' (2004) *Company Lawyer*, 25(5), 132–140.

T. Johnson, 'Civil recovery: Is the erosion of individual rights justified?' (2011) *Civil Justice Quarterly*, 30(2), 136.

Joint Money Laundering Steering Group, *Prevention of Money Laundering/Combating Terrorist Financing: Guidance for the UK Financial Sector: Parts 1–3* (Joint Money Laundering Steering Group: London, 2014).

J. Jones, 'HMRC' (2005) *British Tax Review*, 3, 270–271.

S. Jones, 'Diverse funding and strong accounting give Isis unparalleled wealth' (22 June 2014), available from http://www.ft.com/cms/s/0/21e8c922-f95d-11e3-bb9d-00144feab7de.html?siteedition=uk#axzz35pfchnAb, accessed 27 June 2014.

J. Kaetzler and T. Kordys, 'Fourth money laundering directive: Increased risk management requirements' (2015) *Compliance & Risk*, 4(5), 2–5.

M. Kempa, 'Combating white-collar crime in Canada: Serving victim needs and market integrity' (2010) *Journal of Financial Crime*, 17(2), 252.

A. Kennon, 'Pre-legislative scrutiny of draft Bills' (2004) *Public Law*, Autumn, 477–494.

H. Khil and I. Achek, 'The determinants of tax evasion: A literature review' (2015) *International Journal of Law & Management*, 57(5), 486–497.

P. Kiernan and G. Scanlan, 'Fraud and the law commission: The future of dishonesty' (2003) *Journal of Financial Crime*, 10(3), 199–208.

A. Kokkins, 'The Financial Services Act 2012, the recent overhaul of the UK's financial regulatory structure' (2013) *International Company and Commercial Law Review*, 24(9), 325–328.

J. Koningsveld, 'Money laundering – 'you don't see it, until you understand it': Rethinking the stages of money laundering process to make enforcement more effective' in B. Unger and Dvd Linde (eds.), *Research Handbook on Money Laundering* (Edward Elgar: Cheltenham, 2014).

KPMG, 'Global Anti-Money Laundering Survey' (2014) available from https://www.kpmg.com/KY/en/IssuesAndInsights/ArticlesPublications/PublishingImages/global-anti-money-laundering-survey-v3.pdf, accessed March 15 2014.

KPMG, *Money Laundering: Review of the Reporting System* (KPMG, London, 2003).

A. Kruse, 'Financial and economic sanctions – from a perspective of international law and human rights' (2005) *Journal of Financial Crime*, 12(3), 218.

M. Kubiciel, 'Core criminal law provisions in the United Nations Convention against Corruption' (2009) *International Criminal Law Review*, 9(1), 139–155.

Law Commission, 'Fraud: Report on a reference under section 3(1)(e) of the Law Commissions Act 1965', Law Commission Report No 276, Cm 5560 (2002).

Law Commission, *Legislating the Criminal Code: Corruption No. 248* (Law Commission: London, 1998).

Law Commission, *Legislating the Criminal Code Fraud and Deception – Law Commission Consultation Paper No 155* (Law Commission: London, 1999).

Law Commission, *Reforming Bribery* (HMSO: London, 2008).

Law Commission, *Reforming Bribery: A Consultation* (Law Commission: London, 2007).

Law Commission also published an informal discussion paper in 2000. See Law Commission, *Informal Discussion Paper: Fraud and Deception – Further Proposals from the Criminal Law Team* (Law Commission: London, 2000).

Law Society, *Anti-Money Laundering Practice Note* (The Law Society: London, 2009).

R. Lee, *Terrorist Financing: The US and International Response Report for Congress* (Congressional Research Service, Washington, DC, 2002).

D. Leigh and R. Evans, 'Cost of new economic crime agency could prove prohibitive', available from http://www.guardian.co.uk/business/2010/jun/02/economic-crime-agency-scheme-cost, accessed 12 July 2010.

G. Lennon and C. Walker, 'Hot money in a cold climate' (2009) *Public Law*, January, 37.

A. Leong, 'Chasing dirty money: Domestic and international measures against money laundering' (2007) *Journal of Money Laundering Control*, 10(2), 140–156.

M. Leroux, 'Michael Bright gets maximum seven years from Independent Insurance Fraud' (*The Times* 25 October 2007) available from http://business.timesonline.co.uk/tol/business/industry_sectors/banking_and_finance/article2733660.ece, accessed 10 June 2011.

M. Levi, 'Combating the financing of terrorism: A history and assessment of the Control of Threat Finance' (2010) *British Journal of Criminology*, 50, 650.

M. Levi, 'The Roskill Fraud Commission revisited: An assessment' (2003) *Journal of Financial Crime*, 11(1), 38–44.

M. Levi and J. Burrows, 'Measuring the impact of fraud in the UK: A conceptual and empirical journey' (2008) *British Journal of Criminology*, 48(3), 293–318.

M. Levi, J. Burrows, M. Fleming, and M. Hopkins, *The Nature, Extent and Economic Impact of Fraud in the UK* (ACPO, London, 2007).

M. Levitt, 'Stemming the follow of terrorist financing: Practical and conceptual challenges' (2003) *The Fletcher Forum of World Affairs*, 27(1), 64.

A. Lewis, R. Pretorius, and E. Radmore, 'Outsourcing in the financial services sector' (2013) *Compliance Officer Bulletin*, 106(May), 1–34.

L. Linklater, 'The market abuse regime: Setting standards in the twenty-first century' (2001) *Company Lawyer*, 22(9), 267–272.

C. Linn, 'How terrorist exploit gaps in US anti-money laundering laws to secrete plunder' (2005) *Journal of Money Laundering Control*, 8(3), 200.

E. Lomnicka, 'Making the financial services authority accountable' (2000) *Journal of Business Law*, January, 65–81.

E. Lomnicka, 'The new insider dealing provisions, Criminal Justice Act 1993, part V' (1994) *Journal of Business Law*, March, 173–188.

E. Lomnicka, 'Preventing and controlling the manipulation of financial markets, towards a definition of market manipulation' (2001) *Journal of Financial Crime*, 8(4), 297–304.

P. Lowe, 'Counterfeiting: Linking organised crime and terrorist funding' (2006) *Journal of Financial Crime*, 13(2), 255.

P. Lowe, 'Counterfeiting: Links to organised crime and terrorist funding' (2006) *Journal of Financial Crime*, 13(2), 255.

M. Lunt, 'The extraterritorial effects of the Sarbanes-Oxley Act 2002' (2006) *Journal of Business Law*, May, 249–266.

W. Maclean, 'Shabaab finances face squeeze after Kenya attack' (26 September 2013), available from http://www.reuters.com/article/2013/09/26/us-kenya-attack-shabaab-funding-idUSBRE98P05Z20130926, accessed 27 June 2014.

B. Mahendra, 'Fighting serious fraud' (2002) *New Law Journal*, 152(7020), 289.

J. Masters, 'Al-shabab' (13 March 2015), available from http://www.cfr.org/somalia/al-shabab/p18650, accessed 27 June 2014.

J. Masters, 'Fraud and money laundering: The evolving criminalisation of corporate non-compliance' (2008) *Journal of Money Laundering Control*, 11(2), 103–122.

J.L. Masters, 'Fraud and money laundering: The evolving criminalization of corporate non-compliance' (2008) *Journal of Money Laundering Control*, 11(2), 103.

S. Maylam, 'Prosecution for money laundering in the UK' (2002) *Journal of Financial Crime*, 10, 157–158, at 158.

F. Mazzacuva, 'Justifications and purposes of negotiated justice for corporate offenders: Deferred and non-prosecution agreements in the UK and US systems of criminal justice' (2014) *Journal of Criminal Law*, 78(3), 249–262.

T. McCoy, 'Paying for terrorism: Where does Boko Haram gets its money from?' (6 June 2014), available from http://www.independent.co.uk/news/world/africa/paying-for-terrorism-where-does-boko-haram-gets-its-money-from-9503948.html, accessed 27 June 2014.

R. McDonnell, 'UN anti-money laundering initiatives', in W. Muller, C. Kalin and J. Goldsworth (eds.), *Anti-Money Laundering International Law and Practice* (John Wiley and Sons: Chichester, 2004) 49–56.

M. McKee, 'The proposed EU Market Abuse Directive' (2001) *Journal of International Financial Markets*, 3(4), 137–142

C. McKenna, 'The serious fraud office', available from http://www.law-now.com/law-now/2009/anticorruptionthesfo?cmckreg=true, accessed 29 November 2011.

H. McVea, 'Fashioning a system of civil penalties for insider dealing, sections 61 and 62 of the Financial Services Act 1986' (1996) *Journal of Business Law*, July, 344–361.

H. McVea, 'Plans for compulsory insider dealing legislation by the EEC' (1987) *Company Lawyer*, 8(5), 223–224.

M. Menkes, 'The divine comedy of governance in tax evasion matters: Or not?' (2015) *Journal of International Banking Law and Regulation*, 30(6), 325–329.

Metropolitan Police, 'Man jailed for 30 years for terrorism offences' (18 March 2011), available from http://content.met.police.uk/News/Man-jailed-for-30-years-for-terrorism-offences/1260268719101/1257246745756, accessed 28 June 2011.

Metropolitan Police, 'Operation Overamp: Hassan Mutegombwa' (1 March 2008), available from http://www.powerbase.info/images/6/6c/Metropolitan_Police_Service_Press_Release_on_Conviction_of_Hassan_Mutegombwa.pdf, accessed 28 June 2011.

Ministry of Justice, *Bribery Act 2010, Circular 2011/05* (Ministry of Justice: London, 2011).

Ministry of Justice, *The Bribery Act 2010 – Guidance* (Ministry of Justice: London, 2011).

Ministry of Justice, 'Bribery Act implementation', 20 July 2010, available from http://www.justice.gov.uk/news/newsrelease200710a.htm, accessed 15 December 2011.

Ministry of Justice, *Bribery: Draft Legislation* (The Stationery Office, 2009).

Ministry of Justice, 'Government welcomes new Bribery Law recommendations', 20 November 2008, available from http://www.wired-gov.net/wg/wg-news-1.nsf/0/329BD09E4E75E8138025750700478C2E?OpenDocument, accessed 28 June 2016.

Ministry of Justice Press Release, 'UK clamps down on corruption with new Bribery Act' (30 March 2011), available from http://www.justice.gov.uk/news/press-release-300311a.htm, accessed 29 November 2011.

V. Mitsilegas and B. Gilmore, 'The EU legislative framework against money laundering and terrorist finance: A critical analysis in light of evolving global standards' (2007) *International & Comparative Law Quarterly*, 56(1), 119–140.

C. Monteity, 'The Bribery Act 2010: Part 3: Enforcement' (2011) *Criminal Law Review*, 2, 111–121, at 114.

MSCI The, 'Tax Gap' in the MSCI World (MSCI ESG Research)' (December 2013), available from https://www.msci.com/resources/factsheets/MSCI_ESG_Research_Issue_Brief_The_Tax_Gap_in_the_MSCI_World.pdf, accessed 18 April 2014.

R. Murphy, *The Tax Gap: Tax Evasion in 2014 – and What Can Be Done About It* (Public and Commercial Services Union: London, 2015).

R. Murray-West, 'Barrister sentenced for £600,000 tax fraud' (*The Telegraph*, 26 February 2013), available from http://www.telegraph.co.uk/finance/personalfinance/9895308/Barrister-sentenced-for-600000-tax-fraud.html, accessed 16 March 2016.

National Audit Office, *Tackling Tax Fraud: How HMRC Responds to Tax Evasion, the Hidden Economy and Criminal Attacks* (National Audit Office: London, 2015).

National Commission on Terrorist Attacks upon the United States, *The 9/11 Commission Report* (Norton and Company: New York, 2004).

National Crime Agency, 'About us', n/d, available from http://www.nationalcrimeagency.gov.uk/about-us, accessed 21 August 2015.

National Crime Agency, 'Money laundering', n/d, available from http://www.nationalcrimeagency.gov.uk/crime-threats/money-laundering, accessed 16 June 2015.

National Crime Agency, *Suspicious Activity Reports (SARs) Annual Report 2013* (National Crime Agency: London, 2014).

National Crime Agency, *Suspicious Activity Reports (SARs) Annual Report 2014* (National Crime Agency: London, 2015).

National Crime Agency, 'UK Financial Intelligence Unit' (n/d), available from http://www.nationalcrimeagency.gov.uk/about-us/what-we-do/specialist-capabilities/ukfiu, accessed 25 June 2015.

National Criminal Intelligence Service, *UK Threat Assessment* (National Criminal Intelligence Service, London, 2007).

National Fraud Authority, *Annual Fraud Indicator* (National Fraud Authority: London, 2011).

National Fraud Authority, *Annual Fraud Indicator* (National Fraud Authority: London, 2012).

National Fraud Authority, *Annual Fraud Indicator* (National Fraud Authority: London, 2013).

National Fraud Authority, *National Fraud Authority Annual Fraud Indicator* (National Fraud Authority: London, 2010).

National Fraud Strategic Authority, *The National Fraud Strategy – A New Approach to Combating Fraud* (National Fraud Strategic Authority: London, 2009).

National Fraud Strategic Fraud Authority (2008), 'UK toughens up on fraudsters with new anti-fraud authority', available from http://www.attorneygeneral.gov.uk/NewsCentre/Pages/UKToughensUpOn%20FraudstersWithNewAnti-FraudAuthority.aspx, accessed 2 October 2008.

NBC News, 'The McVeigh Tapes: Confessions of an American terrorist' (15 April 2010), available from http://www.nbcnews.com/id/36135258/ns/msnbc_tv/#.VDJpOU10zIU, accessed 6 October 2014.

R. Nordland and A. Rubin, 'Iraq insurgents reaping wealth as they advance' (20 June 2014), available from http://www.nytimes.com/2014/06/21/world/middleeast/isis-iraq-insurgents-reaping-wealth-as-they-advance.html?_r=0, accessed 26 June 2014.

Office for National Statistics, 'Crime in England and Wales, year ending June 2015' (*ONS* 15 October 2015) available from http://www.ons.gov.uk/ons/rel/crime-stats/crime-statistics/year-ending-june-2015/stb-crime—ye-june-2015.html#tab-Fraud, accessed 12 November 2015.

Organisation for Economic Co-operation and Development, *Action Plan on Base Erosion and Profit Shifting* (OECD, Paris, 2013).

Organisation for Economic Co-operation and Development, 'All interested countries and jurisdictions to be invited to join global efforts led by the OECD and G20 to close international tax loopholes', 23 February 2016, available from http://www.oecd.org/tax/all-interested-countries-and-jurisdictions-to-be-invited-to-join-global-efforts-led-by-the-oecd-and-g20-to-close-international-tax-loopholes.htm, accessed 15 March 2016.

Organisation for Economic Co-operation and Development (2000), 'Business approaches to combating bribery', available from http://www.oecd.org/dataoecd/45/32/1922830.pdf, accessed 24 July 2010.

Organisation for Economic Co-operation and Development (2011), 'Guidelines for multinational enterprises', available from http://www.oecd.org/document/28/0,3343,en_2649_34889_2397532_1_1_1_1,00.html, accessed 24 July 2011.

Organisation for Economic Co-operation and Development, *The Fight against Bribery and Corruption* (OECD, Paris, 2000).

Organisation for Economic Co-operation and Development, *OECD Working Group on Bribery 'Annual Report 2008'* (OCED, Paris, 2008).

Organisation for Economic Co-operation and Development, 'Steps taken to implement and enforce the OECD Convention on Combating Bribery of Foreign Public Officials in International Business Transactions: UNITED KINGDOM', 28 May 2010, available from http://www.oecd.org/dataoecd/17/30/48362318.pdf, accessed 27 March 2012.

D. Ormerod, 'The Fraud Act 2006 – criminalising lying?' (2007) *Criminal Law Review*, March, 193–219.

D. Ormerod, 'Prosecution: Insider dealing – Criminal Justice Act 1993 s.61' (2009) *Criminal Law Review*, 6, 445–449.

G. Osborne, 'Summer budget 2015 speech' (8 July 2015), available from https://www.gov.uk/government/speeches/chancellor-george-osbornes-summer-budget-2015-speech, accessed 16 March 2016.

Oxford Analytica Ltd, 'Country report: Anti-money laundering rules in the United Kingdom' in M. Pieith and G. Aiolfi (eds.), *A Comparative Guide to Anti-Money Laundering a*

Critical Analysis of Systems in Singapore, Switzerland, the UK and the USA (Edward Elgar: Cheltenham, 2004).

E. Parris and S. Briskman, 'The daft communications data bill: An overview' (2012) *E-Commerce Law & Policy*, 14(7), 14.

N. Passas, 'The genesis of the BCCI scandal' (1996) *Journal of Law and Society*, 23(1), 57.

R. Peat and S. Bazley, 'Enforcement briefing' (2009) *Company Lawyer*, 30(12), 380–381.

R. Peat and I. Mason, 'Credible deterrence in action: The FSA brings a series of cases against traders' (2009) *Company Lawyer*, 30(9), 278–279.

R. Picur and A. Riahi-Belkaoui, 'The impact of bureaucracy, corruption and tax compliance' (2006) *Review of Accounting and Finance*, 5(2), 174–180.

Pinsent Masons, 'Amount of extra tax collected via HMRC investigations into "mass affluent" jumps 60% to £137.2 million#' (n/d), available from http://www.pinsentmasons.com/en/media/press-releases/2015/amount-of-extra-tax-collected-via-hmrc-investigations-into-mass-affluent-jumps-60-to-1372-million-1/, accessed 16 March 2015.

E. Podgor, 'White collar crime: A letter from the future' (2007) *Ohio State Journal of Criminal Law*, 5, 247.

T. Pope and T. Webb, 'Legislative comment – the Bribery Act 2010' (2010) *Journal of International Banking Law and Regulation*, 25(10), 480–483.

J. Prober, 'Accounting for terror: Debunking the paradigm of inexpensive terrorism' (1 November 2005), available from http://www.washingtoninstitute.org/policy-analysis/view/accounting-for-terror-debunking-the-paradigm-of-inexpensive-terrorism, accessed 11 August 2014.

A. Proctor, 'Supporting a risk-based anti-money laundering approach through enforcement action' (2004) *Journal of Financial Regulation and Compliance*, 13(1), 10–14.

J. Raynor, 'FSA fines anti-money laundering officer £14k' (20 May 2010), available from http://www.lawgazette.co.uk/news/fsa-fines-anti-money-laundering-officer-14k/55555.fullarticle, accessed 3 July 2015.

G. Rees and T. Moloney, 'The latest efforts to interrupt terrorist supply lines: Schedule 7 to the Counter-Terrorism Act 2008' (2010) *Criminal Law Review*, 2, 127.

J. Rhodes and S. Jones, 'The Proceeds of Crime Act 2002 and tax evasion' (2004) *Private Client Business*, 1, 51–59.

B. Rider, 'An abominable fraud?' (2010) *Company Lawyer*, 31(7), 197–198.

B. Rider, 'A bold step?' (2009) *Company Lawyer*, 30(1), 1–2, at 1.

B. Rider, 'Taking money launderers to the cleaners: Part 2' (1996) *Private Client Business*, 3, 205–206.

G. Robb, *White-Collar Crime in Modern England – Financial Fraud and Business Morality 1845–1929* (Cambridge University Press: Cambridge, 1992).

Lord Eustace Roskill, *Fraud Trials Committee Report* (HMSO: London, 1986).

Royal Institute for Chartered Surveyors, *Money Laundering Guidance* (Royal Institute for Chartered Surveyors: London, 2011).

J. Russell, 'SFO settles Nigeria Bribery case for £7m' (*The Telegraph*, 2011) available from http://www.telegraph.co.uk/finance/newsbysector/industry/8329298/SFO-settles-Nigeria-bribery-case-for-7m.html, accessed 29 November 2011.

N. Ryder, 'Danger money' (2007) *New Law Journal*, 157(7300); Supp (Charities Appeals Supplement), 6, 8.

N. Ryder, 'A false sense of security? An analysis of legislative approaches to the prevention of terrorist finance in the United States of America and the United Kingdom' (2007) *Journal of Business Law*, November, 821–850.

N. Ryder, 'To confiscate or not to confiscate? A comparative analysis of the confiscation of the proceeds of crime legislation in the United States of America and the United Kingdom' (2013) *Journal of Business Law*, 8, 767.

N. Ryder and U. Turksen, 'Banks in defense of the Homeland: Nexus of ethics and suspicious activity reporting' (2013) *Contemporary Issues in Law* (Special Issue on Law, Ethics and Counter-Terrorism), 12(4), 311–347.

N. Ryder, *Financial Crime in the 21st Century* (Edward Elgar: Cheltenham, 2011).

N. Ryder, *The Financial Crisis and White Collar Crime: The Perfect Storm* (Edward Elgar: Cheltenham, 2014).

N. Ryder, *The Financial War on Terror: A Review of Counter-Terrorist Financing Strategies Since 2001* (Routledge: London, 2015).

N. Ryder, *Money Laundering – An Endless Cycle? A Comparative Analysis of the Anti-Money Laundering Policies in the United States of America, the United Kingdom, Australia and Canada* (Routledge: London, 2012).

G. Sacerdoti, 'The 1997 OECD convention on combating bribery of foreign public officials in international business transactions' (1999) *International Business Law Journal*, 1, 3–18.

Salens, (n/d) 'Anti-bribery and corruption: The UK propels itself to the forefront of global enforcement', available from http://www.salans.com/~/media/Assets/Salans/Publications/Salans%20Client%20Alert%20UK%20Bribery%20Act%20Implementation%20Date.ashx, accessed 24 July 2010.

R. Sanyal and S. Samanta, 'Trends in international bribe-giving: Do anti-bribery laws matter?' (2011) *Journal of International Trade Law & Policy*, 10(2), 151–164.

C. Sargeant, 'Two steps backward, one step forward' – The cautionary tale of Bank Mellat (No 1)' (2013) *Cambridge Journal of International and Comparative Law*, 3(1), 111.

R. Sarker, 'Anti-money laundering requirements: Too much pain for too little gain' (2006) *Company Lawyer*, 27(8), 250–251, at 251.

R. Sarker, 'Fighting fraud – a missed opportunity?' (2007) *Company Lawyer*, 28(8), 243–244, at 243.

R. Sarker, 'Guinness – pure genius' (1994) *Company Lawyer*, 15(10), 310–312.

R. Sarker, 'Maxwell: Fraud trial of the century' (1996) *Company Lawyer*, 17(4), 116–117.

G. Scanlan, 'The enterprise of crime and terror – the implications for good business: Looking to the future – old and new threats' (2006) *Journal of Financial Crime*, 13(2), 164.

G. Scanlan, 'Offences concerning directors and officers of a company: Fraud and corruption in the United Kingdom – the present and the future' (2008) *Journal of Financial Crime*, 15(1), 22–37.

F. Schneider, 'The size of the shadow economies of 145 countries all over the world: First results over the period 1999–2003', IZA Discussion Paper No. 143, Forschungsiinstitut zur Zukunft der Arbeit (Institute for the Study of Labor (IZA): Bonn, 2004).

Sentencing Council Fraud, *Bribery and Money Laundering Offences, Definitive Guideline* (Sentencing Council: London, 2014).

Sentencing Guidelines Council, 'Guideline judgments case compendium' (1 March 2005), available from http://sentencingcouncil.judiciary.gov.uk/docs/web_case_compendium.pdf, accessed 6 June 2011.

Sentencing Guidelines Council, *Sentencing for Fraud – Statutory Offences Definitive Guideline* (Sentencing Guidelines Secretariat: London, 2009).

Serious Fraud Office, (2010) 'Approach of the serious fraud office to dealing with overseas corruption', available from http://www.sfo.gov.uk/media/107247/approach%20of%20the%20serious%20fraud%20office%20v3.pdf, accessed 24 July 2010.

Serious Fraud Office, (n/d) 'Bribery and corruption', available from http://www.sfo.gov.uk/bribery—corruption/bribery—corruption.aspx, accessed 23 November 2011.

Serious Fraud Office, 'City directors convicted in £23m "Green bio fuel" trial' (*News Release* 5 December 2014), available from https://www.sfo.gov.uk/2014/12/05/city-directors-convicted-23m-green-biofuel-trial/, accessed 10 February 2016.

Serious Fraud Office, 'City directors sentenced to 28 years in total for £23 million green bio fuel fraud' (*News Release* 8 December 2014), available from https://www.sfo.gov.uk/2014/12/08/city-directors-sentenced-28-years-total-23m-green-biofuel-fraud/, accessed 10 February 2016.

Serious Fraud Office, 'David Green CB QC, Director, at the 10th Annual Corporate Accountability Conference, PricewaterhouseCoopers, London' (14 June 2012), available from https://www.sfo.gov.uk/2012/06/14/10th-annual-corporate-accountability-conference-held-pricewaterhousecoopers/, accessed 26 February 2012.

Serious Fraud Office, 'Innospec Ltd' (Case Information, 12 March 2015), available from https://www.sfo.gov.uk/cases/innospec-ltd/, accessed 10 February 2016.

Serious Fraud Office, 'Innospec Ltd: Two more executives charged with corruption' (Press Release 27 October 2011), available from http://www.sfo.gov.uk/press-room/latest-press-releases/press-releases-2011/innospec-ltd-two-more-executives-charged-with-corruption.aspx, accessed 29 November 2011.

Serious Fraud Office, 'Insider dealing' (2010), available from http://www.sfo.gov.uk/media/99234/insider%20dealing%20web%201.pdf, accessed 4 October 2011.

Serious Fraud Office, 'Medical goods to Iraq supplier jailed for paying kick-backs' (Press Release, 13 April 2011), available from http://www.sfo.gov.uk/press-room/latest-press-releases/press-releases-2011/medical-goods-to-iraq-supplier-jailed-for-paying-kick-backs.aspx, accessed 29 November 2011.

Serious Fraud Office, 'Our cases' (n/d), available from https://www.sfo.gov.uk/our-cases/#aza, accessed 10 February 2016.

Serious Fraud Office, 'Oxford Publishing Ltd to pay almost £1.9 million as settlement after admitting unlawful conduct in its East African operations' (News Release 3 July 2012) available from https://www.sfo.gov.uk/2012/07/03/oxford-publishing-ltd-pay-almost-1–9-million-settlement-admitting-unlawful-conduct-east-african-operations/, accessed 10 February 2016.

Serious Fraud Office, 'Richard Alderman, Speech the Bribery Act 2010 – the SFO's approach and international compliance' (9 February 2011), available from http://www.sfo.gov.uk/about-us/our-views/director's-speeches/speeches-2011/the-bribery-act-2010—the-sfo's-approach-and-international-compliance.aspx, accessed 13 November 2011.

Serious Fraud Office, *Serious Fraud Office Annual Report and Accounts 2011–2012* (Serious Fraud Office: London, 2012).

Serious Fraud Office, 'Serious Fraud Office [SFO] case selection' (n/d), available from http://www.sfo.gov.uk/fraud/sfo-confidential–giving-us-information-in-confidence/serious-fraud-office-[sfo]-case-selection.aspx, accessed 20 August 2015.

Serious Fraud Office, 'SFO agrees first UK DPA with Standard Bank', 30 November 2015, available from https://www.sfo.gov.uk/2015/11/30/sfo-agrees-first-uk-dpa-with-standard-bank/, accessed 26 February 2016.

Serious Fraud Office, 'Smith and Ouzman Ltd' (Case information, 11 September 2014), available from https://www.sfo.gov.uk/cases/smith-ouzman-ltd/, accessed 10 February 2016.

Serious Fraud Office, 'Sweett Group PLC sentenced and ordered to pay £2.25 million after Bribery Act conviction' (19 February 2016), available from https://www.sfo.gov.uk/2016/02/19/sweett-group-plc-sentenced-and-ordered-to-pay-2–3-million-after-bribery-act-conviction/, accessed 26 February 2016.

Serious Fraud Office, 'What we do and who we work with' (n/d), available from http://www.sfo.gov.uk/about-us/what-we-do-and-who-we-work-with.aspx, accessed 20 August 2015.

Serious Organised Crime Agency, *The Suspicious Activity Reports Regime Annual Report 2008* (Serious Organised Crime Agency: London, 2008).

Serious Organised Crime Agency, *The Suspicious Activity Reports Regime Annual Report 2009* (Serious Organised Crime Agency: London, 2010).

Serious Organised Crime Agency, *The Suspicious Activity Reports Regime Annual Report 2010* (Serious Organised Crime Agency: London, 2011).

Serious Organised Crime Agency, *The Suspicious Activity Reports Regime Annual Report 2011* (Serious Organised Crime Agency: London, 2012).

Serious Organised Crime Agency, *The Suspicious Activity Reports Regime Annual Report 2011* (Serious Organised Crime Agency: London, 2013).

S. Sheikh, 'The Bribery Act 2010: Commercial organisations beware!' (2011) *International Company and Commercial Law Review*, 22(1), 1–16, at 3.

S. Sheikh, 'FSMA market abuse regime: A review of the sunset clauses International' (2008) *Company and Commercial Law Review*, 19(7), 234–236.

J. Sidak, 'The failure of good intentions: The WorldCom fraud and the collapse of American telecommunications after deregulation' (2003) *Yale Journal on Regulation*, 20, 207–261.

M. Simpson, 'International initiatives', in M. Simpson, N. Smith and A. Srivastava (eds.), *International Guide to Money Laundering Law and Practice* (Bloomsbury Professional: Haywards Heath, 2010).

S. Simpson, 'White collar crime: A review of recent developments and promising directions for future research' (2013) *Annual Review of Sociology*, 39, 309–331.

J. Simser, 'Money laundering and asset cloaking techniques' (2008) *Journal of Money Laundering Control*, 11(1), 15–24.

J. Simser, 'Tax evasion and avoidance typologies' (2008) *Journal of Money Laundering Control*, 11(2), 123–134.

H. Smith, 'FSA fines bank and its former MLRO for failure to comply with anti-money laundering requirements' (2012) *Law & Financial Markets Review*, 6(4), 311–314.

H. Smith, 'FSA fines MLRO and firm for failure to comply with anti-money laundering requirements' (2009) *Law & Financial Markets Review*, 3(1), 79–82.

S. Smith, *Britain's Shadow Economy* (Clarendon Press: London, 1986).

B. Spalek, 'Exploring the impact of financial crime: A study looking into the effects of the Maxwell scandal upon the Maxwell pensioners' (1999) *International Review of Victimology*, 6, 213.

B. Spalek, *Knowledgeable Consumers? Corporate Fraud and Its Devastating Impacts, Briefing 4.* (Centre for Crime and Justice Studies, London, 2007).

R. Spalek, 'Regulation, white-collar crime and the Bank of Credit and Commerce International' (2001) *Howard Journal of Criminal Justice*, 40, 166–179, at 167.

P. Sproat, 'Counter-terrorist finance in the UK: A quantitative and qualitative commentary based on open-source materials' (2010) *Journal of Money Laundering Control*, 13(4), 315–335.

A. Srivastava, I. Mason, M. Simpson, and M. Litt, 'Financial Crime' (2011) *Compliance Officer Bulletin*, 86(May) 1–23.

G. Sullivan, 'Proscribing corruption – some comments on the Law Commission's report' (1998) *Criminal Law Review*, August, 547–555.

Sunday Times, 'Stars face heft bill over film tax breaks' (1 February 2015), available from http://www.thesundaytimes.co.uk/sto/news/uk_news/People/article1513839.ece, accessed 16 March 2016.

E. Sutherland, 'The white collar criminal' (1940) *American Sociological Review*, 5(1), 2.

E. Sutherland, *White Collar Crime* (Dryden: New York, 1949).

E. Swan, 'Derivatives market manipulation by "wash sales" in violation of the US commodity exchange act' (1995) *Journal of Financial Crime*, 3(1), 53–56.

E. Swan, 'Market abuse: A new duty of fairness' (2004) *Company Lawyer*, 25(3), 67–68.

A. Sykes, 'Market abuse: A civil revolution' (1999) *Journal of International Financial Markets*, 1(2), 59–67.

N. Taylor, 'FSA prosecutions: Offences of money laundering – power to prosecute' (2010) *Criminal Law Review*, 10, 772–775.

S. Teasdale, 'FSA to FCA: Recent trends in UK financial conduct regulation' (2011) *Journal of International Banking Law and Regulation*, 26(12), 583–586.

Telegraph (2011), 'Two al-Qe'eda terrorists jailed for 11 years', available from http://www.telegraph.co.uk/news/1426290/Two-al-Qaeda-terrorists-jailed-for-11-years.html, accessed 28 June 2011.

Times Online (2009), 'Canoe fraudster Anne Darwin to repay nearly £600,000' (*The Times*, 11 November 2009) available from http://www.timesonline.co.uk/tol/news/uk/article6912213.ece, accessed 10 June 2010.

Times Online, 'Conservatives confirm plans for single Economic Crime Agency', available from http://timesonline.typepad.com/law/2010/04/conservatives-confirm-plans-for-single-economic-crime-agency.html, accessed 26 April 2010.

J. Titcomb, 'Insider trading has plummeted since the financial crisis: Here's why' (11 July 2014), available from http://www.telegraph.co.uk/finance/financial-crime/10960400/Insider-trading-has-plummeted-since-the-financial-crisis.-Heres-why.html, accessed 13 January 2016.

M. Tran, 'Isis insurgents attack Iraq's biggest oil refinery' (18 June 2014), available from http://www.theguardian.com/world/2014/jun/18/isis-fighters-iraq-oil-refinery-baiji, accessed 27 June 2014.

Transparency International, 'Corruption statistics', n/d, available from http://www.transparency.org.uk/corruption/statistics-and-quotes/uk-corruption, accessed 16 June 2016.

Transparency International (2010), The global coalition against corruption, 'Corruption Perceptions Index 2010', available from http://www.transparency.org/policy_research/surveys_indices/cpi/2010, accessed 28 June 2011.

Travers Smith Regulatory Investigations Group, 'FSA enforcement action: Themes and trends' (2010) *Compliance Officer Bulletin*, 76(May), 1–32

W. Tupman, 'Where has all the money gone? The IRA as a profit-making concern' (1998) *Journal of Money Laundering Control*, 1(4), 303.

Brigette Unger, *The Scale and Impacts of Money Laundering* (Edward Elgar: Cheltenham, 2007).

United Nations, *Report of the Monitoring Group on Somalia and Eritrea Pursuant to Security Council resolution 2060 (2012): Somalia* (United Nations: New York, 2012).

United Nations Office on Drugs and Crime, *Estimating Illicit Financial Flows Resulting from Drug Trafficking and Other Transnational Organised Crimes* (United Nations Office on Drugs and Crime: Vienna, 2011).

United States Department of State, *Department of State Bureau of International Narcotics and Law Enforcement Affairs Narcotics Control Strategy Report Volume II Money Laundering and Financial Crime* (United States Department of State: Washington, DC, 2010).

United States Federal Sentencing Guidelines, 'Chapter eight – part b – remedying harm from criminal conduct, and effective compliance and ethics program' (1 November 2004), available from http://www.ussc.gov/2007guid/8b2_1.html, accessed 24 July 2010.

C. van Cleef, H. Silets, and P. Motz, 'Does the punishment fit the crime' (2004) *Journal of Financial Crime*, 12(1), 57.

D. Vitkova, 'Level 3 of the Lamfalussy process: An effective tool for achieving pan-European regulatory consistency?' (2008) *Law and Financial Markets Review*, 2(2), 158.

C. Walker and A. Horne, 'The terrorism prevention and investigations measures act 2011: One thing but not much the other?' (2012) *Criminal Law Review*, 6, 421.

C. Walker, 'Terrorism financing and the policing of charities: Who pays the price?', in C. King and C. Walker (eds.), *Dirty Assets–Emerging Issues in the Regulation of Criminal and Terrorist Assets* (Ashgate: Farnham, 2014) 229–260.

C. Walker, *Terrorism and the Law* (Oxford University Press: Oxford, 2011).

J. Walker, 'Modelling Global Money Laundering Flows – some findings' (30 November 1998), http://www.johnwalkercrimetrendsanalysis.com.au/ML%20method.htm, accessed 6 June 2011.

J. Waszak, 'The obstacles to suppressing radical Islamic terrorist financing' (2004) *Case Western Reserve Journal of International law*, 36, 673.

P. Webb, 'The United Nations Convention against Corruption: Global achievement or missed opportunity?' (2005) *Journal of International Economic Law*, 8(1), 191–229.

C. Well, 'Bribery: Corporate liability under the Draft Bill' (2009) *Criminal Law Review*, 7, 479–487.

S. Welling 'Smurfs, money laundering, and the federal criminal law: The crime of structuring transactions' (1989) *Florida Law Review*, 41, 287–339.

M. White, 'The implications for securities regulation of new insider dealing provisions in the Criminal Justice Act 1993' (1995) *Company Lawyer*, 16(6), 163–171.

S. White, 'Freezing injunctions: A procedural overview and practical guide', 2005 available from http://www.parkcourtchambers.co.uk/seminar-handouts/16.11.05%20Commercial-Chancery%20_S%20White_.pdf, accessed 24 June 2011.

The White House, *Progress Report on the Global War on Terrorism* (The White House: Washington, DC, 2003).

C. William, 'Trillion Dollar Bribery' (2011) *New Law Journal*, 161(7447), 25–26.

World Bank, *Reference Guide to Anti-Money Laundering and Combating the Financing of Terrorism* (World Bank: Washington, DC, 2006).

R. Wright, 'Developing effective tools to manage the risk of damage caused by economically motivated crime fraud' (2007) *Journal of Financial Crime*, 14(1), 17–27.

R. Wright, 'Fraud after Roskill: A view from the Serious Fraud Office' (2003) *Journal of Financial Crime*, 11(1), 10–16.

R. Wright, 'Market abuse and market manipulation, the criminal, civil and regulatory interface' (2001) *Journal of International Financial Markets*, 3(1), 19–25.

Majid Yar, *Cybercrime and Society* (Sage: London, 2006).

M. Yeandle, M. Mainelli, A. Berendt, and B. Healy, *Anti-Money Laundering Requirements: Costs, Benefits and Perceptions* (Corporation of London, 2005).

INDEX

anti-money laundering (AML) 11, 22–9, 32, 33, 36, 43, 44, 47, 71, 109, 198, 210, 222–5, 229, 230

Anti-terrorism, Crime and Security Act 2001 69, 75, 76, 81, 173, 183, 225, 226

bribery 9, 22, 30, 38, 100, 114, 171–99, 211–13, 221, 228–30

Bribery Act 2010 22, 98, 171–4, 179, 183–5, 187, 189, 191–3, 195, 198, 228, 229

confiscation order 40, 41, 75, 138, 139, 141, 145, 146, 192, 217

corruption 8, 9, 22, 23, 30, 98, 99, 108, 171–3, 180–99, 211, 228, 229

counter-terrorist financing (CTF) 23, 26, 49, 53, 59, 60, 61, 63–8, 75, 81, 82, 225, 226, 230

Criminal Justice Act 1993 45, 60, 69, 124, 128, 132, 138, 145, 153, 154, 158, 167, 228

Crown Prosecution Service 31, 73, 86, 189, 213, 229

Drug Trafficking Offences Act 1986 33, 59, 69, 224

economic crime agency (ECA) 28, 31, 108, 109, 111, 121, 226

European Union (EU) 5, 21, 50, 66, 92, 131, 148, 182, 223

Federal Bureau of Investigation (FBI) 92

Financial Action Task Force (FATF) 5, 6, 8, 22–4, 50, 58, 64, 71, 72, 224

Financial Conduct Authority (FCA) 1, 28, 29, 32, 33, 35, 41, 43–7, 104–6, 108, 110, 111, 121, 130, 133, 135, 139, 141, 142, 147–9, 152–4, 156–8, 160–7, 169, 172, 184–8, 193–5, 198, 224, 227–9

financial crime 1–11, 23, 24, 27, 29, 30, 31, 33, 38, 41, 49, 53, 66, 68, 82, 84, 91, 93, 94, 97, 100–2, 104–6, 108, 109, 112, 122, 129, 133, 135, 137, 142, 154, 159, 160, 180, 182, 185, 186, 188, 203, 208, 210, 211, 217, 221, 223, 225–7, 229, 230

Financial Intelligence Unit 23, 31, 67, 109, 224

financial penalty 28, 36, 41, 43, 44, 75, 101, 105, 142, 161, 163–5, 168, 187, 190, 212, 224

Financial Services and Markets Act 2000 (FSMA 2000) 27, 28, 136, 137, 147, 149–51, 153–5, 157, 158, 160, 163, 164, 167, 169, 224, 228

Financial Services Authority (FSA) 1, 3, 26–30, 32, 41–6, 100–5, 111, 133–9, 141, 142, 144, 148, 151, 154, 159–2, 164–8, 185, 186, 194, 224, 228

fraud 1, 3–7, 9–11, 27, 30, 31, 33, 38, 45, 46, 49, 55, 66, 73, 84–121, 135, 138, 139, 141, 143, 151, 154, 187, 188, 197, 201–3, 205, 208–13, 215, 218–20, 227, 228

Fraud Act 2006 84, 85, 87, 88, 91, 95, 97, 111, 115, 116, 119–21

Fraud Review 84, 93–5, 109, 121, 227

HM Revenue and Customs (HMRC) 31,
33, 45, 120, 201–21, 229, 230
HM Treasury 20, 23–6, 28, 33, 36, 41, 46,
61, 65, 66, 71, 72, 76–9, 81, 121, 126,
136, 205, 206, 209, 226, 227, 230
Home Office 24–6, 31, 60, 64, 66, 67, 81,
95, 108–10, 121, 225, 227, 230

imprisonment 38, 39, 41, 42, 45, 72–4, 80,
111, 113, 116–19, 139–42, 145, 163, 189,
190, 192, 193, 198, 213, 218, 219
insider dealing 3, 9, 30, 45, 103, 123–47,
148, 149, 153, 155–7, 161–3, 169, 211,
228
Insider Dealing Directive 124, 126, 133, 146
International Monetary Fund (IMF) 3–6, 8,
9, 19, 20, 23, 49
Irish Republican Army (IRA) 60, 81

Law Commission (The) 87, 88, 96, 173, 183

market abuse 1, 3, 9, 45, 124, 135–8, 141,
142, 145, 147, 148–69, 211, 228
Market Abuse Directive (MAD) 132, 135,
148, 228
Market Abuse Regime (MAR) 124, 135, 145,
148, 153, 154, 158, 160, 163, 166, 167, 228
money laundering 1–4, 6–9, 11–47, 49–51,
53, 58–61, 64, 66–73, 84, 90, 94, 95, 99,
101–3, 105, 106, 109, 110, 112, 114, 116,
117, 121, 130, 140, 157, 187, 197, 198,
207, 210–12, 215, 221, 223, 224, 229, 230
money laundering directives 1, 22–4, 34, 46,
223, 225, 230
Money Laundering Reporting Officer
(MLRO) 28, 29, 35, 43, 49, 69, 109, 110,
224

National Crime Agency (NCA) 1, 12,
26, 31, 32, 34, 35, 47, 66–70, 73, 81,
82, 95, 106, 108–10, 118, 121, 224–7,
230
National Fraud Authority (NFA) 5, 33, 93,
95, 106, 107, 116, 121, 227
National Fraud Intelligence Bureau (NFIB)
95, 188
National Fraud Reporting Centre (NFRC)
33, 95

Office of Fair Trading (OFT) 30, 33, 108

Proceeds of Crime Act 2002 13–16, 30, 31,
33, 36, 37, 40, 47, 76, 109, 110, 117, 121,
210, 224, 227

restraint order 41
reverse money laundering 49, 53

serious crime prevention orders 118, 196
Serious Fraud Office (SFO) 30, 31, 53,
97–100, 103, 108, 111, 121, 171, 172,
179, 184, 185, 187–90, 192, 193, 195,
196, 198, 208, 210, 227, 229, 230
Serious Organised Crime Agency (SOCA)
17, 30, 33, 35, 47
Suspicious Activity Reports (SARs) 15, 16,
25, 35, 43, 69, 70, 109, 224, 225

tax evasion 1, 3, 4, 8, 10, 200–21, 229
Terrorism Act 2000 50–3, 59–61, 68–70,
73–5, 81, 109, 160, 225, 226, 230
terrorist financing 1, 3, 9, 23, 34, 35, 44,
49–83, 94, 103, 109, 121, 130, 207,
225–7, 230
Theft Act 1968 85, 86, 95, 96, 98, 104, 111